Nelson's Annual Preacher's Sourcebook

2004 EDITION

Nelson's Annual Preacher's Sourcebook

2004 EDITION

ROBERT J. MORGAN, EDITOR

THOMAS NELSON PUBLISHERS
Nashville

© 2004 by Robert J. Morgan

Published in Nashville, Tennessee, by Thomas Nelson, Inc.

Published in association with the literary agency of Alive Communications, 7680 Goddard Street, Suite 200, Colorado Springs, CO 80920.

All rights reserved. Written permission must be secured from the publisher to use or reproduce any part of this book except for brief quotations in critical reviews or articles.

Unless otherwise indicated, scripture quotations are from the *New King James Version of the Bible*, © 1979, 1980, 1982, 1990, Thomas Nelson, Inc., Publishers.

Verses marked "NIV" are taken from the *Holy Bible: New International Version*, copyright © 1973, 1978, 1984 by the International Bible Society. Used by permission of Zondervan Publishing House. All rights reserved.

Book design by Mark McGarry, Texas Type and Book Works, Dallas, Texas

Typesetting by BookSetters, White House, Tennessee

Morgan, Robert J. (ed.)
  Nelson's annual preacher's sourcebook, 2004 edition.

ISBN 0-7852-5035-2

Printed in Canada

1 2 3 4 5 6 7—07 06 05 04 03

Contents

Introduction		xi
Editor's Preface: Plugged In to the Power		xiii
Create a Sermon Series!		xix
Contributors		xxi
Calendar Pages		xxviii
Sermons and Worship Suggestions for 52 Weeks		1
January 4	*The Lord Bless You and Keep You* Numbers 6:22–27	2
January 11	*Outward, Inward, Upward* Matthew 9:35–38	8
January 18	*Real Revival* 2 Chronicles 7:12–16	16
January 25	*An Amazing Offer* Titus 2:11–14	24
February 1	*The Tender Heart of a Tough Leader* Nehemiah 1:1–11	36
February 8	*The Brother in the Bone Box* Matthew 13:54–56	42
February 15	*To Change the World* Acts 17:6	50
February 22	*Jesus: Full of Compassion* Mark 8:1–13	56
February 29	*Come Now, and Let Us Reason* Isaiah 1:1–31	62
March 7	*The Horrors of Hell* Luke 16:19–31	68
March 14	*A Model for Ministry* 1 Thessalonians 2:1–12	80

Date	Title	Page
March 21	*The Precious Stone* 1 Peter 2:4–12	86
March 28	*Faith in the Face of a Giant* 1 Samuel 17:1–54	92
April 4	*The Triumphal Entry: Tragedy or Triumph?* Mark 11:1–11	98
April 11	*What Easter Gives Us* Romans 1:1–4; 4:24–25; 8:11	106
April 18	*From Rags to Riches* 2 Kings 4:1–7	116
April 25	*Walking with God* Genesis 5:25	124
May 2	*A Life of Integrity* James 5:12	132
May 9	*The Wise Woman* Genesis 2:18–25; Proverbs 31:10–31	140
May 16	*After God's Own Heart* 1 Samuel 13:1–14; 16:1–13	146
May 23	*Stairway to Heaven* Genesis 28	154
May 30	*The Difference a Day Makes* Acts 2:1–38	166
June 6	*The Five B's of Purity* Psalm 24	172
June 13	*What Jesus Says to Frazzled People* Luke 10:38–42	180
June 20	*Ordinary People/Extraordinary Praying* James 5:16–18; 1 Kings 17—18	186
June 27	*Face to Face with God* Genesis 32—33	196
July 4	*Elisha's Last Sermon* 2 Kings 13:14–19	206
July 11	*Lord, Make Us One* John 17:20–25	212

July 18	*Is Your Faith Genuine?* James 2:14–20	218
July 25	*Who Do You Say That I Am?* Mark 8:27–38	228
August 1	*Consider Your Ways* Haggai 1	234
August 8	*A Most Unlikely Evangelist* 2 Kings 5:1–14	240
August 15	*How to Live in the Last Days* Matthew 24:32–35	250
August 22	*Prayer: The Solid Foundation* Philippians 1:1–11	256
August 29	*One Thing I Know* John 9	262
September 5	*A Book and a Blessing* Revelation 1:1–3	270
September 12	*Learning to Be Thankful Whatever Your Circumstances* Philippians 4:4–8	276
September 19	*The Forgotten Secret of Happiness* Psalm 32	282
September 26	*Shaking Off Discouragement* Haggai 2	292
October 3	*Nic at Night* John 3:1–16	298
October 10	*Playing Favorites* James 2:1–7	304
October 17	*You Are What You Eat* Matthew 5:6	310
October 24	*The Marks of Maturity* 1 Corinthians 3:2	318
October 31	*Faith Alone* Ephesians 2:1–9	324
November 7	*The True Lifeline* Isaiah 6:1–10	330

November 14	*Mourning Has Broken: The Gift of Tears* Matthew 5:4	340
November 21	*Solomon's Legacy* 1 Kings 2:1–9	346
November 28	*Thanksgiving Everyday* Psalm 27	354
December 5	*Who Is He in Yonder Stall?* Matthew 1:18–25	362
December 12	*The Bible and the Babe* 2 Corinthians 9:15	368
December 19	*The Peace of Christmas* Micah 5:1–5	374
December 26	*Delayed Re-entry: Why Christ Hasn't Returned Yet* 2 Peter 3:1–12a	380

Children's Sermon Suggestions
January 4, 11, 18; February 8, 21; March 21; April 11, 18; May 30; June 20; August 15, 29; September 19; October 3; November 14; 28

Special Occasion Sermons
A Sanctity of Life Sermon: Value and Dignity of Human Life	22
A Communion Sermon: Three Crosses and Two Choices	104
A Missions Sermon: Will You Give Jesus Your Lunch?	164
A Patriotic Sermon: Red, White, and Blue	202
A Baptism Sermon: The Pleasing Christian Life	246
A Thanksgiving Sermon: Giving Thanks: Developing an Attitude of Gratitude	352

Classics for the Pastor's Library
Gleanings from Thomas Watson	14
Heidi	122
The Knowledge of the Holy	138
E. M. Bounds	248
Two Classics on Ephesians	336

Conversations in a Pastor's Study
The Relationship Between the Pastor and the Minister of Music/ Vernon Whaley	112

The Pastor and His Children's Ministry/Vicki Wiley	178
The Pastor and His Reading/Samuel Logan Brengle	268

Helps for the Pastor's Family

Keeping Marriage on the Front Burner	48
Praying for "Preachers' Kids"	192

Heroes for the Pastor's Heart

James Young Simpson	78
James Renwick	153
Finney's Conversion	224
Isaac Watts	288
Anskar	339

Prayers for a Pastor's Closet

A Prayer from Psalm 86	79
O Master Let Me Walk with Thee	114
A Prayer for Insight	152
Lord, Speak to Me	361

Quotes for the Pastor's Wall

Merrill F. Unger	35
Thomas Chalmers	77
Johann Albrecht Bengle	205
George Herbert	205
R. A. Torrey	227
Dietrich Bonhoeffer	338
Martin Luther	365

Techniques for the Pastor's Delivery

A Voice Teacher's Letter to Her Pastor	130
The Public Reading of Scripture	316

Thoughts for the Pastor's Soul

What Do You Do All Week?	30
A Stale Loaf of Bread	74
The Minister's Zeal	160

Wedding Messages

A Traditional Wedding	386
A Wedding from 1 John 1:7	388
A Wedding Ceremony about Love	390

Funeral Messages

How God Comforts Us — 393
What to Avoid at Funerals — 396
Death Swallowed Up in Victory — 398

Special Services Registry

Sermons Preached — 402
Marriages Log — 404
Funerals Log — 405
Baptisms/Confirmations — 406
Baby Dedication Registration — 407
Wedding Registration — 408
Funeral Registration — 409

Subject Index — 410

Scripture Index — 412

Introduction

This book is designed to give you more time.

In his book *Why Leaders Can't Lead,* Warren Bennis warns of the danger of letting routine work drive out non-routine work, smothering to death all creative planning. We become so overwhelmed with regular daily demands that we have little time for solitude, conceptualizing, dreaming, and creative planning.

Here is a book to help you with the weekly routines of ministry. Chock full of sermon outlines, wedding and funeral ideas, illustrations, children's sermons, and worship planning helps, *Nelson's Annual Preacher's Sourcebook* is designed to take some of the burden off your schedule.

Please let us know if it's helpful. If you have comments, feedback, or suggestions for future volumes, please contact me at www.robertjmorgan.com.

This book would have been impossible without the oversight of Lee Hollaway of Thomas Nelson who gently nudges, nags, improves, suggests, corrects, inspires, and encourages me. Thanks, too, to Joshua Rowe and to Sherry Anderson, my assistants. I'm also grateful to Phil Stoner and Wayne Kinde of Thomas Nelson, and to Greg Johnson of Alive Communications.

My life and ministry was largely shaped through the influence of my pastor, Rev. Winford R. Floyd of Elizabethton, Tennessee. He is now in heaven after a lifetime of "preaching the gospel to the mountains of East Tennessee." This book is dedicated to his memory.

Editor's Preface

Plugged In to the Power

Before a recent speaking engagement to ministers, I asked the sound technician to turn off my microphone. Rising to speak, I quoted John 3:16, but virtually no one heard me. At my signal, the mic was switched on, and I said: "I just gave out the gospel. It was the pure, life-changing gospel, but you didn't hear it because the power wasn't on. My message was not being amplified by the power that was available."

I pressed home my point: "You and I have dedicated our lives to giving the world John 3:16. We're ambassadors for Christ, preachers of the gospel, soul-winners. But the world doesn't seem to be hearing us, or at least they aren't hearing us very well. Perhaps the reason is because the power isn't on. Our message is not being amplified by the power that is available."

Jesus said, "You shall receive power when the Holy Spirit has come upon you" (Acts 1:8). The Lord wants to amplify our message, to give wind to our voice and wings to our words. But we must operate in the power of the Lord Christ who said, "All authority has been given unto me in heaven and on earth. Go...."

One of the best places to learn about this power is in the Book of Ephesians, for the subject of *power* is a prominent sub-theme in this epistle. Paul never veers far from the fact that Jesus Christ exercises authority above and beyond that of Satan, the demonic world, and the human sphere.

The people to whom this epistle was originally addressed had come to Christ from a background of magic, superstition, and demonic influence as followers of the goddess Diana. Upon their conversion, many had burned their books of occultism and sorcery (see Acts 19). In writing to them, Paul kept returning to the true nature of spiritual power. Notice how this works itself out in chapter 1 as Paul prayed for the Ephesians to realize...

> ... the exceeding greatness of His power toward us who believe, according to the working of His mighty power which He worked in Christ when He raised Him from the dead and seated Him at His right hand in the heavenly places, far above all principality and power and might and dominion, and every name that is named, not only in this age but also in that which is to come.

When we think of power, we think of the horsepower of a sports car, the muscles of an athlete, or the military might of an army. But the Bible wants us to conceptualize a different kind of power, *the exceeding greatness of His power toward us who believe.* This passage portrays a fourfold power.

God of Power

First, it is **resurrection power**. According to verse 19, the power available to us is "according to the working of His mighty power which He worked in Christ when He raised Him from the dead."

To reverse the process of death is not easy. I've been preaching through the Book of Ezekiel on Sunday nights, and I was surprised, on coming to chapter 37, at the vision of the valley of dry bones. These bones were the scattered remains of long-decayed people. As Ezekiel watched in astonishment, the bones began moving, reassembling themselves into skeletons. Suddenly tissue began appearing, and the valley of dry bones became a valley of dead corpses. When the breath of heaven entered them, their lungs began breathing, and they stood on their feet, a vast and very great army.

Though this vision was given to express a prophetic truth, it also provides the Bible's most vivid description of the resurrection of the body. How often, when standing by the caskets of friends or loved ones, have we not longed to awaken them?

To bring Christ from death to life, to resurrect Him bodily from the grave—that was impossible for any but the Omnipotent God, who accomplished it on Easter morning.

Paul is telling us that the same power that raised Christ from the grave is available to change our lives, to answer our prayers, to resolve our difficulties, and to empower our ministries. We serve a risen Savior!

The power available to us is also **exaltation power**: "according to the working of His mighty power which He worked in Christ when He raised Him from the dead and seated Him at His right hand in the heavenly places."

Had we a telescope powerful enough to peer into the highest heaven, we would see Christ now seated at the Father's right hand, exalted in layers of light, surrounded by His angels, and enveloped with glory.

The power of the resurrected and exalted Christ is available for us now, to change our lives, to answer our prayers, to resolve our difficulties, and to give us authority in our work of Him.

Third, our ministries are fueled by **lordship power**: "according to the working of His mighty power which He worked in Christ when He raised Him from the dead and seated Him at His right hand in the heavenly places, far above all principality and power and might and dominion, and every name that is named, not only in this age but also in that which is to come."

Jesus Christ is higher than the angels. He is greater than the demons. He lords over the principalities and powers. He rules the world, setting up one and deposing another. We fret and fear the political machinations of earth, but God Most High rules in the affairs of men. He will bring about His purposes and draw history to its pre-appointed end. *Jesus shall reign where'er the sun / does its successive journeys run.* This lordship power of Jesus Christ is available every time you step into the pulpit.

This passage doesn't stop there; it goes on to tell us of Christ's **headship power**: "And He put all things under His feet, and gave Him to be head over all things to the church, which is His body, the fullness of Him who fills all in all" (vv. 22–23).

Jesus is head of His church. He's the boss, the senior pastor, the archbishop, the great shepherd, and our great High Priest. His work in this world is done through His body the church. Our only job is to obey the commands coming from our Head, and as we do so we receive His power.

Ministry of Might

What kind of ministry taps into this kind of power? First, a powerful ministry must be **closet-based**. Jesus told us to go into our closets and talk to our Father who is in heaven. While in London several years ago, my wife and I visited the home of John Wesley. On an upper floor was Wesley's bedroom, adjacent to which was a small room about the size of a closet—Wesley's prayer room. The guide said, "This little room was the powerhouse that fueled the Methodist revival."

Missionary J. O. Fraser said about his work among the Lisu of China:

> I am feeling more and more that it is, after all, just the prayers of God's people that call down blessings upon the work, whether they are directly engaged in it or not. Paul may plant and Apollos water, but it is God who gives the increase; and this increase can be brought down from heaven by believing prayer, whether offered in China or in England. We are, as it were, God's agents, used by Him to do His work, not ours. We do our part, and then

can only look to Him, with others, for His blessing. If this is so, then Christians at home can do as much for foreign missions as those actually on the field. I believe it will only be known on the Last Day how much has been accomplished in missionary work, by the prayers of earnest believers at home.

Second, a powerful ministry must be **Calvary-centered**. The preaching of the cross is foolishness to the world; but to us who are being saved, it is the power of God (1 Cor. 1:18). When evangelist D. L. Moody was preaching in London, a reporter covering the meetings couldn't understand why so many people were coming to hear the uncouth, uneducated American. He finally concluded that it wasn't the worldly rank, wealth, or oratory of the preacher. It was the fact that Moody was lifting up the Cross of Christ.

In 1953, Billy Graham was preaching to crowds of 40,000 each night in Dallas, Texas, but one night few people responded to his invitation to receive Christ. He left the platform dejected, but a friend of his, a German businessman, came alongside, put his arm over his shoulder, and said, "Billy, do you know what was wrong tonight? You didn't preach the cross of Christ." The next night he preached on the blood of Jesus, and a great host responded. There is power in the blood and in the Cross.

Third, a powerful ministry is a **contemporary** one. The word "contemporary" comes from the prefix *con* meaning "with," and the Latin root word *tempo*, meaning, "time"—*with the times.* King David selected advisors who were wise and who understood the times. We aren't going to reach many people in this decade if we use the tools and techniques of previous decades.

This doesn't mean we must discard our heritage and traditions, but we should be mindful of our times and unafraid to change techniques when necessary. When the power of the Holy Spirit is behind your ministry, it propels you to be creative, innovative, and fresh. God's power works in the present tense; it's never out-of-date.

Finally, the power of Christ gives us a **confident** ministry. How can we fail if we have the resurrection, exaltation, lordship, and headship power of Christ behind us? Not that we'll all have mega-ministries. On one occasion, Jesus preached a sermon rippling with the power of the Holy Spirit, and the result was that almost everyone left Him. But that sermon on the cost of discipleship has been changing the world ever since.

After the Civil War, John Broadus was burdened for more preachers to heal the nation's wounds. He prepared a seminary course on homiletics. To his dismay, only one student, a blind man, enrolled in the class. Broadus decided to do his very best anyway, and he taught that one student, conversationally, as earnestly and as thoroughly as if there had been a hundred students enrolled. The lectures were so powerful they later became the classic book, *The Preparation and Delivery of Sermons*, which has been training preachers for over 100 years.

When we labor in the power of the Lord we may not always see immediate success, but we can rest our heads on our pillows at night knowing that sooner or later, in one way or another, to one degree or another, our ministry is going to change the world.

His Word does not return unto Him void. Our labor is not in vain in the Lord. When we minister in the power of the Holy Spirit, we are ministering in a power which is like the working of His mighty strength which He exerted in Christ when He raised Him from the dead and seated Him at His right hand in the heavenly realms, far above all rule and authority, power and dominion, and every name that can be named, not only in the present age, but also in the world to come.

All hail the power of Jesus' name,
let angels prostrate fall.
Bring forth the royal diadem
and crown Him Lord of all.

Create a Sermon Series!

If you would like to publicize and preach a *series* of messages, you can assemble your own by mixing and matching various sermons and sermon outlines in this *Sourcebook.* Here are some suggestions:

Leadership 101
- Qualities of an Effective Leader (January 4)
- The Tender Heart of a Tough Leader (February 1)
- A Model for Ministry (March 14)
- The Marks of Maturity (October 24)

An Offer We Can't Refuse
- An Amazing Offer (January 25)
- Come Now and Let Us Reason (February 29)
- The Precious Blood (February 29)
- What the Gospel Means to Me (April 4)
- Stairway to Heaven (May 23)
- Two Ways of Life (August 29)
- Faith Alone (October 31)

The Disciplines of Life
- The Discipline of Defeat (April 25)
- The Discipline of Delay (May 9)
- The Discipline of Denial (May 23)
- The Discipline of Detour (August 21)
- The Discipline of Distress (October 10)

The Overcoming Life
- Of Whom Shall I Be Afraid? (March 7)
- Truths Regarding Temptation (March 14)
- Faith in the Face of a Giant (March 28)
- Rags to Riches (April 18)
- The Five B's of Purity (June 6)
- What Jesus Says to Frazzled People (June 13)
- When Life Overwhelms Us (September 5)
- The Forgotten Secret to Happiness (September 29)

The Wonderful Names of Our Wonderful Lord
- One Who Fits the Bill (February 1)
- The Precious Name (February 29)
- And That Rock Was Christ (August 29)
- The Prince and the Paupers (September 29)
- The Lord Is My . . . (November 28)
- Her Firstborn Son (December 5)
- King of Kings (December 12)
- The Babe (December 12)

Across the Street and Across the Seas
- Outward, Inward, Upward (January 11)
- Worldwide Witness (February 8)
- To Change the World (February 15)
- Everyday Evangelism (April 25)
- A Most Unlikely Evangelist (August 8)

Contributors

Dr. Timothy K. Beougher
Associate Professor, Billy Graham School of Missions, Evangelism, and Church Growth, The Southern Baptist Theological Seminary, Louisville, Kentucky

A Life of Integrity (May 2)
How Money Can Hurt You (May 16)
Extraordinary Praying for Ordinary People (June 20)
Is Your Faith Genuine? (July 18)
Playing Favorites (October 10)
Why Did He Come? (December 19)

Paul Borthwick
Senior Consultant of Development Associates International (DAI), teacher of missions at Gordon College, Wenhan, Massachusetts, and former Minister of Missions, Grace Chapel, Lexington

Outward, Inward, Upward (January 11)
Will You Give Jesus Your Lunch? (A Missions Sermon)

Samuel Logan Brengle (1860–1936)
Co-founder of the Salvation Army in the United States and writer

Be Obedient (July 11)

Dr. Stuart Briscoe
Minister at Large, Elmbrook Church, Brookfield, Wisconsin

Consider Your Ways (August 1)
Shaking of Discouragement (September 26)

Dr. Dan Chun
Senior Pastor, First Presbyterian Church of Honolulu, Co-Founder and Chairman of the Board of Hawaiian Island Ministries

Nic at Night (October 3)
Hang in There (October 31)
Stay Awake (November 28)

Dr. Michael Duduit
Editor, Preaching Magazine, Franklin, Tennessee

　　A Model for Ministry (March 14)
　　The Triumphal Entry (April 4)

Dr. Ed Dobson
Pastor, Calvary Church in Grand Rapids, Michigan, and Moody Bible Institute's 1993 Pastor of the Year

　　Jesus: Full of Compassion (February 22)
　　Of Whom Shall I Be Afraid? (March 7)
　　When God Has You Waiting (June 20)
　　Lord, Make Us One (July 11)
　　Learning to Be Thankful (September 12)
　　Value and Dignity of Human Life (Sanctity of Human Life Sermon)

Jane Duensing
Voice Instructor for Musical Arts Studios of Columbia College, Palmetto Center for the Arts, and Columbia International University, Columbia, South Carolina

Rev. Michael Easley
Pastor and Teacher, Immanuel Bible Church, Springfield, Virginia

　　Tender Heart of a Tough Leader (February 1)
　　The Forgotten Secret of Happiness (September 19)

Dr. David George
Pastor, Lake Arlington Baptist Church, Arlington, Texas, and Chairman of the Board of Trustees for Golden Gate Baptist Theological Seminary

　　Submission to Authority (January 18)
　　Hearts of Worship (February 22)
　　After God's Own Heart (May 16)

Rev. Peter Grainger
Pastor, Charlotte Baptist Chapel, Edinburgh, Scotland

　　The Winning Team (February 1)
　　Come Now, Let Us Reason (February 29)
　　Are You a Liar? (May 2)

The Parable of the Prodigal Father (May 16)
Growing in the Knowledge of Christ (May 30)
More to Life (June 20)
Who Do You Say I Am? (July 25)
I Have Loved You (August 22)
Two Ways of Life (August 29)
Overcoming Legalism (September 26)
Close Down the Temple (October 3)
I Saw the Lord (October 17)
Profile of a Priest (October 31)
The Light of the World (November 7)
Two Kinds of Talkers (November 14)
The Journey of a Lifetime (December 19)

Frances Ridley Havergal (1836–1879)
English hymn and devotional writer

The Bright Side of Growing Older (July 4)
The Royal Bounty (October 24)

Matthew Henry (1662–1714)
Nonconformist Bible commentator and minister

It Is Finished (April 4)

Rev. Evan Henry Hopkins (1837–1918)
Leading teacher and exponent of Keswick Convention and writer

The Lord in Our Midst (June 27)
What Christ Has Secured (December 26)

Dr. David Jackman
Director, Cornhill Training Course, London, England

An Amazing Offer (January 25)
Isn't He Rightly Named? (March 14)
Why Have You Deceived Me? (April 18)
Stairway to Heaven (May 23)
Face to Face with God (June 27)
Prayer: The Solid Foundation (August 22)

Dr. David Jeremiah
Senior Pastor of Shadow Mountain Community Church, El Cajon, California, and Chancellor of Christian Heritage College

Jacob's Final Thoughts (June 6)
A Book and a Blessing (September 5)
Revelation Revealed (September 5)
Solomon's Legacy (November 21)

Dr. D. James Kennedy
Pastor, Coral Ridge Presbyterian Church, Fort Lauderdale, Florida

To Change the World (February 15)

Rev. Todd Kinde
Minister of Preaching, Grace Bible Church, Grandville, Michigan

You Are What You Eat (October 17)
The Gift of Tears (November 14)

Dr. Woodrow Kroll
President and Senior Bible Teacher of Back to the Bible Broadcast

The Five B's of Purity (June 6)
How to Live in the Last Days (August 15)

Rev. J. J. Luce
Teacher at Keswick Convention

The Marks of Discipleship (November 14)

Dr. Denis Lyle
Pastor, Lurgan Baptist Church, Northern Ireland

From Rags to Riches (April 18)
The Discipline of Defeat (April 25)
The Discipline of Delay (May 9)
The Discipline of Denial (May 23)

The Difference a Day Makes (May 30)
Elijah's Last Sermon (July 4)
The Discipline of Detour (August 1)
A Most Unlikely Evangelist (August 8)
The Sin of Silence (August 22)
The Discipline of Distress (October 10)
Daniel's Prayer (October 24)
Three Crosses and Two Choices (A Communion Sermon)

Dwight Lyman Moody (1837–1899)
American Preacher and Evangelist to America, England, Scotland, and Ireland

What Think Ye of Christ? (September 26)

Morris Proctor
President of Morris Proctor Seminars, Inc.

Who Is He in Yonder Stall? (December 5)

Rev. Kevin Riggs
Pastor, Franklin Community Church, Franklin, Tennessee

Effective Leaders (January 4)
Real Faith in Hard Times (March 7)
Making Wise Decisions (July 25)
The Peace of Christmas (December 19)
Giving Thanks: Developing an Attitude of Gratitude (A Thanksgiving Sermon)

Joshua D. Rowe
Assistant Editor to Robert J. Morgan and graduate of Columbia (S.C.) International University, with degrees in Bible and Biblical Languages

What Are You Running For? (April 18)
Prevailing Prayer (May 23)
The Lord Is My... (November 28)
Fear or Faith (December 26)

The Pleasing Christian Life (A Baptism Sermon)

William Graham Scroggie (1877–1959)
Scottish minister and writer

The Joyful Repose of the Christian Life (January 4)
The Lofty Ideal of the Christian Life (January 25)
The Devout Energy of the Christian Life (March 21)
What the Gospel Means (April 4)
The Grand Uniqueness of the Christian Life (May 2)
Brainstorming the Bible (August 8)
Where to Find Christ (September 12)
The Love Life (October 3)
The Thorn Blessing (November 21)

Richard Sharpe, Jr.
Founder and director of Small Church Ministries in Batavia, New York

Perfect Hearts (July 11)
Disobedient Children (October 17)
The True Lifeline (November 7)

Rev. Charles Haddon Spurgeon (1834–1892)
Pastor, Metropolitan Tabernacle, London

Ponder This (January 11)
A Grand Highway (February 8)
The Precious Blood (February 29)
Healing for the Wounded (December 5)

Dr. Vernon Whaley
Minister of Music at Olive Baptist Church, Pensacola, Florida

George Whitefield (1714–1770)
English evangelist

Walking with God (April 25)

Vicky Wiley
Director of Children's Ministries of First Presbyterian Church of Honolulu, Hawaii, and editor of the Children's Ministry Sourcebook.

Rev. Drew Wilkerson
Pastor, Jersey Shore Church of God, Jersey Shore, Pennsylvania

Spare Change (January 18)
When Life Overwhelms Us (September 5)
Unbroken Cords of Friendship (September 12)

Dr. Melvin Worthington
Executive Secretary, National Association of Free Will Baptists

Real Revival (January 18)
The Model of Marriage (January 25)
Worldwide Witness (February 8)
The Wonderful Word (February 15)
The Horrors of Hell (March 7)
Truths Regarding Temptation (March 14)
Hosanna and Hallelujah (April 11)
Everyday Evangelism (April 25)
The Wise Woman (May 9)
Identifying Immaturity (May 30)
Obligated to Obey (June 6)
Tried, Tested, and Thankful (June 13)
Back to Basics (July 18)
The Sovereign Speaks (August 15)
The Believer's Badge (October 10)
Marks of Maturity (October 24)
The Bible and the Babe (December 12)

All other outlines are from the pulpit ministry of the general editor, Rev. Robert J. Morgan, of The Donelson Fellowship in Nashville, Tennessee. Special appreciation goes to Jerry Carraway, worship leader of The Donelson Fellowship, for his invaluable assistance.

2004 Calendar

January 1	New Year's Day
January 4	
January 5	Epiphany
January 11	
January 18	**Sanctity of Human Life Sunday**
January 19	Martin Luther King, Jr. Day
January 25	**Superbowl Sunday**
January 26	Australia Day
February 1-29	Black History Month
February 1	**National Freedom Day**
February 2	Groundhog Day
February 8	
February 12	Lincoln's Birthday
February 14	Valentine's Day
February 15	
February 16	Presidents' Day
February 22	**Washington's Birthday**
February 25	Ash Wednesday
February 29	**First Sunday of Lent**
March 7	**Second Sunday of Lent**
March 14	**Third Sunday of Lent**
March 17	St. Patrick's Day
March 20	Spring Begins
March 21	**Fourth Sunday of Lent; Mothering Sunday**
March 28	**Fifth Sunday of Lent**
April 4	Passion / Palm Sunday; Daylight Savings Time begins

(all **boldface** dates are Sundays)

April 6	Passover
April 8	Holy Thursday
April 9	Good Friday
April 11	**Easter**
April 13	Jefferson's Birthday
April 18	**Holocaust Remembrance Day**
April 21	Administrative Professionals Day
April 22	Earth Day
April 25	
May 1	
May 2	
May 6	National Day of Prayer
May 9	**Mother's Day**
May 15	Armed Forces Day
May 16	
May 20	Ascension Day
May 23	
May 30	**Pentecost**
May 31	Memorial Day
June 6	**Trinity Sunday**
June 13	
June 14	Flag Day
June 20	**Father's Day**
June 21	Summer Begins
June 27	
July 1	Canada Day
July 4	**Independence Day**
July 11	
July 18	
July 25	Parents' Day
August 1	**Friendship Day**

August 6	Transfiguration Day
August 8	
August 15	
August 22	
August 29	
September 5	
September 6	Labor Day
September 12	**Grandparents' Day**
September 15	Rosh Hashanah begins
September 19	
September 22	Autumn begins
September 24	Yom Kippur begins; Native American Day
September 26	
October 1-31	Pastor Appreciation Month
October 3	
October 10	**Clergy Appreciation Day; Children's Day**
October 11	Columbus Day; Thanksgiving Day (Canada)
October 16	National Boss Day
October 17	
October 24	**United Nations Day; Mother-In-Law Day**
October 27	Reformation Day
October 31	**Daylight Savings Time ends; Halloween**
November 1	All Saints' Day
November 2	Election Day
November 7	
November 11	Veteran's Day
November 14	International Day of Prayer for the Persecuted Church
November 21	
November 25	Thanksgiving Day
November 28	**First Sunday of Advent**
December 5	Second Sunday of Advent

December 7   Pearl Harbor Remembrance Day
December 8   Hanukkah
December 12   **Third Sunday of Advent**
December 19   **Fourth Sunday of Advent**
December 21   Winter Begins
December 24   Christmas Eve
December 25   Christmas Day
December 26   **Kwanzaa begins**
December 31   New Year's Eve

SERMONS AND WORSHIP SUGGESTIONS FOR 52 WEEKS

JANUARY 4, 2004

SUGGESTED SERMON *Date preached:*

The Lord Bless You and Keep You

Scripture: Numbers 6:22–27, especially verse 24: "The LORD bless you and keep you."

Introduction: Let's begin the year on a positive note, with a timely blessing and a timeless benediction. Numbers 6 gives various instructions to Israel's priests. In verses 22–27, they are told how to bless their people. We call this the Priestly Blessing, or the Aaronic Blessing or Benediction. Aaron, Israel's chief priest, was to pronounce it on ancient Israel. But in a special way, it's for you and me at the beginning of this New Year.

1. **A Blessing in Triplicate.** Notice the threefold use of God's name: *The Lord . . . the Lord . . . the Lord . . . .* This represented the fullness of God's blessing. He was blessing and blessing and blessing again. It reminds us of the threefold angelic song in Isaiah 6: *Holy, Holy, Holy is the Lord God Almighty.* The triple use of the word intensifies the reality to an infinite degree. As Ecclesiastes puts it: "A three-fold cord is not quickly broken." But there may be a greater significance to this triune formula. The Israelites didn't understand the doctrine of the Trinity as we do; but the Book of Numbers wasn't written just for them. These passages were written for God's people of all ages. Looking through the lens of subsequent revelation, it seems natural to understand that the three-fold blessing of Numbers 6 suggests the Trinity. Compare the Apostolic Benediction in 2 Corinthians 13:14. Some feel the Aaronic Blessing should be read with the Trinity in mind:

    - God the Father bless you and keep you.
    - God the Son make His face shine upon you and be gracious to you.
    - God the Spirit lift up His countenance upon you and give you peace.

2. **A Blessing from Christ.** While the blessings are from the Triune God, the Bless-er Himself is the Lord Jesus. This was a priestly blessing, given to Aaron as the high priest of Israel representing the Almighty. According to Hebrews 5, Aaron was a foreshadowing of Christ, our Great High Priest. Our Lord's last act of ministry before returning to heaven was to

bless His people (Luke 24:50–51). His nail-pierced hand is lifted over the heads of His children in continual blessing.

3. **A Blessing with Authority.** Christ conveys this blessing to us with authority. This wasn't just an expression of good will or a simple prayer. In Old Testament times, Aaron, endued with the authority of Almighty God and using the Divine Name and the appointed words of God Himself, conveyed God's blessings on the congregation.

4. **A Blessing According to Our Needs.** The six components of this blessing correspond to our needs:

   A. **The Lord Bless You.** "Bless" is a common Old Testament word, occurring (with its derivatives) about 415 times. It implied life, health, and prosperity. These blessings are spelled out for Israel in Deuteronomy 28, and for the Christian in Ephesians 1—3 (see Eph. 1:3).

   B. **The Lord Keep You.** "Keep" conveys the idea of protection. It was used for a shepherd's keeping watch over his flock. Its root meant "to hedge about." The *Theological Wordbook of the Old Testament* defines this term, "to exercise great care over."

   C. **The Lord Make His Face Shine Upon You.** Here the idea is sunshine. We're to soak up the light, joy, radiance, and enthusiasm of Almighty God. We need to be close to Him, in His Word, worshiping and loving Him. As we absorb His light, we begin glowing in the darkness like a child's luminescent object.

>>> sermon continued on following page

APPROPRIATE HYMNS AND SONGS

The Lord Bless You and Keep You, Peter C. Lutkin; Public Domain.

May the Lord Bless and Keep You, John Illg; © 1993 Maranatha Praise, Inc.

Sweet Shalom, Claire Cloninger/Gary Sadler/Chris Springer; © 1994 Juniper Landing Music/Word Music, Inc./Integrity's Hosanna! Music/Integrity's Praise! Music, Admin. by Integrity Music, Inc.

Lift Up Your Hands, Patrick Henderson/Anthony Wilkins; © 1990 Birdwing Music/Patrick Fleming Music, Admin. by EMI Christian Music Publishing.

There Shall Be Showers of Blessing, Daniel W. Whittle/James McGranahan; Public Domain.

D. **The Lord Be Gracious to You**. Gracious here means "kind and beneficent." Prominent in this is the idea of forgiveness.
E. **The Lord Lift Up His Countenance Upon You.** In the Bible, relationships were often expressed in terms of facial expressions. When Cain became angry with Aaron, his countenance fell. When Laban became frustrated with Jacob, his countenance was not favorable toward him. The Lord's lifting up His countenance implies His fellowship and smile.
F. **The Lord Give You Peace.** The Hebrew word for peace is s*halom* (see Is. 26:3).

5. **Blessings Equated to the Name of God.** This Aaronic benediction was equated to the Name of God (v. 27). The blessings of Christ indicate He has put His name on us, we are called by His name. Do you need His blessings? Are you ready to turn from sin and Satan, to give yourself wholeheartedly to Him? Here at the beginning of a new year, may the Lord bless you and keep you. May He make His face to shine on you and be gracious to you. May He lift up His countenance upon you and give you peace.

FOR THE BULLETIN

✽ On January 4, 1528, the brother of Holy Roman Emperor Charles V issued a decree to put the Anabaptists to death. This was first secular mandate forbidding the Anabaptist movement. ✽ Hans Bret, a young believer in Holland was arrested and tortured for his faith. Early on Saturday, January 4, 1577, the executioner clamped an iron screw on his tongue, and seared the end of his tongue with a hot iron so he couldn't preach at his execution. He was burned alive. ✽ January 4, 1581, is the birthday of James Ussher, Archbishop of Armagh, Ireland. He is remembered for his calculations regarding the origin of earth, which he determined was created on November 23, 4004 B.C. ✽ On January 4, 1866, missionary James Chalmers sailed aboard the *John Williams* for a lifetime of successful service in the South Pacific. He was martyred on Easter, 1901, trying to reach a new island with the gospel. His head was cut off and his torso was cooked. News of the attack stunned the West, leading to a flood of new recruits for missions. ✽ Kaj Munk grew up in a pietistic setting and, in 1924, was ordained a priest in Denmark. He became an outspoken opponent of the Nazis, and on January 4, 1944, he was taken from his home by the Gestapo and shot. His Bible was found 20 meters from his body. He is considered Denmark's greatest modern martyr. ✽ On January 4, 1947, Peter Marshall was elected chaplain of the U.S. Senate.

STATS, STORIES AND MORE

The Silver Scrolls
At the beginning of the twentieth century, we didn't have any ancient copies of the Hebrew Scriptures. The oldest extant copy dated from about A.D.1000. The critics, therefore, questioned the accuracy of the transmission of the text. In 1949, the Dead Sea Scrolls were discovered, pushing back the date of our oldest extant Hebrew Scriptures by a millennia. When these Scrolls were compared to more recent texts, the transmission proved very accurate. Then, in 1979, an even older fragment of a biblical text was discovered by Dr. Judith M. Hadley of Villanova University in a burial cave in Jerusalem's Hinnom Valley. Two tiny silver scrolls were found. It took several years for Israeli scientists to clean and unroll them, but when they did, they found the oldest known fragment of Scripture, dating from the Davidic dynasty. Inscribed on those scrolls (now in the Israeli Museum in Jerusalem) is our text today, the Aaronic Blessing.

The Nail-Scarred Hands
It is the Lord Jesus Christ who pronounces on His children the richest gifts of the Trinity. He constantly holds His nail-scarred hands over our heads saying, "The Lord bless you and keep you. The Lord make His face to shine upon you and be gracious to you. The Lord lift up His countenance upon You and give you peace." If we could realize that, what a difference it would make every day. That's why we say, "Surely goodness and mercy shall follow me all the days of my life." That's why we say, "This is the day the Lord has made. I will rejoice and be glad in it."

From Matthew Henry
Matthew Henry said that the idea *lifting up His countenance* is that of sensing God's smile. When a person had an audience in an ancient Middle Eastern court, the monarch might not even look in his direction. Or he might look at the claimant with an expression of wrath. But how pleasant when the monarch looked with pleasure on the one who had come to his throne.

WORSHIP HELPS

Call to Worship:
Behold, bless the LORD, all you servants of the LORD. . . Lift up your hands in the sanctuary, and bless the LORD (Ps. 134:1–2).

Scripture Medley:
Blessed be the God and Father of our Lord Jesus Christ, who has blessed us with every spiritual blessing in the heavenly places in Christ. He has given food to those who fear Him. . . . He has given us rest on every side. . . . He has given us light. . . . He gives power to the weak, and to those who have no might He increases strength. By this, we know that we abide in Him, and He in us, because He has given us of His Spirit. He has given assurance . . . by raising (Christ) from the dead. Be glad then, you children of Zion, and rejoice in the LORD your God; for He has given you the former rain faithfully, and He will cause the rain to come down for you. May you be blessed by the LORD, who made heaven and earth. We will bless the LORD from this time forth and forevermore.
(Eph. 1:3; Ps. 111:5; 2 Chr. 14:7; Ps. 118:27; Is. 40:29; 1 John 4:13; Acts 17:31; Joel 2:23; Ps. 115: 15, 18)

Benediction:
The blessing of the Lord be upon you; we bless you in the name of the Lord! (Ps. 129:8).

Kids Talk

Write the letters B L E S S on five pieces of cardboard or project them on a large screen. Tell the children that Jesus blesses us with many good things. Let the children suggest specific blessings that begin with B, L, E, and S. For example, "B" can stand for birds, balloons, bicycles, the Bible, basketball, bananas, etc. Have your own ideas if the children are stumped. You might ask if anyone's name begins with one of the letters. "Yes, we're thankful for Billy. He's a blessing." With the last "S" say, "This letter stands for *SAYING thank you* to the Lord for His gifts," then lead the children in a prayer of thanksgiving for the blessings they mentioned.

Additional Sermons and Lesson Ideas

Qualities of an Effective Leader
Date preached:

By Kevin Riggs

SCRIPTURE: Titus 1:5–9

INTRODUCTION: To one degree or another all of us are leaders, as parents, husbands, wives, students, employees, employers, and at church. How effective are you as a leader? Titus 1:5–9 gives three essential qualities of leadership.

1. Effective Leaders Are Grounded in Truth (v. 9). Effective leaders recognize the existence of absolute truth, know right from wrong, and are not afraid to stand for what is right.
2. Effective Leaders Are Encouragers (v. 9). To encourage means to "pump" courage into another person. A true leader does not snap a whip, but bends over to serve, for it is through serving we demonstrate the love of Christ.
3. Effective Leaders Live Godly Lives (vv. 5–9). "Blameless" doesn't mean perfection, but consistency over the long haul. A leader needs to live a godly life in the home (v. 6), the community (vv. 6–8), at work (v. 6), and at church (vv. 5–9).

CONCLUSION: What kind of leader are you? That's an important question to ask because people are watching.

The Joyful Repose of the Christian Life
Date preached:

By W. Graham Scroggie

SCRIPTURE: Philippians 1:1–26

INTRODUCTION: Are you haunted by your past? Are you discontent with your life presently? Do you fear the future? Paul, writing from prison, gives the Philippian believers reason to relax, to rest in Christ:
1. Repose in the Promise of the Past (vv. 1–11).
   A. Praise for Progress (vv. 3–7).
   B. Prayer for Perfecting (vv. 8–11).
2. Repose in the Purpose of the Present (vv. 12–18).
   A. By Means of His Bonds (vv. 12–14).
   B. By Means of His Foes (vv. 15–18).
3. Repose in the Plan for the Future (vv. 19–26).
   A. Paul's Ambition, Come Life or Death (vv. 19–20).
   B. Paul's Attitude towards Life and Death (vv. 21–26).

CONCLUSION: If we have surrendered to Christ as Lord, we can rest assured that Christ has redeemed us and that He will use us for His purposes.

JANUARY 11, 2004

SUGGESTED SERMON

Outward, Inward, Upward

Date preached:

By Paul Borthwick

Scripture: Matthew 9:35–38, especially verse 38: "Therefore pray the Lord of the harvest to send out laborers into His harvest."

Introduction: Traveling in other countries is often an overwhelming experience. The city of Delhi, India, for example, has a larger population than all of New England. Mexico City's population is around twenty million. Manila has over ten million people. Many of these over-populated areas have "squatter villages" near city dumps where inhabitants scavenge food. How do we respond to these desperate situations? And the needs are not only global, they are local and very personal. Every day, people around us are in crisis. What can we do to help? Jesus gives us the answer in today's text.

1. **Our Outward Response (v. 36).** "But when (Jesus) saw the multitudes, He was moved with compassion for them, because they were weary and scattered, like sheep having no shepherd." The word compassion means to "suffer alongside." God's eyes are eyes of compassion. As we watch the nightly news each evening, it's easy to become apathetic, seeing the same stories and accepting them without thinking of the people involved. Do we realize that even terrorists are sinners who need Christ? Jesus saw tax collectors and prostitutes as needy people. What about that person with whom you work—the one who drives you crazy? The one who blocked your promotion or attacked your integrity? Can you see the need behind that person's action, the hurt behind his or her words? We must look outwardly with compassion, reflecting the concern God has for people.

2. **Our Inward Response (v. 38).** If the word "compassion" describes the vision we should have outwardly, the word "laborer" describes the commitment we should have inwardly. The Bible describes us as workers, laborers, servants, stewards, soldiers, and ambassadors. All these words convey our position: We are at the disposal of our Master. When the Old Testament heroine, Esther, went to the king to lobby on behalf of her captive people, she was willing to die because her life was not her own (Esth.

4:16). Paul said, "Let a man so consider us, as stewards . . . of Christ . . . " (1 Cor. 4:1). This is the attitude we should have. Unfortunately, many of us have a "back-pocket Jesus," an "open-in-case-of-emergency Jesus," or an "ATM Jesus." We go to Him when we have a need rather than realizing we were bought with a price. We must view ourselves as people at the disposal of our Master, Jesus Christ. What role does He want you to play in His global and local work?

3. **Our Upward Response (v. 38).** In light of the need of people in verse 36 and the need for workers in verse 38, Jesus tells us to pray. Prayer reminds us we have a Master and it is His harvest. Many believers constantly lie to one another about prayer. I wonder how many times, "I'll pray for you" is spoken and immediately forgotten. As we remember our position as laborers, we should remember whom we serve, the Lord of the harvest. We all are called to pray, but many of us are strangely apathetic about prayer. Maybe we are afraid that if we pray for the Lord to send laborers, we'll end up being called ourselves! We are an integral part of God's global purpose. Perhaps the lack of workers in our church and the low numbers of young people going into vocational Christian service is the result of our failure to obey Jesus' command here in verse 38—to pray for laborers to be raised up.

Conclusion: In a city dump in the Philippines is a "squatter village" called "Smokey Mountain" with needy people everywhere; but in the middle of the

>>> *sermon continued on following page*

APPROPRIATE HYMNS AND SONGS

Christ For the World We Sing, Samuel Wolcott/Felice De Giardini; Public Domain.

Go Forth and Tell, James E. Seddon/Michael Baughen; © 1964 Hope Publishing Company.

Heart for the Nations, Martin J. Nystrom/Gary Sadler; © 1994 Integrity's Hosanna! Music.

Heart to Change the World, Debby Kerner Rettino; © 1987 Kerner-Rettino Music, Admin. by Word Music Group, Inc.

Lord Lay Some Soul Upon My Heart, Mack Weaver/B.B. McKinney; © 1940 Sunday school Board of the Southern Baptist Convention, Admin. by Genevox Music Group.

dump stands a new building with a banner over it, saying: "Welcome to Smokey Mountain." It is the "Smokey Mountain" headquarters of Youth With A Mission. These youth teach about health, give inoculations, and run literacy programs. If you were to ask them why they're located in the middle of a dump, they'd say, "The Lord of the Harvest sent us. We wanted to be obedient. We know God loves these people, though circumstances are forcing them to live in a dump." This is a symbol of our church—a beam of hope in the middle of a hopeless world. It's also a symbol of you and me, ambassadors for Christ in the midst of the moral dump of this city. Let's be His laborers, viewing people compassionately, submitting and praying to Christ as Master, and allowing Him to use us for His global purpose.

> **FOR THE BULLETIN**
>
> ✤ Muhammad arrived in Mecca on January 11, 630, with ten thousand troops. ✤ St. Paulinus of Aquileia, a favorite preacher of Charlemagne, died on this day in A.D. 804. He had been born into a family of Italian farmers, but his brilliant mind, godly heart, and gifted oratory propelled him into the ministry. During his lifetime, he fought heresy and promoted missions. ✤ It's well known that Dorothy Carey, the first wife of William Carey, suffered severe mental illness, aggravated by William's insistence on being a missionary in India. On this day in 1796, William's colleague, John Thomas, discussed the problem in a letter to supporting pastor Andrew Fuller: "Mrs. C has taken it into her head that C (William) is a great whoremonger; and her jealousy burns like fire unquenchable. . . . (She) declares in the most solemn manner that she has catched him with his servants, with his friends, with Mrs. Thomas, and that he is guilty every day and every night." ✤ January 11, 1782, marks the birth of Robert Morrison, first Protestant missionary to China. Arriving there, he lived in a cellar and was rarely seen until he mastered the language. The number of his converts during his twenty-seven years in China was no more than five, but he paved the way for future missions work in that country. ✤ On January 11, 1813, the first pineapples are planted in Hawaii. ✤ Today marks the death of Timothy Dwight, who passed away in 1817. As president of Yale University, Dwight led many of the students to faith in Christ. His chapel sermons are published under the title *Theology Explained and Defended*, and he is the author of the hymn, "I Love Thy Kingdom, Lord." ✤ Christian lawyer, statesman, and hymnist, Francis Scott Key, died on this day in 1843. ✤ The Church of God, headquartered in Cleveland, Tennessee, adopted its current name on this day in 1907, although its history goes back to the late 1800s.

STATS, STORIES AND MORE

A Dangerous Assignment
Missionaries Martin and Gracia Burnham, seized by guerrillas in the Philippines in May, 2001, were held for 376 days. Just before a military raid led to Martin's death and Gracia's freedom, Martin said, "The Bible says to serve the Lord with gladness. Let's go out all the way. Let's serve Him all the way with gladness."

The Need
About six hundred million people in the world claim a personal, saving relationship with Jesus Christ, leaving about 1.4 billion "cultural Christians" who associate in some way with the Christian religion but don't necessarily follow Jesus as Savior and Lord. Another 2.5 billion people are non-Christian, but have some access to the gospel message by various means. More than 1.6 billion people have virtually no access to the gospel, a church, Scripture, or followers of Christ. Forty-one countries have populations that are 99 percent non-Christian.

Support Base
In his book, *The Great Omission,* Robertson McQuilkin points out that in the days before William Carey, the father of the modern Protestant missionary movement, the Moravians from Herrnhut considered a support base of four adequate to keep one missionary at the front. Using that formula, America's forty million evangelicals could support ten million overseas workers.

Using a more modern standard, it was said that during World War II fifteen personnel were needed to keep one man at the front. Using that as a basis, the American evangelical church could support a missionary force of 2,666,666.

But evangelical churches of the United States, perhaps the wealthiest group of Christians in history, now have about thirty-seven thousand career foreign missionaries, about nine thousand of whom are engaged in full-time evangelism.

"The truth is," says McQuilkin, "less than 1 percent of full-time Christian workers are engaged in evangelistic ministry among the unevangelized of the world. Is this the way the Commander-in-Chief would assign His troops? Or is someone not listening?"

Compassion
If we could only read the secret history of our enemies, we would find in each man's life sorrow and suffering enough to disarm all hostility.
—Henry Wadsworth Longfellow.

WORSHIP HELPS

Call to Worship:
Jesus said to them again, "Peace to you! As the Father has sent Me, I also send you" (John 20:21).

Pastoral Prayer:
Father, so often we present our prayer requests and forget about those things for which You Yourself have requested prayer. You've told us in Psalm 122 to pray for the peace of Jerusalem. You've asked us to pray for rulers and for those in authority over us. And You've bid us pray to You, the Lord of the harvest, for workers for Your fields. Lord, we do need more workers in this church. Your church around the world needs more preachers and pastors, more teachers and leaders, more missionaries and evangelists. Will You not raise up a new generation for Christ!

Responsive Reading:

Leader:	The Lord is gracious and full of compassion, slow to anger and great in mercy. The Lord is good to all, and His tender mercies are over all His works.
People:	His compassions fail not. They are new every morning; Great is Your faithfulness.
Leader:	Should you not also have had compassion?
People:	Be of one mind, having compassion for one another; love as brothers, be tenderhearted.

(Taken from Ps. 145:8–9; Lam. 3:22–23; Matt. 18:33; 1 Pet. 3:8)

Kids Talk

Take a picture of a street person and put on a little table. As the children gather around you, get up and walk to one side of the picture. Criticize the man in the picture. Call him worthless and lazy. Then stop talking and walk around to the other side of the picture. This time, speak compassionately about the man. This poor man. . . perhaps his father abandoned him; perhaps his mother was mean to him; who knows what problems and troubles he has had. He needs someone to pray for him. Then sit down in front of the picture, and ask the children which response is the one Jesus would approve.

Additional Sermons and Lesson Ideas

Ponder This
Date preached:

Based on a message by Charles Spurgeon

SCRIPTURE: Luke 2:19

INTRODUCTION: This blessed woman—Mary—exercised three parts of her being:

1. Her Memory. She kept all these things. Beloved, remember what you have heard about Christ and what He has done for you. Let your memory treasure everything about Christ that you have felt, known, or believed.
2. Her Affections. She kept them in her heart. Let your affections hold Him forever. Open the alabaster box of your heart and let the precious ointment of your affections stream over His pierced feet.
3. Her Intellect. She pondered them. Meditate on what you read about Jesus in Scripture. Don't stop at the surface, but dive into the depths. Be not like a bird that does not touch the water with its wings, but be like a fish that penetrates an ocean's depth.

CONCLUSION: If your mind cannot grasp the Lord Jesus in your understanding, embrace Him in the arms of affection.

Seven Incorruptible Things
Date preached:

SCRIPTURE: Romans 1:23

INTRODUCTION: In a world of decay and change, it's good to know that some things are incorruptible. This word literally means "incapable of death or decay," and it occurs exactly seven times in the Bible, referring to:

1. God Himself (Rom. 1:23).
2. The King of Kings. 1 Timothy 1:17 says, "Now to the King. . . immortal (the Greek word there is the same—incorruptible)."
3. The Incorruptible Word of God (1 Pet. 1:23).
4. The Christian's Reward. 1 Corinthians 9:25 speaks of our incorruptible (imperishable) crown.
5. The Inner Beauty of the Spirit-Transformed Soul (1 Pet. 3:4).
6. Our Heavenly Home (1 Pet. 1:4).
7. Our Transformed Resurrection Bodies (1 Cor.15:42).

CONCLUSION: The hymn writer said: *Change and decay in all around I see; / O Thou who changest not, abide with me.*

CLASSICS FOR THE PASTOR'S LIBRARY

Gleanings from Thomas Watson

It was tough being an evangelical pastor in seventeenth-century England.

As the government seesawed between Catholic and Protestant-leaning monarchs, the Puritans and Dissenters were hounded, hunted down, and harried out of the land. In 1662, a series of Parliamentary acts further plagued the Puritans. The Act of Uniformity, for example, required all English ministers to either use the government-sanctioned *Book of Common Prayer* in their services or leave their pulpits. As a result, on August 17, 1662, two thousand ministers preached their farewell sermons and were expelled from their churches.

Among them was Thomas Watson.

I wish we knew more about Watson, for he is among the most readable and quotable of the Puritans. His writings brim with practical, biblical truth. He could grasp doctrine like J. I. Packer, craft a sermon like John Stott, and turn a phrase like Vance Havner.

His date and place of birth are unknown to us, and little information has survived about his upbringing. We know that in 1646, following his training at Cambridge, he married a minister's daughter and the two of them moved to the City of London, where Thomas became rector of the parish of St. Stephen's, Walbrook.

There the popularity of his sermons was excelled only by the renown of his deeply moving, extemporaneous prayers. Crowds came, souls were converted, and his influence spread through London and across England. His ministry at St. Stephens continued, with brief interruptions (he was once thrown into the Tower of London for his political views), until the aforementioned Act of Uniformity in 1662.

Ejected but not dejected, he continued teaching and preaching in barns, homes, kitchens, and wooded groves, quietly and always at risk. After the Declaration of Indulgence restored his freedom to minister in 1672, he publicly resumed preaching in the great hall of a friend's mansion.

His failing health finally forced his removal to the village of Barnston, where he died in 1686 while engaged in prayer.

If you've never read any of the Puritans, *Gleanings from Thomas Watson* is an excellent starting place. It's an assortment of irresistible, pithy truths culled from Watson's writings, first compiled and published in 1915 by Central Bible Truth Depot in London. It has recently been reprinted by Soli Deo Gloria Publishers.

Here are some samples from my own underlined and dog-eared copy:

- "True grace holds out in the winter season. That is a precious faith, which, like the star, shines brightest in the darkest night."

- "Other physicians can only cure them that are sick, but Christ cures them that are dead. He doth not only cure them but crown them. Christ doth not only raise from the bed, but to the throne. He gives the sick man not only health but heaven."

- "The world is fading not filling."

- "If God be our God, He will give us peace in trouble. When there is a storm without, He will make peace within. The world can create trouble in peace, but God can create peace in trouble."

- "Who would have thought to have found adultery in David, and drunkenness in Noah, and cursing in Job? If God leave a man to himself, how suddenly and scandalously may sin break forth in the holiest men of the earth! 'I say unto all, Watch.' A wandering heart needs a watchful eye."

- "Prayer delights God's ear, it melts His heart, it opens His hand: God cannot deny a praying soul."

- "The world is but a great inn, where we are to stay a night or two, and be gone; what madness is it so to set our heart upon our inn, as to forget our home."

Charles Spurgeon called Watson "one of the most concise, racy, illustrative, and suggestive" of those who made the Puritan age the "Augustan period of evangelical literature."

I wouldn't call Watson "racy"—he was, after all, a Puritan—but he has certainly become one of my favorite authors.

I hope you'll make his acquaintance, too.

JANUARY 18, 2004

SUGGESTED SERMON

Real Revival

Date preached:

By Melvin Worthington

Scripture: 2 Chronicles 7:12–16, especially verse 14: "If My people who are called by My name will humble themselves, and pray and seek My face, and turn from their wicked ways, then I will hear from heaven, and will forgive their sin and heal their land."

Introduction: Why disturb the status quo? Do we need revival? Millions belong to churches across America. Publishing houses fill the marketplace with Christian books and magazines. Christian colleges number in the thousands. Religious activities make front-page news. The media is clogged with religious programming. What more do we need? We need revival. God's people have become forgetful and formal. Carnality, carelessness, and compromise have stolen the testimonies of many churches and Christians in this confused, corrupt world. Our greatest need is not more men, money, or methods. The greatest need is for spiritual revival, a divine infusion of life into the church which declares itself through an inflowing, outflowing, and overflowing of the Holy Ghost. This troubled society with its tired saints must have revival. Real revival will make a difference in our churches and society at large.

1. **Revival Misconceptions.** The very word *revival* suggests restoration, renewal, and return. The process that leads to revival always begins with man's rebellion, continues with his remorse and climaxes with his repentance and restoration. The pattern and process is amplified in the Book of Judges. Revival comes from heaven. It cannot be worked up. It must be prayed down. It is not man's doing but God's miracle. Methods, organizations, and publicity are not revival and do not produce revival. Only revival that comes from the bosom of God can awaken, arouse, and activate God's people. *Emotionalism* and *enthusiasm* are not revival, although emotions and enthusiasm are certainly involved when God moves among His people. *Evangelism*, simply sharing the gospel, is not revival. Genuine revival that results in a love for lost men everywhere always manifests itself in evangelism, but evangelism alone is not revival. *Education* is not revival. Learning how to get the job done by mental discipline and moral principles is a poor

substitute for heaven-sent revival. *Enlargement* is not revival. Church growth alone is not an indication of real revival.

2. **Revival Mandates.** Real revival *commences with brokenness.* Believers must get alone with God. He speaks and they tremble at His Word. There is conviction, confession, and cleansing. Revival begins with God's people. Revival *continues with beseeching.* Prayer is a vital element in the channel of revival. When we pray we commune with God. No work of God is of lasting value without prayer. Revival *continues with a burden.* After being confronted with our sin, after beseeching our Heavenly Father for cleansing, we are then burdened for the will of God. We want more than anything else to find, follow, and finish God's will for our lives. Revival *culminates in behavior.* Revival climaxes in a change of behavior. Saints turn from stubborn, slack, and sinful ways to obedience. When saints obey, then Jesus is exalted in our hearts, our heads, and our habits. Revival that does not affect our beliefs and our behavior is man-made, not heaven-sent. The mandates for a heaven-sent revival are set forth in 2 Chronicles 7:14, "If my people which are called by my name, shall humble themselves, and pray, and seek my face, and turn from their wicked ways; then will I hear from heaven, and will forgive their sin, and will heal their land."

3. **Revival Manifestations**. Some undeniable traits of revival are a humble spirit, hatred of sin, hunger for the Scriptures, holiness in saints, honesty among servants, and a harvest of souls. We are rightly concerned about church growth, evangelism, youth conflicts, Christian schools, family life, and discipleship training. Let us add one more concern—the biblical

>>> *sermon continued on following page*

APPROPRIATE HYMNS AND SONGS

If My People, Don Wyrtzen; © 1974 Singspiration Music, Admin. by Brentwood/Benson Music Publishing, Inc.

If My People Who Bear My Name, Graham Kendrick; © 1987 Make Way Music, Admin. by Music Services.

Answer Us, Andy Park; © 1995 Mercy/Vineyard Publishing.

Flow O Mighty Holy River, Connie Boerner; © 1989 Integrity's Hosanna! Music.

Revive Us Again, William P. MacKay/John J. Husband; Public Domain.

teaching on revival. John Wesley many have handed us the revival key when he said, "Give me one hundred preachers who fear nothing but sin and desire nothing but God, and I care not a straw whether they be clergymen or laymen. They alone will shake the gates of Hell and set the kingdom of Heaven upon the earth."

Conclusion: Real revival is desperately needed in the Church of Jesus Christ. We must not settle for the counterfeits. Genuine revival will make a difference. It will disturb the status quo. Much of that which is called revival in the world today has produced no change of behavior. The evidences of real revival among the saints include a humble spirit, hatred of sin, hunger for the Scriptures, holiness in the saints, honesty among servants, and a harvest of souls. When God's people get serious about their spiritual condition and meet God's conditions for revival, real revival will come from God.

FOR THE BULLETIN

✱ After the outbreak of the Protestant Reformation in 1517, Roman Catholic officials convened the Council of Trent to articulate the principles of the Counter-Reformation. The first meeting took place in 1545, and met periodically for years as decisions were made and published. The third era of these periodic sessions convened on this day in 1562, with all hope of reconciliation with the Protestants gone. ✱ On January 18, 1674, Scottish "Worthy" James Mitchell was executed after having been tortured for his faith. Being led to the Grassmarket in Edinburgh to be hanged, he was forbidden from preaching to the crowds, so he flung a manuscript of his message to the crowd. It said in part: "I am brought here that the work of God may be made manifest for the trail of faith, that I might be a witness for His despised truths and interests in this land, where I am called to seal the same with my blood. . . . Farewell to all earthly enjoyments; and welcome Father, Son, and Holy Ghost into whose hands I commit my spirit." ✱ Taylor University was established in Fort Wayne, Indiana, by Methodists on January 18, 1846. ✱ Today marks the birthday of John Stam (1907), who, along with his wife Betty, was murdered by the Communists in China in 1934. ✱ Andrew Murray, Dutch Reformed pastor in South Africa and famous devotional writer, died on this day in 1917. Missionary Amy Carmichael died on January 18, 1951.

Kids Talk

Today's message is about unity in the church. Gather the children around and show them the way to construct a church with one's hands, repeating the words: "Here's the church and here's the steeple. Open the doors and see the people." Show them how intertwined the people are, how we are all "in this thing together." Remind them of the value of loving each other and of spending time together.

STATS, STORIES AND MORE

If My People Pray

How should we pray when God burdens us for something in particular? How should we pray when we need revival in our nation and in our own hearts? How should we pray when a loved one is troubled? How should we pray for those things that only God can provide? We should give ourselves no rest and we should give the Lord no rest until he answers our prayers and fulfills his promises (Is. 62:6–7).

Missionary John Hyde of India, who later became known as "Praying" Hyde, grew up in Carthage, Illinois, in a minister's home. At McCormick Theological Seminary, he committed himself to overseas evangelism, and, following graduation, he went to India. His itinerant ministry took him from village to village, but his preaching produced few converts until he discovered the truth of Isaiah 62:6–9, and took these words literally.

At the beginning of 1908, he prayed to win at least one soul to Christ every day. By December 31, he had recorded over four hundred converts. The following year, the Lord laid two souls per day on his heart, and his prayer was again answered. The next year he prayed for four souls daily with similar results.

Once, stopping at a cottage for water, Praying Hyde pleaded with God for ten souls. He presented the gospel to the family, and by the end of his visit all nine members of the family had been saved. But what of number ten? Suddenly a nephew who had been playing outside ran into the room and was promptly converted.

Hyde's great missionary work flowed from his prayer life like water from a fountain, and he finally wore himself out in prayer, staying on his knees, night after night, year after year, reminding God of His promises and giving the Lord no rest. Christians in India still speak of his lasting impact.

WORSHIP HELPS

Call to Worship:
To Him be glory in the church by Christ Jesus to all generations, forever and ever. Amen. (Eph. 3:21).

Offertory Comments:
The great American revivalist, Charles Finney, was far more outspoken than most of us pastors today. He once wrote a chapter on the subject, "What Hinders Revival," and in it he warned his readers about failing to give of their tithes and offerings. He said: *When Christians refuse to render to the Lord according to the benefits received; this is a fruitful source of religious declensions. God has opened the windows of heaven to a church and poured them out a blessing, and then he reasonably expects them to bring in the tithes into his storehouse and devise and execute liberal things for Zion; and lo! they have refused; they have not laid themselves out accordingly to promote the cause of Christ; and so the Spirit has been grieved and the blessing withdrawn, and in some instances a great reaction has taken place because the church would not be liberal when God has been so bountiful."* Even though those words are a little blunt, what would happen if we really took them to heart?

Suggested Scripture Readings:
Acts 2:41–47
Ephesians 4:1–16
1 Corinthians 13

Benediction:
Now may amazing grace of the Master, Jesus Christ, and the extravagant love of God, and the intimate friendship of the Holy Spirit, be with you all. Amen. (Adapted from 2 Corinthians 13:14, *The Message*).

Additional Sermons and Lesson Ideas

Spare Change
By Drew Wilkerson

Date preached:

SCRIPTURE: Luke 21:1–4

INTRODUCTION: It seems the more money some people have the more they want. With others, however, the more they have the more they give. What does God think about our financial resources? A widow helps us gain the understanding we need.

1. God is concerned with how we handle our money.
2. God's desire is not "equal giving." God's concern is "equal sacrifice."
3. The issue is not about how much money we have. The issue is what we do with what we have.

CONCLUSION: God takes it personally when we are stingy with our resources. He doesn't want our spare change. He wants all that we have. When we give with an attitude of selfless joy, we will never be able to out-give God.

Submission to God's Authority
By David George

Date preached:

SCRIPTURE: 1 Samuel 15:1–23; especially verse 22; 1 Samuel 24:1–13, especially verse 6.

INTRODUCTION: How can we, like David, become people after God's own heart? The dynamics between Saul and David show the necessity of submission to God's authority.

1. Submission is more important than worship (15:1–22). Saul assumed authority over God, sacrificing what God said to destroy. God accepts our praise as sacrifice (Heb. 13:15), but rejects it if we disobey.
2. Never violate God's law to implement God's plan (15:22). Like Saul, many times we think, "the end justifies the means." It is impossible to disobey God for *His good*.
3. Failure to submit causes you to lose a favorable role in God's plan (15:23). Because Saul did not submit to God's authority, God rejected him as king. Have you decided your way is better than God's?
4. Submit to the humans who represent God's authority. Saul repeatedly attempted to kill David (1 Sam. chs. 18—26). Although David could have killed Saul, he submitted to God's anointed (1 Sam. 24:6). Do you submit to God's authorities on earth (Rom. 13)?

CONCLUSION: Submission to God's authority should dominate our lives, in worship, in obedience, in leadership, and in respect towards human leaders.

SANCTITY OF LIFE SERMON

Value and Dignity of Human Life
Date preached:

By Ed Dobson

Scripture: Various; especially Genesis 2:7: And the LORD formed man of the dust of the ground, and breathed into his nostrils the breath of life; and man became a living being.

Introduction: In our culture, have we lost our sense of the value of life? We hate traffic and busy shopping malls. We want a three-bedroom house for two people. The fewer the better, right? We abort the young and euthanize the old. Humans are no longer viewed as an asset, but as an inconvenience. Let's look at how this warped view of human life compares with Scripture.

1. **Where Does Human Life Come from?** (Gen. 2:7). Life is a gift from God. Adam, the first man, is the Hebrew word *Adom* which means *man*. It comes from a word which means "red dirt." But God breathed into the dirt the breath of life, His own breath, and what was just dirt became a living, breathing human being. To get from dirt to all of us here this morning requires the supernatural, creative intervention of God. Distinct from every other created thing, humans have God's image (Gen. 1:27).

2. **When Does Human Life Begin?** (Matt. 1:18–20; Luke 1:41; Ps. 139:13). From a biblical viewpoint, human life begins at conception. Notice in Matthew 1:18–20 that the Holy Spirit brought about conception within Mary's womb. In Luke 1:41, Elizabeth's baby leaps in response to the presence of Mary and the unborn Christ, and the Holy Spirit comes upon him. Psalm 139:13 says God is involved in the formation of an unborn baby in the womb. Are you being careless about your diet, or smoking, or drinking while pregnant? The life within you is already greatly valued by God.

3. **When Does Human Life End?** (Ps. 139:16). This text tells us that, before our birth, God plans our steps. God alone has the right to end life. I may shorten my life through reckless living and sinful choices (1 Cor. 11:27–31). On rare occasions God may even extend life (Is. 38:1–5). The larger truth of Scripture is that none of us know when we will die, but God knows. Life ends in the plan, purpose, and timing of God.

Application:

1. **Value Life.** We should value life as God does. How much does God value life? Think of the Cross. He sent His only Son as a sacrifice for our sins, so that if we believe we can have eternal life (John 3:16).

2. **Respect Life in its Various Stages and Forms.** The young and the old seem to be the most often discarded in our society. Because abortion is so often discussed and so controversial, I would like to further discuss this subject:
   A. **Abortion Violates the First Commandment** (Gen.1:28). I am not referring to the first of the Ten Commandments, but to the first commandment ever given to man, to multiply and increase in number. God encourages reproduction of people made in His image!
   B. **Abortion Violates the Sixth Commandment** (Ex. 20:13). The sixth of the Ten Commandments reads, "You shall not murder." Abortion violates this command. Severe endangerment of the mother's life is the only possible exception I can ponder. I'd like to add a few comments on this difficult issue:
   - **God Is Forgiving.** If anyone here has gone through the tragedy of aborting a child, God will receive you with open arms if you repent and ask His forgiveness (Luke 15:20; 1 John 1:9).
   - **God Is Just.** Also, if you have lost a child, through abortion, miscarriage, SIDS, or any other way, trust God concerning their salvation. David's baby was lost due to his sin, but he remained confident that God would allow his child into heaven (2 Sam. 12:23).
   - **God Is Able.** If you are in this congregation and you are considering abortion, I beg of you before God who gives life, seek help. Don't take the life of your child, but trust God; seek help from us in this congregation. God will help us bear any burden (1 Cor. 10:13), and as believers, we are commanded to help you (Gal. 6:2).

3. **Protect Life.** We are not to use violence to push our cause; bombing abortion clinics is *just as bad as abortion*! Be someone who helps. Teach biblical truth: the value of human life, and the forgiveness of God. Support a Christian pregnancy center. Make sure nursing homes are safe. Vote against legalization of abortion and euthanasia. If you're not a part of the solution, you're part of the problem.

Conclusion: Let's thank God for life. Thank You, Lord, for life abundant. Thank You, Lord, for life eternal. Thank You, Lord, for life today.

JANUARY 25, 2004

SUGGESTED SERMON

An Amazing Offer
By David Jackman

Date preached:

Scripture: Titus 2:11–14, especially verse 11: "For the grace of God that brings salvation has appeared to all men . . ."

Introduction: Why should anyone believe Christianity? Where do we find its credibility? The Book of Titus is concerned with that very question. The context for this epistle is the pagan island of Crete where Paul and Titus have been planting churches. Christianity was coming to Crete for the first time, and Paul left Titus to "set in order the things that are lacking and appoint elders in every city" (Titus 1:5). The standards for the elders were very high, and clearly it wasn't going to be easy to find people like that in Crete (Titus 1:6—10:13). In the first century, there was a verb in Greek literature—to Crete-inize—and it meant "to lie." That's why the issue for Titus was credibility. People wanted to know, "Is this Christian message really credible?" It was a culture very much like our own in which you couldn't really believe anything that anybody said. It was full of liars. So why should anybody believe the Christian preachers? Why should anyone believe the gospel in Crete, or in our world today? Well there is one irrefutable argument. The proof of the pudding is in the eating. If this Good News actually transforms people's lives—if "liars, evil beasts, and lazy gluttons" (1:12) became self-controlled, upright, holy, and disciplined people (1:8)—then the credibility of the message will be secured. And that is the function of the Gospel of Grace as it is presented in Titus 2:11-15.

1. **God's Grace Meets Humanity's Universal Requirement.** "The grace of God brings salvation. . . ." This is a major theme of the Book of Titus. There are five references in this letter to God as our Savior, our Rescuer (see 1:3–4; 2:10; 2:13; 3:4). That presupposes that we are in a condition of needing to be saved. Titus 3:3 tells us what we need to be rescued from: Foolishness, disobedience, deception by the spurious attraction of temptations, being consumed by lusts and pleasures, living in malice and envy, hating and being hated. By definition, we are rescued when the danger is

great and when our own ability is insufficient. There is a coming Day of Judgment, hell is as great a reality as heaven, and we need to be rescued.

2. **God's Grace Provides God's Unique Remedy.** "The grace of God that brings salvation has appeared to all men." I need to be rescued because I can't dig myself out of my own pit. I don't have the will or the moral strength to do it. Unless a power of righteousness greater than my own acts on my behalf, there is no hope. God, of course, does not need to do that—except that He is a God of grace and love. His grace is His free favor that we cannot and do not deserve. In grace, God does not give us what we deserve; He gives us what we don't deserve. This salvation is potentially for everyone, since all are equally in need. But go back to the original question: What credibility does this message have? Is it just comforting fiction? No, there is a verb in this verse that is very important. The grace of God that brings salvation *has appeared*. That is a historical verb. Something happened in time and space, in history, when the grace of God ceased being just an idea and became visible, tangible, a reality. It appeared. And that grace has been accessible to everybody ever since. Verse 13 defines it as the "appearing of our great God and Savior Jesus Christ." God's plan is rooted in the historical appearing of Jesus Christ, who was born of the Virgin Mary in Bethlehem, who gave His life as an atoning sacrifice for the world. Everyone who will accept that grace gains peace with God and a restored relationship with Him. It's all about God's grace. Jesus appeared to rescue sinners.

>>> *sermon continued on following page*

APPROPRIATE HYMNS AND SONGS

Amazing Grace, John Newton; Public Domain.

He Giveth More Grace, Annie Johnston Flint/Hubert Mitchell; © 1941. Renewed 1969 Lillenas Publishing Company, Admin. by The Copyright Company.

Wonderful Grace of Jesus, Haldor Lillenas; Public Domain.

Shout to the North, Martin Smith; © 1995 Curious Music UK, Admin. by EMI Christian Music Publishing.

Grace Alone, Scott Wesley Brown/Jeff Nelson; © 1998 Maranatha! Music.

Conclusion: The amazing offer of God's grace is still on the table for us today. Why do we find it so hard to live by grace? When the message is so amazing, what is there within us that rejects it? It has something to do with the humbling nature of the message. We have to admit we're failures; we cannot save ourselves. But Christ can save us. He is the Rescuer, and today He is making you an amazing offer: For the grace of God that brings salvation has appeared to you, to transform your life.

FOR THE BULLETIN

✺ In Christian tradition, this day commemorates the conversion of St. Paul to Christianity. ✺ The Roman Emperor, Nerva, dying suddenly on January 25, A.D. 98, was succeeded by his adopted son, Trajan, who proved a tireless and able administrator. It was Trajan who sent his advisor Pliny the Younger to Bithynia in 110, to check out disturbances relating to Christian activity. Pliny wrote back his famous letter, which is now our earliest extant Roman document regarding Christianity. It said, in part: *On an appointed day, they meet before daybreak, recite a hymn antiphonally to Christ, as to a god, and bind themselves by an oath to abstain from theft, robbery, adultery and breach of faith. After the conclusion of this ceremony it was their custom to depart and meet again to take food.* ✺ On January 25, 1527, Felix Manz, 30, became the first Swiss Anabaptist to die for the faith. He was drowned by followers of Zwingli in the Limmat River in Zurich. ✺ Mendelssohn's "Wedding March" was presented for the first time on this day in 1858, as the daughter of Queen Victoria married the Crown Prince of Prussia. ✺ January 25, 1949, marks the death of Scottish-born Peter Marshall, chaplain to the United States Senate. ✺ On January 25, 1959, Pope John XXIII announced the Second Vatican Council to bring Roman Catholic worship and practice up to date. He attributed the idea of convening such an assembly to a sudden inspiration by the Holy Spirit. ✺ President John F. Kennedy was buried in Arlington National Cemetery on January 25, 1963.

STATS, STORIES AND MORE

More from David Jackman
Titus 2:11–14 is a great jewel lying at the heart of this little pastoral letter to Titus. These verses are remarkable because they constitute one of the clearest summaries of authentic first-century Christianity that we have in the whole of the New Testament, and they resonate very clearly to our world today. This gives us God's master plan. Here, God both lays out His purposes for our world, and He also expands the methodology by which the reality of that plan has credibility in our world.

Amazing Grace
After his mother's death when he was about seven, John Newton alternated between boarding school and the high seas. At times he sought to live a Christian life through his own efforts, but his resolve always collapsed, and he went deeper into sin. Pressed into service with the British Navy, he deserted, was captured, and after two days of suspense, was flogged. His subsequent thoughts vacillated between murder and suicide. "I was capable of anything," he recalled. More voyages, dangers, toils, and snares followed. It was a life unrivaled in fiction. Then, on the night of March 9, 1748, John, 23, was jolted awake by a brutal storm that descended too suddenly for the crew to foresee. The next day, in great peril, he cried to the Lord. He later wrote, "That tenth of March is a day much remembered by me; and I have never suffered it to pass unnoticed since the year 1748—the Lord came from on high and delivered me out of deep waters." His hymn, "Amazing Grace," is his testimony.

More on Amazing Grace
Here's a nearly forgotten verse that Newton added near the end of "Amazing Grace":

> *The earth shall soon dissolve like snow, the sun forbear to shine;*
> *But God, who called me here below, will be forever mine.*

Quotes about Grace:
Grace is but glory begun, and glory is but grace perfected.
—*Jonathan Edwards*
Grace is free, but when once you take it you are bound forever to the Giver.
—*E. Stanley Jones*
I need Thy presence every passing hour; / What but Thy grace can foil the tempter's power?
—*Henry Francis Lyte*

WORSHIP HELPS

Call to Worship:
Behold the throne of grace, / The promise calls us near, / There Jesus shows a smiling face / And waits to answer prayer.—John Newton

Pastoral Prayer:
We thank you, O God, for your amazing grace revealed in Jesus Christ our Lord. And we thank you that He now appears in heaven to intercede for us, and will appear a second time as the Great God and Savior who comes to judge the world. Thank you so much for His coming in grace, for His Throne of Grace, for His all-sufficient grace. Please help us to marvel at it today and to find it meets all our deepest needs. May the grace of our Lord Jesus Christ be with us all. Amen.—David Jackman

Responsive Reading from Titus 2:1–8:

Leader:	But as for you, speak the things which are proper for sound doctrine.
Men:	That the older men be sober, reverent, temperate, sound in faith, in love, in patience.
Women:	The older women likewise, that they be reverent in behavior, not slanderers, not given to much wine, teachers of good things—that they admonish the young women to love their husbands, to love their children.
Leader:	To be discreet, chaste, homemakers, good, obedient to their own husbands, that the word of God may not be blasphemed.
Men:	Likewise, exhort the young men to be sober-minded, in all things showing yourself to be a pattern of good works; in doctrine, showing integrity, reverence, incorruptibility, sound speech that cannot be condemned.
All:	That one who is an opponent may be ashamed, having nothing evil to say to you.

Benediction:

Sweet Savior, bless us ere we go;
Thy Word into our minds instill,
And make our lukewarm hearts to glow
With lowly love and fervent will.
—Frederick W. Faber

Additional Sermons and Lesson Ideas

The Model Marriage
By Melvin Worthington

Date preached:

SCRIPTURE: Genesis 2:18–25

INTRODUCTION: Marriage was conceived in the mind and heart of God to bring together a man and a woman in a wonderful relationship.

1. Marriage Is a Divine Institution. God ordained marriage for our good.
2. Marriage Is a Defined Institution. God set the parameters for marriage—one man and one woman in a lifetime relationship is the ideal marriage.
3. Marriage Is a Designed Institution. God designed marriage for male and female. Men and women were created differently to complement the other.
4. Marriage Is a Directed Institution. The directives for a happy, harmonious, and holy home are found in the Bible. The relations of husband and wife are clear and concisely delineated in the Word of God.

CONCLUSION: The proper concept of marriage can make a significant difference in every home, and couples will greatly benefit by carefully reading God's marriage blueprint.

The Lofty Ideal of the Christian Life
By W. Graham Scroggie

Date preached:

SCRIPTURE: Philippians 1:27—2:30

INTRODUCTION: An incredibly "lofty" and difficult standard is set forth for believers in our text. Is it really possible to live worthy of the gospel as these verses suggest? Besides, the standard is Jesus Christ. We have in these passages a standard set, but also living examples of those who lived up to them.

1. The Standard Appointed (1:27—2:16).
   A. Steadfastness in Suffering (1:27–30).
   B. Harmony by Humility (2:1–11).
   C. Effectiveness through Earnest Effort (2:12–16).
2. The Standard Approached (2:17–30).
   A. The Example of Paul (2:17–18).
   B. The Example of Timothy (2:19–24).
   C. The Example of Epaphroditus (2:25–30).

CONCLUSION: Jesus is the supreme standard for living a life worthy of the gospel. Our lives should shine in suffering, humility, and works. Paul is an example of sacrifice. Timothy lived as a servant. Epaphroditus worked diligently as a soldier. To live worthy of the gospel is possible, but requires dependence upon God and hard work. Are you living worthy?

THOUGHTS FOR THE PASTOR'S SOUL

What Do You Do All Week?

"What do you do all week?" the man asked me in a tone of incredulity. I think he was wondering why anyone would pay me a full-time salary for speaking a half-hour once a week. That's a hard question to answer, not because we pastors do so little but because we do so much. Where does one begin? But it's a fair question. If people pay our salaries out of their own they should know we're laborers worthy of our hire.

One of the best descriptions of a pastor's duties is found in the tiny Book of Jude. This book was written by a man whose busy life reflected his status as a leader in the early church. As the son of Joseph and Mary, he had grown up living in the same house as Jesus. They had played together in Nazareth's haunts, and had worked side-by-side in shop and field. Following a period of skepticism and intellectual doubt (John 7:5), Jude had become a convinced and converted disciple, and had joined the band of early believers (Acts 1:14). He had married, had become a father and a traveling evangelist, and was everywhere recognized as "the Lord's brother," which gave him great prominence in the early church (1 Cor. 9:5; see also the writings of Eusebius).

In verse 3 of his book, Jude states the purpose of his letter, and in so doing gives us a description of what a pastor, minister, or Christian leader should be doing all week: *Beloved, while I was very diligent to write to you concerning our common salvation, I found it necessary to write to you exhorting you to contend earnestly for the faith which was once for all delivered to the saints.*

We Love Our People

The first word in verse 3 is *beloved*—*agapatos* in the Greek. Jude uses the same form of address again in verses 17 and 20. He loved those to whom he was writing, and he wasn't ashamed to express that love. He wasn't just a brilliant preacher or a respected leader. He was a warm, accessible shepherd who held his flock deeply in his heart. I read of a young minister who found that he loved the limelight of preaching, but one day his sermon royally flopped, and shortly thereafter he experienced a heart-crisis in ministry. An older Christian put his arm over his shoulder, saying, "Son, it's one thing to love to preach to people; it's another thing to love the people to whom you preach."

Jesus loved His own who were in the world, and He loved them to the end (John 13:1). It was the driving force of divine love that enabled the apostle Paul to withstand the jeering, the floggings, and the fatigue of ministry (2 Cor. 5:14).

We pastors need to ask ourselves plainly, "Do I love this church—these people—who sit before the pulpit every week? Do I love the ones that don't show up? Do I love the ones that cause me trouble? Do I love the children, the teens, the adults? Do I really love this flock?"

Contrary to popular opinion, love is not having a trouble-free relationship with someone. Love is caring deeply about the other person *even if* you're having stress in your association. And love means putting up with the faults, flaws, and failures of others. Love is being proactive in trying to avoid or correct the problems you may be having in the relationship.

Once, entering a pastorate, I was warned that a particular lady would almost certainly call us as soon as we had unpacked and invite us over for a meal. She would be sizing us up, I was told. She had been a thorn in the side of several pastors, I was told.

That evening, I picked up the telephone and invited her to have supper at our house next week. I told her that, being new to the church, I'd like to get to know my people. Since she had been in the church for many years, perhaps she could share some of the history of the church, how it began, how its former pastors had faired. Her tone of voice told me she wasn't quite sure what to make of these turned tables. Nonetheless, she and another lady came to supper the next week and we had a lovely meal and a profitable chat. From that day she was an ally rather than an enemy.

Romans 12 says: *If it is possible, as much as depends on you, live peaceably with all men.* And with all women, too.

We Manage Our Schedules

Second, Jude managed his schedule. Look again at the way he puts it in verse 3: *Beloved, while I was very diligent to write to you concerning the common salvation, I found it necessary to write to you, exhorting you to contend earnestly for the faith which was once for all delivered to the saints.*

Notice the first phrase: . . . *while I was very diligent to write you.* The key word that is used here in the original Greek means "haste, in a hurry." This indicates Jude was very busy in the ministry. He said, in effect, *I've been trying to get around to . . . I've been busy trying to get*

THOUGHTS FOR THE PASTOR'S SOUL—CONTINUED

this done . . . I've been trying to find time to write to you about this . . . In other words, he had eagerly wanted to sit down and write to them, but he not been able to carve out time until the nature of the crisis at hand demanded it.

The Lord's work is never done. I never go to bed at night with that satisfying sense of a day's work being finished. There's always a phone call or a visit I didn't make. There's always another hour I should have put into my sermons or lessons. There's always a sick person I didn't visit, someone needing counseling I didn't see.

Beyond those pastoral obligations, our work involves a great deal of administration. We're not just to minister; we're to *ad*-minister. And that involves brainstorming, meetings, planning, paperwork, and staff oversight.

Then there's sermon preparation: I could spend the whole week just studying for sermons and nothing more. I've always been envious of the great preacher, Ambrose.

He was a great preacher and a deft defender of orthodox doctrine. He combated paganism and heresy with diligence, maintained the independence of the church against civil powers, and championed morality. He confronted political leaders, even emperors, when necessary. He wrote books and treatises, sermons, hymns, and letters. He tended Milan like a shepherd.

Perhaps none of that was more important than his influence on a hot-blooded infidel who slipped into town one Sunday to hear him preach. The skeptical Augustine found himself deeply impressed by the power of Ambrose's sermons, and he sought personal counseling from the bishop. But Ambrose was too busy. Visitors were allowed into his room, but he paid scant attention to them. He just went ahead reading, and those who wanted to see him stood along the wall in his study, watching him pore over books, watching him pray, watching him prepare his message. Several times Augustine stood watching him, but Ambrose remained unaware of it. His preaching, however, reached the prodigal, and shortly afterward Augustine was converted.

In a somewhat similar vein, it was the customary habit of British expositors to devote the mornings exclusively to study and to sermon preparation, and to minimize interruptions and interaction before noon.

Not everyone is going to have the same schedule, but the primary thing is to obey the biblical injunction to "redeem the time." I began doing this while in college. When I wasn't in class, I found it easy to flitter away the time, so I took a piece of paper and a ruler, and I made seven columns, one for each day of the week. Then I drew horizontal lines across the paper, marking out the hours of the day. Then, using colored pencils, I shaded in all the hours that were already committed: My class hours, my work schedule, my meal times, and so forth. Then I shaded in time every day for my devotions. Then my church time. Then I looked at what was left, and set aside my study hours, and some hours for exercise.

I didn't fill in every last minute, because we all need some unscheduled time, but most of the chart was nicely filled up. I posted it over my desk, and, for the most part, lived accordingly. To this day, I do virtually the same thing. My time-management tools have improved some, but the basic idea is still at work.

We only have so many hours and days and years, and the Bible tells us to number our days that we might present God a heart of wisdom, for time is short and the task is great.

We Proclaim Our Gospel

Jude's ministry not only involved loving his people and planning his schedule, it involved proclaiming the gospel. He told them he was very eager to write to them about *our common salvation.* The word *common* is the familiar old word translated *koinonia*, which means something special that is shared among two or more people

Jude was saying that if he could write about anything he wanted, he would write on the theme of salvation. He would describe how wonderful salvation is. He would articulate on its nature.

Paul was the same. Most of his letters addressed certain problems facing the early church. But two wonderful books were penned to churches that didn't have huge problems, and Paul was able to write what he really wanted to write. One was his letter to the church at Rome, and the other was his letter to the church in Ephesus. The theme of both letters is salvation. To the Romans, he articulated his understanding of the nature of salvation—we are justified by grace through faith. And to the Ephesians he wrote about the richness of our salvation.

There are many things we like to talk about—sports and work and politics and our hobbies. But those of us who are growing closer to Christ on a daily basis, who are really advancing in the Word . . . for us, there is one thing above all that we should enjoy talking about—our common salvation.

> How wonderful to have such a message! How marvelous to preach such a Savior! No wonder lawyer-turned-preacher Gardiner Spring (1785–1873) said: *Oh, if ministers only saw the inconceivable glory that is before them, and the preciousness of Christ, they would not be able to refrain from going about, leaping and clapping their hands for joy, and exclaiming, I am a minister of Christ! I am a minister of Christ!*
>
> ### We Defend Our Faith
>
> There is a fourth thing we must do, and this brings us right to the heart of Jude's book: We defend our faith. *Beloved, while I was very diligent to write to you concerning our common salvation, I found it necessary to write to you exhorting you to contend earnestly for the faith which was once for all delivered to the saints.*
>
> The word, "faith" here refers, not to the placing of our faith in something, but in that thing in which our faith is place. In other words, this is Jude's synonym for our doctrine, our theology. "Once for all" is one word in the Greek—a word that means, "Once and only once," "once and never again." In other words, God has deposited His truth in our hands. He has inscribed His theology in our Bibles. He has given it to us, and it has already been done. Now, we must guard that doctrine and that theology at all costs. We must contend earnestly for the faith.
>
> Christianity and conservative Christian theology is under bitter attack in the world today, especially as it asserts its exclusivity. Recently I received a document addressed to "The World's Religious Leaders." It was a seven-page letter appealing for a new spirit of harmony and unanimity among the world's great religions. After citing ways in which the world is becoming more unified, the paper suggested that it is high time for the religions of the world to share in this oneness. "In contrast to the processes of unification that are transforming the rest of humanity's social relationships," wrote the authors, "the suggestion that all of the world's great religions are equally valid in nature and origin is stubbornly resisted by entrenched patterns of sectarian thought." The paper urged "renunciation of all those claims to exclusivity or finality that, in winding their roots around the life of the spirit, have been the greatest single factor in suffocating impulses to unity and in promoting hatred and violence. . . . It is evident that growing numbers of people are coming to realize that the truth underlying all religions is in its essence one."
>
> What alarmed me most about this document was not its contents, but its cover letter. It came to me with the endorsement of a local

Christian pastor who called it, "the strongest message I've seen. . . . I'll be urging the leaders of [my denomination] to acknowledge this message and stand in solidarity with it." Another prominent pastor wrote, "I support the message [of this document] and would appreciate the opportunity to think together about how we can encourage interfaith understanding and concerned efforts for peace."

Why would Christian leaders knowingly, willingly gut their gospel of its message, strip Christianity of its authority, and rob the Bible of its exclusive claims? Yet that is the temptation of our age, and much of Christianity has already been lost to modernism. The Fundamentalist/Liberal wars of the early twentieth century may be an unattractive part of our history, but the battle for the Bible is not yet won. It wasn't in Jude's day, and it will not be fully over until Christ comes again.

Until then, we are called on to love our people, manage our schedules, proclaim our gospel, and defend our faith. That's what we do all week, all year, in all our ministries until Jesus comes.

Quotes for the Pastor's Wall

" A love for the Word in the pulpit is bound to produce a love for the Word in the pew. "

—Merrill F. Unger

FEBRUARY 1, 2004

SUGGESTED SERMON   *Date preached:*

The Tender Heart of a Tough Leader
By Michael Easley

Scripture: Nehemiah 1:1–11, especially verse 11: "O Lord, I pray, please let Your ear be attentive to the prayer of Your servant, and to the prayer of Your servants who desire to fear Your name; and let Your servant prosper this day, I pray, and grant him mercy in the sight of this man."

Introduction: How do we respond to bad news? The phone call late at night? The conference with your child's teacher? The meeting with the lawyer? The report from the medical lab? None of us are immune to bad news; the secret is in the way we learn to respond to it, and that's where today's text can help us.

Background: As Nehemiah was tending to business in the citadel of Susa (probably the winter residence of the Babylonian kings), his brother and some other men from Judah came with news. Nehemiah asked for a report concerning the Jews in Jerusalem, and the news was not good. The remnant of Jews in Jerusalem was in great distress. The walls of Jerusalem were broken down, its six gates burned with fire. The people were vulnerable and demoralized, and there seemed to be no one to lead them. Nehemiah's reaction is described in detail. He sat down and bitterly wept. He mourned for days (Compare Ezra 10:1). He was brokenhearted, crushed, shocked, and heavyhearted. That the bad news broke his heart reveals something of his piousness, something of his devout nature as a God-fearing Jew. The heart of this tough leader suggests a mature and confident relationship with God that had developed over the years. Nehemiah's prayer is one of the most revealing in Scripture. It isn't just a well-written composition or a polished piece of religious verse. It is the result of days of fasting and prayer. In his prayer, Nehemiah didn't just bemoan the circumstances, He compared the broken walls of Jerusalem with the great and awesome God. Notice how he addressed God: *Lord God of Heaven, O great and awesome God, You who keep Your covenant and mercy.* . . . Nehemiah reflected on God's character, knowing that God loves to be loyal to His covenant and His people.

Nehemiah then confessed Israel's sins and his own (cf. Dan. 9:4–6, and Ezra 9:6–15). Nehemiah proceeded to ask God to remember His own Word, quoting from Deuteronomy 9:29. He ended his prayer by asking God for success and compassion. The chapter ends and the next one begins with a note about Nehemiah's position, which was similar to that described in Genesis 40:2, referring to a butler or to a high official in the royal house. Most likely the importance of this is seen in Nehemiah's frequent access to the king. He was a man of influence in a key place at the right time. What lessons can we learn here about dealing with bad news?

1. **Tough Leaders Are Servants.** The words "servant" and "servants" occur seven times in chapter 1 (vv. 6, 8, 10, 11). Our world applauds the proud, successful, the out-in-front, get-it-done individual. I'm not knocking confident leadership; I am just pointing out how Nehemiah's example is different. Jesus spoke of the servant-role of leaders in Matthew 20:20–28, and it reminds us that God's leaders are not so very concerned about getting themselves out of messes, building their own empires, or enhancing their own reputations. Their concern is for the welfare of God's people and for His kingdom.

2. **Tough Leaders Acknowledge Their Own Sins (vv. 6–7).** When disaster strikes, the heart of a tough leader is tenderized to know his own sins. Nehemiah didn't exempt himself from responsibility, but wept over his own sin and made sure his heart was clean. We can't deal with bad news as spiritual individuals until we have placed our own hearts under the blood of Christ (1 John 1:9).

>>> *sermon continued on following page*

APPROPRIATE HYMNS AND SONGS

A Mighty Fortress, Martin Luther; Public Domain.

God Is the Refuge of His Saints, Isaac Watts; Public Domain.

God Is My Refuge, Judy Horner Montemayor; © 1973 Integrity's Hosanna! Music.

He Will Come and Save You, Bob Fitts/Gary Sadler; © 1995 Integrity's Hosanna! Music.

Hide Me in the Cleft of the Rock, Dennis Jernigan; © 1987 Shepherd's Heart Music, Admin. by Word Music Group, Inc.

3. **Tough Leaders Know Prayer Is Not a Substitute for Action.** "We can't do more than pray before we have prayed, but we can do more than pray after we have prayed." Nehemiah's great prayer in chapter 1 was a holy prelude to the practical steps he was to take in subsequent chapters.

4. **Tough Leaders Maximize Their God and Minimize Their Position.** Nehemiah didn't compare himself with the task; he compared the task with God's awesome power, presence, promises, provision, and providence.

Conclusion: Many of us grossly underestimate how God can use us, but often we do our best work for Him in the face of bad news. Take upon yourself the mind of a servant, confess your sins to God, ask Him what steps He would have you to take in the light of the problem you're facing, then minimize your own position and maximize your great and awesome God.

FOR THE BULLETIN

✺ According to *Foxe's' Book of Martyrs*, Trypho and Respicius, two eminent men, were seized as Christians and imprisoned at Nice. Their feet were pierced with nails; they were dragged through the streets, scourged, torn with iron hooks, scorched with lighted torches, and at length beheaded, on February 1, A.D. 251. ✺ February 1, 435, is the traditional date and the Feast Day for Bridgit, famous Irish Christian and the founder of a monastery. ✺ On February 1, 1738, John Wesley arrived back in England following his unfruitful trip to America. Shortly thereafter at a Moravian meeting on Aldersgate Street, his heart was "strangely warmed." ✺ February 1, 1750 marks the marriage of John Newton and Mary Catlett. They lived together until her death 40 years later, and their love story is one of the most tender in Christian history. John Newton, a British pastor, was the author of "Amazing Grace." ✺ Today is the birthday of Thomas Campbell (1763), founder of the Disciples of Christ. ✺ Julia Ward Howe published her famous "Battle Hymn of the Republic" on February 1, 1862, in *The Atlantic Monthly*. ✺ American missionaries Charles and Lettie Cowman set sail for Japan, as missionaries on this day in 1901. During the course of their ministry, they founded the Oriental Missionary Society which supported mission works in Japan, Korea, Formosa, and China. Mrs. Cowman later became famous for her devotional book, *Streams in the Desert*. ✺ February 1, 1909, is the birthday of George Beverly Shea, America's beloved gospel singer.

STATS, STORIES AND MORE

Bad News?

There's an old story about a Chinese gentleman who lived on the border of China and Mongolia. In those days, there was constant conflict along the perimeter. The Chinese man had a beautiful horse, a mare, who one day leaped over the fence, raced down the road, crossed the border, and was captured by the Mongolians. His friends came to comfort him. "That's bad news," they said sadly.

"What makes you think it's bad news?" asked the Chinaman. "Maybe it's good news."

A few days later the mare came bolting into his corral, bringing with it a massive snow white stallion. His friends crowded around. "That's good news!" they cried.

"What makes you think it's good news?" he asked. "Maybe it is bad news."

Later that week, his son was riding the stallion, trying to break it. He was thrown off and he broke his leg. The friends came. "That's bad news," they cried.

"What makes you think it is bad news?" asked the Chinese gentleman. "Maybe it's good news." The next week, war broke out with Mongolia, and a Chinese general came through town drafting all the young man. He took them all and they were all later killed, except for the young man who couldn't go because his leg was broken.

The Chinaman said to his friends, "You see, the things you thought were bad turned out good; and the things you thought were good turned out bad." And thus we face life. We can't always know if the news is really bad or good. We must trust the Lord to work all things together for our benefit.

WORSHIP HELPS

Call to Worship:

O great and awesome God . . . Let Your ear be attentive and Your eyes open, that You might hear the prayers of Your servants today . . . and grant us mercy. Amen. (Based on Neh. 1:5–6, 11.)

Scripture Medley:

O LORD, I pray, please let Your ear be attentive to the prayer of Your servant, and to the prayer of Your servants who desire to fear Your name; and let Your servant prosper this day, I pray, and grant him mercy . . . Bow down Your ear, O LORD, hear me; for I am poor and

needy ... Give ear to my prayers; and attend to the voice of my supplications. In the day of my trouble I will call upon You, for You will answer me. God is our refuge and strength, a very present help in trouble. Therefore we will not fear, even though the earth be removed, and the mountains be carried into the midst of the sea ... There is a river whose streams shall make glad the city of God ... The LORD of hosts is with us; the God of Jacob is our refuge.
(Neh. 1:11; Ps. 86:1, 6–7; 46:1–2, 4, 7)

Hymn Story:
Psalm 46 has inspired a number of famous hymns, particularly Martin Luther's *A Mighty Fortress is our God*. In that hymn, Luther takes a militant tone to the victory he has in Christ. The English hymnist, Isaac Watts, using the same text, hit a softer note. In his beautiful (but nearly forgotten) hymn "God Is the Refuge of His Saints," he composed these words:

> *God is the refuge of His saints,*
> *When storms of sharp distress invade;*
> *Ere we can offer our complaints,*
> *Behold Him present with His aid.*
>
> *Loud may the troubled ocean roar;*
> *In sacred peace our souls abide;*
> *While every nation, every shore,*
> *Trembles, and dreads the swelling tide.*

Benediction:
> *Heavenly Father, Mighty Savior, Faithful Friend,*
> *Send us forth to fields of labor*
> *As on You our hearts depend.*
> *O Lord, for Thy Name's sake revive my fainting heart;*
> *My soul from trouble take, for just and true Thou art.*
> *Remove mine enemy, my cruel foes reward;*
> *In mercy rescue me who am Thy servant, Lord.*
> —From the hymn, "Lord, Hear Me In Distress," author unknown, a paraphrase of Psalm 143

Additional Sermons and Lesson Ideas

The Winning Team
Date preached:

By Peter Grainger

SCRIPTURE: 1 John 2:1–2

INTRODUCTION: Recall the faces of the players at last week's Superbowl. Some were so exuberant they were dancing; others were so downcast they could barely trudge to the showers. That's the difference between victory and defeat.

1. God's Purpose (v. 1a). That we should not sin. God wants us to experience victory over sin and temptation. He wants us to overcome:
   A. This should be our past and present experience (see 2:13–14; 4:4; 5:4–5).
   B. This is possible through the Word of God that lives in us ("These things I write to you, so that..." (v. 1; see also Matt. 4:1–11).
2. God's Provision (v. 1b)—If we do sin forgiveness is available. Jesus is:
   A. Our Advocate (v. 1)
   B. The "Righteous One" (v. 1)
   C. The Propitiation for our sins (v. 2)

CONCLUSION: Be on the winning side. We are more than conquerors through Him who loved us.

One Who Fits the Bill
Date preached:

SCRIPTURE: Various verses in 1 Peter

INTRODUCTION: A diamond is beautiful because of its many facets, all reflecting different beams of light. The Lord Jesus is a multi-faceted diamond, and one of the ways the various writers of the Bible exhibit Him is by using different names and titles to describe the various elements of His nature and ministry. The Book of 1 Peter uses several different names for our Lord:

1. A Savior. The Lord Jesus Christ (1:1–3); the Lamb without blemish (1:19).
2. A Stone. A Cornerstone (2:4, 6); a Stone of Stumbling and Rock of Offense (2:8).
3. A Shepherd. The Shepherd and Overseer of Your Souls (2:25; 5:4).

CONCLUSION: We need a Savior to rescue us from sin, a Stone on which to build our lives, and a Shepherd to care for us every day. Peter reminds us that the Lord Jesus fits the bill perfectly.

FEBRUARY 8, 2004

SUGGESTED SERMON

The Brother in the Bone Box *Date preached:*

Scripture: Matthew 13:54–56, especially verse 55: "And His brothers James, Joses, Simon, and Judas?"

Introduction: We have wonderful people here in our church, but one member tends to be troublesome. I've had more difficulty with this one than with anyone else. Sometimes this person drives me up a wall. It's me! That's the way that I sometimes feel about myself, and I wonder if that's the way you sometimes feel about yourself. We have so many troubling traits, stubborn temptations, failures, and immaturities that we become discouraged with ourselves. Well, Christ Himself tackles this problem. He helps us to gain altitude, to go upward, to fly higher. (see Ps. 138:8; Phil. 1:6; 2 Cor. 3:18.) Today I'd like to show how this principle worked itself out in an unusual man in the Bible named James, the son of Joseph and the brother of Jesus. He has been in the news in recent years because his ossuary ("bone box") has reportedly been discovered in Jerusalem (see "STATS, STORIES AND MORE"). James took a while to mature, and his development came by fits and starts, going through several stages:

1. **Jesus Is My Big Brother (Matt. 13:54–56).** Here we have the Bible's most complete listings of Jesus' family. In this home were Joseph, Mary, Jesus, and His four brothers and at least three sisters (the use of "all" in verse 56 indicates at least three sisters). So a minimum of eight children in this little house in Nazareth made it a crowded home. It's unlikely that Jesus had his own bedroom. Probably all the boys roomed together, so James, being the next oldest, was always following in the footsteps of his big brother, Jesus. We have a lot of questions about this. What was Jesus like as a 6-year-old, a 16-year-old, a 21-year-old? The Bible is silent, but we can assume James looked up to his older brother. A lot of people look up to Jesus today, but don't really recognize Him as Savior and Lord.

2. **Jesus Is My Ambitious Brother (John 7:1–5).** After Jesus entered the ministry, James grew confused and cynical. He went through a "Jesus is my

ambitious brother" stage. Perhaps he was disturbed that Jesus walked away from a lucrative job and became, for all practical purposes, unemployed. The role of provider fell heavily and suddenly on the shoulders of the second brother. At any rate, James and his brothers determined that Jesus merely wanted to become famous, and they grew cynical. A lot of people today are cynical about the Christian faith.

3. **Jesus Is My Insane Brother (Mark 3:20–21).** Here the boys Christ had lived with in Nazareth, His siblings, thought He had lost His mind. (The Lord's response is in vv. 31–35.) A lot of people think we're crazy to follow Christ. Indeed, subsequent events seemed to bear that out. To James' horror, his brother was nailed to a post and tortured to death. James found himself in a family nightmare he couldn't escape.

4. **Jesus Is My Risen Brother (1 Cor. 15:7).** But now we come to a little verse that explains everything to us, the most important verse in the Bible about James. How we would have loved to have been present when the Risen Savior met his little brother. Perhaps they met in a well-loved, secret spot where they had played as children. We don't know what was said, but whatever it was, it changed James' life, because he instantly was a changed man, and very soon we see him as a leader in the Jerusalem church (see Acts 1:14; 12:17; 15:13; 21:18; Gal. 2:9). The historian Eusebius says James became the pastor or bishop of the founding church of Christendom. That leads us to the final stage in James' life:

>>> sermon continued on following page

APPROPRIATE HYMNS AND SONGS

He Is Lord, Traditional; Public Domain.

He Is Lord, John Barnett; © 1998 Mercy/Vineyard Publishing.

Jesus, I Believe, Bill Batstone; © 1995 Maranatha Praise, Inc., Admin. by The Copyright Company.

All Hail the Power of Jesus' Name, Edward Perronet/Oliver Holden/John Rippon; Public Domain.

Rejoice, the Lord Is King, Charles Wesley/John Darwall; Public Domain.

5. **Jesus Is My Lord (James 1:10).** This little letter near the end of the New Testament was written by this very James whose life we have been studying today. Notice how he identifies himself as a servant of the Lord Jesus Christ. Is Jesus your Lord?

Conclusion: It took a while, and it wasn't a pretty journey, but James finally ended up where he needed to be—recognizing that Jesus was none other than King of Creation and Lord of the Universe. Jesus knew all along what His brother would become. James went from stage to stage until he finally arrived at "Jesus is my Lord." Are you discouraged with yourself today? Are you thinking that you aren't worth much, that you don't count for very much? Jesus didn't give up on James, and He won't give up on you. He doesn't leave us where we are. So don't be discouraged; the Lord isn't finished with us yet.

FOR THE BULLETIN

✺ On February 8, 1587, Mary Queen of Scots (Mary Stuart), age 44, was beheaded. An ardent Roman Catholic, she was viewed as a threat by England's Queen Elizabeth I. The Roman Catholics of England considered Mary the rightful queen and formed many conspiracies to place her on the throne. For alleged complicity in one of these she was executed. Her son later became James 1 of England, for whom the King James Version of the Bible is named. ✺ On February 8, 1693, the College of William and Mary was chartered in Williamsburg, Virginia, for the purpose of training young men for the Anglican ministry. ✺ Evangelist George Whitefield returned home on this day in 1744 after a preaching trip, eager to be reunited with his wife, Elizabeth, and four-month-old son, John. George was met at the door by tearful family members who told him little John had just died of a stroke or seizure. The heartbroken evangelist gathered his family for prayer. He felt he should fulfill a preaching obligation on the day of the child's burial, and he chose for his text Romans 8:28, almost breaking down as he said, *"All things work together for good...."* ✺ February 8, 1865 marks the birth of Louis E. Jones, author of the gospel song, "There Is Power in the Blood." ✺ The Boy Scouts of America was chartered and incorporated on February 8, 1910.

STATS, STORIES AND MORE

James' Ossuary?
The magazine *Biblical Archaeological Review* recently announced the discovery of the possible ossuary (burial bone box) of James. The Jewish people only used ossuaries during a brief time period, from about 20 years before Christ to the destruction of Jerusalem in A.D. 70. On this limestone ossuary are incised the words: "James, son of Joseph, brother of Jesus." If authenticated, it would be a major archaeological find.

What Happened to James?
We have extra-biblical information about James in the writings of Josephus and in the records of Eusebius, the "Father of church history," who writes: "James was called the brother of the Lord since he too was called Joseph's son, and Joseph Christ's father—though the Virgin was his betrothed and before they came together she was found to have conceived by the Holy Spirit . . . This same James, whom early Christians surnamed 'the Just' for his outstanding virtue, was the first to be elected to the bishop's throne of the church in Jerusalem . . . Clement [of Alexandria] . . . puts it as follows: 'Peter, James, and John, after the Savior's ascension, did not contend for the honor because they had been previously favored by the Savior, but chose James the Just as Bishop of Jerusalem.'"

Later we read this in Eusebius: "When Paul appealed to Caesar and was sent to Rome by Festus, the Jews were disappointed in their hope regarding the plot they had devised against him and turned against James, the Lord's brother, to whom the bishop's throne in Jerusalem had been assigned by the apostles. This is the crime they committed. They brought him into their midst and in front of the whole populace demanded a denial of his faith in Christ. But when he, contrary to all expectation, loudly and courageously confessed before them all that our Lord and Savior Jesus Christ was the Son of God, they could not tolerate his testimony any longer, since he was universally deemed the most righteous of men because of the heights he had reached in philosophy and religion. So they killed him. . . He was thrown down from the parapet and clubbed to death."

Kids Talk

Show the children some pictures of yourself when you were a child. Tell them you were once their age. And so was Jesus! He lived in a house with at least seven other brothers and sisters, and it was very crowded. But He loved God and obeyed His parents, and in so doing grew up to be a great teacher and Savior.

WORSHIP HELPS

Call to Worship:
> *Awake, my soul, and with the sun*
> *Thy daily stage of duty run;*
> *Shake off dull sloth, and joyful rise,*
> *To pay thy morning sacrifice.*
> —Thomas Ken (1674)

Exhortation to Worship:

Have you ever tried to cut up vegetables or meat with a dull knife? Then you know what it's like to worship God with a dull heart. Missionary Amy Carmichael wrote: "Dullness of spirit is sin; there is no way out of that conclusion." Francis Scott Key, author of our national anthem, was a Christian attorney who wrote hymns as a hobby. One of them is a prayer speaking to this, and it's a timely exhortation for us today:

> *Lord, with glowing heart I'd praise Thee,*
> *For the bliss Thy love bestows,*
> *For the pardoning grace that saves me,*
> *And the peace that from it flows:*
> *Help, O God, my weak endeavor;*
> *This dull soul to rapture raise:*
> *Thou must light the flame, or never*
> *Can my love be warmed to praise.*

Pastoral Prayer:

Our Lord and our God, we read of the amazement of the crowds in Galilee who whispered among themselves, "What manner of man is this?" May we, too, be full of wonder and worship. May we, too, be amazed by the power of Your presence. May we sense today that You are here, in this very place, filling this very room, here, at this very moment, among us. Pierce through our lethargy, O Lord, and banish all dull thoughts. Quicken us! Revive us! Awaken us! Amaze us! In Jesus' name. Amen.

Additional Sermons and Lesson Ideas

Worldwide Witnesses
By Melvin Worthington

Date preached:

SCRIPTURE: 2 Corinthians 5:17–21

INTRODUCTION: Our commission is to preach the gospel to the entire world. The challenge has not diminished. God is still calling ambassadors, witnesses and servants. Worldwide witnesses must be aware of three basic things.

1. The Truth (v. 20). God uses people to advance His Church. The Holy Spirit does not flow through methods, but through men and women. He does not come on machinery, but on men.
2. The Traits (v. 17). Those who proclaim the gospel must practice it. As ambassadors and witnesses, we preach the gospel by precept and practice. Our conduct conforms to our creed; our deportment duplicates our doctrine.
3. The Task (vv. 18–21). God's ambassador has *the ministry of reconciliation* (v. 18) and a *message of reconciliation* (v. 19). We are *models of reconciliation* (v. 21).

CONCLUSION: God's ambassador must say with the apostle Paul, "Be ye followers of me, even as I also am of Christ" (1 Cor. 11:1). Being an ambassador for the Almighty is the highest calling one can receive.

A Grand Highway
By Charles Haddon Spurgeon

Date preached:

SCRIPTURE: Luke 3:5

INTRODUCTION: We must pay attention to the Master's proclamation and give Him a road for our hearts. There are four directions in this text that must have our attention:

1. Every Valley Shall Be Filled. Low and sordid thoughts of God must be given up. Doubt and despair must be removed. Self-seeking and sensual delights must be forsaken. Across these deep valleys a glorious causeway of grace must be constructed.
2. Every Mountain and Hill Brought Low. Proud self-assurance and boastful self-righteousness must be leveled to make a highway for the King of kings.
3. The Crooked Places Shall Be Made Straight. The undecided, double-minded heart must mark a straight path of decision for God and holiness. Make sure that in everything you are honest and true.
4. The Rough Ways Smooth. Stumbling blocks of sin must be removed. Thorns and briars of rebellion must be dug up.

CONCLUSION: Lord, find in my heart a highway of holiness, made ready by Your grace.

HELPS FOR THE PASTOR'S FAMILY

Keeping Marriage on the Front Burner

Over the years, my wife, Katrina, and I have enjoyed a long-simmering romance, but it really heated up when we began spending time in the kitchen together.

It all started when I spent some time with an elderly couple in Geneva, Switzerland. One evening, I followed them to their tiny kitchen, where, for the next half-hour, I watched them cook. My friend Ramon sliced vegetables with the flair of a French chef, tossing them into a nearby pot of water. His wife, with no less flourish, trimmed the meat and kneaded the dough, occasionally offering me a shy smile.

I couldn't help noticing how much fun they were having. They huddled over ingredients. They borrowed one another's utensils. They playfully argued what spices should be added to the sauce. They took turns tasting it, making expressions of disdain or approval. It occurred to me that this timeless couple possessed an important ingredient in the recipe for a savory marriage. They enjoyed a joint hobby and a common pastime: cooking.

Returning home, I described my trip with relish to Katrina.

"Why don't we collaborate on some meals?" I offered. "After all, the couple that stirs together stays together. It will add spice to our marriage."

Katrina arched her eyebrows.

"We can melt in each other's arms and boil with passion," I continued. "We can savor the moments. We can satisfy our deepest appetites."

Katrina thought I was laying it on a little thick. "You're *so* corny," she groaned.

"I expect corn to be one of my main ingredients," I chirped. Still, I had to win her over. The kitchen, after all, had been her dominion for decades. She excelled at making delicious meals for our family of five: Finnish bread every Thursday, cinnamon rolls on Saturday morning, and homemade pizzas every Sunday night—all from scratch.

But soon she discovered that I posed little threat, and we started sizzling together. My first effort, cinnamon-carrot soup, was spurned, but the meal was saved by Katrina's roast. My next effort, cherry pie, was the pits.

So I went back to the basics: the patio grill. I perused local meat markets until I found an economy cut of lean meat. I bought a half-dozen steaks, drenched them in a mysterious marinade I made, and slowly grilled them.

Katrina's comments were encouraging—more or less. "Except for being as tough as jerky," she said between chews, "these steaks are pretty good."

My girls smiled wanly as their jaws kept moving. But soon I got the hang of this cooking. My next meal wowed them: chilled orange soup served with Polynesian fish on a bed of wild pineapple rice.

Gradually, Katrina and I became a team. We read cooking magazines together in bed, fantasizing over recipes and meals. We flirted with calories and enticed each other with rich, sensuous desserts.

But we also had to watch over each other's figures, so we searched for low-salt, low-calorie, low-cholesterol, low-fat recipes. Our girls called such meals "low taste."

But I trudged on, and since I'm a pastor, we allowed our hobby to assume ministerial dimensions. We cooked for couples who were throwing rolling pins at each other. We entertained singles who had been burned by bad relationships. We welcomed denominational officials digesting new responsibilities and church members sifting through problems.

And Katrina and I drew closer. We boiled, broiled, and baked together. We hugged and kissed in the kitchen—and helped each other wash the dishes.

All this may be hard to swallow, but it's food for thought. Cooking became a hobby that Katrina and I could sink our teeth into, and it helped us get our marriage off the back burner.

All this has given me a new slant on the apostle Paul's advice: "It's better to marry than to burn."

FEBRUARY 15, 2004

SUGGESTED SERMON

To Change the World

Date preached:

By D. James Kennedy

Scripture: Acts 17:6: But when they did not find them, they dragged Jason and some brethren to the rulers of the city, crying out, "These who have turned the world upside down have come here too."

Introduction: The president of one of our great theological seminaries, at a meeting with the chairman of an accreditation committee, was asked what the purpose of their institution was. The president replied without hesitation, "The purpose of this institution is to change the world." The secular chairman didn't particularly care for that idea, but repeated questioning failed to shake the gentleman from his position. He was there for the singular purpose of changing the world. Our purpose as individuals and as a church should be nothing less than to change the world. I expect this world will be different when I leave it than when I came into it because of the power of the gospel of Jesus Christ and the might of the Holy Spirit. It was said about Paul and Silas that they turned the world upside down. I wish the world today looked at us Christians the same way.

1. **The Secret of Spiritual Multiplication.** You might be saying, "But I'm 'just a layman.' I might teach a Sunday school class or something, but I couldn't really think about changing the world." Perhaps such a thought went through the mind of Edward Kimball. He taught a Sunday school class of teenage boys. One day he decided he would speak personally to one of them about Christ. He went to the shoe store where the lad had a part-time job. In the back room, he succeeded in winning the young man to Christ there among the shoeboxes. His name: Dwight L. Moody. Moody became one of the greatest preachers and evangelists in American history. When Moody was later preaching in England, he influenced a young man named F. B. Meyer, who also became a great preacher of the gospel. Meyer came to America where he influenced J. Wilber Chapman, who in turn became a great evangelist. Chapman influenced his assistant, Billy Sunday, whose preaching changed the face of this nation. Sunday went to Charlotte in 1924

and conducted a great evangelistic meeting. A number of men who were converted formed an organization and in 1932 they invited as speaker Mordecai Ham. During Ham's campaign, 16-year-old Billy Graham was converted. Who could begin to number the millions who have been influenced by all those great ministers down though the years because Edward Kimball shared the gospel one day in the back of a shoe store?

2. **The Importance of Being Concerned.** Those who change the world are those who are concerned. In April, 1964, the nation was shocked by a story out of New York City that a young lady was attacked in front of her apartment building, and for thirty minutes she screamed for help before bleeding to death. A reported thirty-nine people heard her cries, and not one assisted her, no one even called the police. How tragic! Yet many of us sit by daily, yearly, watching people die and face everlasting torment without doing anything to help them.

3. **The Command to Be Witnesses.** Jesus Christ calls every one of us to be a witness for Him. There is a gospel that must be proclaimed (see 1 Cor. 15:1–4). I'm convinced that we can't have faith and love and not witness for Christ.

4. **The Blessing of Holy Boldness.** One of the reasons many people don't witness is because they are afraid. But God can deliver us from fear (see Acts 4:13). We must keep short accounts with God and repent of the daily sin in our lives. We need for our hearts to be filled with joy and delight.

>>> *sermon continued on following page*

APPROPRIATE HYMNS AND SONGS

Come, Let Us Worship and Bow Down, Dave Doherty; © 1980 Maranatha Praise, Inc., Admin. by The Copyright Company.

A Charge to Keep I Have, Charles Wesley/Lowell Mason; Public Domain.

Break Out, O Church of God, Wesley L. Forbis/Aaron Williams; © 1990 Broadman Press, Admin. by Genevox Music Group.

Carry the Call, Danny Chambers/Lincoln Brewster/Jillian Chambers; © 1998 Praise On the Rock Music/Integrity's Praise! Music, Admin. by Integrity Music, Inc.

You Have Called Us, Lynn DeShazo/Martin J. Nystrom; © Integrity's Hosanna! Music, Admin. by Integrity Music, Inc.

One of the inevitable results of enjoyment is the desire to share with others: "Isn't that beautiful? Wasn't that a magnificent sunset? Did you ever see such a beautiful picture?" If we know the joy of daily communion with Christ our overflowing hearts will want to share that enjoyment with others (see Matt. 12:34b).

Conclusion: During the reign of Oliver Cromwell, lord protector of England, there was a shortage of silver coinage. Cromwell sent some soldiers to a cathedral in search of silver. They reported, "The only silver we can find is in the statues of the saints standing in the corner." "Good!" exclaimed Cromwell, "We'll melt down the saints and put them into circulation!" Would to God that we could melt the hearts of all the saints of God and put them into circulation. Out of a burning heart, a believing heart, a loving heart, we would be constrained by the love of Jesus Christ to share the gospel with others.

FOR THE BULLETIN

❂ February 15, A.D. 37 marks the birthday of Nero (Claudius Drusus Germanicus Caesar Nero), the Roman emperor who condemned Peter, Paul, and a multitude of Christians to death for their faith. ❂ February 15, 1497, is the birthday of Philipp Melanchthon, German reformer and Martin Luther's closest associate. ❂ On February 15, 1386, King Jagiello of Lithuania was baptized, making Lithuania the last European people to leave organized Paganism. ❂ The Italian scientist, Galileo, was born on this day in 1562. ❂ The eloquent British preacher, John Donne, preached his last sermon on this day in 1631. It was entitled, "Death's Duel." Five weeks later he passed away. He is chiefly remembered as the dean of St. Paul's Cathedral in London where he often preached before King Charles I. ❂ America's first foreign missionary, Adoniram Judson, found himself imprisoned in Burma, accused of spying. He was placed in a dark cell filled with vermin. Every evening he was hanged upside down with only his head and shoulders resting on the ground. His wife, Ann, was pregnant. On February 15, 1825, eight months after his arrest, she showed up at his prison carrying a small bundle, their newborn daughter Maria. Unfortunately, both Ann and Maria were later to die of fever. ❂ On February 15, 1860, Wheaton College is chartered in Wheaton, Illinois, "for Christ and His Kingdom." ❂ Lew Wallace died on this day in 1905 at age 77. He was a military leader, a lawyer, and a novelist who authored *Ben Hur: A Tale of Christ*.

STATS, STORIES AND MORE

More from D. James Kennedy

Aunt Sophie was a converted scrubwoman. She hadn't much education, but she was a dear lady and her heart was filled with a song. Whenever she could she would share the love and grace of Christ with another. She was getting old and one day someone made fun of her by saying that she was seen talking about the love of Christ to a wooden Indian standing in front of a cigar store. When Sophie heard this, she replied, "Perhaps I did. My eyesight is not good. But talking about Christ to a wooden Indian is not as bad as being a wooden Christian and never talking to anybody about the Lord."

A certain church noticed that not one single person had been brought to Christ in a whole year. The pastor gathered the officers together and said, "Let us make a covenant that if the Lord cannot use us to bring in some souls for Him in the near future, all of us will resign." The next morning one of the officers went to his store with a heavy heart. He invited the first clerk that he met into his office. They had a heart-to-heart talk and soon the clerk had accepted Christ. Then another and another was called in. By late afternoon eleven people had been led to Christ. The other officers had also been busy and the following Sunday thirty men were received into the church on confession of faith in Jesus Christ—because the officers had become genuinely concerned about the lost estate of their fellowmen.

Statistics from George Barna

58 percent of born-again Christians claim they have shared their faith with a non-Christian during the past year (2002).

Americans living in the South feel more of a responsibility to share their faith with others than do adults in other regions of the country, with 47 percent of southerners feeling a sense of responsibility to share their faith with others, compared to 32 percent in the Midwest, 29 percent of those living in the West, and 28 percent of those living in the Northeast (2002).

WORSHIP HELPS

Call to Worship:
Oh come, let us worship and bow down; let us kneel before the LORD our Maker. For we are the people of His pasture.
(Ps. 95:6–7a)

Scripture Medley:
Lord, if it is You, command me to come to You . . . So He said, "Come!" . . . Come to Me, all you who labor and are heavy laden. Let him who thirsts come. Whoever desires let him take the water of life freely. . . . Oh come, let us sing to the Lord! Let us shout joyfully to the Rock of our salvation. Let us come before His presence with thanksgiving. . . . Do not be afraid, for I know that you seek Jesus who was crucified. He is not here; for He is risen, as He said. Come, see the place where the Lord lay. And go quickly and tell . . . Go into the highways, and as many as you find, invite. Go home to your friends, and tell them what great things the Lord has done for you, and how He has had compassion on you. Go therefore and make disciples of all the nations. . . . And lo, I am with you always, even to the end of the age.
(Matt. 14:18–19; Matt. 11:29; Rev. 22:17; Ps. 95:1–2a; Matt. 22:9; Mark 5:19; Matt. 28:19–20)

Offertory Verses:
Some of the heads of the father's houses, when they came to the house of the Lord which is in Jerusalem, offered freely for the house of God—Ezra 2:68
I will freely sacrifice to You—Psalm 54:6
Freely you have received, freely give—Matthew 2:8

Benediction:
Father, may our hearts be broken over the pain and loss of those that are perishing. May we, having been given another opportunity to witness for Christ, take advantage of it so we may not have to come into Your presence without one soul with which to greet You. Amen.
—D. James Kennedy

Additional Sermons and Lesson Ideas

The Wonderful Word
Date preached:

By Melvin Worthington

SCRIPTURE: 2 Timothy 3:14–17

INTRODUCTION: The Bible is an amazing book, a living book. It provides information which can be found in no other book.

1. The Nature of the Bible (2 Tim. 3:16; Ps. 119; 1 Pet. 1:20–21). The attributes which make the Bible a unique book include its *author, authority, accuracy, adequacy, appeal, and agenda.*
2. The Need for the Bible (1 Pet. 1:23–25; James 1:18; John 5:24). The Bible addresses all the needs of the human being. It is essential for *life, likeness, liberty, light, and labor.*
3. The Nourishment from the Bible (1 Pet. 2:2). The Bible reveals and regulates *the development God planned, the diet God provided, the disposition God prescribed, and the diadem God promised.*
4. The Neglect of the Bible (1 Cor. 3:1–2). Neglect of the Bible leads to *dullness, drifting, disobedience, despising, denouncing, and departing* from the Lord.

CONCLUSION: Christians need to peruse, ponder, and pray over the Scriptures. This takes time, thought, toil, and tenacity. We need to pray—Father help me hear, heed, hold, honor, and herald the Word of God.

Deep and Wide
Date preached:

SCRIPTURE: Ezekiel 47:1–12

INTRODUCTION: God loves rivers. He created four of them to water the Garden of Eden. He created the Jordan to run through the land of Israel. According to Revelation 22, a crystal river will flow through the Golden City. And Ezekiel 47 pictures the river that will flow from Jerusalem during the Millennium. This river also gives us an excellent picture of the role of the Holy Spirit that flows like rivers of living water (John 7:38).

1. The Source of the River. From the temple, from the presence of God. Jesus promised that the Father would send on us the Holy Spirit.
2. The Force of the River. First, to ankles, then to knees, then to waist, then to swim. As we grow in Christ and yield ourselves more and more to Him, we experience more and more of the Spirit. Too many are wading in the shallow end of the Christian experience when we should be submerged in it.
3. The Course of the River—to the Dead Sea. Everything this river touches is transformed, including the Dead Sea. It brings life and healing to all.

CONCLUSION: Are you filled with the Spirit? Are the waters of the Spirit flowing through you and me?

FEBRUARY 22, 2004

SUGGESTED SERMON

Jesus: Full of Compassion

Date preached:

By Ed Dobson

Scripture: Mark 8:1–13, especially verse 2: "I have compassion on the multitude, because they have now continued with Me three days and have nothing to eat."

Introduction: If you were asked to choose ten words to describe yourself, would one of them be *compassionate?* Just what is compassion? Is it simply a feeling? How do we react when a homeless person asks us for money? Do we say, "God bless you," and walk away? How are we to treat the boss when he doesn't recognize hard work, but only criticizes? Jesus answers these questions in our text today.

1. **The Compassion of Jesus (v. 1–2).** The word *compassion* used here to describe Jesus is actually two words put together: a word that means to feel sympathy for someone and a second word that means one's "gut." The idea is that Jesus was moved to the very core of His being. What Jesus felt for the crowd He feels for us this morning. Did you know that? Whatever your need, where ever you are on your journey, whatever struggle you're facing this morning, Jesus feels for you from His heart. He's not only aware of your need; He's concerned about your need. And He's not only concerned about your need, He is sympathetic toward your need.
   A. **Compassion that Prompted Action (vv. 2–8).** Whenever the word compassion is associated with Jesus, it's always followed by action. In Mark 1:40–41, Jesus was, "moved with compassion, (and) stretched out his hand and touched him . . ." In Mark 6:34 Jesus saw a crowd and was moved with compassion so He began to teach them. Jesus not only feels compassion for you, but He will always act on it.
   B. **Compassion that Was All-Inclusive (vv. 2, 11).** Jesus' compassion reached out to the critical (v. 2) and the critics (v. 11). Jesus saw that the crowd's need was critical, "And if I send them away hungry . . . they will faint on the way . . ." (v. 2). Are you wondering how you will make it through another week? Jesus cares about you. He desires to give you the strength and nourishment to make it. He also cares about the critical. The reli-

gious leaders came to argue with Jesus (v. 11), but instead of yelling or fighting, Jesus sighed deeply (v. 12). I think it was a sigh of compassion. He loves those in critical need and those who are critical of Him.

C. **Compassion Rooted in Personal Experience (Matt. 4:1; Heb. 4:15).** Remember that Jesus fasted 40 days (Matt. 4:1); He knew what hunger was. The compassion of Jesus is rooted in His own human experience (Heb. 4:15). He understood what it meant to be hungry. What needs or temptations are you struggling with? He knows and understands them all.

2. **The Action of Jesus (vv. 5–7).** You may want to circle the verbs in this section: *He took ... He blessed ... He broke ... He gave.* What a pattern for our lives!
    A. **Given to Jesus (v. 6).** If you and I want to be used by Jesus, the first step is the complete surrender of ourselves to Jesus, giving ourselves completely, without reservation, without holding back.
    B. **Blessed by Jesus (v. 7).** Much is mentioned of material or spiritual blessings from God, but the core of what it means to be blessed by Jesus is not only to be taken by Him, but to be set apart by Him for His purpose, for His objective, for His will, for whatever He wants to do in our lives. Don't ask Jesus to bless you if you are unwilling to surrender everything to Him.
    C. **Broken by Jesus (v. 6).** Brokenness is the model Jesus set for us. How does He "break" us? Through circumstances, through sickness and disease, through disappointment, through criticism, through opposition, through failure, through the demands of everyday life. In a sense, we cannot be multiplied until we are broken.

>>> *sermon continued on following page*

APPROPRIATE HYMNS AND SONGS

O To Be Like Thee, Thomas O. Chisholm/William J. Kirkpatrick; Public Domain.

The Lord Is Gracious and Compassionate, Graham Ord; © 1998 Vineyard Songs, Admin. by Mercy/Vineyard Publishing.

The Servant Song, Richard Gillard; © 1977 Scripture in Song, Admin. by Integrity Music, Inc.

New Every Morning, Scott Underwood; © 1995 Mercy/Vineyard Publishing.

Jesus Has Lifted Me, Avis B. Christiansen/Haldor Lillenas; Public Domain.

D. Given to Others (v. 6). We are blessed and broken in part for our benefit, but primarily for the benefit of others. What God gives us back is blessed, broken, and forever altered and changed. Why? So we can give that away to bless others. Are you ministering to others? If we are not, we need to go back to being surrendered.

Conclusion: The all-inclusive, all-understanding compassion of Christ always prompts action. If we are to have His compassion, we are to surrender to Him as He blesses us for His purpose, even breaking us to serve Him and His people better. Remember that Jesus is affected by and able to meet *all* our needs.

O to be like Thee! full of compassion,
Loving, forgiving, tender and kind,
Helping the helpless, cheering the fainting,
Seeking the wandering sinner to find.

FOR THE BULLETIN

● On February 22, 1661, Scottish Covenanter James Guthrie was placed on trial for his faith in Christ. In his defense, he said: "I beseech you to ponder well what profit there is in my blood... My blood, bondage, or banishment will contribute more for the propagation of these things than my life in liberty would do, though I should live many years." He was hanged in Edinburgh on June 1, 1661. ● February 22, 1680, marks the death of famed English Nonconformist preacher, Thomas Goodwin, 79. His last words were: "Ah, is this dying? How I have dreaded as an enemy this smiling friend." ● George Washington was born on this day in 1732. ● February 22, 1805 is also the birthday of hymnist Sarah F. Adams, born in Harlow, Essex, England. Sarah was a noted London actress, but when her career was disrupted by poor health she began writing poetry and hymns, her best known being "Nearer, My God, to Thee." ● On February 22, 1807, as William Wilberforce watched, the second reading of his bill to ban slavery in the British Empire was read in Parliament. He had written in his diary that morning, "God can turn the hearts of men," but prospects for victory were uncertain. To his amazement, the entire House rose, cheering and applauding his lifelong efforts. The motion carried 283 to 16. ● On February 22, 1906, the African-American evangelist, William J. Seymour, arrived in Los Angeles. He began holding revival meetings there, and the famous "Azusa Street Revival" broke out under his leadership, launching the Pentecostal movement in America.

STATS, STORIES AND MORE

Someone Once Said...

If we could only read the secret history of our enemies, we would find in each man's life sorrow and suffering enough to disarm all hostility—*Henry Wadsworth Longfellow*

He who feels no compassion will become insane—*Hasidic saying*

The Cost of Compassion

Eusebius, the "Father of Church History," quotes long passages from Dionysius, Bishop of Alexandria in the third century. In one of those passages, Dionysius spoke of how Christians responded to a terrible outbreak of the plague following a war: "Most of our brethren showed love and loyalty in not sparing themselves while helping one another, tending to the sick with no thought of danger and gladly departing this life with them after becoming infected with their disease. Many who nursed others to health died themselves, thus transferring their death to themselves. The best of our own brothers lost their lives in this way—some presbyters, deacons, and laymen—a form of death based on strong faith and piety that seems in every way equal to martyrdom. They would also take up the bodies of the saints, close their eyes, shut their mouths, and carry them on their shoulders. They would embrace them, wash and dress them in burial clothes, and soon receive the same services themselves."

Dionysius continued: "The heathen were the exact opposite. They pushed away those with the first signs of the disease and fled from their dearest. They even threw them half dead into the roads and treated unburied corpses like refuse in hopes of avoiding the plague of death, which, for all their efforts, was difficult to escape."

WORSHIP HELPS

Call to Worship:
"Through the LORD's mercies we are not consumed, because His compassions fail not. They are new every morning. Great is Your faithfulness." (Lam. 3:22–23a)

Readers' Theater from Matthew 25:34–40:

Reader 1: Then the King will say to those on His right hand...

Readers 2: Come, you blessed of My Father, inherit the kingdom prepared for you from the foundation of the world, for I was hungry and you gave Me food; I was thirsty and you gave Me drink; I was a stranger and you took Me in; I was naked and you clothed Me; I was sick and you visited Me; I was in prison and you came to Me.

Reader 1: Then the righteous will answer Him, saying...

Reader 3: Lord, when did we see You hungry and feed You, or thirsty and give You drink? When did we see You a stranger and take You in, or naked and clothe You? Or when did we see You sick, or in prison, and come to You?

Reader 1: And the King will answer and say to them...

Reader 2: Assuredly, I say to you, inasmuch as you did it to one of the least of these My brethren, you did it to Me.

Kids Talk

Today's message provides a good opportunity to tell the children about some aspect of the church's ministry of compassion. "We are followers of the Lord Jesus Christ, and that means we should be compassionate like He was. That means that we feel badly when others are hurting, and we want to help them. Maybe you know someone who is hurting that you can help. As a church, let me tell you about some children we are helping in India (or some flood victims in your own area, etc)." End your **Kids Talk** by praying for those in need.

Additional Sermons and Lesson Ideas

Contending for the Faith

Date preached:

SCRIPTURE: Jude 1–25

INTRODUCTION: If you want to win football games, you have to have not one but two teams—an offensive team and a defensive team. Christianity is under attack today, and the Book of Jude reminds us that we must contend for the faith, having a good offensive and a good defensive. Key to Jude: Verse 3.

1. Salutation (vv. 1–2).
2. Christianity on Defense (vv. 3–16).
3. Christianity on Offense (vv. 17–23).
4. Benediction (vv. 24–25).

CONCLUSION: A. W. Tozer said, "Great saints have always been dogmatic." J. I. Packer wrote, "There can be no spiritual health without doctrinal knowledge." Dr. Martyn Lloyd-Jones said, "We cannot have the benefits of Christianity if we shed its doctrines." Paul predicted, "The time will come when they will not endure sound doctrine." That's why Jude tells us: "Contend earnestly for the faith."

Hearts of Worship
By David George

Date preached:

SCRIPTURE: 2 Samuel 6:12–22; 22:1–5; 24:18–25; Psalm 23

INTRODUCTION: David, a man after God's heart, frequently displayed his heart of worship (2 Sam. 6:12–22; 22:1–5; 24:18–25). If we are to be people after God's heart, we are to have hearts of worship. David gives us insight into what it means to worship in Psalm 23.

1. A heart of worship grows out of a healthy sense of belonging to God (Ps. 23:1). Throughout Scripture, sheep indicate belonging, unlike wolves or goats which are intruders. The shepherd indicates ownership. David recognized he was owned. Do you?
2. A heart of worship is expanded as we follow God's leadership (Ps. 23:2–3). David's sense of worship flowed from an understanding of God's control over his life (Ps. 91). Worship is not always public or planned. It grows from our walk with the Lord.
3. A heart of worship is confident (Ps. 23:6). Living a life owned by the Father, following His leadership, results in an unshakeable confidence. Are you living a life of worship? Do you have David's confidence that you will dwell with the Lord forever?

CONCLUSION: People after God's heart have hearts of worship. Do we worship on Sunday morning only, or do our lives reflect God's leadership and ownership?

FEBRUARY 29, 2004

SUGGESTED SERMON

Come Now, and Let Us Reason
Date preached:

By Peter Grainger

Scripture: Isaiah 1:1–31, especially verse 2: "Hear, O heavens, and give ear, O earth! For the Lord has spoken."

Introduction: When we have visitors in Edinburgh, we take them atop Blackford Hill for a panoramic view of Edinburgh, a wholly different perspective from the one on Princes Street. A prophet like Isaiah is, in a sense, someone who sees things from a different perspective because his vantage-point is higher. Isaiah had "eagles' eyes" (Is. 40:31), and his book tells what he saw. His message is focused on a tiny nation in the Middle East through whom the Lord had promised to bless the earth. Israel was in danger, but the Lord had not given up on her. Striking parallels exist between Isaiah's day and ours. We see a world in turmoil; and God's people, who hold the key to His purposes, are in disarray. Isaiah's opening chapter contains three themes that recur throughout his long ministry.

1. **An Alarming Accusation (vv. 1–17).** The scene is a courtroom. The universe is called to attend, the Judge is the Lord, and His people are in the dock. The charges are very serious, a deadly cocktail of outright rebellion and outward religion.

    A. **Outright Rebellion (vv. 2–10).** God says with amazement that even oxen and donkeys recognize their master's voice, but His children have rejected His authority. Rebellion often flourishes during prosperity, and Isaiah began his ministry during the reign of Uzziah, a period of peace and prosperity. Yet it had been used by the rich to exploit the poor. Justice was bought and sold to the highest bidder, gaps in society widened, and bloodshed was common. The people had prostituted themselves (vv. 21–23). The crucial question for those of us who are Christians is: Do we live under the authority of the Lord and of His Son? We rebel against His authority by refusing to submit every area of life to His Lordship. It's only a matter of time, unless something is done about it, that sons become rebels and rebels become harlots.

B. **Outward Religion (vv. 11–17).** Despite their rebellion, the Israelites didn't abandon religion, but the Lord could no longer bear rituals (vv. 11–14) which were prescribed in the Law of Moses to give outward expression to inner obedience. The Lord would sooner they suspended their religion than indulge in hypocrisy (Rev. 3:15–16). Notice how seriously the Lord regards sin in His people. But that is not, thank God, the sum of Isaiah's message. In the middle of this chapter, and running like a silver thread through the book, is a message of hope.

2. **An Incredible Invitation (vv. 18–20).** Verse 18 is one of the great texts of the Bible, especially when read in context, because of its tone and its terms.
   A. **Its Tone**. Its tone is one of reason rather than demand. The righteous judge is also the loving Father. In fact, His tone all along has been one of sorrow over His children's sin (vv. 5–6). The Son of God would later express the same anguish (Luke 13:34). What an amazing thing that God reasons with us when we stray. How incredible that the Lord Jesus knocks at the door of His lukewarm church (Rev. 3:20).
   B. **Its Terms.** Stepping from His bench, the Judge offers the accused full pardon. Both wool and snow are white by nature; the Lord is offering to give His people a new heart and nature. Neither the sacrifices of animals nor the multitude of rituals can ever pay the debt owed. The judge had to descend from His throne, become a human being, and suffer in our stead (see Is. 53). But there is a condition. A change of direction—repentance—is required (vv. 19–20). In subsequent chapters, the Israelites refused to repent. Was that, then, the end of the Lord's plan for them? No. The chapter finishes with a third theme:

>>> *sermon continued on following page*

APPROPRIATE HYMNS AND SONGS

Come Let Us Reason, Ken Medema; © 1971 Word Music, Inc.

According to Thy Lovingkindness; Robert C. Savage; © 1958 Singspiration Music, Admin. by Brentwood-Benson Music Publishing, Inc.

I Must Tell Jesus, Elisha A. Hoffman; Public Domain.

Jesus, I Come, William T. Sleeper/George C. Stebbins; Public Domain.

Jesus, You're All I Need, Darlene Zschech; © 1997 Darlene Zschech (Hillsong), Admin. by Integrity Music, Inc.

3. **A Painful Purification (vv. 21–31).** Though they were like Sodom, Judah's fate would be different. The Lord, Isaiah said, will come in judgment, but for purification, not annihilation. Those who persist in doing evil would be judged through a process whereby Israel would be purged of its sin and refined, for God wants His people to declare His character and draw others to Himself (vv. 26–28).

Conclusion: It was all fulfilled when Christ came to His own, though they did not receive Him. The consequence was judgment, and only a remnant was preserved. But God's great plan, conceived in eternity and executed in time, was fulfilled as Gentiles were grafted into God's people. Christians are "a chosen generation, a royal priesthood, a holy nation, His own special people" (1 Pet. 2:9). God is seeking to reason with us, the choice is ours, and the time is now: "Come, now, and let us reason together."

FOR THE BULLETIN

✿ Patrick Hamilton was born about 1504 to a wealthy family near Glasgow, Scotland. His mother told him Bible stories, and her lessons lived in his heart till the close of his life. As a teen, Hamilton attended the Sorbonne in France where he heard the sensational news of Luther's Reformation. Graduating in 1520, he returned to Scotland and continued his studies at the University of St. Andrews, eventually joining the faculty. There he accepted Reformation and began proclaiming views. The Scottish Parliament had condemned anyone possessing Reformation books or beliefs, and Archbishop David Beaton, rabid foe of Protestantism, began seeking Hamilton's life. Hamilton was eventually arrested, and at high noon on February 29, 1528, he was chained to a post and burned. The flame didn't catch well, and Hamilton suffered for six long torturous hours. When it finally appeared the fire was doing its work, he cried, "How long, O God, shall darkness cover this kingdom." The flames of those fires sparked the Reformation in Scotland. ✿ The Salem Witch Trials began on this day in 1692 in Massachusetts. ✿ Ann Lee was born on this day in 1736. She grew up in Manchester, England, working in the textile mills. As a young person she turned away from a worldly life and began seeking inner peace. She joined a group who worshiped with such inner intensity that they shook, and they became known as "Shaking Quakers," or Shakers. Ann emigrated to New York, and under her leadership, the Shaker movement in the United States began. ✿ On February 29, 1956, Pakistan proclaimed itself an Islamic republic.

STATS, STORIES AND MORE

Amnesty
The word *amnesty* comes from the word from which we get *amnesia*. It means to forget. When God washes away our sins, they are forgotten. We're left whiter than snow, purer than wool.

Whiter Than Snow
Evangelist E. Howard Cadle (1884–1942), was converted from a debauched life through the power of Isaiah 1:18. He was the black sheep of four children in a Christian family who started drinking at age twelve. He became addicted to alcohol, gambling, and sexual adultery, becoming known as the "Slot Machine King" in much of the Midwest because of his gambling enterprises. He attempted to murder a man, only narrowly escaping the penitentiary. Broken in finances and health, he finally "hit bottom" and returned home and collapsed into his mother's arms, saying, "Mother I'm tired of sin. I've broken your heart, betrayed my wife, broken my marriage vows—I'd like to be saved, but I've sinned too much." His mother replied, "Son, I've prayed for 12 years to hear you say what you've just said." Getting out her Bible, she turned to Isaiah 1:18, and on that morning, March 14, 1914, E. Howard Cadle was converted. He later became a powerful and popular evangelist and radio preacher.

WORSHIP HELPS

Call to Worship:
Bless the LORD, O my soul; and all that is within me, bless His holy name! Bless the LORD, O my soul, and forget not all His benefits: Who forgives all your iniquities, who heals all your diseases, who redeems your life from destruction, who crowns you with lovingkindness and tender mercies, who satisfies your mouth with good things, so that your youth is renewed like the eagle's (Ps. 103:1–5).

Offertory Comments:
If you use humor in your service, consider this story passed along by Pastor David Jeremiah: Two men were shipwrecked on an island, and one of them started screaming, "We're going to die. There's no food. There's no water. We're going to die." The other man was propped against a palm tree acting so calmly it drove the first man crazy. "Don't you understand we're going to die?" the first man said. "No we won't," replied his companion. "I make a $100,000 a week." The first man looked at him with amazement and said, "So? We're on an island with no food or water. We're going to die." The second man answered, "You don't get it. I make $100,000 a week. I tithe. My pastor will find me." Well, today, we're looking for tithers.

Responsive Reading from Psalm 51:

Leader:	Have mercy on me, O God, according to Your lovingkindness; according to the multitude of Your tender mercies, blot out my transgressions.
All:	Wash me thoroughly from my iniquity, and cleanse me from my sin.
Leader:	For I acknowledge my transgressions, and my sin is always before me.
All:	Against You, You only, have I sinned, and down this evil in Your sight.
Leader:	Purge me with hyssop, and I shall be clean; wash me, and I shall be whiter than snow.
All:	Create in me a clean heart, O God, and renew a steadfast spirit within me.

Additional Sermons and Lesson Ideas

The Precious Blood
Date preached:

By Charles Haddon Spurgeon

SCRIPTURE: 1 Peter 1:9

INTRODUCTION: Standing at the foot of the cross, we see His hands, feet, and side, spilling crimson streams of precious blood.

1. Christ's blood is precious because of its cleansing power (1 John 1:7).
2. Christ's blood is precious because of its preserving power (Ex. 11:5). We are safe from the destroying angel under His sprinkled blood.
3. Christ's blood is precious because of its sanctifying power (Heb. 13:12). The same blood that justifies by taking away sin also awakens the new nature and leads us to subdue sin and to be set apart of God's purposes.
4. Christ's blood is precious because of its overcoming power (Rev. 12:11).

CONCLUSION: The blood of Jesus! Sin dies at its presence. Heaven opens before it. There is power in the blood!

The Precious Name
Date preached:

SCRIPTURE: Revelation 1

INTRODUCTION: Most of us have two or three names, but Jesus has hundreds of names, titles, and descriptions given to Him in Scripture. Notice how He is introduced in the first chapter of Revelation.

1. Jesus
2. Christ
3. The Faithful Witness
4. The Firstborn from the Dead
5. The Ruler over the Kings of the Earth
6. Him Who Loved Us and Washed Us
7. Alpha and Omega
8. The Beginning and the End
9. He Who Was and Is and Is to Come
10. The Almighty
11. The Son of Man
12. He Who Lives and Was Dead

CONCLUSION: His name, which is above every name, deserves and demands our worship.

MARCH 7, 2004

SUGGESTED SERMON
The Horrors of Hell
Date preached:

By Melvin Worthington

Scripture: Luke 16:19–31, especially verse 23: "And being in torments in Hades, he lifted up his eyes . . ."

Introduction: One of the most solemn doctrines in the Bible is eternal punishment. During recent years, little has been written or preached on the subject of hell despite its prominence in the Bible, but we dare not neglect this matter. Jesus spoke more of hell than of heaven, and this passage is one of His plainest statements on the subject. It's also the only passage in Scripture that describes the feelings of the unconverted after death.

1. **The Place.** The Bible identifies hell as a specific place. Bishop J. C. Ryle noted, "The Lord Jesus tells us plainly that after death the rich man was in hell, tormented with flame." Albert Barnes defined hell as "that dark, obscure, and miserable place, far from heaven, where the wicked shall be punished forever." (see 2 Pet. 2:4 and Rev. 20:13–15).

2. **The Portrait (Luke 16:19–31).** This provides insight into the horror, hopelessness, and helplessness of those in hell. Consider the rich man's *Daily Merriment* (v. 19). Before death, he enjoyed the fine things of life. Every day was a banquet. He wore the finest clothes and feasted constantly. Albert Barnes said, "This was a mark of great wealth, and in the view of the world, evidence of great happiness."

   Consider the rich man's *Dying Moment* (v. 22b). The Bible simply says, " . . . the rich man also died and was buried." Wealth does not secure one from death. The rich as well as the poor go down to the grave. Death is the common end to which all classes of mankind must come. Although death is a fact that all acknowledge, few live their lives facing this reality. Most people eat, drink, talk, and plan as if they were going to live on earth forever.

   Consider the rich man's *Described Misery* (vv. 23–25). Hell is a place of *punishment*. The man cried out, tormented in the flame. Hell is a place of *pain*. Barnes says, "The suffering of the wicked in hell will be indescribably great.... Remember that all this is but a representation of the pains of the damned, and that this will have not intermission day or night, but will continue from year to year, and age to age, without end...." The *permanence* of hell adds immeasurably to the torment. There is no possibility of getting out. Once in hell, we are in hell forever. The *partition* that separates man from God is one of the devastating things about hell. As R.C.H. Lenski wrote, "The sense of the statement is that death decides forever, it is either Heaven or Hell." Barnes concludes, "There will never be any escape from those gloomy regions. There is a gulf fixed—fixed, not movable. Nor can any of the damned beat a pathway across this gulf to the world of holiness."

Consider the rich man's *Desired Mercy* (v. 24). He wanted Lazarus to come and put a drop of water on his tongue in order to cool it.

Consider the rich man's *Disturbing Memory* (v. 25). He was challenged to remember that in his lifetime he had lived sumptuously. One of the horrors of hell will be remembering what we might have been had we responded to the call of God.

Consider the rich man's *Deadly Mistake* (v. 30). He disbelieved, disregarded, despised, and disobeyed the writings of Moses. God has given us sufficient warning to prepare for death. He has sent His Word, His prophets, His Son; He warns us by His Spirit and by the pleas of friends.

>>> *sermon continued on following page*

APPROPRIATE HYMNS AND SONGS

Clap, Clap Your Hands, Jennifer Randolf; © 1990 Integrity's Hosanna! Music.

O Lord, the Clouds Are Gathering, Graham Kendrick; © 1987 Make Way Music, Admin. by Music Services.

Jesus Is Tenderly Calling, Fanny Crosby/George C. Stebbins; Public Domain.

Kind and Merciful God, Bryan Jeffery Leech; © 1973 Fred Boch Music Company, Inc.

For Your Mercy, Danny Daniels; © 1995 Mercy/Vineyard Publishing, Inc.

Consider the *Divine Message* to the rich man. When he requested someone be sent to warn his brothers he was reminded that his brothers had the writings of Moses and the prophets. If they would not believe them, they would not believe even if someone returned from the dead. Barnes concludes, "God will give us nothing farther to warn us. No dead man will come to life to tell us of what he has seen. If he did, we would not believe him."

3. The Population. The Bible gives a comprehensive list of those who will populate hell in 1 Corinthians 6:9–12, Galatians 5:19–21 and Revelation 21:8.

Conclusion: What about you? Are you a believer? Have you placed your faith in the finished work of Christ for salvation? God has given His Son, the Scriptures and His Spirit to bring us to Christ. Are you willing to come today?

FOR THE BULLETIN

- March 7, 322 B.C. marks the death of the Greek philosopher, Aristotle.
- The young Christian maid, Perpetua, died on March 7, 202. Emperor Septimus Severius had issued an edict against Christians, and presently Perpetua was placed under house arrest. When her father begged her to recant, she pointed to a waterpot and asked, "Father, do you see this vessel? Can it be called by any other name than what it is? So also I cannot call myself by any other name than what I am—a Christian." She and a handful of other believers were marched into the arena where Perpetua was gored and thrown by a savage heifer. Shortly thereafter, a gladiator pierced her with his sword. Her death for Christ so inspired the Christians in North Africa that she personified Tertullian's famous quote, "The blood of the martyrs is the seed of the church."
- The long and bitter dispute between Pope Gregory VII and Emperor Henry V culminated with the second excommunication of the king on March 7, 1080.
- This day marks the death of Thomas Aquinas. While traveling to the city of Lyon, he fell and injured his head. He died in the Cistercian abbey of Fossanova on March 7, 1274. He was 48.
- On March 7, 1526, the Zurich City Council took action against the Anabaptist movement by decreeing that anyone who allowed himself to be rebaptized would be drowned. Under this decree, Felix Mantz was later drowned.
- On March 7, 1804, the British and Foreign Bible Society was formed in London.
- On March 7, 1835, Fanny Crosby arrived at the New York School for the Blind as a student.
- On this day in 1981, missionary Chet Bitterman was executed by terrorists in Columbia, South America.

STATS, STORIES AND MORE

Someone Once Said...

There is no doctrine which I would more willingly remove from Christianity than this (hell) if it lay in my power. But it has the full support of Scripture and, especially, of our Lord's own words; it has always been held by Christendom; and has the support of reason.—*C. S. Lewis*

Wisdom directs us to admit that there is no biblical alternative to the biblical doctrine of eternal punishment.—*J. I. Packer*

As the Lord liveth, sinner, thou standest on a single plank over the mouth of hell, and that plank is rotten. Thou hangest over the pit by a solitary rope, and the strands of that rope are breaking.—*Charles Spurgeon*

A hard look at this doctrine should first change our view of sin. Most believers do not take sin as seriously as God does.—*John Thomas*

As hell was becoming for many no more than a swear word, sin was also an accepted way of life. . . . If people can ignore what the Bible calls sin, then they can quite logically discount what it says about the reality of hell.—*Billy Graham*

My congregation would be stunned to hear a sermon on hell.—*Mary Kraus, pastor of Dumbarton United Methodist Church in Washington, D.C.*

Time/CNN Polling Data

A telephone poll of 1,018 American adults, conducted by Time/CNN by Yankelovich Partners, Inc., asked these questions:

· Do you believe in hell, where people are punished forever after they die?
- Yes: 63%
- No: 30%

· Do people get into heaven based mostly on the good things they do or on their faith of God, or both (asked of 809 who believe in heaven):
- Good things they do: 6%
- Faith in God: 34%
- Both: 57%

· Immediately after death, which of the following do you think will happen to you? (asked of 809 who believe in heaven):
- Go directly to heaven: 61%
- Go to purgatory: 15%
- Go to hell: 1%
- Be reincarnated: 5%
- End of existence: 4%

WORSHIP HELPS

Call to Worship:
Oh, clap your hands, all you peoples! Shout to God with the voice of triumph! (Ps. 47:1)

Pastoral Prayer:
Our heavenly Father, we know that You are not willing for any to perish, but for all to come to repentance. We know that You loved this world so much You sent Your only begotten Son, that whoever believes in Him shall not perish, but have eternal life. But we also know that the issues of life and death, of heaven and hell, of hope and horror are very real, and we ask today that You will give us a sense of urgency. Impress us, Lord, with Your call to salvation. Impress us, Lord, with Your commission to evangelize. Awaken us from lethargy, and make us a people who live in the light of eternity, who labor with the earnestness of those who understand eternal things. We pray in Jesus' name, Amen.

Scripture Reading from Revelation 22:14–17 (NLT):
Blessed are those who wash their robes so they can enter through the gates of the city and eat the fruit from the tree of life. Outside the city are the dogs—the sorcerers, the sexually immoral, the murderers, the idol worshipers, and all who love to live a lie. "I, Jesus, have sent my angel to give you this message for the churches. I am both the source of David and the heir to his throne.? I am the bright morning star." The Spirit and the bride say, "Come." Let each one who hears them say, "Come." Let the thirsty ones come—anyone who wants to. Let them come and drink the water of life without charge.

Offertory Comment:
The Amplified Bible renders 2 Corinthians 9:7: "Let each one [give] as he has made up his own mind and purposed in his heart, not reluctantly or sorrowfully or under compulsion, for God loves (that is, He takes pleasure in, prizes above other things, and is unwilling to abandon or to do without) a cheerful (joyous, prompt-to-do-it) giver—whose heart is in his giving."

Additional Sermons and Lesson Ideas

Real Faith in Hard Times

By Kevin Riggs

Date preached:

SCRIPTURE: 1 Kings 19:1–18

INTRODUCTION: Living by faith means that during hard times you have Someone to lean on. Elijah was a prophet who stood for righteousness during a wicked time. After his defeat of the prophets of Baal on Mt. Carmel, Queen Jezebel vowed to kill him. Elijah fled and became discouraged. God spoke to him and encouraged him. From his experience we learn what to do, and what not to do, during difficult times.

1. What not to do during hard times.
   A. Don't throw a pity party (vv. 4, 9, 10).
   B. Don't become a loner (v. 3).
   C. Don't whine and complain (vv. 4, 10, 14).
   D. Don't give up (v. 4).
2. What to do during hard times.
   A. Realize the situation you are in.
   B. Draw yourself closer to God (vv. 11–13).
   C. Fellowship with other believers (vv. 15–18).

CONCLUSION: Tough times come and go, but tough people come and grow.

Of Whom Shall I Be Afraid

By Ed Dobson

Date preached:

SCRIPTURE: Psalm 27

INTRODUCTION: We all deal with fear, and in the time in which we are now living, fear is multiplied over and over. What's the cure for fear? The only medicine that deals with fear is faith. I would like to suggest three steps for dealing with fear and cultivating your faith:

1. Faith is a choice (vv. 1–3, especially the end of v. 3).
2. Faith is cultivated through an intimate relationship with God (vv. 4–6).
3. Faith is strengthened through prayer (vv. 7–12).

CONCLUSION: I began the sermon with the thesis that faith is the key to fear. I want to finish the sermon with another truth. God, who is good, is on your side (v.13). So if you are afraid, choose to have faith. Continue in your relationship with God, continually praying, and, "Wait on the LORD . . . and He shall strengthen your heart . . ." (v. 14).

THOUGHTS FOR THE PASTOR'S SOUL

A Stale Loaf of Bread

Have you ever had the common reoccurring dream of the overworked pastor—that you're late for a speaking engagement?

On the eve of a recent obligation at a local college, I dreamed I was running late. I sped across town in a panic, arriving to find the chapel filled with students who had been singing hymn after hymn while awaiting me. As I ascended the platform, a sickening feeling came over me; I had forgotten my Bible. I quickly grabbed one from a professor, but when I stood in the pulpit to open it, what I had in my hands was a large loaf of stale and moldy bread.

The memory of that dream stayed with me, and it bothered me. "Lord," I prayed, "may I never stand in Your pulpit with dry, moldy, stale bread. May my messages from You always be fresh."

After twenty-five years in ministry, I know the only way for my messages to be fresh is to cycle them through my heart in a personal way. I have to sit at the feet of Jesus, listen to His Word, get His food for my own soul, then be excited enough to pass it on. What does this require of us pastors?

1. Constantly Remembering Our Great Calling. Sometimes my calling doesn't seem so great. My zeal tends to flag when problems arise, offerings are off, attendance is down, dissension is up, and my to-do list is long. I suffer pangs of failure and wonder whether the stress and strain is really worth it. But then I remember what the Lord said to the Levites in Numbers 16:9–10: "Is it a small thing to you that the God of Israel has separated you from the congregation of Israel, to bring you near to Himself, to do the work of the tabernacle of the LORD, and to stand before the congregation to serve them?"

It is *not* a small thing. It may sometimes seem that I'm in a small place, laboring with scant resources to a small audience with limited results. But it's a huge privilege with eternal ramifications, for God has promised that our labor will never be in vain in the Lord, and that He will use us in ways we may not fully understand till we get to heaven.

"Oh," wrote Gardiner Spring, pastor of the Brick Church in New York City for 63 years, "if ministers only saw the inconceivable glory that is before them, and the preciousness of Christ, they would not be able to refrain from going about, leaping and clapping their hands for joy, and exclaiming, 'I am a minister of Christ! I am a minister of Christ!'"

2. Keeping Our Quiet Time. An effective work for God is impossible without an intimate walk with God. Meeting the Lord each morning for private Bible study and prayer is the most important habit in my Christian life, and without it my Sunday sermons would be hollow words. Jeremiah criticized the shepherds of his day because they spoke well-crafted words, but they didn't get those words by standing in the counsel of Jehovah. "But if they had stood in My counsel," declared the Lord in Jeremiah 23:22, "and had caused My people to hear My words, then they would have turned from their evil way and from the evil of their doings."

Our souls are receptacles for God's living waters; our sermons are the overflow. We cannot give out more than we're taking in. As one financial advisor put it, "If your output exceeds your intake, your upkeep will be your downfall."

3. Guarding Our Saturday Nights. I've always stolen away on Saturday nights to prepare myself for Sunday ministry, but recently I became so busy with writing projects that I began to "cheat"—a few minutes here, proofing a manuscript, and a little time there, scribbling ideas for an article. Occasionally I'd sit down and watch a Saturday night television show. It didn't take long for me to feel less prepared and less confident on Sunday mornings, not only with my sermon but with my soul. Just as the Jewish Sabbath actually began at sundown on the night before, the tone of our Sunday ministry is set by our hearts and habits on Saturday night. Realizing this, I confessed my lapses to the Lord and renewed my commitment to re-sanctify the hours of seven to nine on Saturday nights, and to retire shortly thereafter in order to be well-rested for Sabbath labor.

4. Rising Early on Sunday Mornings. For years, I went to my office early on Sunday to focus all my energies on being well-prepped for the day's obligations. My wife faithfully got our children out of bed, fed and dressed, and on to church without my help. Our children are grown now, but I'm unable to keep my old routine due to Katrina's multiple sclerosis. I have to help her dress; and since she can no longer drive, we both come to church together. This is no small loss, but I've learned that faithfulness to God in one area is as important as in another. If I

THOUGHTS FOR THE PASTOR'S SOUL — CONTINUED

fill the bedroom with Christian music on Sunday mornings as we're getting ourselves ready, if I help her with shoes and socks and zippers, and if I sit beside Katrina in the service, participating in worship, by the time I rise to speak my heart is ready.

5. Preparing Our Hearts. Preparing my sermon is only half the job; the other half is preparing my soul to deliver the sermon. If I'm not moved by the truths I'm going to preach, how do I expect others to be impacted? Preaching isn't a matter of giving lectures. It's a matter of becoming a live conduit for God's electricity. This requires making sure my soul is plugged into the current, which only happens through prayer and meditation. Given the choice, I'd rather stand to preach with a heart full of passion and love and extemporize from a few verses than to stand with a well-crafted sermon but an unprepared heart. I can improvise the sermon, but I can't fake the fire.

6. Resting. Having passed the mid-century mark, I've noticed that it's easy to work so hard on Saturday, my supposed "day off," that I'm exhausted on Sunday and can barely summon the energy necessary for pulpit work. This we can't allow, for nothing drains our energy like preaching. We feel "virtue" go out of us, as Jesus put it in Mark 5:30, and most of us don't have an abundance of "virtue" to spare. We have to conserve our physical strength. Physical exertion is important, but should be undertaken so that it *imparts* energy and doesn't *deplete* it. Exercise is useful as long as it doesn't cross the line of diminishing returns. So this year I'm going to hire a boy to help me with some of the yard work. My workaholic tendencies are nearly impossible to control, but moderate exercise, some time away, regular vacations, a few evenings off, an occasional morning without the alarm clock—these are necessary for longevity in the pulpit.

7. Dedicating Our Sermons to God. My mentor, Rev. Winford R. Floyd, taught me that, having prepared my sermon on paper, I should lay my notes before the Lord and dedicate the message to Him. It needs God's unction and power.

Some years ago, when *Sunset Boulevard* was enjoying a long run on Broadway, someone asked its star, Betty Buckley, how she kept her performance "fresh" night after night. Her answer sounds almost sacrilegious for an actor but strangely appropriate for a preacher. She said that she views each performance as a ritual, as an offering to something higher and as an opportunity to touch the sacred. Each performance, she said, is an opportunity to connect deeply with the character and with the audience.

Preaching is an offering of fire, designed to form a deep connection between the speaker (God) and, through us, the listener.

Charles Spurgeon referred to preaching as "logic set on fire." To put it a bit differently, preachers are people who pile the firewood of Scripture in their hearts before dousing themselves with the kerosene of prayer, and setting themselves on fire while an audience gathers to watch the blaze. Like Moses' burning bush, we're burning but never consumed. There we are next Sunday to repeat the spectacle, again and again.

How do we keep the crackling flames from dying into a smoldering heap? It isn't by might nor by power. Not by the giftedness of a sharp mind, the eloquence of clear outlines, or the force of a vivacious personality.

It is by His Spirit alone, which, like oil from a hidden, limitless reservoir, feeds the flame of passion and keeps the blaze going.

> *Jesus, the Truth and Power divine,*
> *Send forth this messenger of Thine;*
> *My hands confirm, my heart inspire,*
> *And touch my lips with hallowed fire.*
> —Charles Wesley

Quotes for the Pastor's Wall

" To fill the church well, we must fill the pulpit well. "

—Thomas Chalmers

HEROES FOR THE PASTOR'S HEART

James Young Simpson

Visitors to Edinburgh, flocking to see the monuments of the great in Princess Street Gardens, sometimes look at one giant figure, seated sternly in a chair of bronze, and ask, "Who's that?"

That, my friend, is one of the most remarkable Christian physicians and scientists of all time, one who is responsible for saving you much suffering if you've ever had surgery.

James Young Simpson was born to a baker and his wife in a Scottish town in 1811. So brilliant was he that he enrolled in the University of Edinburgh at age 14, and graduated in 1832. He was one of the world's most outstanding physicians and obstetricians. He was also a committed and devout Christian who was deeply concerned about the sufferings of those who had to undergo surgery.

Imagine surgery before the day of anesthesia. Patients were strapped down while scalpel and saw cut through tissue and bone, every slice and turn of the knife causing unimaginable pain.

Dr. Simpson became Senior President of the Royal Medical Society of Edinburgh when only twenty-four, and in time received virtually every possible honor and position. He dreamed of finding a way of putting patients to sleep during surgery. On Monday evenings, Simpson periodically invited small groups of physicians to his home to experiment with chemicals, crystals, and powders, which were placed over a burning brazier while the doctors inhaled the fumes. Nothing worked until November 4, 1847. One of the men had purchased a crystal called chloroform in Paris. As the doctors sniffed the burning substance, they fell to the floor unconscious.

Simpson had his answer, but he soon encountered another problem. He was attacked by fellow Christians who claimed that pain was a God-ordained part of life. Freedom from pain comes only in heaven, and it is immoral to devise dangerous ways of escaping it on earth.

Sir James went to the Scriptures, seeking answers. He no sooner opened his Bible than he came to this verse: "And the Lord God caused a deep sleep to fall on Adam, and he slept; and He took one of his ribs, and closed up the flesh in its place." Carefully studying the text, Simpson wrote an article entitled, "Answer to the Religious Objections Advanced Against the Employment of Anesthetic Agents in Midwifery and Surgery." He ended his paper saying, "We may rest fully assured that whatever is true in point of fact or humane and merciful in point of practice, will find no condemnation in the Word of God."

His critics were silenced, and a new day dawned in medical science. After Queen Victoria used this anesthetic during the birth of Prince Leopold in 1853, it became generally accepted throughout Great Britain and soon around the world.

PRAYERS FOR A PASTOR'S CLOSET

A Prayer from Psalm 86

Father,

I praise You for the years of health and joy You've given me, for my family and friends, for my ministry and message. Thank You for Your own sweet love and companionship through Jesus Christ my Lord.

I also present my prayer to You today, asking as the writer of Psalm 86:

- **Be merciful to me, Lord (v. 2).** Wash away my faults, failures, and foolishness in the flood of Your blood. Keep me from anguishing over what You've forgiven, and may Your hand restrain me from sinning against You.

- **Rejoice my soul, Lord (v. 4).** Thank You for the way its put here: "Rejoice the soul of Your servant." Infuse me with Your gladness. Pump Your joy into me.

- **Attend to my prayers (v. 6).** Hear and heed my requests made daily to You, O Lord. May this be a season of answered prayer.

- **Teach me Your way, O Lord (v. 11).** Give me Your wisdom on a constant, on-going basis; may I see things from Your standpoint.

- **Give me Your strength (v. 16).**

- **Show me a sign for good (v. 17).** Teach me to recognize the token of Your goodness daily spread across my pathway. May I daily recognize the blessings You so graciously and freely give me, Father, O You who daily loads me with benefits.

And in the process, may my whole life be a testimony to Your goodness and a reflection of Your grace. May I glorify You in body, heart, mind, and soul. In Jesus' name, Amen.

MARCH 14, 2004

SUGGESTED SERMON
A Model for Ministry

Date preached:

By Michael Duduit

Scripture: 1 Thessalonians 2:1–12, especially verse 4: "As we have been approved by God to be entrusted with the gospel, even so we speak, not as pleasing men, but God who tests our hearts."

Introduction: A young pastor was conducting the funeral of a war veteran. The dead man's military friends, wanting a part in the service, asked him to escort them to the casket, stand with them for a moment of remembrance, then lead them out through the side door. The pastor did precisely that, but not being familiar with the funeral home, he picked the wrong door. They marched with military precision into a janitorial closet! That story says two things about leadership. First, if you're going to lead, you'd better know where you're going. Second, if you're going to follow, you'd better follow someone who knows where he's going. Thousands of books, articles, and conferences focus on leadership, yet we have few outstanding leaders. We need examples of integrity. This passage gives us such a model. Paul, Silas, and Timothy came to Thessalonica to establish a church, but the religious officials drove them from town. Even so, Paul demonstrated a model of leadership in which the fledging church there could have confidence.

1. **Christian Leaders Prioritize on God.** Paul's opponents impugned his motives, but they weren't successful because his ultimate priority was God's approval, not the approval of man. Authentic leadership places its focus on God: His approval, purpose, and will above all else. How do we recognize such leaders?
    A. **Their motives come from God (v. 3).** Paul faced three accusations: First, that he was teaching incorrectly: Our *exhortation did not come from error*.... Paul reminded them that his teaching and leadership came from God's truth. Too often we ask, "Will it work?" rather than "Is it true?" A second charge was: ... *or uncleanness*. This was probably an accusation of sexual immorality. In a pagan culture like Thessalonica, such a charge was not uncommon. If Paul could be dis-

credited here, Christianity could be disdained. Paul denied the accusation, and later, in chapter 4, underscored the issue of sexual purity. It's vital for leaders to be pure and faithful. A third accusation involved manipulation or trickery—*nor was it in deceit.* This word was used of catching a fish with bait. But Paul renounced handling the Word of God deceitfully (2 Cor. 4:2). He was above reproach.

- B. **Their model comes from God (v. 4).** Christian leaders serve so as to meet God's test. Sometimes we're duped by so-called leaders, but God cannot be fooled. Paul wasn't trying to please men but God, who tests the heart. Who are you trying to please? That's an important question because it determines how high we set our standards. Suppose I said I could jump twelve feet in the air. If I used my own measuring standard in which an inch equals a foot, I might make it! We tend to set our own standards, and the moral judgments of our culture are easy to achieve, but they won't stand the test of eternity.

2. **Christian Leaders Convey God's Love (vv. 7–9).** Leadership is more than talents and techniques; it is caring for those we're leading. Notice the images in verses 7 and 11: "we were gentle . . . as a nursing mother . . . as a father. . . ." In verse 9, Paul says he supported himself on behalf of the church. If we're going to be leaders in God's service, it can't be done from a distance. We must lower our defenses and love people for Christ's sake.

3. **Christian Leaders Focus on God's Kingdom.** Good leaders don't get sidetracked. In his biography of Ronald Reagan, Edmund Morris observes

>>> *sermon continued on following page*

APPROPRIATE HYMNS AND SONGS

Jesus Shall Reign, Isaac Watts; Public Domain.

The Lord Reigns, John Sellers; © 1989 Maranatha Praise, Inc., Admin. by The Copyright Company.

How Clear Is Our Vocation Lord, Fred Pratt Green/C. Hubert H. Perry; © 1982 Hope Publishing Company.

In the Service of the King, Bentley D. Ackley/Rev. Alfred H. Ackley; Public Domain.

Guide Me O Thou Great Jehovah, William Williams/Harry E. Fosdick/John Hughes/Peter William; Public Domain.

that Reagan decided to have two or three primary objectives in office. Lots of issues could have waylaid him, but he focused on those major goals. As a result, he accomplished much of what he set out to do. Paul kept his eyes on the prize, maintaining a focus on God's Kingdom in all he did.

A. **Leaders have "kingdom focus" in their lifestyle (v. 10).** Paul and company were (1) devout in their behavior toward God; (2) just in their behavior toward the Thessalonians; (3) blameless in their behavior toward themselves.

B. **Leaders have a "kingdom focus" in their message (v. 11–12).** Christians encourage others to experience Christ, helping them live "worthy of God."

Conclusion: Management guru Peter Drucker remembers when he was thirteen. A teacher asked his class, "What do you want to be remembered for?" When none of the boys answered, the teacher said, "I didn't expect you to be able to answer that now. But if you can't answer it by the time you're fifty, you'll have wasted your life." Knowing how you want to end up makes the difference in how you get there. What do you want to be remembered for?

FOR THE BULLETIN

❖ March 14, 840, marks the death of Einhard, the Frank historian and biographer of Charlemagne. He was born into a wealthy family and educated at the monastery of Fulda and, later, under Alcuin. His latter days were spent as an ordained presbyter. ❖ In the early 1870s, word from missionary/explorer David Livingstone ceased, and the world held its breath, wondering if he were still alive. Finally the *New York Herald* sent reporter Henry Stanley to find him. Stanley, an infidel, organized five caravans and plunged into the jungle. He finally located Livingstone near Lake Tanganyika. He bowed and uttered his famous words, "Dr. Livingstone, I presume." Stanley stayed with Livingstone four months, and the two men grew attached. Stanley later reported, *I went to Africa . . . as the worst infidel in London. But I saw this solitary old man there, and I asked myself, "What is it that inspires him?" For months I found myself listening to him, wondering at the old man carrying out the words, "leave all and follow me." Little by little . . . I was converted by him.* Their parting on March 14, 1872, was very painful. They would not see each other on earth again, but Stanley himself later became a Christian missionary. ❖ George Mueller was buried on this day in 1898. His biographer said, "His earthly remains were laid in the grave of his first and second wives at Arno's Vale Cemetery. . . . The man who in life sought not his own glory, became in death the one to whom all classes delighted to show respect and honor," as thousands came to pay their respects.

STATS, STORIES AND MORE

More from Michael Duduit
It's not that we don't recognize the value of leadership. Just imagine what might have happened in World War II if England had not had a leader like Winston Churchill. We might still be singing "God Save the Queen" if the American colonies had not had a leader like George Washington. How many companies and organizations have become great successes because of talented, visionary leaders? Likewise, how many efforts have failed for the lack of a good leader?

Someone Once Said. . .
Personal leadership is not a singular experience. It is, rather, the ongoing process of keeping your vision and values before you and aligning your life to be congruent with those most important things.—Stephen Covey

Great leaders are almost always great simplifiers, who can cut through argument, debate, and doubt to offer a solution everybody can understand.
—Colin Powell

The key to being a good manager is keeping the people who hate me away from those who are still undecided.—Casey Stengel

The Greatest General
A man died and met Saint Peter at the gates of heaven. Recognizing the saint's knowledge and wisdom, he wanted to ask him a question. "Simon Peter," he said, "I have been interested in military history for many years. Tell me, who was the greatest general of all times?"

Peter quickly responded, "Oh, that is a simple question. It's that man right over there."

The man looked where Peter was pointing and answered, "You must be mistaken. I knew that man on earth, and he was just a common laborer."

"That's right," Peter remarked, "but he would have been the greatest general of all time—if he had been a general." (Mark Twain quoted by John Maxwell).

WORSHIP HELPS

Call to Worship:
The Lord shall reign forever and ever. Say among the nations, "The Lord reigns." The kingdoms of this world are become the kingdoms of our Lord, and of His Christ; and He shall reign for ever and ever (Ex. 15:18; Ps. 96:10; Rev. 11:15).

Offertory Comments:
King David's words in 1 Chronicles 29:14 were put into verse form by William W. How in 1864. They make a good recitation before the offering:

> We give Thee but Thine own,
> Whate'er the gift may be;
> All that we have is Thine alone,
> A trust, O Lord, from Thee.
>
> May we Thy bounties thus
> As stewards true receive,
> And gladly, as Thou blessest us,
> To Thee our firstfruits give.
>
> And we believe Thy Word,
> Though dim our faith may be;
> Whate'er for Thine we do, O Lord,
> We do it unto Thee.

Benediction:
Lord, may we leave here Your men, Your women, Your youth, Your children, in Your care, for Your glory, in Your Name we pray, Amen.

Additional Sermons and Lesson Ideas

Isn't He Rightly Named?
By David Jackman

Date preached:

SCRIPTURE: Genesis 27:18–40; especially 27:36.

INTRODUCTION: We must let the God of this story be God in our lives. He is faithful and trustworthy, making and keeping promises.

1. God's Plans Overthrow Human Convention (25:23). The Lord is overthrowing the conventional rights of primogeniture (the older has the birthright and the blessing). We have many similar social structures, but God is not restricted by them.
2. God's Plans Overrule Human Scheming (ch. 27). Despite the promise, Isaac attempts to give his older son rule (vv. 1–4) but Esau gets nothing. Rebekah helps Jacob deceive Isaac (vv. 5–10, 13, 15–17); her beloved Jacob later must flee from Esau. How often we think we know better than God, but our schemes gain nothing!
3. Rebellion Is Met by Grace. Isaac and Rebekah die in faith and are numbered with those who eternally belong to God (Matt. 22:32). Esau and Jacob later meet as very different men (see Gen. 35). The God of Jacob always works out His promises, not in spite of, but even *through* the rebellion of sinful human beings like us.

CONCLUSION: The Cross of Jesus is the supreme example that God works through human rebellion, making and keeping promises. But isn't He rightly named the Lord Jesus Christ, King of kings, Anointed Ruler, and Savior of all who turn to Him!

Truths Regarding Temptation
By Melvin Worthington

Date preached:

SCRIPTURE: -Matthew 4:1–11

INTRODUCTION: Temptation is a reality in the life of every human, as Paul affirms in 1 Corinthians 10:13.

1. The Source of Temptation (Matt. 4:1, 3, 5, 8 10, 11). Temptation comes from the devil. He is a liar and deceiver.
2. The Scope of Temptation (Matt. 4:3–10). The scope of temptation includes *human appetite* (vv. 3–4), *human applause* (vv. 6–7) and *human assets* (vv. 8–10).
3. The Season of Temptation (Matt. 4:10; Luke 4:13). Following the temptation the devil departed for a season.
4. The Succor in Temptation (Matt. 4:10). The angels came and ministered unto him.

CONCLUSION: Temptation is a reality we all must face. The temptation of Christ provides an example of how to overcome temptation.

MARCH 21, 2004

SUGGESTED SERMON

The Precious Stone
Date preached:

Scripture: 1 Peter 2:4–12, especially verse 7: "Therefore, to you who believe, He is precious."

Introduction: Is anyone here wearing jewelry? Any diamonds? Any rubies or emeralds? Any precious stones? We wouldn't normally think of using that word "precious" to describe a rock or a stone, yet we've all heard the phrase "precious stones." Well, three times in this passage, Peter uses the word "precious" to describe our Lord Jesus (vv. 4, 6, and 7), and strangely, he portrays Christ as a precious stone.

1. **As We Come to Christ, He Becomes Our Cornerstone (vv. 4–7).** Peter begins with the assumption that we have come to Christ for salvation. Verse 4: *Coming to Him as to a living stone.* . . . The word "come" is a word of obedience. This is one of the first commands taught in dog obedience school. The word "come" appears in the Bible 1,706 times. Jesus says, "Come!" It's an invitation, but also a command. We can turn toward Him and run into His embrace, or we can turn on our heels and run in the other direction. Jesus has been saying, "Come!" to people of every generation, and He calls the same to you and me today. As we come to Christ, He becomes our Cornerstone. Verse 7 tells us He is a cornerstone others have missed: *The stone which the builders rejected has become the chief cornerstone.* This quote from Psalm 118:22–23 is repeated five times in the New Testament as referring to Christ. Jesus used it in Matthew 21:42, Mark 12:10, and Luke 20:17. Peter preached from it at the beginning of his ministry in Acts 4:11, and quoted it near the end of his life here in 1 Peter 2:7. German theologian Johann David Michaelis felt this was referring to an event that reportedly took place during the building of Solomon's temple. It's said there was no sound of hammers or pounding, the temple being erected in relative silence. The plans were so exact that each stone was perfectly shaped at the quarry. Arriving at the site, each fit perfectly into place. But one huge stone didn't seem to fit anywhere, and the builders placed it to the side. Eventually it got in the way, and workmen

pushed it over the bank and it rolled into the Kidron Valley. After the foundation had been laid, the time came to hoist the cornerstone into place. Word was sent to the quarry, but the masons replied that it had already been delivered. It was that rejected stone! Being retrieved, it slid perfectly into place, serving as the stone that held all the others in position. When we come to Christ, He becomes the Cornerstone for our lives and for our church. That leads to the second part of the equation:

2. **If He Is Our Cornerstone, We Are His Construction Project (vv. 4–5).** Ever heard the phrase: "Please be patient; God is not finished with me yet"? We're all under construction. The Lord is building "a spiritual house;" and the emphasis isn't just on His work in us as individuals, but as a church. Notice how Peter described the church: Living stones being built into a spiritual house, a holy priesthood, a chosen people, a royal priesthood, a holy nation, a people belonging to God, aliens and strangers in the world. That leads us to the third part of the equation:

3. **If We Are His Construction Project, We Have Divine Purpose (v. 9).** No one ever constructed a temple or cathedral without having a vision for it— of what it could be for the glory of God. What does God intend for us? What function and role has He designed for us? Verse 9 says: ". . . that you may proclaim the praises of Him who called you out of darkness and into His marvelous light."

4. **If We Have Divine Purpose, We Should Live Accordingly (vv. 11–12).** The word "abstain" means to refrain from doing certain things, going certain

>>> *sermon continued on following page*

APPROPRIATE HYMNS AND SONGS

I Will Sing to the Lord Forever, Joey Holder; © 1990 Integrity's Hosanna! Music.

O Come and Magnify, Kevin Singleton; © 1991 Kevin Singleton.

Precious Cornerstone, Graham Kendrick; © 1989 Mercy/Vineyard Publishing.

Jesus Take Me As I Am, Dave Bryant; © 1978 Kingsway's ThankYou Music; Admin. by EMI Christian Music Publishing.

O Worship the King, William Kethe/Johann Michael Haydn/Robert Grant/William Gardiner; Public Domain.

places, indulging in certain habits. The Christian life is a restrictive life. Jesus talked about self-denial, and the Bible frequently uses the words "discipline" and "self-control." Many things may be fun for the moment, but only at the expense of our welfare and testimony. But the positives of self-discipline outweigh the negatives, and the blessings are far greater than anything we give up.

Conclusion: If we come to Christ, He becomes our Cornerstone. If He becomes our Cornerstone, we become His construction project. If we become His construction project, our lives have divine purpose. And if our lives have divine purpose, we should live accordingly. For to us who believe, He is precious.

FOR THE BULLETIN

❉ In the early years of Christianity, a controversy arose about the dating of Easter. Believers in Asia celebrated one day, Christians in Europe another. The issue came to a vote at the famous Council of Nicaea in 325. Easter, declared the council, should be celebrated on the first Sunday following the first full moon after March 21, the vernal equinox. Easter then is a "movable feast" that may occur as early as March 22 or as late as April 25. The matter wasn't entirely settled, but believers seemed to realize that it wasn't the date, but the significance that gave Easter its magnificence. ❉ Archbishop Thomas Cranmer was the first Protestant Archbishop of Canterbury, author of the Book of Common Prayer and the Thirty-Nine Articles. During the reign of "Bloody Mary," he was burned at the stake on March 21, 1557, in Oxford, at the same spot where the reformers Ridley and Latimer had previously died. ❉ March 21, 1685, is the birthday of Johann Sebastian Bach. ❉ March 21, 1794, is the birthday of Emily Tubman, a Virginia resident who married a wealthy Englishman and became one of the richest women of her generation. Deeply committed to Christ, Emily used her vast fortune to help finance the work of Alexander Campbell and the Disciples of Christ. ❉ On March 21, 1871, journalist Henry Stanley began his expedition to Africa to locate Scottish missionary David Livingstone. Stanley was a skeptic and an infidel, but upon finding Livingstone and spending time with him, he was converted. He later himself became a far-famed missionary. ❉ The great Chinese Christian, Watchman Nee, was baptized on March 21, 1921. ❉ On March 21, 1957, Christian thinker and writer C. S. Lewis married Joy Gresham.

STATS, STORIES AND MORE

To You Who Believe...

Scottish preacher James Durham was born nearly four hundred years ago into a wealthy family, and as a young man he inherited his family estate and lived an aristocratic life. He wasn't a Christian, and had no interest in becoming one. He married, and one Saturday he and his wife were visiting her mother, who was a devout Christian. There was a special service at the older woman's church that evening, and she persuaded them both to attend. James was deeply impressed by the sermon and seriousness of the preacher, a Mr. Melvill. The next morning, to everyone's surprise, he rose and went to Sunday services. Mr. Melvill preached that day from 1 Peter 2:7—*to you who believe, He is precious*. That very day, James Durham heard the Lord Jesus saying to him, "Come!" And he came. Almost instantly he developed a hunger and thirst for Bible study. He had a special chamber built for himself on his estate where he could study the Bible without disturbance or interruption, and he became a powerful preacher from that time on, until his early death at age 36.

Difficult Stones

Perhaps you've visited the museum in Florence, Italy, which houses Michelangelo's famous statue of David. It's an enormous work of art, carved from a block of marble eighteen feet high. But perhaps you didn't know that Michelangelo wasn't the first person to attempt to craft a statue from that marble. There was an earlier artist named Agostino di Duccio who selected that stone forty years earlier and had begun working on a statue of either David or an Old Testament prophet. But it was a difficult piece of marble with which to work, quite thin and misshapen. Di Duccio gave up, reportedly saying, "I can do nothing with it." In 1501, when Michelangelo was commissioned to create the David by authorities at the Cathedral in Florence, he used it and with his superior skill carved the David that has thrilled the world for 500 years. You and I are difficult, misshapen blocks of marble, but Jesus Christ is a Master Sculptor, and He is chipping away, carving, polishing, and making us into His own image.

Kids Talk

Show the children some pictures of your church building while it was under construction. Tell them how the foundation was first laid, then the walls, then the roof. Then remind them that the building isn't the real church. The real church is made up of the people who come into the building, and that they are under construction, too. God is building His church. We are His construction project. Tell them that God is making, developing, growing, and building them, too.

WORSHIP HELPS

Call to Worship:
Oh, magnify the LORD with me, and let us exalt His name together. Honor the LORD with me! Proclaim with me the LORD's greatness. Celebrate His great name. Let us praise His name together.
(Ps. 34:3, NKJV, CEV, and TEV)

Suggested Scripture Readings:
Psalm 18:30–32
Psalm 138:7–8
Matthew 16:13–18
Ephesians 4:11–16

Pastoral Prayer:
Heavenly Father, we often grow discouraged with ourselves, for how easily we yield to temptation. How often we lose our temper. Many of us are overextended and underdeveloped. Our thoughts tend to be devilish and our emotions childish. How often we're given to anxiety or alarm. But You, O Lord, are patient with us, molding us, making us into Your image, transforming us day by day by Your Spirit. A bruised reed You will not break, and a smoldering wick You will not snuff out. You have promised to perfect that which concerns us and to bring to completion the work You've begun in us. You are Jehovah-M'Kaddesh—The God Who Sanctifies. Lord, please work in us what is pleasing to You, and encourage our hearts in Your ability to bring us to maturity, both as individuals and as a church. In Jesus' name we pray, Amen.

Benediction:
We have come here, O Lord, to follow You. May we leave here, O Lord, as fishers of men. In Jesus' name, Amen.

Additional Sermons and Lesson Ideas

Growing in the Grace of Christ
By Peter Grainger

Date preached:

SCRIPTURE: 2 Peter 1—3, especially 3:18

INTRODUCTION: The Christian life, it has been said, is like riding a bicycle: unless you keep moving, you fall off. Peter tells us to keep *growing* in grace, or we will fall into sin.

1. Past Grace: Those of us who have given our lives to Christ have experienced God's *saving* grace (Eph. 2:8–9), that's G-R-A-C-E: God's Riches (Eph. 1:3–14) At Christ's Expense (2 Cor. 8:9).
2. Present Grace: Peter makes it clear we must make every effort to *grow* in God's grace (2 Pet. 1:3–8).
    A. Relying on God's Power (1:3).
    B. Relying on God's Promises (1:4).
3. Future Grace: We should continue relying upon God's grace to *finish* well. Peter sets forth two contrasting destinies depending on how we react to God's grace:
    A. Far Worse Off: Falling into Sin (2:1–22).
    B. Far Better Off: Godly Living (1:10–11; 3:13).

CONCLUSION: Grow in grace, praising God *for* it and relying *on* it.

The Devout Energy of the Christian Life
By W. Graham Scroggie

Date preached:

SCRIPTURE: Philippians 3:1—4:1

INTRODUCTION: Are you trying to be saved through doing good? If you are saved, how can others tell? The gospel is opposed to both salvation through works (Judaism) and salvation without works (Antinomianism). Paul explains to his contemporary audience what someone once said, "We are saved by faith alone, but the faith that saves us is never alone."

1. Christianity Is Opposed to Judaism (3:1–16).
    A. The Peril of the Christian (vv. 1–6).
    B. The Passion of the Christian (vv. 7–11).
    C. The Progress of the Christian (vv. 12–16).
2. Christianity Is Opposed to Antinomianism (3:17—4:1).
    A. The Course to Pursue (3:17–19).
    B. The Claim of Faith (3:20–21).
    C. The Call to Stand Fast (4:1).

CONCLUSION: Christians can only be saved by faith (Eph. 2:8), but faith is always naturally accompanied by good works (Eph. 2:10; James 2:17). We should passionately serve Christ who saved us through faith.

MARCH 28, 2004

SUGGESTED SERMON

Faith in the Face of a Giant

Date preached:

By David George

Scripture: 1 Samuel 17:1–54, especially v. 45: Then David said to the Philistine, "You come to me with a sword, with a spear, and with a javelin. But I come to you in the name of the LORD of hosts, the God of the armies of Israel, whom you have defied."

Introduction: Don't you love the fresh-faced enthusiasm and confidence of a kid who has just joined the little league baseball team? He hasn't even played his first game but he wants to sleep in his uniform. Though inexperienced, he believes there's no ball that can get by him. David was like that. He was the youngest of his brothers, the runt, the shepherd with a few sheep, yet he was called a man after God's own heart. Against all odds, David had faith, even to face a giant. David was sent to give food to his brothers as they fought against the Philistines. As he approached the battle scene, he saw the Israelites standing opposite to the Philistines with a dried up riverbank between. The Philistine champion, Goliath, about 9 feet 9 inches tall, taunted and challenged the Israelites to send a champion to fight. How do we react to giants in our lives? We need:

1. **Simple Faith (v. 26).** There is never a thought in David's mind that this Philistine wouldn't be defeated. He only asked about what good would come to the one who killed Goliath. Where did David get this mindset? He was probably raised hearing stories of God's victory: the parting of the Red Sea, or Israel's victory at the walls of Jericho. It never occurred to David that this pagan could possibly defeat the soldiers of God. We should teach our children that God cannot be defeated. We must believe it as well.

2. **Living Faith (v. 32).** Faith matters not only at church, but when your bills are due and you have no money, when a loved one dies, or when you're persecuted at work; faith through life's circumstances is living faith. David's faith was born from defending his sheep against a lion and a bear, so David knew God would also fight Goliath through him (vv. 34–37). Without everyday use of our talents and abilities for God, we cannot face big projects or obstacles. Many of us disobey, refusing to be baptized or to tithe. We will never grow if we consistently refuse to live out our faith.

3. **Crisis Faith (vv. 45–47).** God gives us the ability to stand when no one else will during a moment of crisis. David was granted this type of faith as he faced Goliath, saying, "You come to me with a sword, with a spear, and with a javelin. But I come to you in the name of the Lord of hosts . . ." (v. 45). "Lord of hosts" can be translated, "The Lord of our extremity." When we've reached the end of our human abilities, we come to the Lord of hosts, asking for His strength. Overcoming, overwhelming faith bears forth in the moment of crisis from the foundation of simple, living faith. What giant are you facing? A financial giant? A hurting relationship? An addiction? Whatever it is, take these practical steps from David's example.

   A. **Your encouragement cannot come from the defeated.** As David faced the Philistines, he saw the Israelites afraid (v. 24), but they were no help. If you have a drug or alcohol problem, get away from other addicts. If you have relationship problems, don't hang around divorced people who tell you how great it is. Seek encouragement from victorious Christians.

   B. **Remember your past victories.** The enemy is quick to oppose us, and we tend to be quick to tremble in fear. David called on his past victories for confidence (vv. 34–37). We need to remember times when God has answered our prayers, when He has pulled us from hard situations, when He has provided.

   C. **You cannot trust someone else's army.** Someone else's strategy may not work for you. Samuel tried to give David his armor. It wouldn't work. He wouldn't use spear or javelin, but preferred a simple shepherd's sling. God wants to take *your* history, *your* abilities, and *your* talents and add *His* power to accomplish *His* purposes.

   >>> sermon continued on following page

APPROPRIATE HYMNS AND SONGS

How Firm a Foundation, George Keith/Anne Steele/John Rippon/Joseph Funk; Public Domain.

Living by Faith, James Wells/R.E. Winsett; © 1918. Renewed 1946 by R.E. Winsett/Ellis J. Crum.

The Name of the Lord, Clinton Utterbach; © 1988 Polygram Island Music.

Blessed Be the Rock, Daniel Gardner; © 1985 Integrity's Hosanna! Music.

Cover Me, Danny Daniels; © 1987 Mercy/Vineyard Publishing.

D. The threats of the enemy are just threats. God granted David success in the face of the enemy's mockery! Greater is He that is in you than he that is in the world (1 John 4:4).

Conclusion: We must become people after God's heart through simple, living faith, faith which will not fail in crisis. Practically, we must gain encouragement from the victorious, remembering our victories, allowing God to use our genuine selves, despite circumstances or obstacles.

FOR THE BULLETIN

❂ March 28, 1515, is the birthday of Theresa of Avila, Spanish mystic, writer, and saint. ❂ March 28, 1592, is the birth date of John Amos Comenius, "father of modern education." His *The Great Didactic,* published in 1632, was a breakthrough work in the area of Christian education in which Comenius laid out a plan for a complete system of education from primary school to university. The goal of schooling, Comenius believed, was to mold students into the image of Christ. He later became a bishop of the Bohemian Brethren, but is chiefly remembered for his contributions to the theory and practice of education. ❂ March 28, 1758, marks the death of Jonathan Edwards, American theologian whose sermon, "Sinners in the Hands of an Angry God" helped spark the Great Awakening. ❂ On March 28, 1796, the Bethel African Methodist Church of Philadelphia became the first US-African church in America. ❂ After a few years of relative peace, Christians on the African island of Madagascar came under renewed persecution on this day in 1849, when nineteen believers from influential families were condemned to death. Fifteen of them were dropped from a high cliff into a ravine 150 feet deep. As they were held over the precipice by ropes they were asked, "Will you worship your Christ or the queen's gods?" When each one answered Christ, the ropes were cut, and the martyrs plunged to their deaths. ❂ The Salvation Army begins its work in the United States on this day in 1885. ❂ The inimitable African-American preacher, John Jasper, died on March 28, 1901. ❂ Billy Graham preached his first sermon on this day in 1937.

STATS, STORIES AND MORE

From a Dad's Journal
My child was safe and sound last night, but I wasn't sure, and I was scared... nervous... ill at ease. Fretted all evening—the very thing the Lord condemns. This morning's Bible reading took me to 1 Samuel 17: David and Goliath. Though I know the story, I've never seen it quite like I have today. There was something new: The real lesson of 1 Samuel 17 is not the comparison between David and Goliath—but between young David and old apostate King Saul.

King Saul's reaction is in verse 11: When Saul and all Israel heard these words of the Philistine, they were dismayed and greatly afraid. Saul compared himself with the giant instead of comparing the giant with God. He was worried and anxious. Ill at ease. Fretting. Dismayed and greatly afraid. Exactly like me.

David's take on the situation is in verse 47: The battle is the Lord's. He didn't underestimate the difficulty, but neither did he underestimate his Ally. "The Lord, who delivered me from the paw of the lion and from the paw of the bear, He will deliver me from the hand of this Philistine" (vs. 37).

Lord, thank you for reminding me that both the battle and the victory are Yours. Forgive my Saul-ishness. May I be a David, a man after your own heart, trusting, calm, confident, wise, waiting for your arm to win the victory.

And show me how to use that spiritual slingshot as needed.

The Coal
You cannot get encouragement from a defeated army. You need to be around victorious people! Charles Spurgeon visited a church member who had stopped attending. It was a cold day so they were sitting around a fire. Spurgeon picked up a poker and stirred up the fire. He pulled out a white-hot coal and set it on the hearth. In a few minutes it was black, much cooler than before. Then he replaced it and it became red-hot again. The man got the point.

WORSHIP HELPS

Call to Worship:
Come, let us join with one accord / In hymns around the throne: / This is the day our rising Lord / Has made and called His own.
—Charles Wesley

Suggested Scripture Readings:
Psalm 37:1–6
Matthew 21:20–23
Hebrews 11:1–7

Hymn Story:
"How Firm a Foundation"

John Rippon pastored Carter's Lane Baptist Church in London for 63 years, beginning in 1775. He had been born in 1751, so he was in his mid-twenties when he first mounted the Carter's Lane pulpit following his education at the Baptist College in Bristol, England. During the years of Carter's Lane, John developed a vision for a church hymnal, which he edited, assisted by his Minister of Music, Robert Keene. The resulting volume, *A Selection of Hymns from the Best Authors, Intended to Be an Appendix to Dr. Watt's Psalms and Hymns,* was published in 1787. It was a runaway hit, especially among the Baptists, going through eleven British editions during Rippon's lifetime. An American edition appeared in 1820.

"How Firm a Foundation" first appeared in this hymnal. No one knows its author, for the line reserved for the author's name simply bore the letter "K." Many scholars attribute the composition to Keene.

The unique power of this hymn is due to the fact that each of the seven original stanzas were based on various biblical promises. The first verse established the hymnist's theme—God's Word is a sufficient foundation for our faith. The author then selected precious promises from the Bible, and converted these into hymn stanzas, among them: Isaiah 41:10; Isaiah 43:2; 2 Corinthians 12:9; and Hebrews 13:5.

No wonder this hymn was first published under the title, *"Exceedingly Great and Precious Promises."*

Benediction:
Lord, we believe! Help Thou our unbelief. Give us greater faith—simple faith, living faith, crisis faith—faith to move mountains this week. In Jesus' name, Amen.

Additional Sermons and Lesson Ideas

Allegiance to the King
By Frances Ridley Havergal

Date preached:

SCRIPTURE: Psalm 44:4

INTRODUCTION: The Psalmist says, "You are my King, O God." This passage should cause us self-examination. We should ask ourselves:

1. Can I Say It? Is Jesus in deed and truth my King? Where is the proof of it? Am I living in the kingdom of righteousness, peace, and joy in the Holy Spirit (Rom. 14:17)? Am I speaking the language of that kingdom and obeying its laws?
2. Ought I Say It? Should there even be a question about that? The King who came to purchase me from my tyrant and His foe; the King who laid aside His crown and His loyal robes and left His kingly palace and came down Himself to save a rebel? There is no question that I ought to own Him as King, for God has called me unto His Kingdom and glory (1 Thess. 2:12).
3. Do I Say It? Am I ashamed or afraid to confess my allegiance in plain language among His friends or before His foes? Is the seal on my brow so unmistakable that always and everywhere I'm known as His subject (Acts 4:13)?

CONCLUSION: Let us come to Jesus as our King. Let us, in solemn heart-surrender and in open life-confession, yield ourselves to Him as our Lord and Master. What a glorious life of victory and peace opens before us when we do this.

Trust in the Lord

Date preached:

SCRIPTURE: Psalm 31:1

INTRODUCTION: The bulk of our depression, anxiety, and fear would be greatly reduced if we grasped the significance of these four words: Trust in the Lord. How should we trust in the Lord?

1. "Trust in the Lord with all your Heart" (Prov. 3:5).
2. "Trust in the Lord and Do Good" (Ps. 37:3).
3. "Trust in the Lord Forever" (Is. 26:4).

CONCLUSION: "Whoever trusts in the Lord, happy is he" (Prov. 16:20).

APRIL 4, 2004

SUGGESTED SERMON

The Triumphal Entry: Tragedy or Triumph?
By Ed Dobson *Date preached:*

Scripture: Mark 11:1–11, especially verse 9: "Hosanna! Blessed is He who comes in the name of the Lord."

Introduction: For centuries, this Sunday before Easter has been set aside to commemorate the Triumphal Entry of Jesus into Jerusalem. Look at this story with me:

1. **The Setting**

   Verse 1: One can still walk this route from Bethany to Jerusalem. Beside an ancient church in Bethany is a door leading down to an old tomb believed to be that of Lazarus. From there, one can walk to Bethphage where an ancient stone commemorates Jesus' mounting the donkey. Then, crossing the top of Mount Olivet, we pass the tombs of the prophets, descend into the Kidron Valley, and ascend into the old city of Jerusalem where, step-by-step, we walk the Via Dolorosa.

   Verse 2: Why an animal that had never been ridden? In the Old Testament, Jews were told to sacrifice a red heifer that had never been used for plowing; it was for a sacred purpose. So with the donkey. Donkeys were important in the first century, a kind of "pickup truck" for the times. In this case, it was to be one that had never been ridden; it was set aside for sacred use.

   Verses 4–8: When they brought the colt to Jesus and threw their cloaks over it, He sat on it. Many spread their cloaks and palm branches on the road, as they did when royalty entered town (so the king wouldn't get his feet dirty on the dusty streets). This was the ancient parallel to rolling out the red carpet.

   Verses 9–10: The behavior of the people was a curious mix of two Jewish traditions.

   A. **The Feast of Tabernacles.** When Israel possessed Canaan after 40 years of living in tents in the desert, God was concerned they would forget His faithfulness during their wanderings. He appointed a summer festival in which they cut branches and built temporary shelters. The whole nation went camping, as it were. Afterward they would take the branches

and march in procession to the temple, singing Psalm 118 (see Ps. 118:1–4, 15, 19–24, and especially 25–26). Hosanna isn't just an expression of praise; it's a prayer to God: O LORD, save us (Hosanna)."
   B. **The Feast of Hanukkah.** As Jesus rode into the city, perhaps the people remembered another person—Judas Maccabeus—who rode into the city, breaking foreign oppression and liberating them (see **STATS, STORIES AND MORE**). Perhaps they were thinking, "If the Maccabees could defeat the Syrians, think what Jesus will do with the Romans. He has just raised Lazarus from death. Think of His power to defeat Rome." So the crowds were caught up with powerful images that day.

2. **The Shouts**. Three cries rose from the crowd:
   A. **"Hosanna!"—"Lord, save us."** There was recognition of their need, an understanding that God must do what only He can do. This was a prayer of desperation.
   B. **"Blessed is He who comes in the name of the Lord!"** At Passover time, hundreds of thousands of Jews from around the world came to Jerusalem on pilgrimage. Arriving at the Temple, they would greet each other, saying: "Blessed is he who comes in the name of the Lord." This was the official greeting at the temple, and it had messianic implications, for the Jews referred to their coming Messiah as "The One Who is Coming."
   C. **"Blessed is the coming kingdom of our father David . . . Hosanna in the highest!"** The prophets had foretold the Messiah would reign on David's throne forever. This Passover, unlike previous ones, there was a hope that maybe this Jesus was He who was coming to sit on David's throne. You say, "What a wonderful moment of triumph." Well, there was a bit

>>> sermon continued on following page

APPROPRIATE HYMNS AND SONGS

We Cry Hosanna Lord, Mimi Fara/Claire Cloninger; © 1975, 1987 Celebration.

Blessed Is He Who Comes, Carman; © 1984 Lehsem Music.

Hosanna, Loud Hosanna, Jennette Threlfall; Public Domain.

All Glory, Laud and Honor, Theodulph of Orleans; Public Domain.

He Comes In the Name of the Lord, David Ritter; © 1993 Van Ness Press, Admin. by Genevox Music Group.

of triumph; we give the crowd credit because they recognized their need, and they knew where to go to have the need met. But the tragedy is they had the wrong Messiah in mind. A donkey is an animal of peace. A horse is an animal of war. Revelation 19 speaks of Jesus returning, not on a donkey, but on a white horse. He will battle Satan and the armies of earth. He will establish the kingdom of David, and righteousness will encircle the world. But on this day, Jesus was not coming to sit on the throne, but to die on His cross. He was lowly, riding on a donkey (Zech. 9:9).

Conclusion: What kind of a Jesus are you shouting about this morning? Some are pushing a "social" Jesus, some are pushing a "political" Jesus, some are shouting about a "healing" Jesus. He is a saving Jesus. He came in humility that I, a lost, hell-deserving sinner, could be forgiven and find peace with God. Is that your Jesus?

FOR THE BULLETIN

✺ On April 4, 397, the church father Ambrose died during the wee hours of the night. ✺ Isidore of Seville was a church leader who compiled history's first encyclopedia. It became the most used textbook of the Middle Ages, containing entries on medicine, arithmetic, grammar, history, science, and theology. Four days before his death, Isidore asked friends to carry him to the church of St. Vincent the Martyr. Once there, he raised his hands and prayed, confessing his sins and pleading for grace. A crowd assembled, and Isidore preached to the people about love. Returning home, he took to his bed and died peacefully on April 4, 636. ✺ On April 4, 1507, Martin Luther was ordained as a priest in the Roman Catholic Church. ✺ On this day in 1741, the theological disagreement between Arminian evangelist John Wesley and Calvinist George Whitefield came to a head while they rode together in a coach. The two men parted company, no longer friends or partners. ✺ Today marks the conversion of Charles Simeon, powerful British preacher and revivalist, who was converted on Easter Sunday, April 4, 1779. ✺ On April 4, 1793, William Carey, the "father of modern missions," left his pregnant wife and two little children to board the *Oxford* on the Thames to begin his voyage to India. A series of delays allowed him to shortly return home and persuade his wife to accompany him, though the hardships of the trip later contributed to her mental illness. ✺ When missionary/explorer David Livingstone died on May 1, 1873, in a village in Zambia, his heart was removed and buried in Africa. His body was returned to England and buried in Westminster Abbey on April 4, 1873. ✺ On April 4, 1968, Rev. Martin Luther King, Jr., was assassinated in Memphis, Tennessee.

STATS, STORIES AND MORE

Ed Dobson on Hanukkah

Between the Testaments, a Syrian king named Antiochus conquered Israel and tried to force on the Jews the Greek language, laws, philosophy, and religion. Jews were killed for possessing a copy of the Torah or trying to circumcise their baby boys. Antiochus turned the courts of the temple into brothels, placed a statue of Zeus in the middle of the temple, and offered a pig on the sacred altar. But one man, Judas Maccabeus, began fighting Antiochus. In 163 B.C. the Syrians were defeated, and Judas rode into Jerusalem in triumph. There was a huge procession and he was welcomed into the city where he cleansed and rededicated the temple. Today the Jews celebrate this victory during their Feast of Hanukkah, the Feast of Lights.

Some History about Palm Sunday from *The Catholic Encyclopedia*

The Greeks celebrate the day with great solemnity; they call it *kyriake* or *heorte ton baion* or *heorte baiophoros* or also Lazarus Sunday, because the day before they have the feast of the resuscitation of Lazarus. The Latin liturgical books call it Dominica in Palmis, Dominica or Dies Palmarum. From the cry of the people during the procession the day has received the name Dominica Hosanna or simply Hosanna (Ozanna). Because every great feast was in some way a remembrance of the Resurrection of Christ and was in consequence called *Pascha*, we find the names *Pascha floridum*, in French *Pâques fleuries*, in Spanish *Pascua florida*, and it was from this day in 1512 that the state of Florida received its name.

A Palm Sunday Poem by James Gilkey (1915)

Outside the Holy City
Unnumbered footsteps throng,
And crowded mart and streets of trade
Fling back a swelling song.
The voices echo nearer,
In flaming hope they sing:
"Throw down your branches at His feet!
Hosanna to the King!"

WORSHIP HELPS

Call to Worship:
This is the day the Lord hath made; / He calls the hours His own; / Let heav'n rejoice, let earth be glad, / And praise surround the throne.—*Isaac Watts*

Pastoral Prayer:
Jesus, this morning I'm thankful that you are not caught up in the enthusiasm of a crowd that saw you in political and military terms. But you had a larger and greater purpose to redeem not just Jews, but Jews and Gentiles alike. Thank you, Lord, for saving our soul. Thank you, Lord, for making us whole. Thank you, Lord, for giving to us your great salvation so rich and free." Amen.—*Ed Dobson*

Scripture Medley:
Moses said to the people, "Remember this day—the day on which you left Egypt, the place where you were slaves. This is the day the LORD brought you out by His great power . . . I will praise You, for You have . . . become my salvation. The stone that the builders rejected has become the chief cornerstone. This was the LORD's doing; It is marvelous in our eyes. This is the day the LORD has made; We will rejoice and be glad in it. Surely this is the day we have waited for; we have found it, we have seen it! This is the day commemorating the Atonement, cleansing you in the Lord's eyes from all of your sins. For this is the day of the Lord GOD of hosts. We have blessed you from the house of the LORD. God is the LORD, and He has given us light . . . You are my God, and I will praise You; You are my God, I will exalt You. Oh, give thanks to the LORD, for He is good! For His mercy endures forever.
(*Ex. 13:3* GNB; *Ps. 118:21–24*; *Lam. 2:16*; *Lev. 16:29* TLB; *Jer. 46:10*; *Ps. 118:27–29*)

Additional Sermons and Lesson Ideas

What the Gospel Means to Me
By W. Graham Scroggie

Date preached:

SCRIPTURE: Romans 1:16

INTRODUCTION: Looking toward the capital of the Roman Empire the thing that impressed the apostle Paul was not the authority of Caesar, but the power of the gospel. How his soul was thrilled as he wrote this verse. His testimony was: "I am not ashamed of the gospel."

1. The Definition of the Gospel—*the power of God*
2. The Design of the Gospel—*unto salvation*
3. The Scope of the Gospel—*to everyone*
4. The Reception of the Gospel—*who believes*

CONCLUSION: The efficacy of this message was unchallengeable, for Paul himself was the example and witness of its saving power.

It Is Finished
By Matthew Henry

Date preached:

SCRIPTURE: John 19:30

INTRODUCTION: When Jesus gasped those final words, "It is finished!" what did He mean? What was "It"?

1. The Malice of His Persecutors was now finished.
2. The Command of God concerning His sufferings was now fulfilled.
3. The Types and Prophecies of the Old Testament were now accomplished.
4. Sin was finished. Christ made an end to transgression by bringing in an everlasting righteousness (Dan. 9:24; Heb. 9:26).
5. His Sufferings were now finished.
6. His Life was now finished (John 17:11), even as Paul said, "I have finished my course (2 Tim. 4:7).
7. The Work of our Redemption and Salvation is now completed (John 17:4).

CONCLUSION: God always finishes what He begins. When we come to Christ, we begin a life that God will bring to completion in glory.

COMMUNION SERMON

Three Crosses and Two Choices Date preached:
By Denis Lyle

Scripture: Luke 23:32–43, especially verse 43: And Jesus said to him, "Assuredly, I say to you, today you will be with Me in Paradise."

Introduction: All of us have sin *in* us, but we are divided when it comes to sin *on* us. Some have the penalty of sin resting on them; others have, by grace, shifted it over to Christ. The great question is this: Is your sin *on you* or *on Christ* who paid its penalty? On the hill of Calvary, there were three crosses and three men. One man died *in* sin, one man died *to* sin, one man died *for* sin. Over the first cross, we envision the word:

1. **Rejection.** Sometimes we forget that there were two thieves. It has been said, "One thief was saved that no sinner might despair; one thief was damned that no sinner might presume." These two men had the same opportunity, they heard and saw the same things, yet one died and went to heaven, and the other died and went to hell. Over this first cross we have the word *rejection*. He was a man who:
   A. **Despised the Presence of Jesus Christ (vv. 34–38).** The first thief should have *heard Jesus' prayer*: "Father, forgive them; for they do not know what they do" (v. 34). This man should have *read Jesus' title*: perhaps the first gospel tract that was ever written hung over the head of Christ, "JESUS OF NAZARETH, THE KING OF THE JEWS" (v. 38; John 19:19). Instead, he despised the presence of Christ. Is that what you have done? Has the Lord laid you low in order that you might think of Him? Has God allowed peculiar trials to cross your path? Even in trials, Jesus extends to us His salvation; don't despise His presence!
   B. **Despised the Person of Jesus Christ (v. 39).** This thief was no different from those who bypassed the cross and taunted Jesus (Mark 15:29). Imagine, a man on the brink of eternity, on the very precipice of hell, mocking the Savior's person! Yet has your action or attitude been any different from this man? Perhaps the only time you take the Savior's name on your lips is not in prayer, but in mockery.
   C. **Despised the Power of Jesus Christ (v. 39).** Again, on the brink of eternity, the same thief challenges the power of God, saying in effect, "If you are the Anointed One demonstrate your power!" I wonder is this

one of the problems you have in becoming a Christian. Are you unsure whether Christ has the power to save you forever? Over the first cross is "rejection," but over the third cross we envision the word:

2. **Reception.** This man believed on Christ's name in faith, so Jesus saved him (vv. 42–43; see John 1:12). At first he insulted the Lord Jesus, but then:
   A. **He Began to Look at the Savior (vv. 34–38).** He looked at the face of the Son of God, that face so marred. He saw holiness and peace there! He saw Deity stamped on that noble brow. He saw the crown of thorns, the spiky emblem of the curse. He read the title the Romans nailed to the cross. Perhaps he began to remember the teaching of his boyhood days, the words of the prophet Isaiah (Is. 53:5). Have you looked to Jesus in faith (see John 3:14–15)?
   B. **He Began to Listen to the Savior and His Mockers (vv. 34–39).** The second thief listened as Jesus forgave His enemies (v. 34), and it seems that he heard the gospel from Jesus' mockers (vv. 34–39; Matt. 27:40–42)! He believed in the innocence of Jesus (v. 41), the ability of Jesus (v. 42), and in the royalty of Jesus (v. 42). This man was not sitting in a comfortable seat, listening to God's plan of salvation, surrounded by Christians. He did not have a single page of the New Testament. He was racked with fearful pain, yet he believed because he *looked at* and *listened to* Christ in faith. Finally, over the center cross, we envision the word:

3. **Redemption.** One man died *in* sin, one man died *to* sin, but Jesus died *for* sin, purchasing our freedom, becoming our redemption:
   A. **The Basis of Redemption: *Through His Blood* (Eph. 1:7).** Only the precious blood of Christ could purchase us out of the slave market of sin.
   B. **The Blessing of Redemption: *The Forgiveness of Sins* (Eph. 1:7).** Are your sins forgiven and blotted out by Jesus (Is. 43:25)?

Conclusion: Over the first cross is the word *rejection*. Is that you, still rejecting the Savior? Over the second, the center cross is the word *redemption*. Jesus made our redemption possible, through faith in His blood (Rom. 3:25). As we commemorate the sacrifice of His body through the Lord's Supper, let's check ourselves to be sure that, like the thief on the third cross, we have *received* Jesus.

> *Was it for crimes that I have done*
> *He groaned upon the tree*
> *Amazing pity, grace unknown*
> *And love beyond degree.*

APRIL 11, 2004 – EASTER

SUGGESTED SERMON

What Easter Gives Us

Date preached:

Scripture: Romans 1:1–4, 4:24–25, and 8:11, especially 1:3–4: "Declared to be the Son of God with power . . . by the resurrection from the dead."

Introduction: Just after World War II, a Methodist leader in London named William Sangster contracted a disease that gradually paralyzed him. Eventually even his vocal cords were paralyzed. On Easter Sunday—his last Easter on earth—his daughter came to visit. Using stiffened fingers, he scribbled a message: "How terrible to wake up on Easter and have no voice with which to shout, 'He is risen!'" Then, pausing a moment, he added, "Far worse to have a voice and not want to shout." We feel like shouting today because this is Easter, and Christ has risen from the dead. But just what does that mean to us here, now, in this twenty-first century? The answer is in the Book of Romans, Paul's definitive statement of Christian truth. Three times in Romans the apostle Paul cites the great implications of Easter.

1. **Easter Gives Us Confirmation of Christ's Identity (Rom. 1:1–2).** Paul begins his letter to the Romans with a significant reference to Easter: "Paul . . . separated to the gospel of God which He promised before through His prophets in the Holy Scriptures, concerning His Son Jesus Christ our Lord, who was born of the seed of David according to the flesh, and declared to be the Son of God with power according to the Spirit of holiness, by the resurrection from the dead." How do we know Jesus Christ was truly human—a man? He descended from the seed of David. How do we know He was truly divine—God? The Resurrection verified it. Many people have the misconception that other founders of the world's religions claimed to be God, but that isn't so. Abraham and Moses, the founders of Judaism, didn't claim to be God. Mohammed, founder of Islam, didn't claim to be Allah. Buddha didn't claim to be God, and neither did Zoroaster. Among the leaders of the world's best-known religions, only Jesus claimed to be God. But what proof did He give? If a police officer knocked on my door late at night, I'd ask to see his credentials before letting him into my house. Just because people claim to be

something doesn't mean they are. Christ claimed to be God, but what were His credentials? He said, "Destroy this temple (referring to His body), and in three days I will raise it up" (John 1:19). He said, "For as Jonah was three days and three nights in the belly of a huge fish, so the Son of Man will be three days and three nights in the heart of the earth" (Matt. 12:40). He taught that the Son of Man must suffer many things and be rejected and killed, and after three days rise again (Mark 8:31). Easter fulfilled those promises and validated His claims of divinity.

2. **Easter Gives Us the Cancellation of Sin's Penalty (Rom. 4:24–25).** "Jesus our Lord . . . was delivered up because of our offenses, and was raised because of our justification." As the *Bible Knowledge Commentary* puts it: "Christ's death as God's sacrificial Lamb (John 1:29) was to pay the redemptive price for the sins of all people (Rom. 3:24) so that God might be free to forgive those who respond by faith to that provision. Christ's resurrection was the proof (or demonstration and vindication) of God's acceptance of Jesus' sacrifice (Rom. 1:4). Thus because He lives, God can credit His provided righteousness to the account of every person who responds by faith to that offer."

3. **Easter Gives Us the Celebration of Life Eternal (Rom. 8:11).** "But if the Spirit of Him who raised Jesus from the dead dwells in you, He who raised Christ from the dead will also give life to your mortal bodies through His Spirit who dwells in you." (See also Rom. 6:1–9.) Those who know and follow Christ have certain hope of a resurrection of our own,

>>> *sermon continued on following page*

APPROPRIATE HYMNS AND SONGS

My Redeemer Lives, Reuben Morgan; © 1998 Reuben Morgan/Hillsongs Publishing, Admin. by Integrity's Hosanna! Music.

Jesus Is Alive, Ron Kenoly; © 1987 Integrity's Hosanna! Music.

Christ Arose, Robert Lowry; Public Domain.

Christ Is Risen, Graham Kendrick; © 1989 Make Way Music, Admin. by Music Services.

Blessing, Honor and Glory, Geoff Bullock/David Reidy; © 1990 Word Music, Inc./Maranatha! Music, Admin. by Word Music Group.

of eternal life. Robert Ingersoll, the skeptic, rejected belief in the Resurrection, but at the casket of his brother he speculated as to whether or not something might lie beyond the grave. "We cry aloud," he said, "and the only answer is the echo of our wailing cry." But Jesus said, "I am the resurrection and the life. He who believes in Me, though he may die, he shall live. And whoever lives and believes in Me shall never die" (John 11:25–26).

Conclusion: Easter gives us everything our hearts and minds need—confirmation of Christ's identity, cancellation of sin's penalty, and celebration of life eternally. All of it is yours for the taking, for the believing, for the accepting. Will you come to Christ today?

FOR THE BULLETIN

❋ On April 11, 1506, the cornerstone of St. Peter's Basilica was laid by Pope Julius, who descended a rope ladder to do the job. ❋ On April 11, 1612, Separatist Edward Wrightman was executed in London, the last religious martyr to be burned at the stake in English history. His execution was ordered by King James I (of King James Version fame). Wrightman was actually burned at the stake twice. The first time, he began screaming unintelligible words, and the authorities thought he was recanting his faith, so they doused the flames and released him. But when he continued preaching, he was again arrested and burned, this time to ashes. ❋ On April 11, 1661, Scottish Coventanter James Guthrie made his defense before the "Drunken Parliament," saying: "My conscience I cannot submit. But this old crazy body and mortal flesh I do submit, to do with it whatsoever ye will, whether by death, or banishment, or imprisonment, or anything else; only I beseech you to ponder well what profit there is in my blood." He was executed on June 1, and his head suspended above Netherbow Port. ❋ Richard Allen was appointed the first bishop of the African Methodist Episcopal Church on this day in 1816. ❋ April 11, 1836, English philanthropist George Mueller opened his famous orphanage on Wilson Street in Bristol. ❋ Daniel Payne, African-America pastor in Washington, made an appointment to see President Abraham Lincoln on April 11, 1862. Lincoln was facing a decision about signing a law abolishing slavery in the District of Columbia. The black pastor reminded Lincoln that African-Americans were praying for him fervently.

STATS, STORIES AND MORE

Park Rangers
If you became lost in the Great Smoky Mountains National Park, where the undergrowth is so deep and dense that in some areas you might never be found again, what would you do? Suppose you came upon two park rangers, both of them wearing their traditional green uniforms. But suppose one of them was alive, and the other was dead from a heart attack. Which would you want to follow out of the woods? When it comes to eternal matters, who are you willing to follow? The dead leaders of the world's religions or the only founder of a major religion who claimed to be God and who proved it by raising from the dead. *(Adapted from a sermon by Josh McDowell.)*

Goliath's Sword
When the shepherd boy David knocked out the giant Goliath with a stone from his slingshot, he rushed over to the fallen man and, taking the giant's own sword, cut off his head. Jesus did that with Satan. Using the devil's own weapon, death, He defeated him. Hebrews 2:14–15 says: " . . . that through death He might destroy him who had the power of death, that is, the devil, and release those who through fear of death were all their lifetime subject to bondage."

Gone, Gone, Gone, Gone
Pilgrim's Progress by John Bunyan tells the remarkable story of a man who set out from the City of Destruction, hoping to journey toward the Celestial City. As he trudged out of town, beginning his journey, he bore a heavy burden on his back. It weighed him down. It was the burden of sin and guilt. But then the pilgrim met a man named Evangelist who pointed him in the right direction. Coming to a hill called Calvary, the pilgrim knelt at the Cross. The burden fell from his back, rolled down the hill, and disappeared forever into the empty tomb.

WORSHIP HELPS

Call to Worship:
Remember that Jesus Christ, of the seed of David, was raised from the dead. God raised Him from the dead. Christ is risen from the dead, and has become the firstfruits of those who have fallen asleep. Alleluia!
(2 Tim. 2:8; Acts 3:15, NIV; 1 Cor. 15:20; Rev. 19:1)

Pastoral Prayer:
Our Heavenly Father, how our hearts grieve for those who have not heard or who do not believe in the Resurrection of Jesus Christ from that virgin tomb on Easter Sunday. How can some say there is no resurrection of the dead? If there is no resurrection of the dead, then Christ was not risen. And if Christ was not risen, then our preaching is empty and so is our faith. We are liars, false witnesses of God, because we *do* testify and proclaim that Christ has risen from the dead. But we know that Christ *has* risen from the dead and has become the firstfruits of those who sleep in Him. Lord may the entire world hear! May all the earth believe! And may our own hearts perceive more fully, enjoy more completely, and proclaim more loudly today than ever before that He is risen from death. He is risen indeed. It is in His marvelous Name that we pray. Amen.

Benediction:
May the presence of the risen Christ, both personal and powerful, both intimate and infinite, go with us both now and forevermore. Amen.

Kids Talk

Ask the children if they have heard of an Easter Parade. In earlier generations, people in large cities would celebrate Easter by putting on new clothes and bonnets. Then they would march to church. Ask the children if any of them have on new "Easter clothes." Tell them Jesus came out of the grave in new clothes. His old clothing was taken by the soldiers who crucified Him, and His grave clothes were left behind in the tomb. God gave Him new clothes, bright and white and beautiful. But we don't have to have new clothes to celebrate Easter. We just need new hearts.

Additional Sermons and Lesson Ideas

Without Him
Date preached:

SCRIPTURE: John 15:5

INTRODUCTION: What would our lives be without Easter? What would we do without a Risen Jesus? The Bible pictures Him as:

1. A Prophet Without Honor (Matt. 13:57).
2. A Lamb Without Blemish (Ex. 12:5; Heb. 9:14; John 8:7).
3. A High Priest Without Sin (Heb. 4:15; also see John 8:7).

CONCLUSION: Jesus said, "Without me, you can do nothing" (John 15:5). Praise God for Easter, for Jesus, for our Prophet, our Lamb, our High Priest.

Hosanna and Hallelujah
By Melvin Worthington
Date preached:

SCRIPTURE: John 14:19

INTRODUCTION: Every chapter in John's gospel presents Jesus Christ in a unique manner. For example, He is seen as the Eternal Son (ch. 1), the Miracle Worker (ch. 2), the Divine Teacher (ch. 3), the Soul Winner (ch. 4), and so forth. In chapter 14, He is the Royal Comforter and verse 19 is critical to His message of hope:

1. The Truth Asserted. *I Live...* On the eve of His Crucifixion, Jesus is predicting His Resurrection.
2. The Truth Affirmed. *You shall live also.* There was hope for the hurting, grieving, frightened disciples, and for us, too!
3. The Truth Applied. *Because... Also.* Because Christ lives, Christians will live also. We can enjoy His presence, embrace His promises, expect His provision, exemplify His precepts, execute His program, engage His power, encourage His people and emulate His pattern.

CONCLUSION: The fact that Jesus lives is a pledge that all who believe in Him shall be saved. He has power over our spiritual foes, and He can deliver us from the hands of our enemies and from all temptation.

CONVERSATIONS IN A PASTOR'S STUDY

The Relationship Between the Pastor and the Minister of Music

An interview with Dr. Vernon Whaley,
Minister of Music at Olive Baptist Church,
Pensacola, Florida

What is the ideal relationship between the minister of music and the pastor?

It's a partnership. The pastor is really the chief worship leader. The precedent is set in the Old Testament, and as the pastor's heart for worship enlarges, the heart of the minister of music needs to enlarge as well. The two work side-by-side, and it cannot be done independently. It must be a partnership, not only on the platform, but in the preparation. A minister of music functions best if the pastor plans well in advance, and communicates those plans to the minister of music. It helps to know what the preaching schedule will be several weeks or even months in advance; otherwise the minister of music is taking stabs in the dark as he or she plans the service, hoping against hope that the worship and music will correspond with the theme and tone of the message from Scripture.

What does the minister of music need from the pastor?

Focus and direction. The minister of music doesn't have to be micromanaged, but it helps to know the preaching schedule in advance. The worship service I plan may not be on exactly the same theme as the sermon, but there will be coordination. The music and the message don't need to duplicate each other, but they should complement each other. They should have the same basic focus. If the pastor is preaching from the Book of Romans, for example, I would design my core subjects—drama, Scripture readings, music, whatever—around the pastor's direction. I believe that from the time I step onto the platform until the final benediction, there should be one connected worship time.

How do you accommodate things like announcements?

Well, it's interesting you should ask that. I serve at the pastor's pleasure and my pastor likes to include a welcome time during the service. In my opinion, announcements and shaking hands and the like are not in and of themselves worship. Those are fellowship activities. If I had my way about it, I would start the service with a significant worship time and let it go right into the pastor's sermon, and I would use multi-media, drama, music, etc., without interruptions for things like shaking hands, making announcements, or appealing for money before the offering. I would provide other times for those things, perhaps before the service begins or at the end of the hour. My pastor likes to have a welcome time in the middle of the service, and since he is in charge, I design the service so that we can come in and out of it with a minimum of disruption to the flow of worship.

How often should the pastor and the minister of music meet?

We meet at some length every few weeks and sketch out the preaching/service schedule for the months ahead; and then we meet informally every few days. We also communicate a lot by e-mail. This morning, Monday morning, I sent my pastor a note telling him that I'm putting the finishing touches on Sunday services, and asking if there are any surprises. I meet with our tech team and our worship planning team on a weekly basis. And then on Sunday morning we have a really official and very important time—a platform meeting one hour before the services. We meet for fifteen minutes, and everyone who is on the platform is required to be there. The pastor presides. We make sure everyone knows where they are to be, when they're to enter the platform, where they are going to stand, when the lights go up and go down. We have some unique needs since we are on TV, but even if we weren't, we would have some sort of similar meeting so that we would all know what is happening during that worship service.

What trends do you see in congregational worship?

Over the next two or three years, we're going to see more and more use of multi-media, more integration of drama, and more broadening of music in our churches. Every church has its own emotional and cultural profile. Our church here in Florida came out of an old Southern tradition and we have a lot of older people; we're trying to broaden out, and what works best for us is a blending of musical styles. I think this will become the norm, no matter the culture you're in. It's exciting, really, because people today have a heart for worship. They want to gather each week in their churches to praise their God and Father. It's our responsibility to help make that time meaningful and fulfilling.

PRAYERS FOR A PASTOR'S CLOSET

"O Master, Let Me Walk with Thee"

Only a few hymns provide pastors with beautiful worded prayers for their ministries. Chief among åthem is Frances Havergals, "Lord, Speak to Me," and a gospel song entitled "Power for Service" by Elisha Hoffman.

Perhaps the greatest ministerial prayer-hymn was written by Washington Gladden, a Congregational pastor during the post-Civil War industrial era. Christians of all denominations have sung his hymn and shared his prayer, many of them without realizing that Gladden is remembered today as the father of the Social Gospel in America.

Gladden poured his energy into campaigns for political and moral reform, especially in industry and commerce, in support of "the common man." His liberal political views also were reflected in his support for the liberal-leaning biblical criticism that conservatives opposed as "modernist." He wrote that "The Bible is not an infallible Book in the sense in which it is popularly supposed to be infallible. The book is not infallible historically. . . . It is not infallible scientifically. . . ."

Not surprisingly, conservative Christians criticized his ideas very publicly. During a period of particularly heavy criticism, he sat alone in his church and wrote this hymn. Ironically, all sorts of Christians have embraced the hymn as an expression of their own prayer for over a century. Whether or not we agree with Gladden's theology, we can offer this prayer again and again as we labor for the Master in a world desperately needing the transformation of Christ.*

*Adapted from the author's book, Then Sings My Soul (Nashville: Thomas Nelson Publishers, 2003), 203.

O Master, let me walk with Thee,
In lowly paths of service free;
Tell me Thy secret; help me bear
The strain of toil, the fret of care.

Help me the slow of heart to move
By some clear, winning word of love;
Teach me the wayward feet to stay,
And guide them in the homeward way.

Teach me Thy patience; still with Thee
In closer, clearer, company,
In work that keeps faith sweet and strong,
In trust that triumphs over wrong.

In hope that sends a shining ray
Far down the future's broadening way,
In peace that only Thou canst give,
With Thee, O Master, let me live.

APRIL 18, 2004

SUGGESTED SERMON
From Rags to Riches
Date preached:

By Denis Lyle

Scripture: 2 Kings 4:1–7, especially verse 7: *Then she came and told the man of God. And he said, "Go, sell the oil and pay your debt; and you and your sons live on the rest."*

Introduction: Have you ever felt like throwing in the towel and quitting? Have you ever come to your wit's end? Are you there now, ready to give up? When the curtain lifts in 2 Kings chapter 4, a scene of misery, impoverishment, and despair is brought before us. As the story progresses, however, this widow finds the way from rags to riches.

1. **The Trouble Was Brought to Elisha (v. 1).** By turning to God's prophet, Elisha, this woman was turning to God in her trouble; Elisha was God's representative (Heb.1:1). She brought her problems to Elisha *fervently*, she "cried out" indicating her desperation. She also stated her problems *frankly*, honestly relating the facts. She conveyed her problems *fully*, telling her whole story to Elisha. Do you bring your problems to the Lord this way? Let's take a look at her problems:
    A. **There Was Death in the Family (v. 1).** Her human *provider*, her human *protector*, her human *partner* was gone and she felt it! The Hebrew language contains at least 30 words that describe various kinds of trouble. What kind of trouble are you in? Have you brought that trouble and laid it at the Savior's feet?
    B. **There Was Debt in the Family (v. 1).** This woman had seen all her belongings sold to meet the demands of her creditor, and now she faced the dreadful possibility of having to part with her two sons. All that was left in her home was a pot of oil! Is your problem financial? Worried about your job or your business? This family faced death, debt, and possibly:
    C. **There Was Doubt in the Family (v. 1).** The language of verse 1 hints that this woman was perplexed, perhaps even questioning God's wisdom in allowing such affliction to fall upon her home. Are your circumstances causing you to question His Wisdom and doubt His Love?

2. **The Truth Was Taught by Elisha (vv. 2–4).** Here was a preacher with a genuine concern for this widow (see Ps. 68:5; 146:9; Deut. 10:18). Do you have a *heart of compassion* and a *hand of practical helpfulness* for orphans and widows (1 Tim. 5:3; James 1:27)? Elisha gave this widow his full attention. At this stage, however, the situation does not look promising, for she has but a little flask containing a little oil! This proved to be the key to the situation! God, through Elisha, was trying to teach her principles we should also learn:

   A. **She Had to Do as She Was Told (vv. 5–6).** Notice the widow obeyed *immediately* after instructions were given, *implicitly* despite the unusual instructions, and *inclusively*, following his orders step-by-step. Do you take God at His word this way?

   B. **She Had to Use What She Had (vv. 5–6).** It seemed silly, pouring out her few fluid ounces of oil from one vessel to another, but she used what she had. She stepped out with little, which God turned into much (see Luke 17:6). Do you feel too small to accomplish anything? God delights in using little things for His big purposes.

   C. **She Had to Prepare in Abundance (vv. 3–6).** Elisha told her to prepare for abundance. Today we think that a church of 250 people is a big church. We often think small; we believe small and our expectations are trivial. Our expectancy may be the only limitation on what God is prepared to do for us!

>>> *sermon continued on following page*

APPROPRIATE HYMNS AND SONGS

Arise My Soul, Arise, Charles Wesley; Public Domain.

All Your Anxiety, Edward Henry Joy; © 1953 Salvationist Publishing & Supplies, Ltd., Admin. by The Copyright Company.

Draw Nigh to God, Colbert Croft/Joyce Croft; © 1981 Dayspring Music, Admin. by Word Music Group.

Farther Along, W.B. Stevens/J.R. Baxter, Jr.; © 1937 Stamps-Baxter Music, Admin. by Brentwood-Benson Music.

Go With God, Wesley Forbis; © 1990 Van Ness Press, Admin. by Genevox Music Group.

3. **The Triumph Was Wrought for Elisha (v. 7).** She returned to Elisha with her story of victory. Imagine the headlines in the local newspaper: "Company Widow Discovers Oil!" This was a woman who:
   A. **Proved the Adequacy of God.** This woman went from house to house with her small vessels, until one day, there were no more vessels to fill!
   B. **Proved the Ability of God (v. 7).** She found that God was able to meet her *critical need*, to pay her debt, her *constant need*, to pay daily living expenses, and her *collective need*, to provide for her family.

Conclusion: Whether you are facing the death of a loved one, debt, or even doubt, remember that God is able to provide (Phil. 4:19), to deliver (Ps. 50:15), to strengthen (2 Cor. 12:9), to save (Heb. 7:25), and to do more than we could ever ask or imagine (Eph. 3:20).

FOR THE BULLETIN

- April 18, 1480, is the birthday of Lucretia Borgia, illegitimate daughter of the infamous Pope Alexander VI.
- On April 17, 1521, Martin Luther appeared before the Diet of Worms to defend his positions. He stood in simple garb before the Emperor, the royal advisors, the leaders of the church, and dignitaries from various nations. Apparently overawed, Luther seemed nervous and requested a recess. During the night, he strengthened himself in prayer. The next morning, April 18, he appeared again before the Diet, this time bold, heroic, and undaunted, saying, "I cannot and will not recant anything, since it is unsafe and dangerous to do any thing against the conscience."
- April 18, 1587, marks the death of John Foxe, who determined to compile a record of the persecution of God's people that occurred during the reign of Queen (Bloody) Mary. Living on the edge of poverty, Foxe spent every spare moment on his project. He labored by day in a printing shop to support his family, but by night he pored over his manuscript, which was published in 1559.
- Lilian Hamer, missionary to Thailand for China Inland Mission, was shot on April 18, 1959. It was later learned that her death had been planned by the local witch doctor.
- On April 18, 1977, rebels in the nation of Zaire placed missionary doctor Glenn Eschtruth on "trial" for "capitalistic crimes." He wrote the words of Romans 8:28 in the flyleaf of a Bible. His body was later found. He had been shot to death.

STATS, STORIES AND MORE

From Denis Lyle:

Arthur John Gossip was an outstanding Scottish preacher who died in 1954. When he was pastor of the Beechgrove Church in Aberdeen, Scotland, his wife died. The year was 1927. On the first Sunday after he had buried his wife, Dr. Gossip preached in his church as usual. The message he brought that morning was entitled, "But when life tumbles in, what then?" It was probably the best message he had ever preached. Sustained by his strong faith, the lonely heart-broken pastor told his people, "I don't think you need to be afraid of life. Our hearts are very frail and there are places where the road is very steep and lonely. But we have a wonderful God." An old Arabic proverb puts it like this: "Sooner or later the black camel kneels in front of every life." Life has never been easy. This world is a battleground, not a playground. The Lord Jesus said, "In the world ye shall have tribulation, but be of good cheer, I have overcome the world" (John 16:33, KJV).

Disaster Site

A minister was called to the scene of a coal pit disaster. Someone placed in his hands a beautiful piece of embroidery on which the words "God is love" had been wrought. The minister held this up so that the stricken people could see the message which had been so perfectly worked according to a plan. Then he turned the canvas round and all they could see where the tangled ends of thread that certainly did not seem to make any sense at all.

The Backside

A preacher came to C. H. Spurgeon and said, "Mr. Spurgeon, I am seeing very few people saved." Spurgeon said, "Do you expect to see folk saved every time you preach?"
"Why, no," the preacher replied.
Spurgeon said, "That's why you don't!"

Kids Talk

Ask the children if they have ever heard the story of the Magic Porridge Pot. Briefly tell them the story of the old woman who was given a special pot that would cook porridge whenever she said, "Cook, pot, cook!" Unfortunately, one day she couldn't get it to stop cooking and she flooded the town with porridge. Tell the children that the story is a fairy tale that didn't really happen. But there is a similar story—a much better one—that really did happen. Then tell them the story of 2 Kings 4:1–7.

WORSHIP HELPS

Call to Worship:
To Him who is able to keep you from stumbling, and to present you faultless before the presence of His glory... To God our Savior, who alone is wise, be glory and majesty, dominion and power! (Jude 24–25)

Responsive Reading:

Leader:	God is able.
People:	God is able to make all grace abound to you.
Leader:	Our God whom we serve is able to deliver us from the burning fiery furnace.
People:	He is able even to subdue all things to Himself.
Leader:	He is able to aid those who are tempted.
People:	He is able to keep what I have committed to Him until that Day.
Leader:	(He) is able to do immeasurably more than all we ask or imagine, according to His power that is at work within us.

(Rom. 11:23; 2 Cor. 9:8; Dan. 3:17; Phil. 3:21; Heb. 2:18; 2 Tim. 1:12; Eph. 3:20)

Offertory Comments:
Today we're going to study a remarkable oil pot that never ran dry. Through a miracle of God, that jar of oil continued producing for a needy widow and her family. It is a symbol of our pockets and our offerings. God keeps giving and giving to us, filling our pockets and meeting our needs. For two thousand years He has financed His work by giving to His people all they need, and then moving them to return a portion to Him for His church. His blessings to us and through us are a never-ending supply of grace.

APRIL 18, 2004 / 121

Additional Sermons and Lesson Ideas

What Are You Running For?
By Joshua D. Rowe

Date preached:

SCRIPTURE: Hebrews 12:1-2

INTRODUCTION: What makes you run? Being late for work or class? A chance at Superbowl tickets? We can learn from great biblical characters what's worth the run:

1. Running to Face Challenges. Jacob ran to meet Esau (Gen. 33:4). David ran to meet Goliath in battle (1 Sam. 17:48).
2. Running to Find Refuge. The Lord empowered Elijah to run for his life (1 Kin. 18:46). The righteous run to the Name of the Lord for refuge (Prov. 18:10).
3. Running from Temptation. Joseph ran from Potiphar's beautiful wife as she attempted to seduce him (Gen. 39:11-12).
4. Running to Follow Jesus. Crowds ran to follow Jesus (Mark 6:33). Zacchaeus ran ahead of Jesus to climb a tree and watch Him (Luke 19:4).
5. Running to Tell about Jesus. The two Mary's ran to tell the disciples of the risen Christ (Matt. 28:8). Philip ran to evangelize the Ethiopian eunuch (Acts 8:30). Paul referred to His ministry to the Gentiles as "running (his) race" (Gal. 2:2).
6. Running to Reconcile. Moses and Aaron ran to make atonement for Israel's sin (Num. 16:47). The prodigal son's father ran to forgive and accept him (Luke 15:20).

CONCLUSION: Live an eager life. Be enthusiastic about facing challenges, following Christ, telling others, and accomplishing all the other elements that make us contagious Christians. Run with endurance the race set before you.

Why Have You Deceived Me?
By David Jackman

Date preached:

SCRIPTURE: Genesis 29—31

INTRODUCTION: There's a line in *Hamlet* that runs like this, "There's a divinity doth shape our ends, rough hew them how we will." In these central chapters of Jacob's life, "rough hewing" is obviously going on. But in the midst of all the scheming and bitterness, we see the shaping hand of God working out His greater purposes.

1. Twenty Years of Human Confusion (chs. 29—30). This account is filled with constant deception, trickery, bitterness, and hardship. His father-in-law, Laban, deceives him into marrying both daughters who end up in a

bitter race to bear children. Laban continues scheming to profit from Jacob's work.

2. Twenty Years of Heavenly Control (ch. 31). Jacob was disciplined through this experience, forced to become dependent on the promise of God's presence (28:15). He obeyed God's words, to return home (31:3). He was then protected by God's intervention (vv. 22–24) and he acknowledged God's provision and presence through it all (v. 42).

CONCLUSION: Are you facing a difficult period in your life? Does it seem your boss always wants more from you despite your hard work? At school, do your classmates let you do all the work in group assignments? Despite the circumstances, we are to obey God and trust in the promise of His presence (Matt. 28:20; Gal. 3:14) and, as He did for Jacob, in our lives He will certainly protect and provide.

CLASSICS FOR THE PASTOR'S LIBRARY

Heidi

Johanna Spyri (pronounced "Spee-ree") grew up on a postcard. She was born on a high Swiss plateau on July 12, 1827, in the village of Hirzel, not far from Zurich. From her window, she saw Lake Zurich in the distance, all around her were Alpine meadows, and, above her, the Alps. Her father, Johann Jacob Heusser, was a doctor, surgeon, and care-giver for the mentally ill. Her mother, a pastor's daughter, was a nurse and a writer of hymns.

Thus Johanna grew up amid the splendor of God's artistry and in a home that breathed with His presence. As a child, she attended public school in Hirzel, and was tutored by the village pastor, Rev. Salomon Tobler. But approaching adulthood, Johanna pulled away from the piety and faith of her home and family. In 1852, she married Bernhard Spyri, a young lawyer, and moved to Zurich. Bernhard became a successful civic leader, and the two enjoyed an active social life. But in her heart, Johanna suffered growing despondency. In the grip of depression, she returned to the Lord and found there a solid foundation for mental and emotional health.

At age 43, Johanna begin to write stories set in the Alps, drawing from childhood memories, painting vivid word pictures, and conveying Christian truth. Her first stories and poems, published anonymously, were well received, and paved the way for the international success of *Heidi*, published in 1880. Until her death in 1901, she was unimpressed with fame and wealth, semi-reclusive, and she devoted much of the proceeds of her writings to Christian causes, specifically to ministries for orphans and war refugees.

If you've only seen the movie versions of *Heidi*, you've missed the real story, for Hollywood has effectively exorcised its explicitly Christian message. In the novel, Heidi, a handicapped orphan, goes to live with her grandfather in the Alps, hoping the pure air and fresh sunshine will restore her health. Her grandfather, as it turns out, is an embittered old man who hasn't been to church in decades, due to a congregational misunderstanding that occurred in his youth. Heidi, whose own Christian faith is nurtured by a neighboring family, slowly influences him and eventually reads him the story of the Prodigal Son from her Bible picture book.

"Isn't that a beautiful story, grandfather?" asked Heidi, when he sat in silence and she had expected him to be delighted and surprised.

"Yes, Heidi, the story is beautiful," said her grandfather; but his face was so serious that Heidi became quite still and looked at her pictures. She quietly pushed her book in front of her grandfather and said, "See, how happy he is!" and pointed with her finger to the picture of the son's return home, where he stands in fresh garments beside his father, and once more belongs to him as his son.

A few hours later, when Heidi had long been in deep sleep, her grandfather climbed a little ladder; he put his lamp beside Heidi's bed so that the light fell on the sleeping child. She lay there with folded hands, for Heidi had not forgotten to pray. On her rosy face was an expression of peace and blessed trust that must have appealed to her grandfather, for he stood there a long, long time without moving or taking his eyes from the sleeping child. Then he, too, folded his hands and half-aloud, with bowed head, said: "Father, I have sinned against heaven, and before Thee, and am no more worthy to be called Thy son!" and great tears rolled down his cheeks.

When my three daughters were younger, I sat in the hallway between their rooms night after night, reading *Heidi* aloud to them from Helen Dole's translation. Now I'm waiting for my grandchildren to get a little older so I can repeat the pleasure. Every child should get to know Heidi, not from the movies or from condensed little picture books, but from the unabridged novel. It is Christian fiction at its simplest and finest.

APRIL 25, 2004

SUGGESTED SERMON

Walking with God

Date preached:

Adapted from a sermon by George Whitefield

Scripture: Genesis 5:25: And Enoch walked with God; and he was not, for God took him.

Introduction: Obeying the commands of God is not easy, so excuses are plentiful. One of the most common: the Lord's commands are not practical; they are contrary to the flesh. People naturally delight in selfish behavior, but the Lord detests it. Consequently, many agree with the lazy servant in Matthew 25:24, that the Lord is "a hard man." Do we walk with God or make excuses? The Old Testament is full of examples of those who walked with God. Hebrews 11 recalls these heroes—among them is Enoch, who pleased God. We have a short account both of his behavior in this world, "Enoch walked with God," and his entrance into the next, "and he was not, for God took him." My purpose, however, is not to expound upon the life of Enoch, but to examine how to live as he did, walking with God in order to please Him.

1. **Reconciliation.** Walking with God requires that a person be reconciled to God. God lived on earth in the form of Jesus Christ. Because of our rebellion against God, we deserve death, but Jesus paid this penalty; He died for us. Not only this, but He rose from death and ascended into heaven that He might dwell with us in Spirit until He returns to gather His people into eternal fellowship with Himself. If we believe in Jesus, turning away from rebellion and allowing Him to have control, then and only then may we have peace with God to walk with Him.

2. **Submission.** Walking with God implies that we have put aside our rebellious nature. All of us, like our ancestor Adam, instinctively choose satisfaction of our desires over submission to God's direction. When God sought Adam in the garden, why did Adam not run to Him with open arms? His disobedience created an unimaginable hindrance to his walk with God. Believers associate with Paul's words in Romans 7—we want to do good, but our sinful nature makes it difficult. While this may be true,

sin's *prevailing* power has been broken by Christ. John asserts that, to the believer, "... His commandments are not burdensome. For whatever is born of God overcomes the world..." (1 John 5:3–4). Sin's power is weakened as Christ is given control.

3. **Communication.** Walking with God implies an abiding communion and fellowship with God. This is what John would explain as walking as Jesus walked, and what is particularly meant by the passage, "Enoch walked with God." We are called to maintain a holy, settled, consistent communication and fellowship with God, a determined and habitual dependence upon His power and promise.

4. **Progression.** Walking with God indicates making progress in the divine life. Walking, by definition, supposes progressive motion. Peter exhorts Christians to "... grow in the grace and knowledge of our Lord and Savior Jesus Christ" (2 Pet. 3:18). We must be reconciled, submissive, interactive, and active to progress in our walk with Christ. In practical terms, to keep up and maintain our walk with God we must dedicate ourselves to:

   A. *Reading and meditation.* When we sit at Jesus' feet and listen, meditating on His words, we will find them to be spirit and life, food and drink for our souls (John 5:39; Ps. 119:105; 1 Tim. 4:13; Josh. 1:8; 2 Tim. 3:16).

   B. *Secret Prayer.* O prayer! It brings and keeps God and man together. If we would keep up our walk with God; we must pray without ceasing (Eph. 6:18; Matt. 6:46; Matt. 26:41; Luke 9:28).

>>> *sermon continued on following page*

APPROPRIATE HYMNS AND SONGS

O For a Closer Walk With God, William Cowper; Public Domain.

Sometimes a Light Surprises, William Cowper/Bobby L., Huguley; © 1982 Lillenas Publishing Company, Admin. by The Copyright Company.

A Passion for You, Dave Hollen; © 1992 Mercy/Vineyard Publishing.

Aspiration Canon, Bruce Greer; © 1986 Word Music, Inc.

I Build My Life On You, Ken Bible/Randall Dennis; © 1994 Pilot Point Music (Lillenas) Admin. by The Copyright Company.

C. **God's Work.** Believers maintain their walk with God by watching and noting his providential dealings with them (Matt. 10:29–30; Josh. 4:4–9).

D. **Obedience.** Believers must not look at commands as a burden, but as conduits of blessing (Luke 1:5–6; Matt. 28:19–20; Ps. 112:1).

E. **Fellowship.** We do not walk alone. Believers are to provoke one another to good works, encourage one another in love, and carry each other's burdens (Prov. 27:17; 1 Cor. 15:33; Heb. 10:25; Gal. 6:2; 1 Tim. 5:11–14).

Conclusion: Walking with God is honorable, pleasant, and profitable; you will find it so by experience, more so each day. Like Enoch, let us strive to walk with God. The closer we walk with Lord, the more prepared we will be when, in our death or His return, He calls us to his side.

FOR THE BULLETIN

❋ Pope Leo III was kidnapped during a parade on St. Mark's Day, April 25, A.D. 799. The Pope was leading the parade, praying for God's blessings on the Italian farms and fields. As the procession turned the corner, a band of armed men snatched him from his horse and spirited him to a Greek monastery as a hostage. Behind the intrigue was the previous pope, Adrian I. ❋ The Augsburg Confession, the Lutheran Statement of Faith written largely by Philip Melanchthon, was read publicly for the first time on April 25, 1530, at the Diet of Worms. ❋ Knowing he was dying, John Calvin penned his Last Will and Testament on this day in 1564. ❋ April 25, 1800 marks the death of hymnist William Cowper. ❋ Missionary Henry Martyn arrived in India on April 25, 1806. ❋ April 25, 1887, is the birthday of Charles Fuller, pioneer radio evangelist. ❋ The distance between the two great Victorian London preachers, Charles Spurgeon and Joseph Parker, widened on this day in 1890, when Parker published an open letter to Spurgeon in the influential *British Weekly*, in which he said, "Let me advise you to widen the circle of which you are the center. You are surrounded by offerers of incense. They flatter your weakness, they laugh at your jokes, they feed you with compliments. My dear Spurgeon, you are too big a man for this."

STATS, STORIES AND MORE

Walking
The Benefits of Walking (from "thewalkingsite.com"): Walking burns calories, strengthens back muscles, slims your waist, is easy on your joints, strengthens your bones, lowers blood pressure, allows time with family and friends, shapes and tones your legs, cuts cholesterol, reduces risk of heart disease, diabetes, and more, reduces stress, aids sound sleep, improves mood and outlook on life, it can be done almost anywhere, requires no equipment, AND it's free!

Meditation
HWLW is an old slogan going back to the early days of Dawson Trotman, founder of the Navigators. The letters stand for *His Word the Last Word*. Trotman developed a great system of discipling men in the military. Occasionally he would take the men he was training on week-long retreats. As the men lay in their bunks at the end of the day, instead of saying, "Good night" or "Sleep well," Trotman would shout out *HWLW—His Word the Last Word*. It would be a reminder for the men to go to sleep thinking about and meditating on some verse God had given them that day. Trotman knew that the last dominant conscious thought in the human mind at the end of the day would inevitably simmer in the subconscious during sleep and help shape the attitude and personality of the heart. And he was right. If you want to hide God's word in your heart, go to sleep while meditating on a verse of Scripture. It seeps into your subconscious mind and helps shape your soul. You'll sleep better, and wake up the next morning more refreshed. Charles Spurgeon used to say that Bible verses make good pillows.

Data from Researcher George Barna
Women (42%) are more likely than are men (32%) to have read the Bible in the past week. (2001).

85% of evangelical Christians have read the Bible in the past seven days. (2001).

Three out of five born-again Christians (60%) have read the Bible in the past week, compared to 22% of non-Christians. (2001).

WORSHIP HELPS

Call to Worship:

"Hear this, you kings! Listen, you rulers! I will sing to the LORD, I will sing; I will make music to the LORD, the God of Israel" (Judg. 5:2).

Hymn Story:

The theme of today's sermon on "Walking with God" is reflected in a hymn written by William Cowper (pronounced Cooper) who died on this day in 1800. Cowper reminds us of the Psalmist who cried, "Why are you cast down, O my soul?" (Ps. 42:5). He was a melancholy man, subject to depression, but out of his tender soul came such classic hymns as "There is a Fountain Filled with Blood," and "God Moves in a Mysterious Way." On one occasion a dear friend of his, Mary Unwin, fell ill and appeared to be dying. Mary, quite a bit older than William, was a mother-figure to him. He prayed earnestly for her, and it was during this time that, examining his own spiritual condition, he wrote "O For a Closer Walk With God." The words say:

> *O for a closer walk with God,*
> *A calm and heavenly frame,*
> *A light to shine upon the road*
> *That leads me to the Lamb!*
>
> *Where is the blessedness I knew,*
> *When first I saw the Lord?*
> *Where is the soul refreshing view*
> *Of Jesus and His Word?*
>
> *What peaceful hours I once enjoyed!*
> *How sweet their memory still!*
> *But they have left an aching void*
> *The world can never fill.*
>
> *The dearest idol I have known,*
> *Whate'er that idol be*
> *Help me to tear it from Thy throne,*
> *And worship only Thee.*

Benediction:

Walking, growing, working, winning, dear Lord, let us leave this place to serve You 'till we meet again. Amen.

Additional Sermons and Lesson Ideas

The Discipline of Defeat
By Denis Lyle

Date preached:

SCRIPTURE: Joshua 7:1–26, especially verse 12.

INTRODUCTION: Remember Hans Christian Andersen's amusing tale of "The Princess and the Pea?" The Princess could not sleep because of one tiny lump. Likewise, sin, great or small, always irritates and eventually causes defeat. We can learn from Israel how to deal with defeat caused by sin in our lives:

1. Its Cause (vv. 1–5).
   A. Self-Confidence (vv. 2–3).
   B. Prayerlessness (vv. 2–5).
   C. Disobedience (v. 1).
2. Its Cognizance (v. 11).
   A. God Does Not Treat Sin Lightly (v. 25).
   B. Sin Always Affects Others (vv. 5, 24–26).
3. Its Cure (vv. 12–21).
   A. Sin Must Be Identified (vv. 14–21).
   B. Self Must Be Crucified (vv. 12–13; see Col. 3:5).

CONCLUSION: Have you experienced defeat because of sin in your life? Learn to have victory, even in your defeat; confess and crucify your sin!

Everyday Evangelism
By Melvin Worthington

Date preached:

SCRIPTURE: Acts 8:26–40

INTRODUCTION: When Philip caught up with the chariot in Acts 8, he left no doubt about what it takes to put effective evangelism into practice Notice in this story four important ingredients in everyday or effective evangelism.

1. The Servant. Effective evangelism involves a *sensitive, submitted, and skilled* servant. The value of the human instrument surfaces immediately when Philip sees the question on the Eunuch's face.
2. The Sinner. Effective evangelism requires that the sinners have an *interest* in being saved, acknowledge their *ignorance* of spiritual things, and a readiness to receive biblical *instruction.*
3. The Scriptures. The Scriptures are indispensable when one engages in effective evangelism. The Scriptures must be properly *heralded, heard,* and *heeded.*
4. The Spirit. The Holy Spirit always leads the servant to the sinner. God prepares the soil as well as the sower.

CONCLUSION: People are not converted by philosophical husks, preachers' homilies, physical hardship, or psychological hammering, but by the Word of the Living God.

TECHNIQUES FOR THE PASTOR'S DELIVERY

A Voice Teacher's Letter to Her Pastor

Dear Pastor,

Please let me take a moment to thank you for all your dedicated work for our Lord Jesus. Every week, the Lord uses what you say (and live) in my daily walk. You are a blessing in my life and I am very thankful.

Last Sunday I mentioned my concern for your chronic hoarseness and vocal weakness after services. You expressed your anxiety over a constant "scratchiness," nagging dry cough and soreness while swallowing. Thank you for being open to some suggestions from a veteran voice teacher.

Since we spoke, I have been praying for wisdom as I prepared some information that might be helpful for you. Please remember that I am offering this information from my experience as a singer, speaker, and voice teacher; not a speech pathologist or medical doctor.

Some basic information about vocal maintenance and techniques could address and reverse your current discomfort.

General Guidelines for a Healthy Voice

1. Maintain good sleeping and eating habits. No, I'm not from the Land of Oz. My husband is our minister of music and full time chorus teacher; I understand 9 P.M. dinners and early morning computer work. Just try to balance your work with some rest, especially during busy speaking times like Sundays, prayer meetings, revivals, conferences, etc.

2. Keep your voice moist and hydrated. Keep water, or your favorite beverage close by for sipping. Try to include something without caffeine. You can also use hard candy or throat lozenges. Be careful to avoid using menthol-based products for this hydration because they will actually dry your throat. My favorites are Cream Savers and Luden's Sugar Free Cough Drops.

3. Avoid talking in noisy atmospheres like open play in the gym (aargh!), ballgames, concerts, family night suppers, etc. If you need to talk with someone, simply walk over to them so you can speak in a normal voice.

4. Do not EVER yell or scream! Try to remember that we only get one voice. If we don't take care of it, who will?

General Vocal Techniques

1. Posture. Good posture is a pre-requisite for correct vocal productions. Since your body houses your vocal instrument it is important that it is properly aligned so that no negative tension is transferred to the voice. Your feet should be comfortably apart, no wider than a hip-width wide. Never lock your knees. Keep them slightly bent to avoid circulation problems. The rib cage should be expanded broadly to allow the lungs to fill correctly. Notice the space between your hip and armpit while extending your arms at shoulder height. Roll shoulders back and down and allow the weight of your arms to fall out of your fingertips. Make sure you are relaxed between the shoulder blades. The neck should be an extension of the spine, not too forward, or too back. Keep the chin level. This is so important in eliminating stress in the throat.

2. Breathing. The breath is the energy that drives the voice. The control of the breath will determine the quality of voice you produce. As you breathe in (inhale), the diaphragm lowers to allow your lungs to fill with air. As you speak (exhale), the diaphragm raises and causes the air to flow through your throat. In order to control your breath, the muscles about the diaphragm (the intercostals) must be strong. The diaphragm is the largest muscle in the body. It is a dome shaped intrinsic muscle that lowers during inhalation making the abdomen move outward or "get fatter." And as the diaphragm raises during speaking, the abdomen contracts or "gets skinnier."

3. Warming up the voice. Just as a runner warms up his muscles before a race, the speaker must prepare the vocal chords for speaking. Before speaking, make time for your voice. Put it in your routine to hum at least four verses of a hymn, sing three verses of Amazing Grace, and read your Scripture for the morning.

Remember, I am praying for you as you continue to serve the Lord. I stand ready to help you as you work to maintain and protect your voice if you need instruction. Should our schedules be incompatible, there are countless teachers and singers close by that I can direct you to. May God bless you richly as you continue to serve Him.

Always Singing,
Jane Duensing

MAY 2, 2004

SUGGESTED SERMON

A Life of Integrity

Date preached:

By Timothy Beougher

Scripture: James 5:12: But above all, my brethren, do not swear, either by heaven or by earth or with any other oath. But let your "Yes" be "Yes," and your "No," "No," lest you fall into judgment.

Introduction: Someone suggested the top ten lies told in America: 10) Your table will be ready in a minute. 9) One size fits all. 8) This will hurt me more than it hurts you. 7) I'm sorry I'm late; I got stuck in traffic. 6) The check is in the mail. 5) This offer is limited to the first 50 callers. 4) It's not the money; it's the principle of the thing. 3) I need just five minutes of your time. 2) I'll start my diet tomorrow. 1) I'm from the IRS and I'm here to help you. Our culture doesn't place much value on integrity, but Scripture does. James helps us sort out what characterizes a life of integrity:

1. **Avoid the Use of Fine Print (v. 12a).** Verse 12 is James' final exhortation concerning worldliness: in this case, worldliness as expressed by our tongues. James has already dealt with the tongue at length in previous verses, but as he concludes his discussion on worldliness, he again returns to a sin of the tongue. In this case he particularly refers to the abuse of oaths. Let's take a closer look at this idea of oath taking:

    A. **The Use of Oaths in Biblical Times.** In an era before written contracts, oaths served to bind agreements between people. An oath is simply an affirmation attached to a statement designed to give it the certainty of truth, designed to call as witness some independent person or thing to testify to the validity of our words or actions. An oath, in and of itself, was useful, even encouraged in the Old Testament (see Deut. 10:20; 23:21; Ex. 22:10–11; Num. 30:2). Paul used a form of an oath on several occasions (see Rom.1:9; 1 Cor. 1:23; Phil. 1:8). This form of oath taking isn't condemned by James.

    B. **The Abuse of Oaths in Biblical Times.** Unfortunately, by the time of the New Testament the biblical teaching on oaths had suffered tremendous abuse. Some rabbis taught that an oath was not binding if it omitted God's name. The Pharisees began to use other terms, terms that Jesus referred to in Matthew 5:34. Instead of appealing to the name of God, they would say, "Heaven is my witness" or, "Earth is my witness" or "I swear by Jerusalem." Appealing to a substitute for God (heaven, earth, or Jerusalem) was like adding *fine print* into the oath as means of lying and deceiving others. This form of oaths is condemned by Scripture.

- C. **The Use and Abuse of Oaths in Modern Times.** Some religious groups avoid taking oaths in court. However, this type of oath is not condemned by Scripture. In fact, Jesus subjected Himself to an oath at His own trial (see Matt. 26:63–64). The abuse of oaths is still in the form of *fine print.* Have you ever been victimized by high interest rates hidden by *fine print?* Are you using *fine print?* Making promises with your fingers crossed? Calling in to work *sick* when you're only *sick of working?* Are you making excuses based on any half-truth? This may be normal in our society, but Scripture calls us to a life of integrity.

2. **Apply the Practice of Plain Speaking (v. 12b).** James is exhorting us to be so truthful in our speech that we don't need an oath. We should be people who "say what we mean and mean what we say," because deception is dangerous: James concludes this verse to say, "(Speak truthfully) lest you fall into judgment." The word of a Christian should be so trustworthy, so beyond question, that his "yes" always means "yes," and his "no" means

>>> *sermon continued on following page*

APPROPRIATE HYMNS AND SONGS

Clean Hands, Pure Heart, John Slick/Mark Gersmehl; © 1986 Paragon Music Corporation, Admin. by Brentwood-Benson Music Publishing, Inc.

Nothing Between, Charles Albert Tindley; Public Domain.

Keep Your Tongue From Evil, Frank Hernandez; © 1990 Birdwing Music, Admin. by EMI Christian Music Publishing.

All That Thrills My Soul Is Jesus, Thoro Harris; © 1931 Mrs. Thoro Harris. Renewed 1959 Nazarene Publishing House, Admin. by The Copyright Company.

"no." Imagine the testimony Christians would hold if they were known for their honesty in the midst of such a *fine print*, deceptive culture!

Conclusion: Some people say integrity is "what you are when no one is watching." The key to living a life of integrity is to understand that there is never such a time. Integrity is "what you are when *only God* is watching," for we can never escape the Lord's presence (Ps. 139:7–12). We are to avoid deception and to speak plainly and truthfully. If we live this way, surely we will *boldly* stand out in the midst of the *fine print* of our deceptive culture.

FOR THE BULLETIN

❋ Athanasius, third-century defender of the faith, died quietly on this day in A.D. 373. He stoutly began defending the doctrines of the deity of Christ and of the Trinity against the followers of Arius following the Council of Nicea. As Bishop of Alexandria, he battled heresy for forty-six years, and was deposed from his church four times due to his orthodox stands. He is considered one of the church's finest leaders. ❋ Martin Luther was ordained a priest on this day in 1507. ❋ Leonardo Da Vinci died on this day in 1519. He was a genius of creativity—a painter, sculptor, architect, engineer, inventor, and scientist. He is most famous for his painting of the Last Supper, and for his Mona Lisa (now in the Louvre in Paris). ❋ On May 2, 1559, fiery reformer John Knox returned to Edinburgh, just as Mary of Guise, queen regent and mother of young Mary, Queen of Scots, was railing against Protestants. Civil war was threatening. Knox's presence and preachments so inspired the people that the English ambassador reported, "The voice of one man is able in one hour to put more life in us than five hundred trumpets continually blustering in our ears." ❋ May 2, 1764, is the birthday of Robert Hall (1764–1831), prominent British Baptist pastor. So powerful a preacher was he that his audiences would frequently rise to their feet and remain standing in rapt attention until his sermon was done. ❋ May 2, 1840, is the birthday of Theodor Herzl, founder of the Zionist Movement.

STATS, STORIES AND MORE

Oaths in Court
Pastor and theologian Geoff Thomas commented:

"I would urge you if you are going to appear in court that you do choose to take an oath rather than make a civil declaration. I feel it is sad that some people reject the God of the Bible before whom they are going to say some solemn words. For the Christian it is an honour to appeal to the living God before who knows whether his words are true. Bring him praise. He is your God. You know Him as your Father even if you are the only one in the court who does so."

The Trap of Deception
A woman once entered a butcher's shop and asked for a chicken. The butcher only had one left, so he brought it out and placed it on the scale; it weighed two pounds. The woman said, "I was hoping for one a little bigger." The butcher returned to the freezer, pretending to get another, but brought the same chicken back and placed it on the scale, pushing down a little with his thumb so that it weighed three pounds. The woman said, "Perfect, I'll take them both!"

The Next-Door Neighbor Principle
There once was a little boy who watched his father mow the grass each Saturday, eager to be big enough to push the mower himself. Finally, the big day came, and under his dad's supervision, he began to mow. The young boy didn't know the exact boundaries of his yard and mowed a crooked path into the lawn of his perfectionist neighbor. Frightened, the boy turned off the mower and looked to his father. His dad swiftly marched him next door, saying, "If you try to hide it, waiting until he sees, he's going to be angry. Tell him what you did and apologize." The boy quivered in his speech as he confessed and apologized, but the neighbor looked surprised and said, "OK, that's all right." Many times throughout his life, the same young man remembered and practiced the principle he learned that day. He often kept his testimony strong by immediately admitting his faults rather than hiding them. We should all learn to follow the "next-door neighbor principle."

WORSHIP HELPS

Call to Worship:
Make a joyful shout to God, all the earth! Sing out the honor of His name; Make His praise glorious (Ps. 66:1–2).

Scripture Reading:
Psalm 15:1–4

Lord, who may abide in Your tabernacle?
Who may dwell in Your holy hill?
He who walks uprightly,
And works righteousness,
And speaks the truth in his heart;
He who does not backbite with his tongue,
Nor does evil to his neighbor,
Nor does he take up a reproach against his friend;
In whose eyes a vile person is despised,
But he honors those who fear the Lord;
He who swears to his own hurt and does not change.

Benediction:
And now, Lord, let us be, in all things, a pattern of good works; in doctrine, showing integrity, reverence, incorruptibility, and in sound speech that cannot be condemned, that one who is an opponent may be ashamed, having nothing evil to say about us (From Titus 2:7–8).

Additional Sermons and Lesson Ideas

Are You a Liar?
By Peter Grainger

Date preached:

SCRIPTURE: 1 John 1:3— 2:11.

INTRODUCTION: In his first letter, the apostle John challenges our claims to see if they are genuine in regard to our relationship with God and in our relationship with other Christians (1:3). Let's look at each in turn:

1. The Claim to Have Fellowship with God (1:5—2:8).
   A. The Proof (1:7): "If we walk in the light . . ."
   - Obedience and Behavior (2:3–6).
   - Confession and Cleansing (1:9).

   B. The Lie (1:6): "If we . . . walk in darkness . . ."
2. The Claim to Have Fellowship with Other Christians (2:9–11).
   A. The Proof (2:10): "He who loves his brother . . ."
   - Not Taking His Life from Him (3:11–15).
   - Laying Down His Life for Him (3:16–18).

   B. The Lie (2:9): "He who . . . hates his brother . . ."
3. Application: The Lord's Table (1 Cor. 11:17–34), the place for:
   A. Examination
   B. Restoration

CONCLUSION: Do you claim to walk with Jesus but live in consistent rebellion? Are you living with your boyfriend or girlfriend? Are you addicted to pornography? Do you hate anyone here? Do you hold a secret grudge? Or do you gossip about someone else whom you dislike? If any of these are true, we must seek forgiveness from God and others, otherwise our claim to walk with Jesus is a lie.

The Grand Uniqueness of the Christian Life
By W. Graham Scroggie

Date preached:

SCRIPTURE: Philippians 4:2–23

INTRODUCTION: Is it possible that in our constant exposure to secularism that we become comfortable in it? Are we any different? Paul gives us examples of the unique life we have been given.

1. Its Selflessness (vv. 2–7).
   A. Unity of Mind and Purpose (vv. 2–3).
   B. Unreserved Delight in God (vv. 4–7).

2. Its Spirituality (vv. 8–9).
   A. The Heart's Employment (v. 8).
   B. The Heart's Encouragement (v. 9).
3. Its Sufficiency (vv. 10–20).
   A. Satisfaction in Christ (vv. 10–13).
   B. Supply through Christians (vv. 14–20).

CONCLUSION: God's people are called to selflessness. We should be unified in our love for God, meditating on things of God, as we look to Scripture for guidance. Jesus is our sufficiency despite our circumstances; our financial stewardship should reflect this truth. Our grand, unique lives should point others to our grand, unique God (Matt. 5:16).

CLASSICS FOR THE PASTOR'S LIBRARY

The Knowledge of the Holy

A. W. Tozer isn't for cowards. There is something very intense about his writings. His words are pungent. Warren Wiersbe, who heard him many times in person, said that listening to Tozer preach was about as safe as "opening the door of a blast furnace." But if you want to know God better, live straighter, think clearer, and meet problems head-on, take a deep breath and open one of his books.

You might start with *The Knowledge of the Holy.*

I've read it repeatedly—only quote from it in sermons—and it's perhaps the best devotional treatment of the attributes of God to be found. The preface alone is worth memorizing. Tozer says: "It is impossible to keep our moral practices sound and our inward attitudes right while our idea of God is erroneous or inadequate. If we would bring back spiritual power to our lives, we must begin to think of God more nearly as He is."

Tozer suggests that we tend by a secret law of the soul to move toward our mental image of God. We are becoming whatever we envision God as being. Knowing God theologically, personally, and accurately is therefore the most important thing about us.

What, then, is God really like? Tozer describes the Holy One's self-sufficiency, His infinitude, His wisdom, His goodness, His mercy, His justice, His holiness.

Here is a sampling:
- "To say that God is omniscient is to say that He possesses perfect knowledge and therefore has no need to learn. But it is more: it is to say that God has never learned and cannot learn . . . . God knows instantly and effortlessly all . . . ."

- "With the goodness of God to desire our highest welfare, the wisdom of God to plan it, and the power of God to achieve it, what do we lack?"

- "The Lord God omnipotent can do anything as easily as anything else. All His acts are done without effort. He expends no energy that must be replenished."

- "The vague and tenuous hope that God is too kind to punish the ungodly has become a deadly opiate for the consciences of millions."

- "(The holiness of God) stands apart, unique, unapproachable, incomprehensible, and unattainable. The natural man is blind to it. He may fear God's power and admire His wisdom, but His holiness he cannot even imagine."

- "Because we are the handiwork of God, it follows that all our problems and their solutions are theological."

Aiden Wilson Tozer (1897–1963) grew up on a farm in Pennsylvania, where as a boy he put in long hours of physical labor. His education was limited. Economic pressures forced the family to move to Akron, Ohio, when he was 15, and there he began working for the Goodrich Rubber Company. Walking home after work one afternoon, Tozer heard a street preacher say, "If you don't know how to be saved . . . just call on God." Arriving home, Tozer crawled into the attic and asked Jesus Christ to be his Savior and Lord.

Shortly after, he joined the Missionary Alliance Church. In time, he was ordained and began ministering in the Christian and Missionary Alliance denomination. From 1928 to 1959, he pastored the Southside Alliance Church in Chicago, where his congregation grew from 80 to 800. But his greatest and most lasting ministry was arguably as editor of the *Alliance Weekly*. His words were read, reread, reprinted, and republished. Many people subscribed to the magazine just to read his editorials. By the time he died of a heart attack at age 66, his columns, articles, and sermons had become best-selling books.

"It is not a cheerful thought," says Tozer, "that millions of us who live in a land of Bibles, who belong to churches and labor to promote the Christian religion, may yet pass our whole life on this earth without having once thought or tried to think seriously about the being of God."

The Knowledge of the Holy aims to correct that.

MAY 9, 2004

SUGGESTED SERMON

The Wise Woman

Date preached:

By Melvin Worthington

Scripture: Genesis 2:18–25 (see also Prov. 31:10–31, especially v. 30): Charm is deceitful and beauty is passing, But a woman who fears the LORD, she shall be praised.

Introduction: Mother's Day provides an occasion for celebrating what the Bible says about women. In a day when some movements rush to make men and women just alike and other movements seek to make one inferior or superior to the other, it is important to understand the biblical teaching on this subject. Genesis 1 and 2 is a good place to begin. Following a general account of man's creation in Genesis 1:26–31, the Bible gives a detailed account of the creation of woman in Genesis 2:18–21. Wise and happy are those women who understand where they originated, why they were created, and what a wonderful contribution they make to God's plan.

1. **The Need for Woman (Gen. 2:18–20).** A woman is a unique creation because there are needs only she can meet. God said it was not good for man to be alone. Man needed someone to converse and commune with, a companion and one to comfort him. Woman was God's answer to Adam's loneliness. No other creature was suitable for or meet for Adam. Albert Barnes caught a glimpse of the wonder of woman when he wrote, "God did not create man a nonsocial being. He, knowing better than man the social nature of man, voices it in a word spoken for man's guidance. In every way the normal thing for man is to go through life in fellowship with a wife. Man needs her." The creation of woman was not an afterthought with God but vital in His divine plan for man's good. She was created to meet man's need. She was needed, is needed, and will continue to be needed by man. Eve met Adam's need for a lover. She met his need for a listener. No other creation in God's universe could do for Adam what Eve could do. She loved. She listened. She comforted. She understood. She was the perfect answer to a perfect man's dreams. This truth provides women with deserved dignity, delight, and dedication to fill the role God designed for them. A woman clothed in the dignity of knowing who she

is walks in incredible strength. As Proverbs 31:10 says, "Who can find a virtuous wife? For her worth is far above rubies."

2. **The Nature of Woman (Gen. 2:21–22).** The nature of a woman makes her a unique person unlike any other. It is as bad for woman to be alone as for man. Women and men are incomplete without each other. Since Eve was taken from Adam's side, this suggests that woman is neither superior to nor inferior to man. She is on the same level with him in the plan and providence of God.

3. **The Name of Woman (Gen. 2:23–25).** The name of woman makes her a unique person. When God brought Eve to Adam, He declared, "This is now bone of my bones and flesh of my flesh; She shall be called Woman, because she was taken out of Man." Eve provided Adam with companionship, totally unlike the brute creatures. She was near at hand and a part of his own body and shared his same nature. We read the account of woman's creation with a sense of appreciation, awe, and adoration. Joseph Parker wrote, "Perseverance for womanhood will save any civilization from decay. Beautiful and tender is this notion of throwing man into a deep sleep to take a rib from him as the starting point of a blessed companionship. A good wife is from the Lord... He who made the lock will also make the key... This cometh from the Lord of Hosts, which is wonderful in counsel and excellent in working... O woman, love thy maker!

>>> *sermon continued on following page*

APPROPRIATE HYMNS AND SONGS

A Christian Home, Barbara Hart/Jean Sibelius; © 1965, 1986 Singspiration Music, Admin. by Brentwood-Benson Music Publishing, Inc.

In the Circle of Each Home, Bryan Jeffery Leech; © 1976 Fred Bock Music Company.

Lord, Make Our Homes, Bob Burroughs/Esther Burroughs; © 1982 Broadman Press, Admin. by Genevox Music Group.

When Love Is Found, Brian Wren; © 1983 Hope Publishing Company.

Would You Bless Our Homes and Families, Walter Farquharson/Ron Klusmeier; © 1974 Worship Arts, Admin. by Ron Klusmeier.

Thou art the most wonderful instrument He made in the earth; see to it that the music of thy life be all given to His holy praise."

Conclusion: How thankful we are that God created women! Proverbs 31 warns that few women are really fulfilling God's plan. Verse 10 asks, "Who can find a virtuous wife. . ." but they're in *our church*, in *our homes*. We have a God who wants us all to meet the needs of others, to reflect the Divine Nature, and to live up to the name He gave us as men and women and most of all as Christians.

FOR THE BULLETIN

❂ May 9, 1265, is the birthday of Dante Alighieri, author of *The Divine Comedy*. ❂ The Synod of Dort ended on this day in 1619. It affirmed the authority of the Heidelberg Catechism and led to the dismissal of approximately 200 Arminian clergy. ❂ On May 9, 1672, John Bunyan was licensed to preach the gospel by British Baptists. ❂ About midnight on Sunday, May 9, 1760, a dying Count Nicholas Ludwig von Zinzendorf told his son-in-law, John Watteville: "My dear John, I am about to go to the Savior. I am ready. I am resigned to his will, and he is satisfied with me . . . I am ready to go to him. Nothing more stands in my way." Watteville began praying, "Lord, now lettest thou thy servant depart in peace. The Lord bless thee, and keep thee. . . . The Lord lift up his countenance upon thee and give thee peace." At the word "peace" Zinzendorf stopped breathing. ❂ Missionary William Carey married Lady Charlotte Rumohr on May 9, 1808. His first wife, Dorothy, who had suffered mental illness, had died several months earlier. Lady Rumohr was an aristocratic woman of Danish stock, and their marriage so soon after Dorothy's passing caused tongues to wag. They were ideally suited to each other, however, and spent 13 happy years together until Charlotte's death in 1821. ❂ May 9, 1828, is the birth of Andrew Murray, South African Dutch Reformed pastor, devotional writer, and powerful exponent of the Victorious Christian Life. ❂ On May 9, 1983, Pope John Paul II reverses the 1633 decision of the Roman Catholic Church condemning Galileo for his views on the nature of the solar system.

STATS, STORIES AND MORE

Mother Knows Best
A mother was once playing tag with her young children on the lawn, when her husband yelled out the door, "Be careful not to hurt the grass!" She responded, "We're not raising grass, we're raising children."

Far Above Rubies
Rubies are very hard gemstones, almost as hard as diamonds, but much more colorful. They are considered today as being more rare and expensive than even diamonds. The most famous source of fine rubies is Burma (Myanmar). In the ancient world rubies were called the "King of Precious Stones," and they were the rarest and most beautiful of precious stones. Solomon imported rubies into his kingdom, along with vast amounts of gold, silver, and precious stones. In his writings in Proverbs, he used rubies as the standard for comparing the value of other things. Three things are specifically more precious than rubies: First, the ability to speak prudently (Prov. 20:15). Second is wisdom (Prov. 8:11), and third is the Godly woman (Prov. 31:10).

Statistics and Quotes about Mothers
In 1995, there were 27,000 births nationwide attended by physicians, midwives, or others, which did not occur in hospitals, down from 39,000 ten years earlier (U.S. Census Bureau: www.census.gov).

The number of single mothers in America rose about 60 percent between 1980 and 1997: from 6.2 million to 10.0 million (U.S. Census Bureau: www.census.gov).

"I remember my mother's prayers and they have always followed me. They have clung to me all my life."
—*Abraham Lincoln*

"My mother was the most beautiful woman I ever saw. All I am I owe to my mother. I attribute all my success in life to the moral, intellectual, and physical education I received from her."
—*George Washington*

WORSHIP HELPS

Call to Worship:
Bless the Lord, O my soul! O Lord my God, You are very great: You are clothed with honor and majesty, Who cover Yourself with light as with a garment, Who stretch out the heavens like a curtain... Bless the Lord, O my soul! Praise the Lord! (Ps. 104:1–2, 35).

Offertory Comments:
Perhaps one of the most vivid and touching offerings in history comes from a wonderful mother from Scripture. In 1 Samuel chapters 1 and 2 we read about Hannah, a grief-stricken, barren woman who wanted so badly to conceive a child that she went to the Tabernacle year after year asking God to open her womb. She was once praying so earnestly that Eli, the priest, thought she was drunk. She told the Lord that if He granted her a son, she would dedicate him fully to His service as a priest. The Lord granted her request, and she fulfilled her commitment, giving her son to full service in ministry. Has the Lord provided for your needs faithfully? Pray earnestly, and seek what God would have you offer for His kingdom this week. Hannah was not only granted her request, but she was ultimately blessed with *three sons* and *two daughters*! We believe the same God will abundantly bless us for our sacrificial giving as well!

Benediction:
The grace of the Lord Jesus Christ, and the love of God, and the communion of the Holy Spirit be with you all. Amen (2 Cor. 13:14).

Additional Sermons and Lesson Ideas

The Discipline of Delay
By Denis Lyle

Date preached:

SCRIPTURE: John 11:1–46, especially verses 4–5

INTRODUCTION: Too often we worry when we should wait, and we resist when we should resign. Often God's delays are explained in that God wishes to teach us our need of patience (see Hebrews 10:36). In our text, Lazarus was on his deathbed and yet Jesus delayed (see vv. 1–6). Why?

1. Was Jesus Ignorant? No, see verse 11.
2. Was Jesus Indifferent? No, see verses 8–9 and 35.
3. Was Jesus Impotent? No, see verses 33–34.
4. Why Was Jesus Involved?
    A. To Receive Greater Glory for God (vv. 4, 40).
    B. To Remedy Feeble Faith of His Followers (vv. 15, 21–26, 37, 40–42, 45).

CONCLUSION: Have you been praying for your lost loved one for years? Waiting on the funds to come in for your ministry? Allow the Lord to refine you through the discipline of delay (Is. 30:18).

Has an Angel Helped You This Week?

Date preached:

SCRIPTURE: Acts 12

INTRODUCTION: Has an angel helped you this week? Hebrews 1:14 says that angels are ministering spirits sent to serve those who inherit salvation. The early Christians benefited from angelic ministry. Angels are mentioned in the Book of Acts in chapters 1, 5, 6, 7, 8, 10, 11, 12, 23, and 27. In Acts 12, we have three fascinating insights about this angelic ministry.

1. The Delivering Angel (vv. 7–11).
2. The Personal Angel (v. 15). Luke passes along the comment, "It is his angel," without comment, leaving unanswered the question about the Jewish belief that each of God's children has an angel assigned to him or her. (see Matt. 18:10; Dan. 10:21; Ps. 91:11).
3. The Death Angel (vv. 20–24). Angels can kill people. They are sometimes God's instruments of judgment.

CONCLUSION: We may not be able to see them, and we aren't sure of all their activities, but we know the angels of God are watching over us.

MAY 16, 2004

SUGGESTED SERMON

After God's Own Heart
By David George

Date preached:

Scripture: 1 Samuel 13:1–14 and 1 Samuel 16:1–13, especially 1 Samuel 13:14: *The Lord has sought for Himself a man after His own heart.*

Introduction: It was the best of times and the worst of times, as Dickens said in his *Tale of Two Cities*. In her early history, Israel was a coalition of twelve tribes, seeking unity. When the people demanded a king, God said, "Give them a king," and Samuel began looking. When King Saul proved a disappointment, Samuel sought out another man—one "after God's own heart." What does it mean to be a person after God's heart?

1. **There Needs To Be Self-Consciousness.** Though there was already a king, the Bible indicates that when the anointing oil flowed over David's head he began thinking as if *he* were king. We need to capture a vision of what God wants us to be, a vision of what He wants to do with His church—a dynamic, organized, evangelistic army of God. He wants to expand our vision and help us release our lives into His will.
   A. **Understand your limits.** Until age five or six, we think the whole world revolves around us. If your world centers around you, you're acting like a five-year-old. If your every thought needs to be considered, your every whim needs to be respected, your every desire needs to be met, there's an immaturity that needs to be dealt with. You're not the center of the universe. You have to be aware of your limits.
   B. **Be aware of your role in the world.** How do you fit in with your family? Your community? What gifts and talents has God given you?
   C. **Know your possibilities.** Sometimes we believe we're limited by what our parents and grandparents did in raising us or by our background experiences. Let God remove those limits! He created and gifted you. He has called and anointed you. David had to realize he had been called, anointed, and gifted to be king. When God picks you out, it doesn't matter what your granddaddy did, what your mother was like, what kind of education or economics you had. God can use a crooked stick to hit

straight licks if you'll be obedient. Even if you're facing the consequences of past sins, that doesn't hinder God's ability to take and use you if you'll obey Him. You don't have to be subservient to the poor choices you've made in the past. Christ came to forgive sin, to redeem and redirect.

2. **There Needs To Be God-Consciousness**
   A. **We must desire God's plan for our lives.** I wonder if David sat on the hillside and dreamed of being a successful sheep rancher? With his leadership skills, he was probably plotting to take over the family business. But when God called him as king, he resigned his own plans for God's. How many of you know in your heart that you've said "No" to God somewhere in the past? That can be undone in a moment, in the twinkling of an eye, by just saying "Yes" to His call, whatever it is.
   B. **We must begin living as though God's promises were true.** In Romans 4, when Abraham believed God would do as He had promised, he began living as though he were already a father. When the Bible says we are blessed, we should act accordingly. When it says God wants to use us, we ought to begin living as though He *were* using us. Live as though you had enough love for your husband though he appears unlovable. Raise that child believing God will provide the needed wisdom.
   C. **We must walk through open doors.** When we develop inner desires to be used by God, they are frequently matched with talents and abilities. Add to that your experience and training. When those things are in place, the opportunities come in God's timing. *Dave, would you like to give your*

>>> *sermon continued on following page*

APPROPRIATE HYMNS AND SONGS

And Can It Be, Charles Wesley/Thomas Campbell; Public Domain.

Christ in Me, Michael O'Brien; © 1998 Designer Music, Admin. by Brentwood-Benson Music Publishing, Inc.

Glorious Is Thy Name Most Holy, Ruth Elliott/William Moore; © 1961 The Hymn Society, Admin. by Hope Publishing Company.

I Give My Life, Marc Nelson; © 1988 Mercy/Vineyard Music.

I Would Be True, Howard Walter Arnold/Joseph Yates Peek; Public Domain.

testimony at the youth meeting next week? Janice, come sing in the choir! David had no flashing experience or blinding light... just a door that opened.

3. **There Needs To Be Scripture-Consciousness.** The fact that God has called us doesn't bestow the right to ignore the commands and the other words of God. If you're called to be a dad or mom, a school teacher, a church worker, that does not give you the right to ride roughshod over anyone else. We must submit to God's Word in all things. It's a tragedy that so many pastors are failing morally, that so many dads are walking out on their families, that so many Christians live in daily disobedience.

Conclusion: Every man, woman, boy, or girl here today can be a person after God's heart. It doesn't matter what your background is, or what mistakes you've made. Just say: "God, here are my experiences, my gifts, my talents, my weaknesses. I'm going to submit to you and let you open the doors. I desire to glorify you."

FOR THE BULLETIN

- On May 16, 1532, Sir Thomas More resigned as the Lord Chancellor of England. As a staunch Roman Catholic, he was upset at King Henry VIII's break with the pope and refused to recognize Henry as head of the Anglican Church. For this, he was imprisoned in the Tower of London and executed.
- Henry Martyn was born in Cornwall, England, in 1781. He attended Cambridge, graduating with honors in mathematics. The writings of missionary David Brainard brought him to Christian surrender, and he soon contemplated foreign missions. "Let me forget the world," he said, "and be swallowed up in a desire to glorify God." At daybreak on May 16, 1805, Martyn went ashore at Calcutta and was met by William Carey who soon nudged him into translation work. Martyn lost himself in ministry, preaching, establishing schools, and translating the Bible into three Asian languages. He died at age thirty-one.
- May 16, 1855, marks the conversion of evangelist D. L. Moody.
- May 16, 1929 is the birthday of Warren W. Wiersbe.
- Bible teacher G. Campbell Morgan died on this day in 1945.
- On May 16, 1966, five hundred Baptists from 130 towns in Russia demonstrated for religious rights in front of the Communist Central Committee Building in Moscow. Many of them were arrested the next day, and two of them Georgi Vins and Gennadi Kryuchkov, were tried and imprisoned.

STATS, STORIES AND MORE

Restored Failures
- Above his fireplace in Beverly Hills, Fred Astaire hung a memo from his first tryout: The MGM director wrote, "Can't act. Slightly bald. Can dance a little."
- Ray Kroc was an unsuccessful salesman of restaurant equipment for the majority of his life. He didn't sell a single hamburger until he reached age 52, but from a few hamburger stands, he built the world's largest fast-food chain: McDonalds.
- At age 23, he was defeated in his campaign for legislature, he was defeated in his run for Congress at ages 34 and 39, for Senate at age 46, and for Vice President at age 47, but Abraham Lincoln was elected as the President of the United States at age 51.

God Uses Imperfection
One of the most unique and inspiring missionaries of all times is Raymund Lull of the thirteenth century. He married young and before his conversion was often unfaithful to his wife. During this period of history, the Western world feared and hated the rising tide of Islam. But following his conversion, Lull was filled with compassion for Muslims and became the great pioneer missionary to the Islamic world. He often battled his former selfish ways; once he became so angry with a Muslim slave (who was teaching him Arabic) that he struck him with his fist! The slave retaliated, almost killing Lull, and then committed suicide. This scene haunted him throughout his life, and he resolved never to use violence, but to use the Sword of the Spirit and love to reach the Muslim people. Near his death, he was offered a luxurious life: many wives and possessions, but he refused, exhorting Muslims to give up *their* earthly things to receive treasures in heaven! Raymund Lull was martyred on June 30, 1315.

WORSHIP HELPS

Call to Worship:
I will bless the LORD at all times; His praise shall continually be in my mouth. My soul shall make its boast in the LORD; The humble shall hear of it and be glad. Oh, magnify the LORD with me, And let us exalt His name together (Ps. 33:1–3).

Pastoral Prayer:
Lord, we want to be people after your own heart, so we pray with David: You, Lord, are good, and ready to forgive, and abundant in mercy to all those who call upon You. There is none like You, O Lord, nor are there any works like Your works. All nations whom You have made shall come and worship before You, O Lord, and shall glorify Your name. For You are great, and do wondrous things; You alone are God. Teach us Your way, O LORD; we will walk in Your truth; unite our hearts to fear Your name. We will praise You, O Lord our God, with all our hearts, and we will glorify Your name forevermore. For great is Your mercy toward us, and you have delivered our souls *(from Ps. 86:5, 8–13)*.

Welcome:
Often, visitors are quite reluctant to attend a new church for a number of reasons: maybe they are shy, maybe they don't think they fit in. Today we are studying the story of David, a man after God's own heart. Let me remind you of a brief scene from David's life: the ark of the covenant, the symbol of God's presence, had been stolen, and then left in a village outside Jerusalem. David, seeking God's presence, returned the ark to Jerusalem: it was a glorious day of celebration, and he, the king himself, the man in charge, took off his kingly garments and praised God alongside of the people of Israel. This morning you are an important part of our congregation where *everyone* fits in, and we welcome you to celebrate God's presence with us!

Additional Sermons and Lesson Ideas

How Money Can Hurt You
By Timothy Beougher

Date preached:

SCRIPTURE: James 5:1–6, especially verse 5.

INTRODUCTION: Jesus talked more about money than any other topic, often warning of its danger. James tells us that money can hurt us when:

1. We Value it Wrongly (vv. 1–13). James doesn't condemn money, but the love of money because it is *temporal* and we are to focus on the *eternal* (Matt. 6:19–20; Luke 12:15–21; 1 Tim. 6:17).
2. We Obtain it Wrongly (v. 4). Scripture commands against gaining money deceitfully (see Deut. 24:14–15). Do we lie about taxes or keep the extra $10 the cashier accidentally gave us as change? This type of *temporal gain* will always earn us *spiritual pain*.
3. We Use it Wrongly (vv. 5–6). Those who hoard riches and neglect the needy are pictured as fattened cattle headed for slaughter, unaware of their fate! Enjoy God's provision (Ps. 34:8), but beware if your luxury is to the neglect or oppression of others (Eccl. 5:13)!

CONCLUSION: Be a good steward of God's provision to you!

The Parable of the Prodigal Father
By Peter Grainger

Date preached:

SCRIPTURE: Luke 15:11–32

INTRODUCTION: In this familiar yet wonderful story, let us examine each character:

1. The Rebellious Son
   A. Ruin
   - Leaving Home (v. 13)
   - Living it Up (v. 13)
   - Losing Out (vv. 14–16)

   B. Restoration
   - A Change of Mind (vv. 17–19)
   - A Change of Direction (v. 20)
2. The Resentful Son
   A. Rage
   - At His Brother (vv. 28–30)
   - At His Father (vv. 28–30)

B. Refusal
   - To Accept the Invitation (v. 28)
   - To Join the Celebration (vv. 28–32)
3. The Prodigal Father
   A. Prodigal Love Given to:
   - The Son Who Strayed (vv. 22–24)
   - The Son Who Stayed (v. 31).
   B. Prodigal Love: In Giving His Son (John 3:16; 1 John 4:9–10)

CONCLUSION: Are you a rebellious sinner in the far country? The broad road always leads to death (Matt. 7:13). Are you a resentful sinner, trying to gain favour with God as an employer? The wages of sin is death (Rom. 6:23). Wherever you are, turn back to God and receive His invitation.

PRAYERS FOR A PASTORS CLOSET

A Prayer for Insight

Almighty God, may we not be as fools but as wise, having understanding in the meaning of things, and knowing what Thou art doing in all the days as they brighten and die. Thou art always most surely fulfilling Thy Holy Word—may we be numbered amongst those who are inspired with a great expectation, and who are constantly looking for the Lord's coming. Surely Thou art always coming, Thou are nearer now than ever before; give us the insight which sees Thee in the events of the day, and so ennoble our religious faculty that we may be able to interpret unto others the movements which appear to be common or degraded. Enable us by Thy presence in the soul, so to see what is transpiring, as to acknowledge Thine hand in it, and to be enabled to point out to others the gracious rule of Thy sovereignty. Amen.

—Joseph Parker (1830–1902), pastor of London's City Temple

HEROES FOR THE PASTOR'S HEART

James Renwick

Andrew and Elizabeth Renwick, a young couple, weavers, lived in the hills of Glencairn, Scotland in the 1600s. All their children had died. Andrew accepted his grief, but Elizabeth cried to the Lord day and night for another child.

The Lord answered, and little James was born. The lad was taught the Holy Scriptures from infancy. Growing up, his conscience was tender; his mind, sharp. He excelled at the University of Edinburgh, but was denied a degree because he refused to accept Charles II as head of the Scottish Church.

Remaining in Edinburgh, the young man watched with alarm as non-conformists were martyred, their severed heads and hands nailed to the city gates as a warning to others. He left Scotland for training and ordination abroad, but his heart was still in the highlands, and he soon returned to preach, teach, organize, counsel, and wear himself out on behalf of the Covenanters.

"Excessive travel," he told a friend, "night wanderings, unseasonable sleep and diet, and frequent preaching in all seasons of weather, especially in the night, have debilitated me." He trudged with diligence through moors and mountains, in the cold stormy nights and by day. His study was often a cold glen or cave; his pillow, a rock or log. He managed a hundred escapes, but at length one winter's night in Edinburgh he was captured, put in irons, and convicted of treason.

His widowed mother visited him in prison, her heart breaking apart. "O James!" she cried, "How shall I look up to see your head and hands upon the city gate? I shall not be able to endure it." He comforted her as he could, and on February 16, 1688, smuggled a message to her: *There is nothing in the world that I am sorry to leave but you . . . Farewell mother. Farewell, night wanderings, cold and weariness for Christ. Farewell, sweet Bible and preaching of the Gospel. Welcome, crown of glory. Welcome, O Thou blessed Trinity and one God! I commit my soul into Thy eternal rest.*

The next morning he embraced his weeping mother once more, then went to the scaffold.

He was twenty-six.*

Excerpted from the author's book, *On This Day* (Nashville, Thomas Nelson Publishers, 1997), entry for February 16.

MAY 23, 2004

SUGGESTED SERMON

Stairway to Heaven   *Date preached:*

By David Jackman

Scripture: Genesis 28, especially verse 15: "Behold, I am with you and will keep you wherever you go, and will bring you back to this land; for I will not leave you until I have done what I have spoken to you."

Introduction: A passage in C.S. Lewis's writing in which he expresses his conversion reads, "I was brought into the kingdom of heaven kicking and struggling, the most reluctant convert in all England, but I knew that I was in the net." Jacob would have understood that, but then again so would every Christian. We may have grown up in Christian homes, but resisted the truth. Maybe we saw something different about Christians at work or school, but we didn't want to give up our lifestyle. The story of Jacob is the story of grace triumphing over human artifice. Like many of us, he tried to take control over his own destiny. He stole Esau's (his older brother's) birthright, and thus the blessing of his father. Because of this, he was forced to flee from home to avoid Esau's wrath (see Gen. 27:18–46). In this context, God confronts Jacob in His grace.

1. **God's Grace Takes the Initiative (28:10–14).** Jacob is doing two things by leaving home. First, he is effectively fleeing for his life, but (as we see in vv. 1–2) he is on an unknown journey to find a wife. For the first time, Jacob is on his own (v. 11). At the point of his acute need (see 35:3—Jacob calls this "the day of my distress"), God breaks through with an amazing promise. In the Hebrew, a dramatic change occurs in the text; each part of verse 12 starts with a little exclamation—"behold!" On this ordinary night, suddenly, God breaks through in His grace. As Jacob sees the stairway with angels ascending and descending on it, with the LORD at the top, it creates a clear picture of God's communication with Jacob. Grace loves to encounter the fugitive. God includes Jacob, the deceiver, in the promises given to his ancestors (vv. 13–14). Do you think you are too far gone to return to God and share in His blessings? That there is no way God can forgive you and include you in His purposes? Do you think there

is no hope for your rebellious family member or friend? You couldn't be further from the truth. God's grace takes the initiative; it extends to every rebel.

2. **God's Grace Reveals the Blessing (28:15).** For Jacob it now becomes very personal. God says, "I am with you." Look at all the second-person pronouns in this verse. It shifts the lens from a wide-angle to close-up, taking the covenant promises, and now personalizing them to Jacob's own current situation. Jacob has been very concerned about the blessing, but he must learn that the blessing is not prosperity or wealth, but that, "I am with you," the fellowship and relationship with a personal, living God who keeps His promises. It's true of us; the Spirit will remain in every believer (Heb. 13:5). Nothing can separate us from God's love (Rom. 8:35–39). Do you really believe that the promises made to us under the New Covenant bought by the blood of Christ are any less comprehensive or less real than that? Of course not! There's never a day or hour when His grace, mercy, provision, or working in us is not ongoing.

3. **God's Grace Begins the Process of Change (28:16–22).** The man who didn't know if God was with Him now knows there's nowhere God is not. He wakes and says, " . . . How awesome is this place . . ." (v. 17). He realizes that God should be revered and honored. Jacob wants to commemorate this encounter and express his gratitude and commitment to God. He calls this place the house of God (Bethel) and he makes a vow. Jacob is not bargaining in verse 20, but saying, I believe this will happen, and then

>>> *sermon continued on following page*

APPROPRIATE HYMNS AND SONGS

Calvary Covers It All, Mrs. Walter G. Taylor; © 1934 Mrs. Walter G. Taylor. Renewed 1962 Word Music Group, Inc.

Everlasting Grace, Kelly Carpenter; © 1994 Mercy/Vineyard Publishing.

One True Living God, John Chisum/Chris Springer; © 1994 Integrity's Praise! Music/Integrity's Hosanna! Music, Admin. by Integrity Music, Inc.

Savior, Like a Shepherd Lead Us, Dorothy Al Thrupp/William B. Bradbury; Public Domain.

Your Grace, Andy Parks; © 1998 Mercy/Vineyard Publishing.

you'll be my God. The vow almost exactly mirrors the promise. The man who was out for self gain changed to rely on God. When God breaks through in our lives, two things happen: we start to worship Him as we never have before, and we decide to be devoted and committed to His purposes.

Conclusion: Whether it's a prodigal you're dealing with or if you're wandering yourself, God's grace will triumph. Jesus is the real stairway between heaven and earth; He's our mediator who makes it possible to have peace with God (Heb. 9:15). Think of how He hung on the Cross between heaven and earth to bury our sins so we could enter into the New Covenant, sealed by His blood! Our only response is to give up our small ambitions, turning our backs on our Jacob-like disposition to follow God in faith.

FOR THE BULLETIN

❋ On May 23, 1492, Girolamo Savonarola, the Italian Reformer who set Florence ablaze with his preaching, was hanged and his body burned. ❋ On May 23, 1533, Thomas Cranmer, Archbishop of Canterbury, declared null and void the marriage of King Henry VIII and Catherine of Aragon, setting the stage for the English Reformation. ❋ Seventeenth-century Bohemia was a beautiful area at the center of Europe, encircled by mountains and highlands, home of the Moravians. It was the land of John Hus who died for the Reformation before Luther even launched it. And it was filled with Hussites longing for freedom of worship. But Bohemia was ruled by the Hapsburg king, Ferdinand II, a dedicated Catholic. He unleashed a campaign to re-Catholicize Bohemia, and on May 23, 1618 Bohemian rebels shouting the Protestant cause stormed the palace. They literally threw Ferdinand's governors out the window. The governors landed in a pile of manure, and Ferdinand sent troops against the Protestants. This was the beginning of the Thirty-Year War. ❋ By French edict, from this day in 1633 only French Catholics were allowed into "New France"—Canada—as settlers, ending long efforts by French Protestants (Huguenots) to immigrate to the New World. ❋ May 23, 1862 is the birthday of Hermann Gunkel, father of "Form Criticism."

STATS, STORIES AND MORE

Someone Is Watching
A poor farmer asked his young daughter to come with him at sundown. He took her down the road to another farm. He instructed her to be on the lookout and to tell him if anyone was watching him. He began to steal crops, bagging them up. The little girl said, "Someone is watching." Her father froze, looked around, looked inquisitively at the girl, and kept bagging. As he moved on to another farm, his daughter repeated, "Someone is watching." Again, there was no one in sight. A third time, his daughter said, "Someone is watching." He replied in frustration, "What are you talking about, no one is watching!" She replied, "Daddy, God sees you."

God's Presence
When we live in harmony with the Lord, it is joy and delight to linger in His presence.—*Charles Dickens*

Prodigals
Ruth Bell Graham, wife of Billy Graham, knows about prodigals. Two of her five children were spiritual wanderers. From the pain she experienced, she wrote a book called *Prodigals and Those Who Love Them*, in which she said of Christians, "We must take care of the possible and trust God for the impossible. We are to love, affirm, encourage, teach, listen, and care for the physical needs of our families. But we cannot convict of sin, create hunger and thirst after God, or convert. These are miracles, and miracles are not our department." She wrote a little poem about what it feels like facing other families who haven't experienced this problem.

> *They felt good eyes upon them and shrank within*
> *them, undone*
> *Good parents had good children,*
> *they had a wandering one*
> *The good folk never meant to act smug or condemn*
> *But having prodigals just wasn't done with them*
> *Remind them gently Lord, how you*
> *Have trouble with your children, too.*

WORSHIP HELPS

Call to Worship:
"Let us draw near with a true heart in full assurance of faith, having our hearts sprinkled from an evil conscience and our bodies washed with pure water."

Scripture Medley:
For I say to you, that unless your righteousness exceeds the righteousness of the scribes and Pharisees, you will by no means enter the kingdom of heaven . . . Who, then, can be saved? Salvation belongs to our God who sits on the throne, and to the Lamb! . . . The grace of God that brings salvation has appeared to all men . . . The Word became flesh and dwelt among us, and we beheld His glory, the glory as of the only begotten of the Father, full of grace and truth . . . Now the righteousness of God apart from the law is revealed, being witnessed by the Law and the Prophets, even the righteousness of God, through faith in Jesus Christ, to all and on all who believe . . . As each one has received a gift, minister it to one another, as good stewards of the manifold grace of God.
(Matt. 5:20; 19:25; Rev. 7:10; Titus 2:11; John 1:14; Rom. 3:21; 1 Pet. 4:10)

Pastoral Prayer:
O to grace how great a debtor, daily I'm constrained to be. Let your grace, Lord, like a fetter, bind my wandering heart to thee. So, Lord, we pray that the grace that reached Jacob may reach our hearts, too. We thank you that it is in the Lord Jesus, full of grace and truth, in His death for us, in His Resurrection, in His present reign, in the gift of His Spirit, in all the blessings of the gospel and the new Israel that you've been so good to us when you said, 'I will never leave you or forsake you,' Jesus Christ the Son, yesterday today, and forever. Teach us to trust and not to be afraid for the glory of your Holy Name, Amen.

Additional Sermons and Lesson Ideas

The Discipline of Denial
By Denis Lyle

Date preached:

SCRIPTURE: 2 Corinthians 12:7–10, especially verse 9.

INTRODUCTION: It's often said that, in answering our prayers, sometimes God says "wait" (see John 11:6), sometimes "yes" (see 1 Sam. 1:17), and sometimes "no" as in our text today. He teaches us about His grace through this *discipline of denial*.

1. Difficulty (vv. 7–8)
    A. A Pressure that Seemed Unhelpful (v. 7)
    B. A Prayer that Seemed Unheard (v. 8)
2. Discovery (v. 9)
    A. The Lord's Gracious Purpose
    B. The Lord's Gracious Provision
3. Doxology (v. 10)
    A. Attitude Is Changed
    B. Acceptance Is Complete

CONCLUSION: Have you been asking God to remove some pressure, some problem from your life? To change the circumstances? Perhaps the Lord wants it there to teach you this lesson: with abiding pressure comes abundant provision; His grace is sufficient for you!

Prevailing Prayer
By Joshua Rowe

Date preached:

SCRIPTURE: 1 Samuel 1:1–24

INTRODUCTION: Many of us experience problems that seem to last forever; we should learn from Hannah.

1. The Problem (vv. 1–8). Hannah was barren but earnestly desired a child; her problem was:
    A. Provoked. Hannah constantly received cruel comments and hateful treatment from Elkanah's other wife.
    B. Prolonged. Each year she returned to the Tabernacle with the same request.
2. The Prayer (vv. 9–11). We get a glimpse of Hannah's sorrow; her prayer was:
    A. Persistent. Hannah returned yearly with the same request; how often do you suppose she prayed in between? Do you give up after one prayer? Be persistent (Luke 18:1–5).

B. Passionate. Hannah prayed so earnestly that Eli thought she was drunk! Are your prayers this persistent and passionate?
3. The Promise (vv. 11–28). Hannah promised to give her son to full-time ministry! God, through Eli, promised her a child, and she believed. Are the promises of Scripture your comfort? The promise both:
A. Prevailed. Hannah was given a son; notice her response was sacrifice and worship!
B. Persisted. Hannah was ultimately blessed with three sons and two daughters (see 2:21).

CONCLUSION: Whatever your problem is, don't stop praying about it! Pour out your heart to God and take comfort in the promises of Scripture.

THOUGHTS FOR THE PASTOR'S SOUL

The Minister's Zeal
By Samuel Logan Brengle

(Excerpted from *The Soul-Winner's Secret*, published in 1903)

It is said that General Sheridan went to battle with all the fury of a madman, and recklessly exposed himself to the shot and shell of the enemy. He told General Porter that he never went into a battle from which he cared to come back alive unless he came back as victor. This desperation made him an irresistible inspiration to his own troops, and enabled him to hurl them like overwhelming thunderbolts against his foes. If he became so desperate in killing men, how much more desperate, if possible, should we become in our desire and effort to save them!

It was written of Jesus, "The zeal of Thine house hath eaten Me up;" and so it can be said of every soul-winner.

Not until a man can say with Paul, "Neither count I my life dear unto myself," and "I am ready to die for the name of the Lord Jesus," can he hope to be largely used in winning souls. He that is anxious about his dinner, and eager to get to bed at a reasonable hour, and concerned about his salary, and over-solicitous about his health, and querulous about his reputation and the respectability and financial condition of his appointment, and afraid of weariness and painfulness and headache and heartache and a sore throat, may make a very respectable Officer or Parson, but not a great soul-winner.

There are various kinds of zeal which should be avoided as deadly evils:

1. Partial zeal, like that of Jehu (2 Kin. 10:15–31). God sent him to destroy the wicked house of Ahab and the worship of Baal, and he did so with fury. "But Jehu took no heed to walk in the law of the God of Israel with all his heart; for he departed not from the sins of Jeroboam, which made Israel to sink," and in due time God had to cut off his house as well.

This kind of zeal is frequently seen in those who violently attack one kind of sin, while probably they themselves are secretly indulging in some other sin. Such people are usually not only intolerant of the sin, but also of the sinner, while true zeal makes one infinitely tender and patient toward the sinner, while absolutely uncompromising with his sin.

2. Party zeal, like that of the Pharisees and Sadducees. In these days it takes the form of excessive sectarian and denominational zeal, and makes bigots of men. Zeal for the particular church or organization to which one belongs is right within certain limits. We are converted through the instrumentality of a certain religious organization, and we become children of its spiritual household, or we are led into it by the Holy Spirit through a blessed divine affinity with its members, methods, spirit, and doctrine, and we should in that case be loyal and true to its leaders who are over us in the Lord, and who watch for our souls, and follow them as they follow Christ.

We should also be loyal to the principles of the organization so far as they harmonize with the Word of God, and we should seek in all true ways, by prayer and supplication and ceaseless zealous work, to build up this organization in holiness and righteousness. And this we can do if we do it in the Holy Spirit, with all our might, and can be assured that God is well pleased with us. But we must at the same time beware of a party spirit that would despise or hold in light esteem other work and workers, or tear them down that we may rise on their ruins. Such zeal is from beneath, and not from above.

3. The zeal of ignorance. Paul said of his kinsmen, the Jews, "My heart's desire and prayer to God for Israel is, that they might be saved. For I bear them record, that they have a zeal of God, but not according to knowledge. For they, being ignorant of God's righteousness and going about to establish their own righteousness, have not submitted themselves unto the righteousness of God." (Rom. 10:1-3).

THOUGHTS FOR THE PASTOR'S SOUL— CONTINUED

True zeal is from above. Its source is in the mountains of the Lord's holiness, and its springing fountains in the deep, cool valleys of humility. It is born of the Holy Spirit, and springs from a knowledge of "the truth as it is in Jesus." This knowledge is twofold:

It is the knowledge of the dread condition of the sinner without Christ—his slavery to Satan, the inherited depravity of his nature, his bondage to sin, his love of it, his enmity toward God, of which he is probably not aware; his guilt, his helplessness, and his ignorance of the way back to his Heavenly Father's house and happiness, and his awful danger if he rejects Jesus.

It is the knowledge of the unspeakable gift of God, of the possibilities of grace for the vilest sinner, of the Father's pitying, yearning love; of sins forgiven, guilt removed, adoption into the Father's family; illumination, consolation, guidance, keeping; depravity destroyed, cleansing through the Blood, sanctification by the baptism of the Holy Spirit; of salvation from the uttermost to the uttermost; of unbroken fellowship with the Father and His Son, Jesus Christ, through the Eternal Spirit; of a life of blessed service and fruit-bearing, and of a faith and hope that bear the spirit up over sorrows and trials, and losses and pain and sickness, enabling it at last to cry out in supreme victory and holy triumph, "O death, where is thy sting? O grave, where is thy victory? Thanks be to God, which giveth us the victory through our Lord Jesus Christ."

True zeal makes one faithful to Jesus and the souls for whom He died. It led Paul during his three years' appointment at Ephesus "to warn every one night and day with tears," to "serve the Lord with all humility," to keep back no truth that was profitable for the people, but show them and "teach them publicly and from house to house, testifying both to the Jews and also to the Greeks, repentance toward God and faith toward our Lord Jesus Christ." He was not content simply to get sinners to accept Jesus as their Savior, but taught them that "Christ in you is the hope of glory, whom we preach, warning every man and teaching every man in all wisdom, that we may present every man perfect in Christ Jesus, whereunto I labor, striving according to His working, which worketh in me mightily."

True zeal is sacrificial. Jesus, consumed with zeal for the glory of God in the saving and sanctifying of men, "was led as a lamb to the slaughter." Isaiah, who foresaw the humiliation and sacrificial life and death of Jesus, said, "He is despised and rejected of men; a man of sorrows and acquainted with grief: He was despised and we esteemed Him not. Surely He hath borne our griefs and carried our sorrows: yet we did esteem Him stricken, smitten of God and afflicted. But He was wounded for our transgressions, He was bruised for our iniquities; the chastisement of our peace was upon Him, and with His stripes we are healed. . . . The Lord hath laid on Him the iniquity of us all." He poured out His soul unto death for us, He gave His life a ransom for men. Bless His name!

Just as our Lord offered Himself a sacrifice for men, so in their measure do all soul-winners. They "fill up that which is behind of the afflictions of Christ for His body's sake, which is the Church."

The Devil held a great anniversary, at which his agents were convened to report the result of their several missions. "I let loose the wild beasts of the desert," said one, "on a caravan of Christians; and their bones are now bleaching on the sands."

"What of it" said the Devil; "their souls are all saved."

"I drove the East Wind," said another, "against a ship freighted down with Christians, and they were all drowned."

"What of it" said the Devil; "their souls were all saved."

"For ten years I tried to get a single Christian asleep," said a third, "and at last I succeeded, and left him so!"

Then the Devil shouted, and the night stars of hell sang for joy.

Equip me for the war,
And teach my hands to fight,
My simple, upright heart prepare,
And guide my words aright;

With calm and tempered zeal
Let me enforce Thy call,
And vindicate Thy gracious will
Which offers life to all.

MISSIONS SERMON

Will You Give Jesus Your Lunch?
By Paul Borthwick

Scripture: John 6:1–13, especially verse 9: "There is a lad here who has five barley loaves and two small fish, but what are they among so many?"

Introduction: People are overwhelmed in the face of vast opportunity and need. All it takes is to pick up a Sunday newspaper, or tune in to CNN to find out the latest tragedies. It is easy to feel helpless in the face of such need and opportunity, not knowing how to respond. Remember this question, "Will you give Jesus your lunch?"

1. **The Story.** Where does this question come from? Jesus was in the midst of five thousand hungry men, not counting women and children. It could have been twenty thousand hungry people! The custom in the Middle East was, if people came to you, you fed them. Phillip was practical; he knew they couldn't do it financially. Andrew said in effect, "Here is a small man with five small loaves and two small fish.". If this displayed Andrew's faith, it was small; he added, "What are they among so many?" After the miracle, however, the disciples collected twelve full baskets, one basket for each disciple. When we give everything to Jesus, He will meet our needs. Will you give Jesus your lunch?

2. **Our Response.** This passage is a foundation for five things *we* can give to Jesus to make a global difference this week.
   A. **Availability.** Our first loaf to offer is availability. Isaiah 6:1–8 is a wonderful model for how we should respond to God's holiness. In the context of worship, Isaiah experienced the forgiveness of God, and responded appropriately, "Here am I! Send me." In the midst of our worship, we should respond in the same way. In many cultures, the people worship with their hands in the air, with their palms up towards heaven conveying availability to the Lord. Are we available?
   B. **Experiences.** Our second loaf to offer is our experiences. God wants to redeem our past. Jesus called four of His disciples saying, "I will make

you fishers of men." In effect, "Your patience as a fisherman, the ability to strategize the seas and the weather for fishing, and all the skills you've learned, I will use for the kingdom's sake." If you've spent your lifetime in financial management, domestic chores, or whatever it may be, give it to the Lord and He will use it.

- C. **Prayers.** The third loaf in our lunch basket is our prayers. If we watch the news too long we wonder who is in charge, but I can tell you God is. Prayer is God's gift to remind us He is in charge. That's why Jesus says, to pray to the Lord of the harvest (Luke 10:2). Let me encourage you to have a global prayer list. Choose one foreign country and leader to pray for. Get a prayer list from your church. God works globally through your prayers.
- D. **Pain.** This is the most difficult of our loaves to give. We all have some kind of emotional or physical pains. Sometimes God does not take them away. We should respond, "Lord, here it is. I give my pain to you." Paul wrote to the Corinthians that God's comfort in his affliction helped to convey God's comfort to others (2 Cor. 1:4). Christopher Reeve is a source of hope to many handicapped and paralyzed people, not because he was healed, but because of his pain. God used Jesus' pain for our redemption; we should allow God to use ours.
- E. **Faith.** The last loaf is our faith. God uses us when we allow Him to take us where we don't necessarily have confidence. Many of us want peace and security far more than we want to be used by God. If you want God to use your life, it will require a step of faith. It is ok to be afraid, but fear should not dictate your life; faith should dictate your life. Mary Slessor, a famous missionary to Nigeria, said, "Courage is the conquering of fear by faith."

Conclusion: This week, will you give Jesus your lunch? Respond to Him, "Lord in the light of all these vast needs, I will go. I give myself to You. Use my past, use my prayers, even my pain. Give me courage to take a step of faith."

MAY 30, 2004 – PENTECOST

SUGGESTED SERMON

The Difference a Day Makes

Date preached:

By Denis Lyle

Scripture: Acts 2:1–38, especially verse 2: And suddenly there came a sound from heaven, as of a rushing mighty wind, and it filled the whole house where they were sitting.

Introduction: Can you remember one day that changed your life? Maybe a loved one died, or maybe a child was born. Pentecost was a day that changed the course of history.

1. **The Timing of the Spirit's Advent (v. 1).** Our text begins, "When the Day of Pentecost had fully come . . ." The timing was very important:
   A. **Relating to the Divine Person.** Before the Holy Spirit could come, Jesus had to be crucified (John 16:7) to deal with the plague of sin in the human race. Secondly, Jesus had to be glorified (John 7:38–39).
   B. **Relating to the Divine Promise.** The Father promised the Holy Spirit (John 14:16) because without it their task was impossible. Even with the Great Commission in their hands they would need more than willingness if the world was to be won. In the shelter of the Upper Room they could have no idea of the immeasurable task before them: the stubborn unbelief of men, the entrenched vested interests of government, commerce, and religion that would oppose them, or the cruel persecution that awaited them. Are you trying to do the Lord's work on your own?
   C. **Relating to the Divine Plan.** The Jewish Feast of Harvest, so called because it ushered in the harvesting period (Ex. 23:16), is also known as Pentecost. Remember that Jesus told the disciples to wait in Jerusalem (Acts 1:4). Why there? On this Feast of the Harvest, Jews from all around the known world gathered in this central location; this was the commencement of the divine plan to spread the gospel throughout the Gentile world!

2. **The Meaning of the Spirit's Advent (v. 12).** The Holy Spirit *came* (v. 33) and the people heard the sound of rushing wind and saw tongues of fire. The Holy Spirit *baptized* (1:5) and *filled* the believers, and then *spoke* as

they praised God in various languages. The Spirit *empowered* Peter to preach, and then He *convicted* the listeners so that 3,000 of them trusted Christ and were saved. Notice the question (v. 12), "Whatever could this mean?" Let me suggest three things:

- **A. The Reality of His Presence.** Beginning at Pentecost, the Holy Spirit did a *baptizing* work to form His body (Acts 2:41) and an *indwelling* work to fill believers. He continues His indwelling work in Christians today so that our bodies are His temple (John 14:17; 1 Cor. 6:19). He may be residing in your heart, but is He presiding? Is He the ruler of your life?
- **B. The Availability of His Power.** Jesus promised to give the disciples power through the Holy Spirit (Luke 24:49; Acts 1:8). After the Lord Jesus was crucified, the disciples went into a room and slammed the doors shut out of fear that they might be next to die on a cross. They had no peace, no contentment, and no power. But what a difference a day makes, for the Spirit filled them with power; He empowers us, too (1 Cor. 6:14–17).

3. **The Blessing of the Spirit's Advent (v. 38).** The story of Pentecost is the record of the Spirit's ministry in blessing the lives of thousands of people. Notice for example there was:
   - **A. The Blessing of Repentance in the World.** Simon Peter stood up and preached before thousands of Jerusalem citizens (2:14–39). Do you remember how Peter reacted the night Jesus was arrested? One little servant girl totally intimidated the rugged fisherman. Three times he denied Jesus. But after Pentecost, Peter delivered a powerful message

>>> *sermon continued on following page*

APPROPRIATE HYMNS AND SONGS

Fresh Anointing, Robert D. Wells; © 1990 Tennessee Music and Printing Company, Admin. by SpiritSound Music Group.

Pentecostal Power, Dale Matthews/Michael Frazier; © 1996 New Spring Publishing, Admin. by Brentwood-Benson Music Publishing.

Send the Fire, William Booth/Lex Loizides; © 1994 Kingsway's Thankyou Music, Admin. by EMI Christian Music Publishing.

Spirit of the Living God, Daniel Iverson; © 1935. Renewed 1963 Birdwing Music, Admin. by EMI Christian Music Publishing.

so that, "... they were cut to the heart..." (2:37) and three thousand of them repented and were saved (v. 41)!

B. **The Blessing of Revival in the Church**. In the lives of these early, Spirit-filled believers, we see a fearlessness to speak (2:14), a joyfulness to sing (2:46–47), a holiness to shine (4:13), a willingness to sacrifice (4:34–35), a readiness to serve (6:3), a steadfastness to stand (4:29), and a yieldedness to suffer for Christ (7:60).

Conclusion: In the Gospel accounts, the disciples never really had it all together. On one glorious day the Holy Spirit filled them with the Spirit and they became bold servants and witnesses of Jesus Christ. Maybe you have never yielded your life to Jesus Christ, allowing His Holy Spirit to take control, but what a difference a day can make; today could be the start of your Spirit-filled relationship with Christ.

FOR THE BULLETIN

- This is the probable date of the death of Eusebius, in A.D. 339. He was 74, and is known as the "Father of Church History" because of his fascinating 10-volume record of the early church. ❁ Pope John XXIII was deposed on this day in 1415. He was formerly a soldier, pirate, and lawyer who was crowned Pope in 1410. Unfortunately, there were two other popes vying for dominance and John was eventually deposed and held prisoner in Germany. He was set free in 1419, but died soon afterward. ❁ Jerome of Prague, Bohemian Reformer and friend of John Hus, was condemned and burned at the stake on this day in 1416. ❁ Joan of Arc was burned at the stake on this day in 1431. Her last words were: "Jesus! Jesus!" ❁ In 1516, Desiderius Erasmus published his Greek New Testament. "Would that these were translated into every language," he said. In studying Erasmus's New Testament, ministers found themselves returning to the truth of the Bible. Erasmus's translation became Luther's fodder, and the primary source for his German translation of the Bible (and later, of Tyndale's English Version). Erasmus initially supported Luther, but retreated when he saw the church splitting. On May 30, 1519, he wrote Luther, suggesting that it *might be wiser of you to denounce those who misuse the Pope's authority than to censure the Pope himself.... Old institutions cannot be uprooted in an instant. Quiet argument may do more than wholesale condemnation. Keep cool. Do not get angry.* ❁ The missionary hymn, "From Greenland's Icy Mountains" was written on this day in 1819 by Anglican minister Reginald Heber. ❁ Scottish pulpiteer Thomas Chalmers died on May 30, 1847.

STATS, STORIES AND MORE

Power for Today
See how He came on the day of Pentecost! It is not carnal to pray that He may come again and that the place may be shaken. I believe Pentecost was but a specimen day. I think the Church has made this woeful mistake that Pentecost was a miracle that is not to be repeated. I believe now if we looked on Pentecost as a specimen day and began to pray, we should have the old Pentecostal fire here . . . —Dwight L. Moody

The Difference a Day Makes
On October 31, 1517, Martin Luther nails his ninety-five Theses on the door of the Castle Church in Wittenberg, Germany; the Protestant Reformation is launched. On December 7, 1941, Japanese aircraft attack Pearl Harbor, wiping out American air units; America enters the war. On July 16, 1942, at Los Alamos, New Mexico, a tremendous blast rushes out across the desert; a huge, mushroom-shaped cloud lifts heavenward and nuclear weaponry becomes a reality. On September 11, 2001, the Twin Towers of the World Trade Center in New York collapse after a terrorist attack; thousands lose their lives. What a difference a day makes!—Denis Lyle

Spirit-filled Prayer
The late Vance Havner once said, "We are not going to move this world by criticism of it nor conformity to it, but by the combustion within it of lives ignited by the Spirit of God. We ought to be praying, 'Lord, take the Word; Spirit of God, set it on fire.'"

Kids Talk

Can you think of anything that is invisible? Let's make a list. I can think of some things. (Spray some cologne into the air). Can you see that smell? No, smells are invisible. (Turn on a portable radio). Can you see those radio waves in the air? No, they are invisible, but the radio knows they are there. (Fan the children with a funeral parlor fan). Can you see the wind or the air? No, but we can feel it. Well, in the same way, God is here. His Holy Spirit is in this room, just like a fragrance, just like the wind, just like radio waves. Let's get on His frequency this morning.

WORSHIP HELPS

Call to Worship:
But you shall receive power when the Holy Spirit has come upon you; and you shall be witnesses to Me in Jerusalem, and in all Judea and Samaria, and to the end of the earth (Acts 1:8).

Appropriate Scripture Readings:
Joel 2:28–32
Luke 24:44–49
John 16:5–15
Galatians 5:16–25

Offertory Prayer:
We aren't going to ask for anything in this prayer, Dear Lord, not even for your blessings on this offering, for we know that You always bless that which is rendered wholeheartedly unto You. We just want to thank You today for Your provisions, for our daily bread, for our weekly needs, and for our abundant life in Christ.

Benediction:
Come, Holy Spirit, heavenly Dove, / With all Thy quick'ning powers; / Kindle a flame of sacred love / In these cold hearts of ours.
—Isaac Watts

Growing in the Knowledge of Christ
By Peter Grainger

Date preached:

SCRIPTURE: 2 Peter 1, 3; especially 3:18.

INTRODUCTION: Peter highlights two areas of knowledge concerning Jesus which are of vital importance and are under attack, relating to his First Coming and also his Second Coming:

1. The Facts about His First Coming (1:12–21). Peter reminds his readers of past events which are *facts*, not *fiction*. These create a *firm foundation* for the *faith*!
   A. Evidence from Eyewitnesses: Both Seen and Heard (1:16–18).
   B. Predictions from Prophets: Spoken by Men, Originating with God (1:19–21).
2. The Facts about His Second Coming (3:1–16). Peter reminds his readers of future events to stimulate us towards holiness (see vv. 14–16).
   A. Judgment of the Present Heavens and Earth by Fire (3:3–10, 12).
   B. Renewal of Heaven and Earth (3:13).

CONCLUSION: Grow in knowledge of Jesus Christ or you will fall into error (vv. 17–18).

Identifying Immaturity
By Melvin Worthington

Date preached:

SCRIPTURE: 1 Corinthians 3

INTRODUCTION: Spiritual immaturity is rampant in the church today. While it is normal to enter God's family as an infant (with all the childlike characteristics), it is a tragedy to remain a spiritual infant manifesting the marks of immaturity throughout one's Christian experience.

1. The Problem (1 Cor. 3:1–2). Paul clashes with the problem of spiritual immaturity in 1 Corinthians 3. Their spiritual immaturity limited what Paul could speak to them. *Shallowness, superficiality, selfishness,* and *stubbornness* diaper those who refuse to come to terms with Christian growth.
2. The Portrait (1 Cor. 3:3–4). Paul's portrait of spiritual immaturity is stark but convincing. Such immaturity is characterized by *inability, impulsiveness, insensitiveness, impatience, insecurity, ingratitude, and ignorance.*
3. The Peril (1 Cor. 3:4–23). Paul talks of the perils of immaturity. Spiritual immaturity results in envy, strife, division and false loyalties. Immature Christians walk guided by the principles that govern men rather than by the Spirit of God. Spiritual immaturity brings *division, dissension,* and *disputation.* Spiritual maturity brings *holiness, harmony,* and *happiness.*

CONCLUSION: It is time we grow up. May God give us a spirit of *patience, perception,* and *perseverance* as we seek to become mature Christians.

JUNE 6, 2004

SUGGESTED SERMON

The Five B's of Purity

Date preached:

By Woodrow Kroll

Scripture: Psalm 24, especially verses 3–4a: Who may ascend into the hill of the LORD? Or who may stand in His holy place? He who has clean hands and a pure heart...

Introduction: Whatever happened to purity? It's a rare commodity today, but as believers, we should be reflecting the character of God. We need to be clean because God is clean. The prerequisite for service is cleanliness. It's also the prerequisite for blessing. But how on earth are we going to remain pure in a world like this?

1. **Be Careful What You See (2 Sam. 11:1–5).** David's sin began with simple sight. He rose one night, walked on the rooftop, and looked on the houses below. On the south side of Jerusalem is the little village of Silwan, with houses built one on top of another, directly across the valley from where David's city was located. There David saw Bathsheba. Had he not seen her bathing, he would not have committed this sin. It's true that David didn't go out looking for Bathsheba. He accidentally saw her. But sometimes accidents happen on purpose, don't they, like in a motel room, flipping through the channels on television? You need to be careful what you see (see Job 31:1). Long before the advent of television, philosopher Søren Kierkegaard wrote: "Suppose someone invented an instrument, a convenient little talking tube which, say, could be heard all over the whole land. I wonder if the police would not forbid it, fearing that the whole country would become mentally deranged if it were used." Kierkegaard's words have come true. David Frost, who made his living on television, said, "Television is an invention that permits you to be entertained in your living room by people you wouldn't have in your home." Many movies and TV programs aren't fit for human consumption, let alone for a Christian. We must be careful what we see.

2. **Be Careful Where You Go (Judg. 16:1).** Samson was a great champion for God, but his feet led him into trouble. In this passage, he went to Gaza,

one of the Philistine cities. Samson had no business there. In Gaza, he saw a harlot and went to her. Later he went to the Valley of Sorek where he met Delilah (v. 4). Samson's problem is that he went to all the wrong places. If we go to the wrong places, we'll see the wrong things and become the wrong kind of people. (See 2 Tim. 2:22.)

3. **Be Careful What You Desire (Judg. 14:1–2).** The greatest achievements in life are accomplished by those with passion. Do you remember Bob Feller? As a child, Bob loved to throw a baseball. By age five, he had spent hours every day pitching through a hole in a barn wall. At 10, his father provided him a playing field on the family farm. By thirteen, Bob was pitching for a local team. At age seventeen, he began playing for the Cleveland Indians. During his career, he had 266 wins and set a record 348 strikeouts in one season. Today he belongs to Baseball's Hall of Fame. That's not just due to his abilities, but also to the fact that he had one desire—baseball. What's your desire? What drives your life? If our desire is to be clean before God, we're careful what we see, where we go, and what we want.

4. **Be Careful What You Think About (Eph. 4:21–24).** If being clean before God is not on your list of things to do today, you can think about anything you want. But if losing your purity concerns you, you must be careful what you think. Emerson said, "A man is what he thinks about all day long." Marcus Aurelius said, "A man's life is what his thoughts make of it." The Bible says, "As a man thinks in his heart [his mind], so is he." (See Phil.

>>> *sermon continued on following page*

APPROPRIATE HYMNS AND SONGS

O Love That Will Not Let Me Go, George Matheson/Albert Lister Peace; Public Domain.

A Pure Heart, Rusty Nelson; © 1992 Integrity's Hosanna! Music.

All Creatures of Our God and King, St. Francis of Assisi/William H. Draper; Public Domain.

Breathe on Me Breath of God, Edwin Hatch/Robert Jackson; Public Domain.

Pure in Heart, Don Harris; © 1991 Integrity's Hosanna! Music.

4:8). Are you pleased with the things that have entered your mind this week?

5. **Be Careful Why You Live (1 John 3:1–3).** Does life make sense for you? Or, as Shakespeare said, it is "a tale told by an idiot, full of sound and fury, signifying nothing"? One of the best ways to lose your purity is to have nothing eternal to live for. According to 1 John 1:3, those with who have this hope in Christ purify themselves.

Conclusion: If you don't know Christ as Savior, how wonderful to know He can make you pure. If you're a believer today, how wonderful to know He can keep you pure. He can help us live practical lives of daily purity, for He himself said, "Blessed are the pure in heart, for they shall see God" (Matt. 5:8).

FOR THE BULLETIN

❈ Philip William Otterbein was baptized on this day in 1726, as an infant in Germany. Later, at age 26, Otterbein felt called to immigrate to America to do missionary work. He became a noted pioneer pastor to Germans in America and the father of the Church of the United Brethren in Christ (later part of the Evangelical United Brethren Church and now a part of the United Methodist Church). ❈ John Wesley preached on his father's tombstone at Epworth, England, on this day in 1742, to a "vast multitude gathered from all parts." Remembering the harsh and disappointing times his father, a local minister, had endured in Epworth, Wesley wrote: "O let none think his labor of love is lost because the fruit does not immediately appear." ❈ June 6, 1844, marks the founding of the YMCA in London under the leadership of a local merchant named George Williams who had conducted weekly meetings of prayer and Bible study for young men. The original purpose of London's YMCA was "to seek to win over young men to the faith and love of Jesus Christ." ❈ June 6, 1882, is the date of the composition of "O Love that Wilt Not Let Me Go" by George Matheson (see Worship Helps). ❈ H. C. Dillon and his new wife, Margaret, went to Central America as missionaries. When Dillon died of yellow fever, Margaret remained in Honduras, training local evangelists. Fifteen years passed without a furlough, then she planned a trip home. While packing, she was stricken with yellow fever and was carried 36 miles to a missions station, arriving on June 6, 1913. She died two days later.

STATS, STORIES AND MORE

More from Woodrow Kroll:
Somebody sent this to me; I don't know where it came from: "The TV is my shepherd; my spiritual growth shall want. It maketh me to sit down and do nothing for His name's sake. It keepeth me from doing my duty as a Christian, because it presenteth so many good programs that I must see. It restoreth my knowledge of the things of this world and keepeth me from the study of God's Word. It leadeth me into the paths of failing to attend church. Yea, though I live to be 100, I shall keep viewing my TV so long as it shall work, for it is my closest companion. Its sounds and its pictures, they comfort me. It presenteth entertainment before me and keepeth me from doing important things with my family. It filleth my head with ideas which differ from the Word of God. Surely no good thing will come of my life because of so many wasted hours, and I shall dwell in my regrets and remorse forever."

Woodrow Kroll and Charlie Brown
"Life is a mystery, Charlie Brown," said Lucy. "Do you know the answer?" Charlie Brown replied, "Be kind. Don't smoke. Be prompt. Smile a lot. Eat sensibly. Avoid cavities and mark your ballot carefully. Avoid too much sun. Send overseas packages early. Love all creatures above and below. Insure your belongings and try to keep the ball low." Well, it's obvious that Charlie Brown had a lot of platitudes, but the meaning of life is not just platitudes. We live by the resolve that there is more to life than just 70 or 80 years. There is a whole eternity out there. We want to be clean before the Lord God.

WORSHIP HELPS

Call to Worship:
Consecrate yourselves, therefore, and be holy. As He who called you is holy, you also be holy in all your conduct. (Lev. 20:7 and 1 Pet. 1:15, ESV)

Hymn Story:
Today is the anniversary of "O Love That Wilt Not Let Me Go," by George Matheson. As a teenager, Matheson had battled deteriorating eyesight. During his graduate studies for Christian ministry he became totally blind. The worst blow, however, came when his fiancée, unwilling to be married to a blind man, broke their engagement. George never married, and the pain of that rejection never totally left him. Years later, his sister came to him, announcing her engagement. He rejoiced with her, but his mind went back to his own heartache. He consoled himself in thinking of God's love which is never limited, never conditional, never withdrawn, and never uncertain. Out of this experience it is said he wrote this hymn.

He later related: "My hymn was composed in the manse of Innelan [Argyleshire, Scotland] on the evening of the 6th of June, 1882, when I was 40 years of age. I was alone in the manse at that time. It was the night of my sister's marriage, and the rest of the family were staying overnight in Glasgow. Something happened to me, which was known only to myself, and which caused me the most severe mental suffering. The hymn was the fruit of that suffering. It was the quickest bit of work I ever did in my life. I had the impression of having it dictated to me by some inward voice rather than of working it out myself. I am quite sure that the whole work was completed in five minutes, and equally sure that it never received at my hands any retouching or correction. I have no natural gift of rhythm. All the other verses I have ever written are manufactured articles; this came like a dayspring from on high."

Additional Sermons and Lesson Ideas

Jacob's Final Thoughts
By David Jeremiah

Date preached:

SCRIPTURE: Genesis 48:1–22

INTRODUCTION: The death of Jacob gives to us direction concerning the great issues of aging and preparing for death. Four directions occupied Jacob's attention in Genesis 48.

1. He Looked Backward in Gratitude. As we get older, we reminisce. Jacob took a broad sweeping glance back through his life.
   A. He Remembered Bethel—His Greatest Landmark (v. 3).
   B. He Remembered Rachel—His Greatest Love (v. 7).
   C. He Remembered the Angel—His Greatest Lesson (v. 15).
2. He Looked Upward in Faith (vv. 3, 11, 15, 20–21). Jacob had become a God-centered person in his older years.
3. He Looked Outward in Love (vv. 10–15). He loved his children, especially his grandsons, Ephraim and Manasseh, and wanted to leave them a blessing.
4. He Looked Forward in Hope (v. 21). Jacob had a vision for his family that would reach out into the future.

CONCLUSION: Someday we'll stand where Jacob stood, and I pray I'll be able to look back in gratitude, upward in faith, outward in love, and forward in hope.

Obligated to Obey
By Melvin Worthington

Date preached:

SCRIPTURE: Luke 5:1–11

INTRODUCTION: These verses record the miraculous catch of fishes, a miracle that shows the Lord's complete dominion over the animal creation. Everything is His and everything obeys Him in all things. It teaches us:

1. We Must Hear His Word (vv. 1–4). The *circumstances* (vv. 1–4) include the *place,* the *pulpit,* and the *preaching.* The *command* (v. 4) includes *launch* out, *let* down, and *lift* up.
2. We Must Heed His Word (vv. 5–9). The *compliance* (v. 5) includes *full, faithful, fearless, focused,* and *fervent* obedience. The *catch* (vv. 6–7) includes the *problem* and *partners.* The *confession* (vv. 8–9) includes the *action, attitude* and *astonishment* of Peter.
3. We Must Herald His Word (vv. 10–11). Jesus calmed their fears (v. 10), changed their focus (v. 10) and challenged their faith (v. 11).

CONCLUSION: The Lord Jesus Christ *desires, demands, directs, delights in, and deserves* our obedience.

CONVERSATIONS IN A PASTOR'S STUDY

The Pastor and His Children's Ministry

An interview with Vicki Wiley, Director of Children's Ministries of First Presbyterian Church of Honolulu, Hawaii, and editor of the *Children's Ministry Sourcebook*

Vicki, why is children's ministry important to the success of a pastorate?

Children's ministry is very important to the pastor! The foundation of faith formation lies in what happens with the children while the adults are enjoying worship. When the children are in age-appropriate ministry learning to worship, hearing Bible stories, and being taught what a Christian worldview is all about, the pastorate benefits because the family as a whole is the recipient of ministry.

How can the children's ministry strengthen the whole church?

It's important for the church to look at faith formation as something that begins at birth and is critically important through the childhood years. The foundation of that is having a good children's ministry. Today's parents are very discriminating regarding the kinds of programs and activities they want their children involved in; they are always looking for the very best options for their children. When families come to your church, they look carefully at the children's ministry. If there's an appearance that their children will not only be nourished spiritually but also begin to form Christian relationships and be encouraged in their faith walk, parents will want to bring them. When parents know that their children are being cared for and loved they can relax and concentrate on their own worship experience.

Do children's workers often feel disconnected from the pastor?

Children's ministers can sometimes feel isolated from the pastor. Because pastors are so busy on Sunday, they need to take advantage of other opportunities to connect with the children's ministry staff. My pastor comes to important children's ministry meetings for about 5 minutes just to drop in to say, "You are appreciated," to my staff of volunteers. His words are not nearly as important as his presence—because his very presence makes the workers feel that their ministry is valued and important to the overall ministry of the church.

What can a pastor do to encourage the children's ministry?

My pastor encourages me just by affirming my ministry and my decisions. When I want to try something new, he encourages me to do it. When difficult situations come up, he backs me and has faith in what I decide. He is available when I need to discuss something, no matter how busy he is. At the same time, I respect his schedule and ministry and don't expect him to listen to every little thing from me.

What can we do to better coordinate the Sunday sermon with what the kids are studying?

I've always had a great picture in my mind of the whole family going home on Sunday morning talking about how they all interpreted what was learned at church. Of course, learning the same Bible text each week would be difficult since there are some stories that children have difficulty learning. But if the same "concepts" were present—God's love, His calling in our lives, living the Christian life, etc.,—the whole family could be involved in conversation together. Beginning next year, 2005, the *Preacher's Sourcebook* and the *Children's Ministry Sourcebook* will attempt to do just that. Rob Morgan will suggest the sequence of sermons that will be in the *Preacher's Sourcebook* and I will respond in the *Children's Ministry Sourcebook* with age-appropriate Bible lessons and activities and information that will touch the heart and life of the child. We've got to do all we can to strengthen the whole family and to bring these little ones to a strong faith in Christ.

JUNE 13, 2004

SUGGESTED SERMON
What Jesus Says to Frazzled People

Date preached:

Scripture: Luke 10:38–42, especially verses 41–42: "Martha, Martha, you are worried and troubled about many things. But one thing is needed, and Mary has chosen that good part, which will not be taken away from her."

Introduction: Fatigue in one of our most common complaints. Too many people are juggling multiple responsibilities while getting too little sleep and not enough exercise. Recently the National Transportation Safety Board announced that operator fatigue is a primary cause of one hundred thousand traffic accidents every year in the United States, resulting in fifteen hundred deaths annually. On our American waterways, fatigue accounts for 16% of all accidents; and on our rails, fatigue has caused twenty terrible train wrecks in the last ten years. In today's text, Jesus met a frazzled woman and talked to her about her condition. Martha lived in the town of Bethany, just outside Jerusalem. How hard-working and caring and practical she was. But Martha had some problems—not one single problem, but five overlapping ones that we can uncover by carefully reading this text.

1. **When We're Like Martha, We're:**
    A. **Distracted.** Verses 39–40 say: "But Martha was distracted with much serving." The Greek word is a compound of two smaller terms, the verb *to draw* and the word *around* or *away*. It is the idea of being pulled in every direction. Martha was pulled in every direction. Most of us can identify with that. We allow ourselves to become too busy, busier than God intends, busier than is necessary, busier than is wise. That's why so many people are tired today.
    B. **Doubting.** In verse 40, Martha said something shocking: "Lord, do you not care. . . ?" How often, while being pulled in all directions, do we momentarily doubt God's caring and concern? She was like the Psalmist who wrote: "No one cares for my soul" (Ps. 142:4).
    C. **Feeling Self-Pity.** "Lord," said Martha, "do you not care that my sister has left me to serve alone?" Of course, Martha *did* need help. No one denies that. Many hands make light work. The running of a household and the

entertaining of guests require that every member of the family do his or her part. But Martha's agenda didn't line up with the agenda of Christ. He wasn't so concerned about the seasoning in the beans, the dust on the floor, or the way the napkins were folded. He was concerned that His life-changing Word get out, that those in the house hear what He had to say. That left poor Martha feeling abandoned in the kitchen where she fell into a grudging mood of irritable self-pity.

D. **Worrying**. In responding, the Lord pointed out another difficulty: "Martha, Martha, you are worried. . . ." Someone said: "Worry is a small trickle of fear that meanders through the mind until it cuts a channel into which all other thoughts are drained."

E. **Troubled.** Jesus used the word "troubled" to describe Martha (v. 42). The NIV says, "You are . . . upset about many things." I have the feeling the "many things" included more than just preparations for a meal. Perhaps Martha was encumbered by many burdens we don't know about. No wonder we identify with her—pulled in all directions, questioning God's power and goodness, sinking into self-pity, worried, and upset about many things.

2. When We're Like Mary

Jesus' prescription was a little dose of Mary-ness: "One thing is needed, and Mary has chosen that good part." Mary was sitting at Jesus' feet, hearing His word. That implies three things:

A. **Submission.** The phrase "at his feet" occurs sixteen times in the Bible, and it often implies an attitude of submission and trust. Mary could have sat on the sofa next to Christ, but she had a quiet, trusting, submissive heart, expressed by being at His feet.

>>> *sermon continued on following page*

APPROPRIATE HYMNS AND SONGS

Take Time to Be Holy, William D. Longstaff/George C. Stebbins; Public Domain.

Be Still and Know, Lex Loizides; © 1995 Kingsway's Thankyou Music (Admin. by EMI Christian Music Publishing.)

A Quiet Place, Ralph Carmichael; © 1969 Bud John Songs, Inc. (Admin. by EMI Christian Music Publishing.)

Does Jesus Care, Frank E. Graeff/J. Lincoln Hall; Public Domain.

Rest in Your Love, Gary Sadler; © 1996 Integrity's Hosanna! Music.

B. **Devotion.** See the similar scene in John 12, when this same Mary is at a dinner party, once again sitting at Jesus feet, washing His feet with perfume, and wiping them with her hair.
   C. **Communion.** Mary was listening to His Word. She was having her quiet time, having her Bible study. She was in the prayer closet, feeding on her daily manna. The best way to be fresh and refreshing to others is to learn to sit at the Lord's feet with an open Bible before us, meeting Him personally each day so He can give us a word for our hearts.

Conclusion: The great lesson of this story is that being occupied *with* Christ is more important than being occupied *for* Christ, and it is certainly better than being *pre*-occupied with *self*. Are you so busy and upset that you're neglecting the cultivation of the soul and failing to do that one thing that Jesus was needful of and the most important of all? As the old song says: *Take time to be holy, the world rushes on.*

FOR THE BULLETIN

❋ June 13, 323 B.C., is the date of the death of Alexander the Great in Babylon. ❋ On this day in 1525, Martin Luther married Katherine von Bora, 26, a former nun who had escaped her convent in a fish barrel. The union was a very happy one, and Luther owed much to the calm cheerfulness of his wife. ❋ On June 13, 1793, William Carey set sail from Dover, England, for India, aboard the *Kron Princessa Maria*. His companion, Dr. John Thomas, wrote: "The ship is here! The signal made;—the guns fired—and we are going with a fair wind. Finally, my dear brethren and sisters, farewell! May the God of Jacob be ours and yours by sea and land, for time and eternity." Carey, less bombastically but equally optimistically, wrote: "A large field opens on every side. Oh, that many laborers may be thrust out into the vineyard of our Lord Jesus Christ." ❋ June 13, 1812, is the birthday of John Hunt, missionary to Fiji. ❋ In 1858, John and Elizabeth Freeman, Presbyterian missionaries in India, found themselves stranded in a dangerous area when a nearby military regiment mutinied and murdered British citizens in the region. Elizabeth wrote in a final letter, "Can only say good-bye, pray for us, will write next mail if we live; if not you will hear from some other source." On the morning of June 13, they were shot by national Indians who resented the presence of foreigners in their country. ❋ June 13, 1893, is the birth date of Dorothy Sayers, novelist, in England.

STATS, STORIES AND MORE

If Jesus Came to Your House

Of course Martha was distracted. If Jesus were coming to your house, you'd be distracted, too. When he was president, Jimmy Carter, in his travels to various cities, would sometimes stay in someone's private home. He said that spending the night with a typical American family helped him stay in touch with what was really happening in the nation. He would sit in their living room and talk with them after supper, then sleep in the guest room. It was always a circus, with hundreds of reporters and Secret Service agents and the like, but it wasn't a bad public relations idea. If the President of the United States were coming to spend the night with us tonight, we'd be a nervous wreck trying to get everything ready for him. But what if the most important, the most famous, the most admired man in the history of the human race were coming to your house? Jesus Christ? We are like Martha and identify with her, but we can also learn from her to "beware the barrenness of busyness."

WORSHIP HELPS

Call to Worship:
We give you thanks, O Lord God Almighty, the One who is and who was and who is to come, because You have taken Your great power and reigned (Rev. 11:17).

Pastoral Prayer:
Lord, God of stillness and silence, God of peace and quiet, You have told us to be still and to know that You are God. We recall the words of Jesus to His disciples that they come apart for awhile to rest. We recognize that You have given one day in seven as a blessed Sabbath to refresh and restore the hearts of your children. Forgive our barrenness and busyness, our frantic coming and going. Teach us, O Lord, to seek first Your kingdom and Your righteousness, knowing that everything else we need will be added to us. Calm our souls, and teach us the peacefulness of Your green pastures and still waters. We pray in Jesus name, Amen.

Appropriate Poem:
Though it was written in c. 1882, the words of William Longstaff's poem, "Take Time to Be Holy," seems ideally suited as an exhortation for our own day:

Take time to be holy, the world rushes on;
Spend much time in secret, with Jesus alone.
By looking to Jesus, like Him thou shalt be;
Thy friends in thy conduct His likeness shall see.

Take time to be holy, let Him be thy Guide;
And run not before Him, whatever betide.
In joy or in sorrow, still follow the Lord,
And, looking to Jesus, still trust in His Word.

Take time to be holy, be calm in thy soul,
Each thought and each motive beneath His control.
Thus led by His Spirit to fountains of love,
Thou soon shalt be fitted for service above.

Additional Sermons and Lesson Ideas

Him Who
Date preached:

SCRIPTURE: 1 John 2:13

INTRODUCTION: Jesus Christ is given many names in the Bible, and many titles. One of the most interesting ways of studying the wonders of His person is by noticing the "Him Who's" in the Bible.

1. Him Who Is from the Beginning—1 John 2:13
2. Him of Whom Moses Wrote—John 1:45
3. Him Who Called You Out of Darkness and Into Marvelous Light —1 Peter 2:9
4. Him Who Saved Us and Washed Us—Revelation 1:5
5. Him Who Is Able to Keep You from Stumbling— Jude 24
6. Him Who Is Ready to Judge the Living and the Dead—1 Peter 4:5
7. Him Who Fills All in All—Ephesians 1:23

CONCLUSION: This is "Him Who" we worship and serve today, the Friend of Sinners.

Tried, Tested, and Thankful
Date preached:

By Melvin Worthington

SCRIPTURE: Psalm 100:4; Daniel 6:10; Romans 1:8; Colossians 1:3–5

INTRODUCTION: The apostle Paul begins most of his epistles with thanksgiving. Christians are exhorted to enter His gates with thanksgiving, and into His courts with praise (Ps. 100:4). We're to be thankful for:

1. The Brethren (Believers). In his epistles Paul repeatedly affirmed his appreciation, admiration, and applauded fellow believers.
2. The Buffetings. God's grace is sufficient to see us through times of testing, trials, and temptations.
3. The Beloved, God's unspeakable gift (2 Cor. 9:15).
4. The Blessings. Ephesians 1:3 indicates that Christians have been blessed with all spiritual blessings in heavenly places in Christ Jesus.
5. The Burdens. Christians are sometimes tested and tried by inescapable burdens, but God enables them to bear them with victory.

CONCLUSION: Thanksgiving indicates a personal relationship to, reliance on, and reverence for God. Thanksgiving is more than a formula. It is the spontaneous outburst of praise to God for what He has done for us, to us, in us, and through us.

JUNE 20, 2004 — FATHER'S DAY

SUGGESTED SERMON
Ordinary People / Extraordinary Praying
By Timothy Beougher   *Date preached:*

Scripture: James 5:16–18, 1 Kings 17–18; especially James 5:16b: The effective, fervent prayer of a righteous man avails much.

Introduction: Our verses for today apply to everyone in this congregation, but on this Father's Day we should realize the incredible need for praying dads. I'm sure the fathers here today often question their ability to really make a difference. We read stories of great Bible heroes like Moses, Joshua, Elijah, and Paul, but we think they're out of our league. But notice the first part of James 5:17, "Elijah was a man with a nature like ours . . ." We have a tendency to elevate biblical characters to a super-human status. The Bible is very clear: God doesn't use extra-ordinary people; He uses ordinary people in extra-ordinary ways.

1. **Pray (James 5:17).** Elijah was a man just like us, in all our frailty and weakness. Do we find it hard to pray? So did he, but he prayed. Do we ever doubt? So did he, but he prayed. Do we ever get discouraged? So did he, but he prayed. Do we ever grow weary? So did he, but he prayed. Elijah didn't make excuses, he prayed; so should we. Throughout this epistle, James exhorts us to pray: when we need wisdom, when we are suffering, when we are tempted, before we speak, about the future, when we are joyful, when we are sick, etc. Do we live this way? Is prayer the environment of our life, the climate in which we live? Prayer should be our first choice, not our last resort.

2. **Pray with a Clean Heart (James 5:16).** Elijah is given as an example of a "righteous man," whose prayer is powerful and effective. James does not mean "sinless perfection" when he uses the term "righteous," but a right relationship with God. When we repent of our sins and place our faith and trust in Jesus Christ, He transfers His perfect righteousness to us. Have you trusted Christ? James also refers to a practical righteousness; we should confess our sins to one another. Not to everyone, but to trusted believers who will hold us accountable and build us up in Christ.

3. **Pray Earnestly (James 5:17).** In Elijah's days, King Ahab and Queen Jezebel led Israel away from the true God to worship the false god Baal. Baal was the "god" of rain. The people believed Baal controlled the heavens: the thunder and lightning, and especially the rain. Elijah prayed that God would withhold rain from the land to cause them to turn back to the true God. Notice that he prayed, "earnestly," literally in the Greek, "he prayed in prayer," a deliberate repetition of the words for emphasis. When was the last time you "wrestled with God" in earnest, heaven-moving prayer?

4. **Pray Specifically (James 5:17–18).** Elijah prayed for drought; it came. Elijah prayed for rain; it came. He didn't pray, "Lord, bless the weather," but specifically, for God to withhold the rain. Sometimes we must pray in detail.

5. **Pray in Accordance with God's Will (1 Kin. 17:2; 18:1).** The Lord spoke to Elijah concerning the drought (17:2) and the rain (18:1). He prayed in accordance with God's Word. Sometimes we do know God's will. He has revealed some of His will clearly in Scripture for us to overcome temptation, to be patient in trials, and to be bold witnesses. We can pray these and other prayers with full confidence, but praying that God will give us a new job may or may not be in His will. God will always answer, but sometimes His answer is yes, sometimes no, and sometimes wait. Trust God to answer your prayers according to His will.

6. **Pray with God's Honor in View (1 Kin. 18:36–37).** What was the motivation of Elijah's prayers in 1 Kings 17–18? That God would be glorified and

>>> *sermon continued on following page*

APPROPRIATE HYMNS AND SONGS

Father to Son, Brian Doerkson; © 1994 Mercy/Vineyard Publishing.

In the Circle of Each Home, Bryan Jeffery Leech; © 1976 Fred Bock Music Company.

Prayer for Families, Claire Cloninger/Margaret Moody; © 1991 Word Music Group.

We Will Draw Near, Don Harris/Martin J. Nystrom; © 1996 Integrity's Hosanna! Music.

Sweet Hour of Prayer, William W. Walford/William B. Bradbury; Public Domain.

honored. Elijah prayed that it might not rain because of his zeal for God's glory in the midst of the people's idolatry. Don't we live in an idolatrous generation? What better motivation for our prayers than for God's glory to shine through our sinful society (Pss. 115:1; 83:18)?

Conclusion: Elijah was a man with the same nature as ours and his prayers brought repentance to a nation! Are you an ordinary dad? Think of what your prayers can do! No matter who you are, whether you join a prayer chain or make an altar each morning at your bedside, pray! Then watch God work.

FOR THE BULLETIN

❋ On June 20, 404, John Chrysostom, Archbishop of Constantinople and one of Christian history's greatest preachers, was exiled from the city, never to return. He ended up in the town of Cucusus, in the Armenian mountains, where he wrote: "In spite of endless contrivances, I could not shake off the pernicious effects of the cold . . . I underwent extreme sufferings, perpetual vomiting . . . loss of appetite, and constant sleeplessness." ❋ The Pied Piper of Hamelin was a real man, but there was nothing enchanting about him. Historian William Manchester says, "He was horrible, a psychopath and pederast who, on June 20, 1484, spirited away 130 children in the Saxon village of Hammel and used them in unspeakable ways. Accounts of the aftermath vary. According to some, his victims were never seen again; others told of dismembered little bodies found scattered in the forest underbrush." ❋ George Whitefield was ordained in Gloucester Cathedral on June 20, 1736. ❋ The daughter of Christian philanthropist, George Muller, became ill on this day in 1853. Muller later wrote, "In July, 1853, it pleased the Lord to try my faith in a way in which it had not been tried. My beloved daughter and only child . . . was taken ill on June 20th . . . On July 3rd there seemed no hope for recovery. Now was the trial of faith. But faith triumphed. My beloved wife and I were enabled to give her up into the hands of the Lord . . . . I was enabled to delight myself in the will of God; for I felt perfectly sure, that, if the Lord took this beloved daughter, it would be best for her parents, best for herself, and more for the glory of God than if she lived." The little girl eventually recovered.

STATS, STORIES AND MORE

Praying Dads

Pam Frye, children's pastor at Battlefield Parkway Church of the Nazarene in Fort Oglethorpe, Georgia, is one of eleven children, many of whom strayed badly during the adolescent and early adult years. Her father, however, was a man of prayer who begged the Lord for his children to all be saved and happy in Jesus Christ. "He prayed all his children into the kingdom," Pam said, "the last four coming to the Lord after his death." D. L. Moody once wrote, "Though we may not live to see the answer to our prayers, if we cry mightily to God, the answer will come." Rev. E. M. Bounds said: "Prayers are deathless. The lips that uttered them may be closed in death, the heart that felt them may have ceased to beat, but the prayers live before God, and God's heart is set on them and prayers outlive the lives of those who uttered them; outlive a generation, outlive an age, outlive a world . . . Fortunate are they whose fathers and mothers have left them a wealthy patrimony of prayer."

Answering Prayer

Someone has summarized how God answers different prayers: If the request is wrong, God says no. If the timing is wrong, God says slow. If you are wrong, God says grow. When the request, the timing, and you are right, God says go!

Someone Once Said . . .

God sovereignly delights to answer the passionate prayers of his children. This is not to suggest that he delights in manufactured passion, nor that passion is a meritorious work. Nor are we suggesting that sweaty, frantic prayer is necessarily pleasing to God. But real passion, however it is expressed through the medium of one's personality, is a part of prayer that God is pleased to answer.
—Kent Hughes

It is a wise father that knows his own child.
—William Shakespeare

If the new American father feels bewildered and even defeated, let him take comfort from the fact that whatever he does in any fathering situation has a fifty percent chance of being right.
—Bill Cosby

WORSHIP HELPS

Call to Worship:
All nations whom You have made shall come and worship before You, O Lord, and they shall glorify Your name. For You are great and do wondrous deeds; You alone are God. Teach me Your way, O LORD; I will walk in Your truth; Unite my heart to fear Your name. I will give thanks to You, O Lord my God, with all my heart, and will glorify Your name forever (Ps. 86:9–12).

Scripture Reading Medley:
His disciples said to Him, "Lord, teach us to pray, as John also taught his disciples" I say to you, love your enemies, bless those who curse you, do good to those who hate you, and pray for those who spitefully use you and persecute you . . . When you pray, go into your room, and when you have shut your door, pray to your Father who is in the secret place . . . It is written, 'My house shall be called a house of prayer . . . And whatever things you ask in prayer, believing, you will receive.
(Luke 11:1; Matt. 5:44; Matt. 6:6; Matt. 21:13; Matt. 21:22)

Kids Talk

Ask the children how many of them like to spend time with friends or family. Then ask, "What do you like to do?" Allow a few answers, then ask, "But what if you never talked to them? Would you still be good friends? How would you get to know them better?" Explain that God wants to be our friend; if we don't talk to God and spend time reading about Him, we can't really get to know Him. Then suggest that we pray to Him now and ask Him to help us remember He's always listening.

Additional Sermons and Lesson Ideas

More to Life
By Peter Grainger

Date preached:

SCRIPTURE: Luke 12:16–21

INTRODUCTION: What do you think of as being foolish? Childlike behavior? Daredevil stunts? Criminal activity? Our passage introduces us to the type of person that God calls a fool.

1. He Was Only Concerned with the Material: He ignored the spiritual.
   A. His Possessions (v. 18).
   B. His Productivity (v. 18).
   C. His Pleasure (v. 19).
2. He Was Only Concerned with the Temporal: He ignored the eternal.
   A. The Present (vv. 16–18).
   B. The Future (v. 19).
3. He Was Only Concerned with the Personal: He ignored God.
   A. Personal Plans (vv. 17–18).
   B. Personal Conversation (v. 19).

CONCLUSION: There's more to life than what is visible. Followers of Christ are to be people who are spiritually aware, eternally secure, and always focused on God's purposes above our own: the wise man is one who is rich towards God (v. 21).

When God Has You Waiting
By Ed Dobson

Date preached:

SCRIPTURE: Psalm 130

INTRODUCTION: How do you react to long lines? Airline delays? Our nature is to hurry, but God wants to mold us through waiting for Him in the midst of difficulty.

1. The Dilemma of the Depths (v. 1). The phrase "the depths" is used throughout Scripture to describe problems, anxieties, or dilemmas, described as a sinking or drowning feeling in a bottomless pit (Ps. 62:2, 15).
2. The Desperation of the Depths (vv. 1–2). Like the Psalmist, the depths drive us to desperation. In difficulty, we tend to pray or read Scripture much more. Our desperation tends to deepen our dependence on God.

3. The Delight of the Depths (vv. 3–4). In the middle of his cry for mercy, the Psalmist is reminded that despite circumstances, nothing can separate us from the love and the forgiveness of God.
4. The Defeat of the Depths (vv. 5–7). In these verses, we learn that in the depths we are to wait for the Lord, not passively, but actively hoping in God's Word and character.

CONCLUSION: God uses even the worst difficulties of life to make us desperate for Him. Whatever you're facing, as you wait and hope in the Lord, He will teach you His love and mercy.

HELPS FOR THE PASTOR'S FAMILY

Praying for "Preachers' Kids"

It isn't easy being a "PK," and sometimes the only thing that gets them through is their parents' prayers. Some time ago while worried about my own children, I spoke with a lady in Denver who attended a seminar I was conducting. She was radiant and cheerful, but her smile faded as she told me of her own son, far from the Lord. He had broken her heart. "I prayed for him for a long time," she said, "then I just sort of ran out of prayers. I lost my energy to pray."

At the same seminar, another woman approached me and told me of her daughter who had been deeply ensnared in demonism, witchcraft, and the occult. "When she came back to the Lord," said the woman, "she credited my prayers and those of my circle of friends. She told me, 'I didn't have a chance against your prayers, mom.'"

I later thought of Jesus' words in Luke 18: We *ought always to pray and not lose heart.* I resolved that as long as I lived I would pray for prodigals, and as long as I had a Bible I would never "run out of prayers" for my daughters and for other children for whom I am concerned.

This is a great soul-project for me, since I have a child who is away from the Lord. This one has taught me to pray as never before. In my journal, I've gathered a collection of Bible verses that easily convert into powerful prayers for troubled children. Here is a sampling:

Please be working in my child, both to will and to do Your good pleasure (Phil. 2:13).

Please work in him what is well-pleasing to You (Heb. 13:21).

Bring him to his senses (Luke 15:17, NIV).

Deliver him from evil (Matt. 6:13).

I do not pray that You would take him out of the world, but that You would keep him from the evil one . . . . Sanctify her by Your truth (John 17:15–17).

Lord, draw my child. Draw him out of many waters and deliver him from the strong enemy (Ps. 18:16–17).

Draw her to Yourself with lovingkindness, with gentle cords, with bands of love (Jer. 31:3 and Hos. 11:4).

Lord, Lord, Satan has desired my child, to sift her like wheat. But I pray for her, that her faith should not fail. May she return to You, and afterward be a strength to many (Luke 22:31–32).

Have mercy upon my child, O God, according to Your lovingkindness. Cleanse him from sin. Create in him a clean heart, O God, and renew a steadfast spirit within him (Ps. 51:1–2, 10).

Lord, plant my child's feet squarely on the Highway of Holiness. Teach him Your ways and may he walk in Your paths. May his ears hear a word behind him saying, "This is the way, walk in it" whenever he turns to the right hand or to the left. Make the crooked places in his life straight and the rough places smooth (Is. 35:8; 2:3; 30:21; 40:4).

Prayers From Proverbs

The adolescent years are often as hard on us parents as on our kids, for we begin letting them go at the moment of their greatest vulnerability. Sometimes we can do little more than anxiously watch to see if they'll stand firm while the world tries to sweep them away in a flood of sex, alcohol, drugs, cynicism, entertainment—and freely bestowed credit cards.

But we can pray. To paraphrase J. Sidlow Baxter, our children may sometimes spurn our appeals, question our authority, and doubt our arguments, but they are helpless against our prayers.

One week during my devotions I read through the Book of Proverbs looking for various character traits which God alone could cultivate in the life of my child. My prayer that week became: *Lord, please grant my child . . .*

The good sense to choose her friends carefully (Prov. 12:26).

The wisdom to act prudently (13:16).

HELPS FOR THE PASTOR'S FAMILY — CONTINUED

Godly fear (14:26).

A wholesome tongue (15:4).

Slowness to anger (15:18).

Diligence and industriousness (10:4–5).

Honesty (11:1).

Direction in her steps (16:9).

Wariness of alcohol (20:1).

Purity of heart (22:11).

A tender conscience (20:27).

Wise counsel from others (24:6).

An excellent life's partner (12:4).

Written Prayers

As I've found Scriptural passages and promises to plead for my children, I've noted them in my journal and frequently returned to them, praying them over and over. Just as Elijah prayed seven times for rain, just as the children of Israel marched around Jericho for seven days, I've found that God desires persistence in our prayers.

It isn't that I *read* my prayers to God like endlessly reciting a shopping list, but my notes and verses become "talking points" in my conversations with the Father. Missionary J. O. Fraser once explained that he makes "a short list, like notes prepared for a sermon, before every season of prayer. The mind needs to be guided as well as the spirit attuned. I can thus get my thoughts in order, and having prepared my prayer can put the notes on the table or chair before me, kneel down and get to business."

I recently "got to business," for example, with a prayer I composed for my wife and me from James 1:

Father, grant us moment-by-moment wisdom as we deal with our children. You alone give wisdom—liberally and without reproach!—to all who ask for it. I ask this in faith without wavering, knowing that every good and perfect gift comes from above, from you, the Father of lights, with whom there is no variation or shadow of turning.

Help us to be swift to listen to our teens, slow to speak, and slow to become angry. Remind us that our wrath will not produce Your righteousness.

Positive Prayers

Praying Scriptural prayers for our children also helps us focus on the positives. In his book *Parenting the Prodigal,* S. Rutherford McDill Jr. writes, *"Hope* is believing that what we want to happen will eventually happen, that everything will eventually work itself out and end up okay. Such an attitude allows you to avoid getting so discouraged that you abandon your child when he needs you the most."

The apostle Paul told us to offer our prayers and supplications *with thanksgiving* (Phil. 4:6). According to Malachi 2:15, God seeks a godly offspring. He wants to bless our children, thus in praying for them we find a sympathetic ear. We can love our kids, keep the communication lines open, and give them our best parental support. But only God can convict their hearts, guide their steps, deepen their faith, and bring them to maturity.

"By intercessory prayer," wrote Oswald Chambers, "we can hold off Satan from other lives and give the Holy Ghost a chance with them. No wonder Jesus put such tremendous emphasis on prayer!"

Yes, there will be ups and downs—remember your own teenage years? But don't lose heart. Wise parents turn setbacks into prayer meetings, and their Bibles into prayer books. They ask God for things in keeping with His will, and He has promised to answer in His time. So, as Romans 12 puts it . . .

Lord, help us (parents) to . . .
—rejoice in hope
—be patient in tribulation
—be steadfast in prayer
Let us not to be overcome by evil,
But to overcome evil with good.
In Jesus' name,
Amen.

JUNE 27, 2004

SUGGESTED SERMON

Face to Face with God

Date preached:

By David Jackman

Scripture: Genesis 32—33; especially 32:28: And He said, "Your name shall no longer be called Jacob, but Israel; for you have struggled with God and with men, and have prevailed."

Introduction: Is your life in constant motion, moving from place to place, from school to school, or from career to career? Or do you realize that God is at work in you, changing you through these circumstances? One Christian poet put it this way, "Observe how God ruthlessly perfects, those he royally elects." As we observe Jacob's pilgrimage, we see not only a geographic journey, but a journey from Jacob to Israel—a pilgrimage from selfishness to God-centeredness, from deception to devotion. This journey takes a lifetime.

1. **Jacob Faced the Esau Factor (32:1–21).** God's promise to make a great nation through Jacob and to bring Jacob back to the land (see 28:14–15) is now being fulfilled. God changed Jacob throughout the years to become a very different man, but there remained a past to confront: the Esau Factor. Remember that Esau pledged to kill Jacob because of his deception (see 27:41) causing Jacob to flee from home (27:42–44). The events that follow reflect a lifetime of change. Jacob's obedience in returning home is met by God's provision. The angels of God who met him as he left the land meet him as he returns to the land (32:1–2). Not surprisingly, Jacob, the schemer, had a plan. He sent messengers ahead of him to try to win over Esau (vv. 3–5). This plan didn't yield the results Jacob hoped for; the messengers returned to report that Esau was on his way, along with 400 men! How did Jacob react? With great fear and distress (v. 7). He had God's promise, has been met by God's angels, but when faced by Esau's force of four hundred men, he was scared stiff. He again schemed, planning to divide into two groups or camps (v. 8). But he was a different man, for he also prayed (vv. 9–11). What an incredible change! He asked God to save him by His grace. How like us! We pray and lay things out before God, but panic when we're not sure it's going to work.

2. **God Confronted Jacob (32:22–32).** Jacob's family and possessions crossed the ford at nightfall and Jacob was left alone (v. 22–24). This deliberately echoed Bethel: when he left home, alone, at night, and God came to him (28:10–22). Here was now another nocturnal encounter with God, this time in a wrestling match! As the story began, the identity of the man in verse 24 was unknown. However, this unknown man was more than a man, He was the Lord (see also v. 28), which becomes obvious when He injured Jacob's hip with a touch. Jacob said, "I will not let You go until You bless me!" From his birth, grasping at his brother's heel, Jacob had been desperate for the blessing. The real blessing comes not from schemes, but from God and His grace. Jacob's name needed to reflect the change in his life, so the Lord changed it to Israel, literally the Prince with God (vv. 27–28). Why did this event happen? Jacob needed to learn to wrestle with God before wrestling problems; we must learn the same. Are you facing the Esau factor? Do you need to deal with a family member? A situation? A spouse? Take it to the Lord; wrestle in prayer!

3. **Israel Faced Esau (33:1–17).** Now Jacob (Israel) himself went on ahead, at the front of the entourage, to meet Esau face-to-face (v. 3). His testimony as he met Esau after all these years was of God's gracious provision (v. 5). The Lord went ahead, resolved difficulties, gave victory, and dispensed grace. If you wrestle with God you can deal with the Esau factor as a changed person. The climax occurred when Jacob says, " . . . take my blessing . . . " (v. 11). Jacob, who stole Esau's blessing, now bestowed a blessing. There is recompense, reparation, and reconciliation. The lessons Jacob

>>> *sermon continued on following page*

APPROPRIATE HYMNS AND SONGS

Face to Face, Carrie E. Breck/Grant Colfax Tullar; Public Domain.

Face to Face, Mark Altrogge; © 1987 PDI Praise/Dayspring Music Inc., Admin. by Word Music Group, Inc.

To Seek Your Face, John Wimber; © 1988 Mercy/Vineyard Publishing.

Take My Life That It May Be, Francis R. Havergal/Timothy Hoekman; © 1987 CRC Publications.

Come All Christians Be Committed, Eva B. Lloyd/James H. Wood; © 1958. Renewed 1986 Broadman Press (Admin. by Genevox Music Group).

had learned outside the land bring him home humbled, God-dependent, and grace-dependent. Think of what grace was displayed on the Cross! Is there someone you need to extend grace to?

Conclusion: To enter into the blessings both now and hereafter, we must submit ourselves totally to the touch of God. We must let Him work in us that which takes away our deceit and self-dependence. Take your difficulties to God, wrestle and deal with them, and you will be able to deal with others with the same grace given to you.

FOR THE BULLETIN

* On June 27, 1556, thirteen Protestant believers (eleven men and two women) died at the stake at Stratford Green while "Bloody" Mary was Queen of England. This was the largest number martyred in a single execution in England, but during Mary's reign nearly 300 Protestants went to the flames. Martyrs' Memorial now stands on the spot of their execution, and the names of the victims are used as the names of the streets surrounding the square.
* On this day in 1737, George Whitefield preached his first sermon. His topic was the need of Christians to help one another. With family members sitting nervously in the congregation, Whitefield seemed ill at ease at first, but soon warmed in his delivery. He went on to become one of the most powerful orators in Christian history, whose unaided voice could convict sinners over a mile away.
* On June 27, 1844, Joseph Smith, founder of the Mormons, was killed in a riot in Carthage, Illinois, along with his brother, Hyrum. The riot was caused in part by community outrage over Smith's authorization of polygamous marriages among Mormons.
* Hudson Taylor established the China Inland Mission on this day in 1865.
* June 27, 1880, is the birthday of Helen Keller.
* James Moffatt, best known for his translation of the Bible into modern English, died on this day in 1944.

STATS, STORIES AND MORE

Weighing in at . . .
How would you do against one of the popular wrestlers of the WWF (World Wrestling Federation)? "Rick Rude" was 6'4", 252 pounds; "Mr. Perfect" was 6'3", 257 pounds; "Andre the Giant" was 7'2", an amazing 520 pounds! How would you feel facing off with one of these men? Compare that to the intimidation Jacob must have felt going against God Himself.

Jacob's Strength
We know from the text of Genesis that Jacob was very strong physically: when he met Rachel, he lifted the well cover in order to water her flocks (Gen. 29:10), a cover which normally took three or four men to shift. Jewish tradition holds that Jacob was a giant of a man, a match for most anyone.

Jacob's Prayer
In our text for this week, we have the longest prayer recorded in the Book of Genesis. Jacob laid out his entire problem before God, providing us with a model as to how covenant people should approach God when they're under threat. First, in verse 9, He reminded God of His covenant promises. Then He confessed His total unworthiness in verse 10. He then asked for God's deliverance in verse 11, and again returned to God's promised word in verse 12. If we get stuck, not knowing how to approach God, this is a wonderful pattern.

WORSHIP HELPS

Call to Worship:
Shout joyfully to the LORD, all the earth. Serve the LORD with gladness; come before Him with joyful singing. Know that the Lord Himself is God; it is He who has made us, and not we ourselves; we are His people and the sheep of His pasture. Enter His gates with thanksgiving and His courts with praise. Give thanks to Him, bless His name. For the LORD is good; His lovingkindness is everlasting and His faithfulness to all generations (Ps. 100).

Closing Prayer:
Heavenly Father, in the midst of this strange story about Jacob which we find in some ways quite hard to relate to, we thank You for the clarity of what You were doing in this patriarch's life. When we think of what You've done in our lives, some of the ways in which You've humbled us, some of the times in which we've come to the end of ourselves and our resources, up against the Esau Factor, we want to thank You so much for Your amazing grace. Thank You that You can take Jacob and turn him into Israel. Thank You that You can take people like us and shape us into the likeness of our Lord Jesus Christ. Help us to remember today what it cost Him for us to experience the triumphs of His grace, that we may not resist Your will for our lives, but rejoice even if we enter into Heaven limping. We want to be people, above all, who enter heaven, people living in the light of Your blessing and Your overwhelming grace. Grant it we pray, for Jesus' sake, Amen.

Additional Sermons and Lesson Ideas

The Lord in Our Midst
By Evan H. Hopkins

Date preached:

SCRIPTURE: Zephaniah 3:17

INTRODUCTION: Do you believe that God is always with you? That He delights to save you? In a prophecy to Israel, God (through Zephaniah) expresses how He relates to His people, a description which can encourage us today.

1. The Lord's Presence. God's presence is not an abstract idea, but a reality in our lives; anywhere we go and whatever we do, whether in church or at work, the Lord is with us.
2. The Lord's Favor. Notice the phrase, "the Lord your God." God has undertaken for you, He has called you, He is *your* God.
3. The Lord's Power. This verse describes God as "a victorious warrior." The God who is with you and who favors you is powerful! Grasp this truth! Act on God's word in faith and He will empower you to do His will.
4. The Lord's Salvation. The next phrase is, "The Mighty One, will save." God not only offers salvation: the rest of the verse reveals that God loves us; He rejoices over His people with joy, even with singing!

CONCLUSION: Do you view God as simply a disciplinarian or judge? He favors you; He is always with you in power. He loves His redemptive work. Meditate on that this week.

Greater Than

Date preached:

SCRIPTURE: 1 John 4:4: "Greater is He" (KJV).

INTRODUCTION: Have you ever met a great person? No matter whom you have met in this life, there's someone even greater for you to know. Jesus Christ is described in Matthew 12 as being:

1. Greater than the Temple (Matt. 12:6). He was a living temple who would be destroyed, yet rebuilt in three days as an eternal habitation for His people. He is our indestructible, everlasting sanctuary.
2. Greater than Jonah (Matt. 12:41). Jonah was in the belly of the fish for three days, then emerged to save an entire city from judgment, but Christ was in the belly of the earth for three days, then emerged to save an entire world.
3. Greater than Solomon (Matt. 12:42). Solomon was the wisest man in history, but in Christ are hidden all the treasures of wisdom and knowledge.

CONCLUSION: Don't be too easily impressed by supposed greatness in this life. You know Someone even greater—and His grace is greater than all your sin.

PATRIOTIC SERMON

Red, White, and Blue

Date preached:

Scripture: Isaiah 1:18

Introduction: Our world has never been more dangerous than it is now. There are powerful, hidden, sinister, evil forces in the world today, and none of us knows what lies ahead. In times of national crisis and distress, Americans have always rallied around the flag. It's the theme of our national anthem and of our national consciousness. I'd like to briefly talk about the Star-Spangled Banner—the American flag—and its famous seamstress, Betsy Ross.

1. The Story of the Flag. Did you know that Betsy Ross, who sewed together the first flag, was married to two different soldiers, both of whom perished for our country? In 1680, a man named Andrew Griscom emigrated from England to the New World. He became friends with the Quaker leader, William Penn. Andrew Griscom was a carpenter, and he helped Mr. Penn establish the city of Philadelphia. Andrew's son, Samuel, also became a carpenter who, it is said, helped construct Philadelphia's Independence Hall. Samuel married Rebecca James, the daughter of a wealthy importer, and the couple had a number of children.

One of those children was named Betsy Griscom. Because the Griscoms were devout Christians and Quakers, they believed in equality of education, and quality schooling was provided the girls in the family as well as for the boys. Along with her education, Betsy was taught needlework and became a skilled seamstress. As a teenager, she was apprenticed to a sewing and upholstery shop. In that same shop, also working as an apprentice was a preacher's son named John Ross. His father was assistant pastor at Philadelphia's Christ Episcopal Church. The two young people started dating, and when Betsy was 21, she accepted John's marriage proposal. But there was a problem. John was Episcopalian and Betsy was a Quaker. In those days, the Quakers didn't approve of marriages between denominations, and the Quakers disowned Betsy. Her parents disapproved of the marriage. One night in November of 1773, John and Betsy rowed across the Delaware River and were secretly married in New Jersey. They settled down as faithful members of Christ Church, and the pew they regularly sat in was near the regular pew of another worshiper, George Washington.

The next year, John and Betsy opened their own sewing and upholstery shop, but the Revolutionary War was brewing, and John joined the militia. One day in January, 1776, he was guarding ammunition along the Delaware River. Somehow the gunpowder exploded, and he was badly wounded. Betsy rushed to his side, but his wounds proved fatal and he died on January 21, 1776. They had been married just three years, and at age 23, Betsy was a war widow. But she was strong-willed, and she determined to keep the couple's upholstery business going.

About five months later, Betsy received a secret visit by a committee from the Continental Congress. They had a rough drawing of a flag they had conceptualized for the new nation. Betsy studied it, made some suggestions (especially about the number of points on the stars), and agreed to do the work. The committee liked it so well that they gave her a standing order for more of them. Betsy continued making flags for the United States for the next fifty years.

In 1777, Betsy married again. Her new husband, Joseph Ashburn, also joined American forces and was taken prisoner by the British. For several months, Betsy tried to learn what had happened to him. She finally heard he had died in an English prison. But Joseph had a friend who also had been taken prisoner and was held in the same prison. This friend, John Claypool, survived the war and was able to return to Philadelphia to give Betsy a farewell message from her husband. In the course of time, John and Betsy fell in love and were married, and the two had a happy and long life.

One of the great questions about the flag has to do with its colors. What do the red, white, and blue represent? No one really knows. The Continental Congress left no explanation about the colors. The same colors were later used in the Great Seal of the United States, and on that occasion the Congress explained that white represented purity and innocence; red, valor and hardiness, and blue, vigilance. Today I'd like to interpret those colors in another way, to explain the great single-minded message of the Bible:

1. Red. Red reminds us of blood. If I'd been in the Continental Congress as this subject was discussed, I might have pointed out red represented the blood that had been shed for the securing and protecting of America's freedom. This is also the crimson thread that runs through the Bible. It is the shedding of the blood of Jesus Christ on the Cross that gives us true liberty and everlasting life. The Bible teaches that every human being is guilty of sin before God. We've all become prodigals. We've all sinned and fallen short of His glory, and the Bible warns that sin always results in separation from God and, thereby, death. But

God, still loving us, became a man named Jesus Christ who deliberately died in our place and shed His own blood for our sins (Rom. 5:6–8).

2. White. Isaiah 1:18 says: *Though your sins are like scarlet, they shall be as white as snow.* When I was growing up in the mountains, I would sometimes go with my father to visit relatives back in the hills. We'd park our car alongside the highway and hike into the mountains. The snowdrifts would be as tall as I was, and on those early Saturday mornings after a newly fallen snow, the sun reflecting off the landscape would be so blinding it would hurt my eyes. Underneath were dirt and mud, dead animals and decaying logs. But all of it was washed white by the newly fallen snow. Isaiah compared God's forgiveness to snow that covers and cleanses, that glistens and reflects the sunshine.

3. Blue. Blue represents the promise and assurance of heaven (Rom. 6:23). George Richie is a man who, in December, 1943, completed basic training at Camp Barkeley, Texas. He caught what he thought was a chest cold, and he began to suffer from a fever. When he collapsed, a doctor was called and he was pronounced dead. A soldier was assigned to prepare his body for the morgue. But the soldier noticed a twitch of some sort, and the doctor rushed back and injected adrenaline directly into the muscle of his heart. After he recovered, George Richie (who later became a medical doctor himself and who was a Christian) said that during those moments he left the earth, as it were, and traveled a great distance. Somewhere beyond, he came to a city—a huge city—what a city!—built of light. It was a city in which the walls, houses, and streets seemed to give off life. In the middle of it all was One who radiated light. After he recovered, George Richie read the Book of Revelation and was amazed that the description of the great city of Heaven corresponded exactly to the images he saw during his death-experience. The apostle Paul said, "To live is Christ, and to die is gain."

Conclusion: Everything hinges on our relationship with the One who died for us. Millions are hoping to get to heaven by living a good life or doing good works. But the Bible warns against having a false sense of security. After the jetliner crashed into the North Tower on September 11, 2001, the World Trade Center's emergency loudspeaker system told those in both towers to stay put. The words recalled by most of the survivors were: "The building is secure. Return to your offices. The building is secure." That announcement doomed hundreds of people. No matter what people say, no matter how you feel, this life is not secure without a personal relationship with Jesus Christ. Have you received Him?

Quotes for the Pastor's Wall

> Apply yourself wholly to the text and apply the text wholly to yourself.

—Johann Albrecht Bengle,
eighteenth-century German preacher

Quotes for the Pastor's Wall

> Lord, how can man preach thy eternal word?
>
> He is a brittle crazie glasse:
>
> Yet in thy temple thou dost him afford
>
> This glorious and transcendent place,
>
> To be a window, though thy grace.

—George Herbert, British poet

JULY 4, 2004 — INDEPENDENCE DAY

SUGGESTED SERMON

Elisha's Last Sermon

Date preached:

By Denis Lyle

Scripture: 2 Kings 13:14–19, especially verse 16: Then (Elisha) said to the king of Israel, "Put your hand on the bow." And he put his hand on it, then Elisha laid his hands on the king's hands.

Introduction: What if our armed forces went into each battle afraid, undedicated to the country or the task? We'd lose the war. Our military is taught complete commitment and courage; if they were not, they could never succeed. In the same way, Christians must learn the lesson Elisha gave from his deathbed to a lethargic young king.

1. **The Task (vv. 14–17).** This scene can easily confuse us; but in Eastern lands instruction by means of symbolic actions was common (see 1 Sam. 15:27–28; Acts 21:10–11). King Joash seemed uninspired, and Elisha was symbolically urging him and his nation to victory. The prophet was departing life, but the fight would still go on. Through the symbolic actions seen in this story, Elisha was spurring on Joash to execute a specific task. In effect this was a call to:

    A. **Public Warfare.** The cities which Syria had taken from Israel (see 13:25) needed to be recovered. The king was to act decisively. Elisha was trying to stir up the sluggish, compromised young king with enthusiasm to fight the enemy. He was saying, "Be up and doing; smite the enemies of your country!" That's the Lord's call to every Christian. Too many of us have been on the defensive too long. God calls us to the offense, to attack the fortified places of error and sin in our society and to be proactive witnesses. Is there any way in which your example is seen as God's offensive weapon against sin and evil in our society? Does your light dispel the darkness?

    B. **Personal Warfare.** The apostle Paul frequently likened the Christian life to a personal battle (Rom. 7:23; Eph.6:10; and 2 Cor. 10:3). How are you doing personally as you wage war with that powerful inward foe, your own flesh? Gossip? Sexual sin? Unforgiveness? We are given the Spirit to daily overcome these things (Gal. 5:16).

2. **The Touch (v. 16).** In verse 16, the trembling hands of the monarch are touched by the rugged hands of the prophet. Just as the touch of Elisha was on King Joash, the Lord's touch is on us as we go forth to fight His battles. Joash experienced the alliance of the supernatural. Do you remember that old song, "He touched me! Oh, he touched me!" Jesus often touched people during His ministry, and His touch on our lives conveys His power as we go onward as Christian soldiers. Is the touch of Christ on your life? Offer yourself to Him as Lord, and visualize His hands clasping around your own, just as Elisha's old, rugged hands fell in blessing over those of the young king, signifying:

   A. **God's Presence with Him.** What an encouragement for Joash to know that the Lord of Hosts would accompany him to the field of battle. Imagine how the disciples felt when the Savior placed before them the responsibility of world evangelization. Not only did Christ instruct them, but He encouraged them, "I am with you always . . . " (Matt. 28:20). Do you need to be reminded of that? God is with you in days of blessing and barrenness, of storm and sunshine, of progress and opposition. He will never leave or forsake you (Heb. 13:5).

   B. **God's Power upon Him.** As the prophet's hand closed over the king's hand, so the might of the Lord of Hosts would, through him, defeat the forces of Syria. When His hand is upon us, is anything impossible (Phil. 4:13)?

   C. **God's Purpose through Him.** God's purpose for Israel was victory over Syria (v. 17). Likewise, if we are engaged in the Lord's work, we're on the winning side (Matt. 16:18). Why is it that we fail so often, when the power available is so unlimited?

>>> *sermon continued on following page*

APPROPRIATE HYMNS AND SONGS

Be Strong and Take Courage, Basil Chaisson; © 1985 Integrity's Hosanna! Music.

He Touched Me, William J. Gaither; © 1964 William J. Gaither, Inc., Admin. by Gaither Copyright Management.

Onward Christian Soldiers, Sabine Baring-Gould/Arthur Seymour Sullivan; Public Domain.

Battle Hymn of the Republic, Julia Ward Howe/William Steffe; Public Domain.

America the Beautiful, Katherine Lee Bates/Samuel A. Ward; Public Domain.

3. **The Test (vv. 18–19).** Elisha commanded Joash to shoot his arrows into the ground, but Joash meekly fired three arrows into the dusty earth around the prophet's bed. Why didn't he get excited and shoot six or seven arrows? This was a mock battle that predicted the outcome of the real thing. Did he feel silly? Did he misunderstand? Joash simply didn't believe there could be any connection between firing arrows in private and later seeing total victory in public. Are we not guilty of the same thing? We often limp in our prayer lives; we struggle to believe that a few words launched from our bedside can achieve anything in the real world. After two or three attempts, we give up.

Conclusion: We need to be wholehearted, boldly believing that through us, God will ultimately win the battle against sin in our lives and our world. Are you willing to follow the Lord faithfully, wholeheartedly, and courageously? Remember that because His Hand is on the bow, victory is sure in the end!

FOR THE BULLETIN

- On July 4, 1776, the American Declaration of Independence was signed.
- On July 4, 1802, the U. S. Military Academy at West Point opened.
- July 4, 1812, is the birthday of the great African-American preacher, John Jasper, pastor of the Sixth Mount Zion Church, Richmond, Virginia.
- July 4, 1820, is the birthday of the inimitable frontier evangelist, Robert Sheffey.
- John Adams and Thomas Jefferson, second and third Presidents of the United States, both died on the Fourth of July in 1826.
- On July 4, 1831, "America" ("My Country, 'Tis of Thee"), written by young Samuel Francis Smith, was sung for the first time. It was performed at Boston's Park Street Congregational Church by the Juvenile Choir at a Sunday school Rally. In the years that followed, Smith became a powerful Baptist preacher, pastor, college professor, hymnist, linguist, writer, and missionary advocate. He traveled the world in support of evangelism. But he was always best known as the author of this patriotic hymn.
- Charles L. Dodgson was the oldest of eleven sons by a British clergyman. He grew up "knowing how to use his fists for a righteous cause." He also knew how to use his brain. Uncommonly intelligent, he became a professor at Oxford and the author of several books about mathematics. On July 4, 1862, he started a book of another kind—about a little girl who fell down a rabbit hole. He published *Alice in Wonderland* under the pen name Lewis Carroll in 1865.

STATS, STORIES AND MORE

Courage, Brother!
This old hymn by Norman MacLeod (written in 1857) later became an inspiration for another Norman—General Norman Schwarzkopf:
Courage brother, do not stumble, though thy path be dark as night:
There is a star to guide the humble, trust in God, and do the right.
Let the road be dark and dreary and its end far out of sight.
Face it bravely, strong or weary. Trust God, and do the right.

The Right One for the Job
Mike Cohen, a former Miami Dolphin, was once asked by a coach to do some recruiting. He said, "What kind of player are you looking for, coach?"
The coach said, "Mike, there's a guy when you knock him down, he stays down."

Mike said, "We don't want him, do we, coach?"

"No, we don't. There's also that player when you knock him down, he gets up, and then when you knock him down again he stays down."

Mike replied, "We don't want him either, coach."

"Mike, there's a man you can knock down and he gets up, you knock him down and he gets up, you knock him down and he gets up . . ."

Mike said, "That's the guy we want, coach."

He said, "No, we don't want him either. I want you to find the man who's knocking everyone down. That's the man I want!"

The Battle Is the Lord's
During the American Civil War, a deputation came to see Abraham Lincoln. In their conversation, they expressed the hope that the Lord was on their side. The President replied, "That is not the thing that I am most concerned about." His hearers were astonished; what could be of greater importance than the question of whether God was on their side? They waited for an explanation, "What I am most anxious about," said Lincoln, "is whether we are on the Lord's side."

WORSHIP HELPS

Call to Worship:
I will sing to the LORD as long as I live; I will sing praise to my God while I have my being. Let my meditation be pleasing to Him; as for me, I shall be glad in the LORD (Ps. 104:33–34).

Readers' Theater from 1 Samuel 17 (or Responsive Reading):

Reader 1: Then Saul said to David, "You are not able to go against this Philistine to fight with him; for you are but a youth while he has been a warrior from his youth."

Reader 2: And David said, "The LORD who delivered me from the paw of the lion and from the paw of the bear, He will deliver me from the hand of this Philistine."

Reader 1: Then Saul clothed David with his armor and put a bronze helmet on his head.

Reader 2: David said to Saul, "I cannot go with these, for I have not tested them." And David took them off. . . . His sling was in his hand; and he approached the Philistine.

Reader 1: The Philistine said to David, "Am I a dog, that you come to me with sticks?"

Reader 2: Then David said to the Philistine, "You come to me with a sword, a spear, and a javelin, but I come to you in the name of the Lord of hosts, the God of the armies of Israel, whom you have taunted. This day the Lord will deliver you up into my hands . . . that all earth may know there is a God in Israel . . . for the battle is the LORD's." Thus David prevailed over the Philistine with a sling and a stone.

Benediction:
Did we in our own strength confide,
Our striving would be losing;
Were not the right Man on our side,
The Man of God's own choosing;
Dost ask who that may be?
Christ Jesus, it is He;
Lord Sabboath, His name,
From age to age the same,
And He must win the battle.

Additional Sermons and Lesson Ideas

Proclaim Liberty Throughout The Land

Date preached:

SCRIPTURE: 1 Corinthians 2:1–5

INTRODUCTION: Our most precious national document is our Declaration of Independence, but Christians have an even greater declaration. Paul said, "I came . . . declaring the testimony of God." The word "testimony" (martyrion) has to do with the reliable truth given by a witness. In this case, it is the truth God has given about Jesus Christ, which it is our duty to declare.

1. Our Limitation (v. 1). We do not declare this message with "excellence of speech or of wisdom."
2. Our Determination (v. 2). We determine to have but one message—Christ and Him crucified.
3. Our Trepidation (v. 3). "Weakness, fear, and much trembling."
4. Our Demonstration (v. 4). Our declaring is not done "in persuasive words of human wisdom, but in demonstration of the power and of the Spirit."
5. Our Aspiration (v. 5). " . . . that your faith should . . . be . . . in the power of God."

CONCLUSION: On the front of America's famous Liberty Bell in Philadelphia are the words of Leviticus 25:10: "Proclaim Liberty Throughout all the Land." What a message to declare!

The Bright Side of Growing Older

Date preached:

By Frances Ridley Havergal

SCRIPTURE: Job 11:17 (KJV): "Thine age shall be clearer than the noonday; thou shalt shine forth." Alternate text: 2 Corinthians 4:16.

INTRODUCTION: I suppose nobody ever did naturally like the idea of getting older. There is a sense of oppression and depression about it. The irresistible, inevitable onward march of moments and years without the possibility of one instant's pause—a march that, even while on the uphill side of life, is leading to the downhill side—casts an autumn-like shadow over many a birthday. But how surely the Bible gives us the bright side of everything! In this case it gives us three bright sides.

1. Increasing Brightness (Prov. 4:18). Every year means another year's experience in His love and faithfulness, more light of the knowledge of the glory of God in the face of Jesus.
2. Increasing Fruitfulness (Ps. 92:14).
3. Increasing Intimacy with Jehovah-Jesus (Is. 46:4).

CONCLUSION: "Fear not the westering shadows, O Children of the Day! For brighter still and brighter shall be your homeward way."

JULY 11, 2004

SUGGESTED SERMON

Lord, Make Us One

Date preached:

By Ed Dobson

Scripture: John 17:20–25, especially verse 21: (I ask) that they may all be one; even as You, Father, are in Me and I in You, that they also may be in Us, so that the world may believe that You sent Me.

Introduction: Has anyone prayed for you aloud and, as a result, you felt moved, empowered, or encouraged? Was it a friend? A pastor or Sunday school teacher? A family member? In our passage for today, Jesus Christ Himself prays for you and me. John 17:20 says, "I do not ask on behalf of these alone, but for those also who believe in Me through their word." Jesus prays for those who haven't yet been converted, including us. How incredible! Now Jesus certainly has my attention, so let's look into His prayer, especially His special request for the oneness of His people.

1. **The Model of Oneness (v. 21).** Jesus gives us the perfect model of unity, the relationship between the Father and the Son, "that they may all be one; even as You, Father, are in Me and I in You, that they also may be in Us." What is the relationship between the Father and the Son? They are both God, yet they have different functions. They are equal in substance or essence, diverse in their functions, and united in purpose. For centuries, theologians have attempted to come up with illustrations for the Trinity, but none are perfect. They do, however help us visualize this incredible unity. Saint Patrick illustrated the Trinity using the shamrock, a three-leaf plant, one in its substance and function, yet having three separate parts (leaves).

2. **The Nature of Oneness (v. 21).** The relationship between the Father and the Son is the model, but it's still fuzzy. What does it look like? Jesus says, "... even as You, Father, are in Me and I in You, that they also may be in Us." Throughout Jesus' life, His close and intimate oneness with the Father is obvious. Now He prays that we would be one like He is with the Father, that is, close, intimate, connected. In this passage, unity refers not to being one with church members, but one with the very Trinity (see Eph. 1:3; 2:13, 19).

3. **The Purpose of Oneness (v. 21).** The Father and the Son model close and intimate unity, but why should we model this unity ourselves? What does it accomplish? Jesus continues His prayer, " . . . so that the world may believe that You sent Me." If we live intimately and passionately connected to Christ, the world will notice. When Christ is working in us, the world will see the fruit of our relationship and believe that Christ is a reality.

4. **The Attraction of Oneness (v. 22).** How can we be assured that a close and intimate relationship with Christ will cause others to see the reality of Christ? Jesus continues, "The glory which You have given Me I have given to them, that they may be one, just as We are one . . . " A basic definition of the word "glory" is the outward, physical manifestation of God's character or invisible qualities. When we understand our position in Christ, and as we cultivate intimacy with the Father and the Son, people will look at us and see God; they will see Jesus; they will have a visible, tangible, observable idea of what God is like! So how much do people see God in us? That depends on our intimacy, our unity with God.

Application:
A. **Become a passionate, devoted follower of Christ.** Unity doesn't mean we all look, walk, talk, and live alike. Unity occurs when we choose every moment to be passionate, devoted followers of Christ. Whether you're a physician or an attorney, whether you're a stay-at-home mom or a school teacher, a mechanic, a student, or a professor, it doesn't matter. Just as the Father and the Son are one in purpose and intimacy, we're

>>> *sermon continued on following page*

APPROPRIATE HYMNS AND SONGS

As We Come Together, Stan Pethel; © 1984 Hope Publishing Company.

Make Us One, Carol Cymbala; © 1991 Word Music, Inc./Carol Joy Music, Admin. by Integrated Music Copyright, Inc.

Blest Be the Tie that Binds, John Fawcett/Johann G. Nagelli; Public Domain.

Let the Walls Fall Down, Anne Barbour/John Barbour/Bill Batstone; © 1993 Maranatha Praise, Inc., Admin. by The Copyright Company.

They'll Know We Are Christians By Our Love, Peter Scholtes; © 1966 F.E.L. Publications, Admin. by The Lorenze Corporation.

to be committed to the purposes of God and to our relationship with Christ.

B. Yield yourself continually to the Spirit. The Holy Spirit indwells believers at all times, but moment-by-moment, step-by-step obedience to the Spirit is necessary if we're to be unified.

C. Learn to see others through God's eyes, and choose patience, love, and cheerfulness in your relationships. These qualities can be cultivated. Through the Spirit, let's love our God more deeply and each other more consistently with each passing day.

FOR THE BULLETIN

❋ On July 11, 1533, Pope Clement VII excommunicated England's King Henry VIII for divorcing Catherine of Aragon and remarrying. This set the stage for the political component of the English Reformation. ❋ On July 11, 1656, the first Quakers arrived in America. They were promptly arrested and sent back to England. ❋ James Mitchell tried to kill Archbishop James Sharp on this day in 1668. Mitchell was a Scottish Covenanter, one of the Scottish Presbyterians who vowed to resist English efforts to impose Anglo-Catholic forms on their churches. Archbishop James Sharp had caught, abused, and killed Presbyterians like dogs. On July 11, 1668, as the archbishop sat in his horse-drawn coach, Mitchell pointed a pistol at him and fired through the open door. He missed, hitting another bishop in the hand. Eventually Mitchell was captured, imprisoned, and tortured. He was later taken to the center of Edinburgh for execution. Loud drumming drowned out his last words, but he had hidden away two copies of his final message, and from the scaffold he flung them to the crowd. ❋ July 11, 1838, is the birthday of John Wanamaker, one of America's most successful merchants, creator of the modern department store, and the Postmaster General of the United States. He is chiefly remembered, however, for his soul-winning passion and Sunday school work. ❋ On July 11, 1886, missionary Horace Underwood secretly administered the first Protestant baptism on Korean soil to Mr. Toh Sa No. ❋ On July 11, 1955, "In God We Trust" was officially placed on all U. S. coins by an order of Congress.

STATS, STORIES AND MORE

More from Ed Dobson

"Having studied this prayer from John 17 all week long, a preacher on TV caught my eye. I figured I could gain some insight. The preacher argued that Jesus was teaching there is one true church, not many, just one, and that Jesus is praying that this church, built on the apostles and on their message, would be impacting the world. Since I didn't belong to his particular church, it aggravated me some. Is Jesus suggesting there's only one true church, or that all of us: Calvinistic, Armenian, Charismatic, and traditional churches all should rid themselves of anything that makes them different? The model refers not to our relationship with other churches, but with Jesus Christ Himself; that's what unifies all believers!" —*Ed Dobson*

Illustrations of the Trinity:

- A fire consists of these three ingredients: heat, fuel, and oxygen. Each has a unique function, but together they form one fire.
- An egg has a shell, a white, and a yolk, yet it is one in its purpose and substance.
- Water is found in solid, liquid, and gaseous forms, yet is still hydrogen dioxide.
- A man can be "Joe Smith," in a conversation with a salesman, but at work he is "Dr. Smith," and at home, "Daddy." He has different roles and even different names, but is one unified person.

Some suggest that no example can accurately explain the Trinity; some examples stress unity and others stress the three parts. This occurs not only in theology, however. The nature of light is often debated: one theory says light is small bundles of energy while another holds that light is waves. To understand light, physicists must hold both, seemingly contradicting theories.
Someone once said about the nature of the Trinity, "Try to explain it, and you'll lose your mind; but try to deny it and you'll lose your soul."

WORSHIP HELPS

Call to Worship:
Praise the LORD! I will give thanks to the LORD with all my heart, in the company of the upright and in the assembly. Great are the works of the LORD; they are studied by all who delight in them. Splendid and majestic is His work, and His righteousness endures forever. The works of His hands are truth and justice; all His precepts are sure. They are upheld forever and ever; they are performed in truth and uprightness. He has sent redemption to His people; He has ordained His covenant forever; holy and awesome is His name (Ps. 111:1–3; 7–9 NASB).

Scripture Reading: Psalm 133 (NLT)
How wonderful it is, how pleasant,
when brothers live together in harmony!
For harmony is as precious as the fragrant anointing oil
that was poured over Aaron's head,
that ran down his beard
and onto the border of his robe.
Harmony is as refreshing as the dew from Mount Hermon
that falls on the mountains of Zion.
And the Lord has pronounced his blessing,
even life forevermore.

Offertory Comments:
In the Old Testament, the people of Israel were required to make sacrifices on a regular basis. One of the most interesting offerings mentioned in the Old Testament, though, is the thank offering or the freewill offering (Lev. 22:17–25). If someone had a fruitful harvest or simply felt like giving worship to the Lord, they might bring a free will offering to show their gratitude. This morning, offer thanks to the Lord out of free will, as an act of worship to Him.

Benediction:
On our way rejoicing gladly let us go;
Conquered hath our Leader, vanquished is our foe;
Christ without, our safety, Christ within, our joy;
Who, if we be faithful, can our hope destroy?
—John S. B. Monsell

Additional Sermons and Lesson Ideas

The Obedience Secret
By Samuel Logan Brengle

Date preached:

SCRIPTURE: Acts 26:19

INTRODUCTION: This reveals the secret of Paul's success as a soul-winner. He was not disobedient to the heavenly vision. Those who win others are soldiers who obey orders (Jer. 1:4–7).

1. This Obedience Must Be Prompt. The King's business requires haste (1 Sam. 21:8). If I speak when the Spirit moves me, I can usually introduce the gospel with good results, but if I delay, the opportunity slips by.
2. This Obedience Must Be Exact. Saul lost his kingdom because his obedience was only partial (1 Sam. 15).
3. This Obedience Must Be Courageous. God told Jeremiah and Ezekiel to be unafraid of reactions to their message (Jer. 1:8; Ezek. 2:6). Saul lost his crown because he feared the people more than he feared God (1 Sam. 15:24).
4. This Obedience Must Be Glad. (See Ps. 100:2.)

CONCLUSION: The soul-winner is a servant of God, a friend of Jesus, a prophet of the Most High, an ambassador of Heaven to the sons of men. We must speak Heaven's words and represent Heaven's court, seeking not our own will but His.

Perfect Hearts
By Richard S. Sharpe, Jr.

Date preached:

SCRIPTURE: Psalm 101

INTRODUCTION: How would you describe your heart? Loving? Angry? Prideful? Psalm 101 motivates us to seek a perfect heart in ourselves and in others.

1. The Perfect Heart (v. 2). David first describes a perfect heart. The term "perfect" doesn't mean sinless perfection, but reflects David's commitment to establish God's kingdom by following God's Law. He was going to be a man of integrity.
2. The Perverse Heart (v. 4). David then addresses the hearts of people who are evil or twisted. He did not want men with perverse hearts among his counselors; he knew perverse hearts could not uphold the standards of God.
3. The Proud Heart (v. 5). The third heart mentioned is prideful, arrogant. Proud hearts are described as gossiping, looking down on others. Proud hearts look for advancement, not compassion. David wants to destroy the haughty, and to seek out the humble.

CONCLUSION: Which category do you fall under? Do you surround yourself with perversity or pride? Commit to obedience and surround yourself with faithful friends.

JULY 18, 2004

SUGGESTED SERMON

Is Your Faith Genuine?   *Date preached:*

By Timothy Beougher

Scripture: James 2:14–20, especially verse 17: *Thus also faith by itself, if it does not have works, is dead.*

Introduction: Kent Hughes writes about a cartoon in The New Yorker that showed a large sign out in front of a church which read: "The Lite Church: 24% Fewer Commitments, Home of the 7.5% tithe, fifteen-minute sermons, forty-five-minute worship services. We have only eight commandments—your choice. We use just three spiritual laws. Everything you've wanted in a church . . . and less!" Unfortunately that cartoon paints an accurate picture. Many people today are looking for a "lite church," a "lite faith," and a "lite commitment." In the passage we're studying today, James asks each of us a question, "Is your faith genuine?" How can we know if we have real faith or "lite faith?"

1. **The Argument Stated (v. 14).** In verse 14, James writes "If someone says he has faith. . ." James doesn't say this individual actually does have faith, but simply that this person claims to have faith. The verb translated here, "to claim," or, "to say," is in the present tense, which suggests this person is continually asserting his faith, constantly saying, "I have faith. I have faith," but his words are hollow. No outward evidence supports his claim. So James is referring to the profession of faith, not to the possession of faith. The faith that James denounces is a mere creedal confession, not a faith that entails wholehearted acceptance. James has nothing against faith. In fact, throughout his letter he shows us he is a great supporter of faith (1:3, 6; 2:1, 5), but he wants it to be genuine, wholehearted faith. James would agree with those who say that we aren't saved by faith plus works, but we are saved by a faith that works. It must have follow-through. If there is a root, it will eventually bear fruit; no fruit means no root. Where works do not exist, neither does faith (see v. 18).

2. **The Principle Illustrated (vv. 15–16, 19).** James goes on to illustrate the logical absurdity of faith without works. The "brother" or "sister" is probably a believer, maybe a needy person in the congregation. James attacks those who

only speak kind words to this needy soul. Isn't it enough to be kind? No! The needy person's body is still cold; his stomach is still empty. To make it personal, there are those in this community needing our help. The test for us is how we react to them. Do we simply smile and say, "I hope it gets better," or do we cook them dinner, keep their children, or help them move into their new apartment? Genuine conversion leads to genuine compassion. James gives a further example of false faith in verse 19. His reference to the demons makes a graphic point. No demon is an atheist. They believe in God, they exercise "faith," yet we know they are spiritually dead; we know they are not saved nor have the kind of faith God requires. A kind of belief exists which is not true faith. The man in verse 14 had intellectual faith. Demons not only have this, but they are in full agreement emotionally with the truth of who God is. But they lack the type of faith that "trusts in" or "relies upon" God. Saving faith involves all three components: knowledge, agreement, and trust. That is, the mind, emotions, and will. A belief that does not work is no better than that which the demons have.

3. **The Conclusion Drawn (vv. 17, 20).** What is James' conclusion? Faith that does not evidence itself outwardly is not genuine faith. Faith, by itself, is dead. If it produces no works, it is lifeless and ineffective to justification. Faith alone without works is as dead as a body without breath. If you put a monitor on someone who professes to have faith but displays no outward evidence, the monitor will show a flat line. That person can talk all they want, but they do not have genuine faith. Without the outward evidence of deeds, a mere profession of faith is simply that: a profession without possession, an impostor posing as a believer. Could that be you?

>>> *sermon continued on following page*

APPROPRIATE HYMNS AND SONGS

'Tis So Sweet to Trust in Jesus, Louisa M.R. Stead; Public Domain.

Burdens Are Lifted at Calvary, John M. Moore; © 1952 Singspiration Music, Admin. by Brentwood-Benson Music Publishing, Inc.

Dare to Be a Daniel, Philip P. Bliss; Public Domain.

Holy One, John Barnett; © 1995 Mercy/Vineyard Music Publishing.

I Have Kept the Faith, Paul Baloche; © 1992 Integrity's Hosanna! Music, Admin. by Integrity Music, Inc.

Conclusion: A line from a Rich Mullins song says, "Faith without works is like a screen door on a submarine." It's worthless and it sinks. Do you claim to have faith? Does your life really show it? A workless faith is a worthless faith. We must ask ourselves, "If I were arrested for being a Christian, would there be enough evidence to convict me?"

FOR THE BULLETIN

❂ The crackle of flames attracted the attention of residents near the Circus Maximus in Rome on July 18, 64. Trumpets sounded the alarm, but winds whipped the fire into an inferno that spread across the city. Thousands died, and hundreds of thousands became homeless. Rumors circulated that the fire had been started by 26-year-old Emperor Nero. To divert blame, Nero pointed a finger at Christians, who were put to death with "exquisite cruelty . . . covered with skins of wild beasts, left to be devoured by dogs . . . nailed to crosses . . . burned alive . . . covered with inflammable matter and set on fire to serve as torches during the night." Peter and Paul, according to tradition, were among the martyrs. ❂ July 18, 1100, marks the death of Godfrey of Bouillon, leader of the First Crusade which captured Jerusalem in 1099. ❂ July 18, 1504, is the birthday of Johann Heinrich Bullinger, Swiss Reformer and successor of Zwingli in Zurich. ❂ On this day in 1753, an unwanted baby named Lemuel Haynes was born to a black man and white woman, both of whom abandoned him. At the age of five months, he became an indentured servant in the home of a kindly family who treated him like their own son. There he learned about Christ and the Bible. During the Revolutionary War, Lemuel enlisted as a minuteman and served with George Washington's forces. He became an early, outspoken advocate for the abolition of slavery, and a powerful pastor and evangelist, and the first African-American to pastor a white church in American history. ❂ On July 18, 1870, the infallibility of the pope and the universality of his episcopate were proclaimed as dogma at the Vatican I Ecumenical Council.

STATS, STORIES AND MORE

From the Peanut Gallery
The Peanuts comic strip written by Charles Schulz once featured a brilliant illustration of faith without works: Charlie Brown and Linus come across Snoopy shivering in the snow. Charlie says, "Snoopy looks kind of cold, doesn't he?" Linus replies, "I'll say. Maybe we'd better go over and comfort him." They walk over to the dog, pat his head, and Charlie Brown says, "Be of good cheer, Snoopy." Linus adds, "Yes, be of good cheer." In the final frame, the boys are walking away, still bundled up in their winter coats. Snoopy is still shivering, and over his head is a big "?".

Faith without Works
"No man can come to Christ by faith and remain the same anymore than he can come into contact with a 220-volt wire and remain the same."
—*Warren Wiersbe*

"A person who professes Christ but who does not live a Christ-honoring, Christ-obeying life is a fraud."
—*John MacArthur*

"Faith alone justifies, but the faith that justifies is never alone."
—*Reformer John Calvin*

While being robbed in Philadelphia, Tony Compolo told the burglar, "I'm a Baptist minister." His assailant replied, "Really? I'm a Baptist, too!"

A Story of Fruitful Faith
In the late '60s and early '70s, Keith Green was highly influenced by his culture. As an aspiring and incredibly talented musician on the rise, he experimented with eastern religions and drugs. In 1975, however, he gave his life to Jesus Christ and his music changed to reflect an energetic faith. While inspirational or worshipful, it was also exhortative, asking questions like, "How can you be so dead, when you've been so well fed?" And, "How can you be so numb, not to care if they come? You close your eyes and pretend the job's done; don't close your eyes and pretend the job's done!" His life reflected his faith: he took in the homeless, the drunks, the drug abusers, and anyone else. His Spirit-filled music and ministry to the needy yielded much fruit.

WORSHIP HELPS

Call to Worship:
Hear my cry, O God; attend to my prayer. From the end of the earth I will cry to You, when my heart is overwhelmed; lead me to the rock that is higher than I. For You have been a shelter for me, a strong tower from the enemy. I will abide in Your tabernacle forever; I will trust in the shelter of Your wings . . . So I will sing praise to Your name forever (Ps. 61:1–4, 8).

Scripture Reading Medley:
For by grace you have been saved through faith, and that not of yourselves; it is the gift of God, not of works, lest anyone should boast . . . When the Son of Man comes in His glory . . . He will set the sheep on His right hand, but the goats on the left. Then the King will say to those on His right hand, "Come, you blessed of My Father, inherit the kingdom prepared for you from the foundation of the world: for I was hungry and you gave Me food; I was thirsty and you gave Me drink; I was a stranger and you took Me in; I was naked and you clothed Me; I was sick and you visited Me; I was in prison and you came to Me" . . . For as the body without the spirit is dead, so faith without works is dead. . .For we are His workmanship, created in Christ Jesus for good works, which God prepared beforehand that we should walk in them
(Eph. 2:8–9; Matt. 25:31, 33–36; James 2:26; Eph. 2:10)

Benediction:
Now to Him who is able to keep you from stumbling, and to present you faultless before the presence of His glory with exceeding joy, to God our Savior, who alone is wise, be glory and majesty, dominion and power, both now and forever. Amen.

Additional Sermons and Lesson Ideas

Deep Impact

Date preached:

SCRIPTURE: Acts 28:17–30

INTRODUCTION: No one short of Christ has made a bigger impact on the world than the apostle Paul, and every snapshot of his life contains clues as to why he was so influential. This final paragraph of the Book of Acts gives us a portrait of Paul following his voyage to Rome (chs. 27—28a), living under house arrest, spreading the gospel in the capital city of the Empire.

1. The Importance of Rest (v. 17). Paul took three days to rest before launching into ministry. We have to take care of ourselves.
2. The Importance of Reputation (vv. 17–19). Paul reassured them that he wasn't a criminal, but an unjustly-charged man.
3. The Importance of Relationship (v. 20). "I have called for you, to see you and speak with you." He was entering an extended relationship with some of these Romans.
4. The Importance of Reasoning (vv. 21–23). Paul didn't give them a ten-minute gospel presentation. He reasoned with them from dawn to nightfall, for two years. Notice the verbs in verse 23: explained . . . testified . . . persuading.
5. The Importance of Receiving (vv. 24–31). Some received, but others, by rejecting, were rejected.

CONCLUSION: How can God use your life to make a deep impact?

Back to Basics
By Melvin Worthington

Date preached:

SCRIPTURE: 1 Peter 2:1–2

INTRODUCTION: During my early years in the ministry a wise man advised me to stick with the Scriptures, stand on the Scriptures, speak the Scriptures, and show the Scriptures. It is time for us to get back to the basics regarding Christian living. Five basic things are required if one is to live a faithful, fruitful, fitting, focused, and fulfilling Christian life.

1. The Word of God. The Christian must faithfully feast upon it, partaking of it as a baby partakes of milk.
2. The Worship of God. Living in the fast lane makes it easy to forget to "be still, and know that I am God" (Ps. 46:10).
3. The Will of God. God's will for the Christian is not optional. Every Christian can find, follow, and finish the will of God (Prov. 3:5, 6).
4. The Work of God. Working in God's field requires patience, perseverance, and prayer (1 Cor. 15:58).
5. The Walk with God. A Christian relationship with God is compared to a walk. "And Enoch walked with God and he was not, for God took him" (Gen. 5:24).

CONCLUSION: It's time to get back to the basics.

HEROES FOR THE PASTOR'S HEART

Finney's Conversion

As a young man Charles Finney decided to study law. When he later came to Christ, he used his legal skills to present the gospel as if he were making a case to a jury. He is credited with winning a half million people to the Lord, either directly or indirectly, and with pioneering methods of evangelism that paved the way for the campaigns and crusades of evangelists like D. L. Moody and Billy Graham. The account of his conversion, as recorded in his autobiography and condensed below, is a classic:

On a Sabbath evening in the autumn of 1821, I made up my mind I would settle the question of my salvation at once. I was busy in the affairs of the office, but as providence would have it, I was not much occupied on Monday or Tuesday; and had opportunity to read my Bible and engage in prayer most of the time.

But I was very proud without knowing it. I found I was unwilling to have anyone know I was seeking salvation. When I prayed I would only whisper my prayer, after having stopped the keyhole to the door. I kept my Bible out of sight. I didn't want to see my minister, because I didn't want to let him know how I felt. I could not shed a tear; I could not pray.

Tuesday night I had become very nervous; and a strange feeling came over me as if I was about to die. I knew that if I did I should sink down to hell; but I quieted myself as best I could until morning.

At an early hour I started for the office, but just before I arrived an inward voice said to me, "What are you waiting for?"

I think I then saw the reality and fullness of the Atonement of Christ. I saw that His work was a finished work; and that instead of having, or needing, any righteousness of my own to recommend me to God, I had to submit myself to the righteousness of God through Christ.

Without being distinctly aware of it, I had stopped in the street right where the inward voice seemed to arrest me. How long I remained in that position I cannot say. But the question seemed to be put, "Will you accept it now, today?" I replied, "Yes; I will accept it today, or I will die in the attempt."

North of the village lay a piece of woods in which I was in the habit of walking. Instead of going to the office, I turned toward the woods, feeling I must be alone so I could pour out my prayer to God.

But as I went over the hill, it occurred to me that someone might see me. So great was my pride that I recollect I skulked along under the fence till I got so far out of sight that no one from the village could see me. I then penetrated into the woods and found a place where some large trees had fallen across each other, leaving an open place between. I knelt down for prayer, recollecting, "I will give my heart to God, or I never will come down from there."

But when I attempted to pray I found that my heart would not pray. In attempting to pray, I would hear a rustling in the leaves, as I thought, and would stop and look up to see if somebody were not coming. This I did several times. A great sinking and discouragement came over me, and I felt almost too weak to stand upon my knees.

Just at this moment I again thought I heard someone approach me, and I opened my eyes to see whether it were so. But right there the revelation of my pride of heart was distinctly shown to me. An overwhelming sense of my wickedness took such possession of me that I cried at the top of my voice, and exclaimed that I would not leave that place if all the men on earth and all the devils in hell surrounded me.

Just at that point, this passage of Scripture seemed to drop into my mind: "Then shall ye seek me and find me, when ye shall search for me with all your heart." I instantly seized hold of this with my heart. I had intellectually believed the Bible before; but never had the truth been in my mind that faith was a voluntary trust instead of an intellectual state. I cried to Him, "Lord, I take Thee at Thy word."

I continued thus to pray for a long time, I know not how long. I prayed till my mind became so full that, before I was aware of it, I was on my feet and tripping up the ascent toward the road. I soon reached the road that led to the village and began to reflect upon what had passed; and I found that my mind had become most wonderfully quiet and peaceful. I said to myself, "What is this? I must have grieved the Holy Ghost entirely away. I have lost all my conviction and perhaps committed the unpardonable sin."

It was on the 10th of October, and a very pleasant day. I had gone into the woods immediately after an early breakfast; and when I returned to the village I found it was dinner time. Yet I had been wholly unconscious of the time that had passed; it appeared to me that I had been gone from the village but a short time.

But how was I to account for the quiet of my mind? All sense of sin, all consciousness of present sin or guilt, had departed from me. I said to myself, "What is this, that I cannot arouse any sense of guilt in my

HEROES FOR THE PASTOR'S HEART — CONTINUED

soul, as great a sinner as I am?" I tried in vain to make myself anxious about my present state, lest it should be a result of my having grieved the Spirit away. But take any view of it I would, I could not be anxious at all about my soul.

I went to my dinner and found I had no appetite to eat. I then went to the office, and found that Squire W had gone to dinner. I took down my bass viol, and began to play and sing some pieces of sacred music. As soon as I began to sing those sacred words, I began to weep. It seemed as if my heart was all liquid; and my feelings were in such a state that I could not hear my own voice in singing without causing my sensibility to overflow. I wondered at this, and tried to suppress my tears, but could not.

By evening I made up, in an open fireplace, a good fire, hoping to spend the evening alone. Just at dark Squire W bade me goodnight and went to his home. I had accompanied him to the door; and as I closed the door and turned around, my heart seemed to be liquid within me. All my feelings seemed to rise and flow out; and the utterance of my heart was, "I want to pour my whole soul out to God." The rising of my soul was so great that I rushed into the room back of the front office, to pray.

There was no fire, and no light in the room; nevertheless it appeared to me as if it were perfectly light. As I went in and shut the door after me, it seemed as if I met the Lord Jesus Christ face to face. He said nothing, but looked at me in such a manner as to break me right down at his feet. I have always since regarded this as a most remarkable state of mind; for it seemed to me a reality, that He stood before me, and I fell down at His feet and poured out my soul to Him. It seemed to me that I bathed His feet with my tears; and yet I had no distinct impression that I touched Him, that I recollect.

As soon as my mind became calm enough to break off from the interview, I returned to the front office, and found that the fire that I had made of large wood was nearly burned out. But as I turned and was about to take a seat by the fire, I received a mighty baptism of the Holy Ghost. Without any expectation of it, without ever having the thought in my mind that there was any such thing for me, without any recollection that I had ever heard the thing mentioned by any person in the world, the Holy Spirit descended upon me in a manner that seemed to go through me, body and soul. I could feel the impression, like a wave of electricity, going through and through me. Indeed it seemed to come in waves and waves of liquid love, for I could not express it in any other way. It seemed like the very breath of God. I can recollect distinctly that it seemed to fan me, like immense wings.

How long I continued in this state I do not know. But I know it was late in the evening when a member of my choir came into the office to see me. He was a member of the church. He found me in this state of loud weeping, and said to me, "Mr. Finney, what ails you?" I could make him no answer for some time. He then said, "Are you in pain?" I gathered myself up as best I could, and replied, "No, but so happy that I cannot live."

Quotes for the Pastor's Wall

" I have no dread of preaching now; preaching is the greatest joy of my life, and sometimes when I stand up to speak and realize that He (the Holy Spirit) is there, that all the responsibility is upon Him, such a joy fills my heart that I can scarce restrain myself from shouting and leaping. "

—R. A. Torrey

JULY 25, 2004

SUGGESTED SERMON
Who Do You Say That I Am?   Date preached:
By Peter Grainger

Scripture: Mark 8:27–38, especially v. 29: He said to them, "But who do you say that I am?" Peter answered and said to Him, "You are the Christ."

Introduction: A couple of years ago, the hit game show, *"Who Wants to Be a Millionaire?"* spawned a whole new set of catch phrases, such as, "Three Lifelines," and "Is that your final answer?" By giving a correct series of "final answers," the contestant could win a million dollars. But the questions had little life-significance. Today I'd like to pose a question which requires a correct final answer, and there isn't just a million dollars riding on it. It is a question of eternal significance. Answer correctly and live forever, answer incorrectly and you will be lost forever. Interestingly, in this passage we have three lifelines to help us:

1. **Ask the Audience (vv. 27–28).** For those who have never watched, *"Who Wants to Be a Millionaire?"* the contestants are allowed three lifelines or helps. One is to ask the audience for help on a certain question, perhaps one they don't know or are uncertain about. Each member of the audience votes as to their suggested answer. The percentages are then given to the contestant. Of course, there may be no clear majority, or the majority may be wrong. Notice in our text, Jesus first asked the disciples, "Who do men say that I am?" (v. 27). Jesus had been traveling throughout Israel for almost three years and vast crowds of people had been following His progress. He was the topic of every conversation, the talk of the nation. Who was this Jesus? Everyone had formed an opinion; some thought He was John the Baptist, Elijah, or one of the prophets (v. 28). If you had asked the audience who Jesus was, you would have gotten no clear answer or definitive help. That suits a lot of people, perhaps you. They like a vague Jesus, one in which we can all have our own opinion. But, before you take this easy option, you'd be wise to avail yourself of a second lifeline.

2. **Phone a Friend (v. 29).** *"Who Wants to Be a Millionaire?"* offers another lifeline if the contestant is perplexed: he or she may phone a friend who

then has thirty seconds to offer his or her opinion. In Mark 8, Jesus was not primarily interested in what the audiences thought about His identity. His concern was with the special group of His followers. Jesus put them on the spot, asking, "Who do you say that I am?" (v. 29). Peter immediately answered, "You are the Christ" (v. 29). Christ was the Greek name for the person called the Messiah in Hebrew. Both names mean the Anointed One. The people of Israel looked forward to the day which God had promised when He would send the Anointed One, who would save God's people and bring in God's rule on earth. Peter answered correctly: Jesus is no ordinary man or prophet, not even Elijah, but the One appointed by God to save those who put their faith in Him. So, have you got the right answer or have you been given the right answer? Are you still in the dark as to the identity of Jesus? Jesus went on to explain to the crowds that His identity was of utmost importance.

3. **Fifty-Fifty (vv. 34–38).** On the game show, there are four possible answers to each question: one correct and three wrong. There is a third lifeline called fifty-fifty, in which you take away two of the wrong answers. Now you are left with just two possible answers: the right one and a wrong one. That's where we are today—we all stand before Christ and He asks, "Who am I?" There are only two answers—the right one and the wrong one. Which will you choose? If He is just a legendary figure or a good Teacher, then it means little to follow Him. But if He is the Christ, the Messiah, the Lord of the Universe, it means everything to follow Him. It means denying yourself and taking up your cross, dying to your own preferences and

>>> *sermon continued on following page*

APPROPRIATE HYMNS AND SONGS

How Great Thou Art, Stuart Hine; © 1941, 1953, 1955 Stuart K. Hine, Renewed 1981 Manna Music, Inc.

Awesome God, Rich Mullins; © 1988 BMG Songs, Admin. by BMG Music Publishing.

Come, Thou Almighty King, Charles Wesley/Felice De Giardani; Public Domain.

Creating God Your Fingers Trace, Jeffery Rowthorn/Eugene W. Hancock; © 1979 Hope Publishing Company.

You Are Mighty, Craig Musseau; © 1989 Mercy/Vineyard Publishing.

ambitions and living for Him. The only way to win your life is to lose your life for His sake and for the gospel, to take this Good News to your world (vv. 34–38). Either Jesus is who He claims to be and following Him is worth giving up everything; or He is not.

Conclusion: Consider what your answer is to this question, "Who do you say that I am?" Is He simply another man? A work of fiction? Or is He your Lord and Savior, your master whom you follow despite the cost? Think this question through carefully, and be prepared with your "final answer."

FOR THE BULLETIN

❋ On July 25, A.D. 325, the Council of Nicea, the first ecumenical council in church history, closed. It had convened in Nicea (now Iznik, Turkey) to deal with the Arian Controversy. The Arians followed the teaching of a North African priest named Arius who presented an inferior doctrine of Christ. At Nicea, church leaders established an orthodox Christology, declaring that Jesus was "true God from true God, begotten, not made." ❋ William Romaine was a fiery evangelical in the Church of England. His zeal confounded church leaders, and he lost both friends and positions. In at least one church, officials refused to light the building where he spoke, forcing him to preach by the light of a single candle held in his hand. But Romaine's revivalistic preaching drew larger and larger audiences until all of London was affected. On Saturday, July 25, 1795, Romaine, 81, found himself unable to go down the stairs. He settled on an upstairs couch in great weakness, "giving glory to God." A little later he cried, "Holy! Holy! Holy! Blessed Jesus! To thee be endless praise," before taking his final breath. ❋ July 25, 1817, marks the death of John Fawcett, a Baptist preacher in Wainsgate, Yorkshire, England. In 1772, he was called to pastor the great Carter's Lane Baptist Church in London. He and his family were ready to go when their hearts broke for the little church in Wainsgate and found themselves unable to part. Out of the experience came the famous hymn, "Bless Be the Tie." ❋ July 25, 1899, is the birthday of Stuart K. Hine, author of "How Great Thou Art."

STATS, STORIES AND MORE

Quotes about Jesus
It occurs to me that all the contorted theories about Jesus that have been spontaneously generating since the day of His death merely confirm the awesome risk God took when He stretched Himself out on the dissection table—a risk He seemed to welcome. Examine Me. Test Me. You decide.
—*Philip Yancy*

If Jesus wasn't God, He deserves an Oscar.—*Josh McDowell*

Jesus is God spelling Himself out in language that man can understand.
—*S. D. Gordon*

He stands absolutely alone in history; in teaching, in example, in character, an exception, a marvel, and He is Himself the evidence of Christianity.
—*A. T. Pierson*

James Kennedy and Jerry Newcombe wrote a book entitled, *What If Jesus Had Never Been Born,* in which they listed some of the elements that would be missing in history if Christ had not come to win people to Himself and establish His church, such as:

Hospitals
Universities, most of which were originally started by Christians for Christian purposes
Literacy and education for the masses
Representative government
Civil liberties
The abolition of slavery
Modern science
Benevolence and charity
Higher standards of justice
The elevation of the common man
A high regard for human life
The codifying and setting to writing of many of the world's languages
The greater development of arts and music
Millions of transformed lives.

WORSHIP HELPS

Call to Worship:
Let us come before His presence with thanksgiving; let us shout joyfully to Him with psalms. For the LORD is the great God (Ps. 95:2–3).

Hymn Story:
Today is the birthday of missionary Stuart Hine, author of one of our most famous hymns, "How Great Thou Art." It began in 1886, when a Swedish minister named Carl Boberg, inspired by the grandeur of a thunderstorm on the rugged Swedish coast, wrote a hymn beginning with the words "O Mighty God!" In 1923, Stuart Hine, a British missionary in Russia, heard the Russian rendition of this hymn, and began writing a new English version, adding his own thoughts and weaving into the text his own expressions of worship for the breathtaking scenery he had seen in his travels. He ended up with three verses, yet his English hymn remained "undiscovered." Years passed. During World War II, Rev. and Mrs. Hine returned to England, and immediately following the war, they observed the plight of refugees trying to return home. Thousands had fled to Britain from Eastern Europe during the Nazi invasion, and now were homesick, wanting to return to their native lands. Prompted by this, Hine wrote a fourth verse to the hymn he had translated.

Responsive Reading:

People: For Your name's sake, O Lord, pardon my iniquity, for it is great.

Leader: Great is the Lord, and greatly to be praised; and His greatness is unsearchable. Great is Your mercy toward me. As the heavens are high above the earth, so great is His mercy toward those who fear Him. Oh, how great is Your goodness which You have laid up for those who fear you. Your righteousness is like the great mountains; Your judgments are a great deep. The works of the Lord are great. His merciful kindness is great. The Lord has done great things for us, and we are glad.

People: Bless the Lord, O my soul! O Lord my God, You are very great.

(Pss. 25:11; 145:3; 86:13; 103:11; 31:19; 36:6; 111:2; 117:2; 126:3; 104:1)

Additional Sermons and Lesson Ideas

Making Wise Decisions
By Kevin Riggs

Date preached:

SCRIPTURE: Various Proverbs

INTRODUCTION: Some decisions we make are more important than others, but all need to be made with care. The Book of Proverbs gives us four principles for wise decisions.

1. Place Your Trust Completely in God (Prov. 3:5–6). The closer I am to God the more apt I am to make wise choices (Prov. 16:3).
2. Plan Ahead and Think Things Through—See the examples of the wise ant, the wise son, and the wise housewife (Prov. 6:6–8; 10:5; 31:21).
3. Gather All the Facts (Prov. 13:16).
4. Seek Godly Counsel (Prov. 12:15; 15:22).

CONCLUSION: Are you facing a tough decision? Once you have applied these four principles you can move forward with confidence, keeping two promises in mind: God will never lead you contrary to His Word, and He will not allow you to make a wrong decision if you have been sensitive to His leadership at every point.

Wrestling with Skunks

Date preached:

SCRIPTURE: Acts 24:1–21

INTRODUCTION: Have you ever been unjustly accused of something? That was Paul's situation in Acts 24, when Jewish authorities from Jerusalem came to Caesarea to accuse him of sedition before Governor Felix. Paul's demeanor and defense were surprising.

1. The Accusation (vv. 1–9). Paul was called a plague, creator of dissention, and ringleader of a sect (v. 5).
2. The Accused (vv. 10–21).
   A. His Cheerfulness (vv. 10–13). Paul said, "I do the more cheerfully answer for myself." His optimist attitude wasn't daunted by trials, for he knew the charges wouldn't stick.
   B. His Confession (v. 14). Standing on trial for his life, Paul used the last two words we'd expect to hear from a defendant: "I confess." He said, "I confess to you, that according to the Way . . . I worship the God of my fathers."
   C. His Conviction (v. 15). The hope of the resurrection.
   D. His Conscience (v. 16). His conscience was clear.
   E. His Case (vv. 17–21). Paul finally got around to the charges against him.

CONCLUSION: When you wrestle with skunks, even if you win, you lose! Paul was more concerned about exalting Christ's name than about clearing his own. Every opportunity, even when we're slandered, can become an opportunity for witness.

AUGUST 1, 2004

SUGGESTED SERMON
Consider Your Ways   *Date preached:*
By Stuart Briscoe

Scripture: Haggai 1, especially verse 7: Thus says the LORD of hosts: "Consider your ways!"

Introduction: The term "minor prophet" is given to Haggai and to eleven others because they wrote relatively short prophetic statements in the Old Testament, but there is nothing minor about their messages.

1. **Verse 1.** The man named Haggai is described as a prophet in verse 1; in verse 13, he's called the LORD's messenger; and in verse 12 he's a man whom God has sent. Everybody lives in a culture, and cultures have dominant themes. Sometimes the dominant theme can be dead wrong. Someone needs to stand up at times and blow the whistle on the things that are wrong about the dominant culture. That person is a prophet, and that is what Haggai was.

2. **Verses 2–4.** This sentence introduces Haggai's message, but we need to understand the historical background. When God called Abraham, He promised to give him a special land and to establish his descendants as a great nation. Later, Joshua brought these people into the Promised Land. Under King David they established a great empire and David built himself a great palace in Jerusalem. But he was concerned that the Ark of the Lord was kept in a battered old tent. He wanted to build a temple as the dwelling place of God, but the Lord told him, "Thank you very much, but I want your son, Solomon, to do it." Hence, the great temple of Solomon was built. Years passed, and the Babylonians swept over this Promised Land, besieged the city of Jerusalem, overthrew the king, and destroyed the temple. The people were herded off to distant Babylon, and the land was desolate. But God promised to restore His people to Judah, and the day came when a new emperor—King Cyrus of Persia—issued an edict for the rebuilding of the temple in Jerusalem (see Ezra 1). A delegation of exiles returned to Judah, but rebuilding the temple became a thankless job, and the surrounding peoples fiercely opposed

them. In utter discouragement, the remnant stopped work on the temple and concentrated on building the rest of the city—including their own houses (see Ezra 4). Now the people were finding themselves in need. Famine and drought and poverty were nipping at their heels. Nothing seemed to satisfy their needs.

3. **Verse 7.** Haggai's message to them was, "Consider your ways!" They needed to think about the fact that what they were really telling the Lord was: "We don't have time to rebuild Your house. We've been too busy with our own houses." It's not that the Lord minded them having their own houses. God is the one who gives us richly all things to enjoy (1 Tim. 6:17). The problem was that there was something fundamentally wrong with their lives. They were so busy planting, eating, working, and getting all the things they needed that they were totally neglecting God's priorities for them. As a result, nothing satisfied. They ate, but stayed hungry. They drank, but stayed thirsty. They put on clothes, but stayed cold. They made money, but it went through holes in their pockets. They couldn't find anything that gave them deep, lasting satisfaction. God's message to them was: Stop and think!

4. **Verses 8–9.** The people were not making the connection between what was lacking in their lives and the fundamental spiritual issue at the core of their lives. When things go wrong with us, we turn to experts. If we have a financial problem, we go to a financial expert. We've got a family problem, so we go to a family therapist. These are all legitimate responses unless, of course, the root problem is spiritual. Haggai was saying, "The reason there's blight on your harvest and emptiness in your life is that you

>>> *sermon continued on following page*

APPROPRIATE HYMNS AND SONGS

Be Bold and Be Strong, Martin J. Nystrom; © 1990 Integrity's Hosanna! Music.

Dare to Be A Daniel, Philip P. Bliss; Public Domain.

Led By the Master's Hand, Mosie Lister; © 1954. Renewed 1982 Lillenas Publishing Company, Admin. by The Copyright Company.

Only Trust Him, John H. Stockton; Public Domain.

God Is Here, Don Moen/Paul Overstreet; © 1997 Integrity's Hosanna! Music/Scarlet Moon, Admin. by Copyright Management.

are neglecting God's priorities." The Lord wanted them to do something He could take pleasure in and be gloried by (v. 8), but they were too busy in all their other pursuits.

Conclusion: The people responded to Haggai's message in three ways. First, they recognized the Lord was speaking through him (v. 12). Second, as they listened they were reassured that the Lord was with them (v. 13). Third, the Lord stirred them up and they said, "We have neglected the spiritual dimension of our lives, and as a result we're empty." They refocused on God and began building His temple once again (v. 14). What Haggai said to his people is what the Lord is still saying to us today: Consider your ways!

FOR THE BULLETIN

❋ When Britain's Queen Anne and Parliament passed the "Schism Bill," to take effect August 1, 1714, many predicted it would reestablish Catholicism in England "with mighty gust," and that Baptists and other Dissenters would again be racked and burned. But just before the law was to begin, Queen Anne took ill and died. For years, Dissenters regarded August 1, 1714 as a day of deliverance, the "Protestant Passover," and many historians believe this was the inspiration for the great Isaac Watts hymn: "O God Our Help in Ages Past, Our Hope for Years to Come." ❋ William Carey is ordained into the ministry on this day in 1787. ❋ Today is the birthday of Francis Scott Key, born in 1779. He was a Christian attorney, statesman, Sunday school teacher, and the author of the American national anthem. ❋ August 1, 1808, marks the birth of Octavius Winslow, powerful nineteenth century pastor and author. Most of his ministry was spent in England. He wrote over forty books, many of which are still in demand today. ❋ August 1, 1834, marks the death of Robert Morrison, 52, first protestant missionary to China. ❋ On August 1, 1834, slavery was abolished throughout all the British Empire, largely as a result of the tireless abolitionist efforts of British evangelicals. ❋ Today is the anniversary of one of the saddest catastrophes in the history of missions—the Ku-Cheng Massacre, which occurred on August 1, 1895. Nine missionaries, eight women and a man, were killed by Chinese nationalists. Four of them died when their house was set on fire. Another had her throat slit. Some were speared, and one died from shock.

STATS, STORIES AND MORE

More from Stuart Briscoe
Many years ago, I was invited to speak in Germany at a home for recovering alcoholics. Most of the men in the home were World War II veterans who had been grievously wounded, and had turned to alcohol as a result of their terrible experiences. While I was speaking there, I noticed a huge tapestry the men had made which hung behind the podium. It pictured a river, down which a whole school of fish were moving. And then in the opposite direction there was just one fish. Underneath in German were the words, which translated into English read: "Any dead fish can go with the stream. It takes a live one to swim against it." That's a prophet. That's also a Christian.

Haggai's Impact
Bishop Handley Moule was one of England's most respected churchmen. His conversion to Christ occurred at age 25, during the Christmas season of 1866. Yet some years later when he entered the ministry, he felt spiritually unfit. Writing again to his father, he said, "I sadly feel the need of ten-fold grace before I can hope to be either a very happy Christian or—as a minister of Jesus Christ—a very useful one."

In 1883, some Keswick speakers came along preaching of rest and victory in Christ. Handley attended the meeting, held in a great barn. A Christian businessman, William Sloan, spoke from Haggai 1:6: "You eat, but do not have enough." Sloan said that when "Self" rules our hearts instead of Christ, our souls are lean. Only the life fully committed to Christ is Spirit-filled and victorious.

That evening Moule yielded himself without reservation to be the Lord's bondservant, and he trusted Christ to fill him with power for joyful living and effective service. A peace filled him like the ocean, and from that day until his death in 1920, he was powerfully used for Christ.

WORSHIP HELPS

Call to Worship:
"My Spirit remains among you; do not fear! . . . I will fill this temple with glory," says the Lord of hosts (Hag. 2:5, 7).

Appropriate Scripture Readings:
Matthew 6:19–34
Psalm 27:1–4
Philippians 3:1–14

Word of Welcome:
The word "visitor" comes from the same Latin word as our word "video." It means, "to come to see." Visitors are people who come to see something. If you're visiting with us today, we want you to see our love for you, our joy that you're here, and we want you to see the Lord Jesus Christ among us. Thank you for your presence here.

Closing Prayer:
Lord, we'd like to take a few moments and just think about the ways our lives are turning out. Disappointments, discouragements, disillusionment, deflated dreams, feelings of worthlessness, lack of direction. And our way of handling all this is to get busier and busier. But what You've told us to do is to consider our ways. As we give careful thought to our ways, help us to see that at the root of our problems, more often than not, is a spiritual lack. Show us how we have neglected our spiritual priorities and the spiritual principles You extol. Lord, stir our hearts with these thoughts. Give us the assurance that You are really speaking to us, that You are with us, totally committed to working out your eternal purposes in our lives. Help us to rise up, to move out, and to do what you are telling us to do. In Christ's Name, Amen.
—*Stuart Briscoe*

Additional Sermons and Lesson Ideas

The Discipline of Detour

Date preached:

By Denis Lyle

SCRIPTURE: Exodus 13:17–22, especially verse 17

INTRODUCTION: Comedian Jerry Seinfeld once commented that race horses must be incredibly confused: the jockeys whip and kick them, obviously in a hurry, but they take the longest possible route, all the way around the track, to reach the finish line! In our lives, we face many detours that may seem pointless, but God always has a wonderful purpose. We find this true in our text today:

1. God's Guidance—God Led (vv. 17–18).
2. God's Goal—God Said (v. 17).
3. God's Grace—God Went Ahead (vv. 19–21).

CONCLUSION: God led the Israelites on "the scenic route," to display His power and provision. Is God taking you on a detour? Look to Him for His abundant grace to meet your every need along the way!

Is Religion Worthless?

Date preached:

SCRIPTURE: Mark 7:1–30

INTRODUCTION: This is a religious world, and Christianity is one of the world's major religions. But there's a problem with that, as Mark explains in this passage.

1. The Inner Reality Is Critical (vv. 1–13). The religious leaders of Jesus' day criticized Him for not observing their external religious traditions. Every religion tends toward the external. Christianity can develop certain forms and features, which may not be bad in themselves, but if the inner reality dries up, the outward forms are worthless.
2. The Inner Reality Is Corrupt (vv. 14–23). But if genuine Christianity is primarily an inward reality, there's a problem. Our hearts are corrupt, and from our inner being flows evil thoughts, adulteries, fornications, murders, etc.
3. The Inner Reality Is Changed (vv. 24–30). Mark places the story of the Gentile woman here to contrast her with the religious leaders in the previous verses. She had a simple faith, and that faith resulted in healing and in the Savior's commendation.

CONCLUSION: Christianity isn't a religion; it's a relationship. The heart of our Christian experience is faith in Jesus Christ to forgive, heal, sanctify, and to live His life through us.

AUGUST 8, 2004

SUGGESTED SERMON

A Most Unlikely Evangelist

Date preached:

By Denis Lyle

Scripture: 2 Kings 5:1–14, especially verse 3: Then she said to her mistress, "If only my master were with the prophet who is in Samaria! For he would heal him of his leprosy."

Introduction: If I were to ask this congregation, "What kind of Christian does God use?" I believe the answer would be as varied as the people gathered here. We tend to believe God only uses the "perfect person," but we discover a delightful truth in Scripture God uses little people in big ways.

1. **A Strange Mystery.** The days in which this "little maid," lived were hard and cruel. There was continual warfare between Ben-Hadad, King of Syria, and the King of Israel. The army of Israel was then dispersed and no longer resisted Syria. The result was that marauding bands of Syrians continually invaded the borders of Israel and carried away whatever they wanted (see 1 Kin. 6:24; 20:1; 22:34; 22:36). In our text, a little maid was taken. What a strange mystery, a kidnapping allowed by God, who guards Israel (Ps. 121:4).

2. **Her Home Was Shattered (v. 2).** Can you enter into the feelings of these parents who had their young daughter ruthlessly snatched from them? How would you feel as a mother or father if your daughter was kidnapped? Would you not be sorely tried by this mysterious providence, asking, "Why?" Are you anguished today about something tragic that just doesn't make sense? God works through tragedy.

3. **A Hand Was Shaping (v. 15).** This event, which seemed to originate in the will of man, was the start of a divine plan through which Naaman was physically and spiritually healed! God had a purpose in this trial. We cannot always trace Gods providential dealings in our lives, but we can be sure that God will always work for our good (Rom. 8:28).

4. **A Simple Testimony (v. 3).** Although this girl was small in stature she was big in heart! She could have easily harbored bitterness against her captor.

Instead she directed Naaman toward God's prophet. Where did such faith come from? No doubt this child had often heard the story of God's dealings with her fathers. She must have listened intently as they spoke of the prophet that was in Samaria. Are you seeking to instill the truths of God's Word into the minds and hearts of your children (Deut. 6:7)? This captive maid, because she had been taught to trust and know God, was the means of bringing salvation to the home of her captivity, and of raising up a testimony for God which rang through the whole land of Syria! Note:

5. **How Courageous She Was.** In the midst of this pagan nation, she pointed her master towards God's representative (see Heb. 1:1), His prophet Elisha. This was true of Daniel, who was loyal to God in pagan Babylon (see Dan. 1:8). What about you? Are you being tested at college? At work? We're either conformers to outside pressure or transformers controlled by the inward power of God. Which are you?

6. **How Compassionate She Was.** This maid was an unwilling captive in Naaman's household, yet she could not bear to see her master suffer. She did not return a curse but a blessing to her captors! How do you react to your jerk of a boss? Your pushy landlord? Our compassion towards "enemies" just may soften the hardest of hearts (see Rom. 12:20).

7. **How Confident She Was.** There's not even a hint of doubt in her words! Leprosy had no cure, yet she was confident in her God's power!

>>> *sermon continued on following page*

APPROPRIATE HYMNS AND SONGS

God Who Stretched the Spangled Heavens, Catherine Cameron Arnott/William Moore; © 1967 Hope Publishing Company.

Here I Am, Tom Long/Alan Pote; © 1994 Hope Publishing Company.

I Would Be Like Jesus, James Rowe/Bently D. Ackley; Public Domain.

I'll Serve You, Jeff Reynolds; © 1993 Mercy/Vineyard Publishing.

The Spirit Says Arise, Billy Funk; © 1990 Integrity's Praise! Music.

8. **A Supernatural Recovery (vv. 4–15).** Naaman was healed of leprosy and brought to know God (vv. 14–15). It all began with a maid in captivity who moved her mistress (v. 3); her mistress moved a servant (v. 4); the servant moved the King of Syria (v. 5); the King of Syria moved the King of Israel (v. 7); the King of Israel moved Elisha (v. 8). The result was that Naaman was delivered from leprosy and idolatry. Talk about a most unlikely evangelist! She was the first link in the chain that eventually brought Naaman to the place of salvation.

Conclusion: Missionary Hudson Taylor, as he looked back over thirty years (during which he had seen 600 missionaries respond to his vision to reach China) said this: "God chose me because I was weak enough. God does not His great works by large committees. He trains someone to be quiet enough, and little enough, and then He uses him." The God who used this little maid can and will use you. Step out in faith and trust God to use you!

FOR THE BULLETIN

❋ August 8, 1471 marks the death of Thomas áKempis, Dutch mystic and devotional writer, at age 91. His book, *Imitation of Christ,* is the most famous book of Christian devotions in history. ❋ King Philip II of Spain, a Catholic, wanting to topple Queen Elizabeth of England, a Protestant, readied his navy, the largest and strongest on earth, to invade her land. When the battle was joined on July 21, weather aided the English, and on August 8, 1588, Elizabeth was told there that the danger of invasion was past. The relieved queen addressed her forces, saying: "I know that I have the body of a weak and feeble woman, but I have the heart and stomach of a king." ❋ In Cain Ridge, Kentucky, crowds began gathering on Friday, August 8, 1801, for an old-fashioned camp meeting. To the surprise of the organizers, thousands showed up, and a great revival broke out that changed the course of American church history. ❋ During the Boxer Rebellion in China, eight British Baptist missionaries at Hsinchow fled into the mountains to hide in the caves. When the magistrate at Hsinchow offered them protection if they would return to the city, they returned and were imprisoned. One of them, Rev. Herbert Dixon, said, "We are ready to glorify our Lord, by life or by death. If we die, there will certainly be others to take our place." On August 8, 1900, they were brutally beaten to death. ❋ On Tuesday, August 8, 1995, Norma McCorvey (Jane Roe of Roe v. Wade) was baptized in Dallas. The baptism was to celebrate her newfound faith in Jesus Christ.

STATS, STORIES AND MORE

A Most Unlikely Evangelist

In May of 1855, an 18-year-old boy went to the deacons of a church in Boston. He had been raised in a Unitarian church, ignorant of the gospel. When he moved to Boston to make his fortune, he began to attend a Bible-believing church. In April of 1855, his Sunday school teacher had come into the store where he was working and simply and persuasively shared the gospel and urged the young man to trust in Christ; he did. Now he was applying to join the church. It quickly became obvious that he was almost totally ignorant of biblical truth. One of the deacons asked him, "Son, what has Christ done for us all?" His response was, "I don't know. I think Christ has done a great deal for us: but I don't think of anything in particular as I know of." Years later his Sunday school teacher said of him, "I think the committee of the church seldom met an applicant for membership who seemed more unlikely ever to become a Christian of clear and decided views of gospel truth, still less to fill any space of public or extended usefulness." Nothing happened very quickly to change their minds. The deacons decided to put him on a year long instruction course to teach him basic Christian truths. Not only was he ignorant of spiritual truths, he was only barely literate and his spoken grammar was atrocious! At his second interview, there was only a little improvement in the quality of his answers. Since it was obvious that he was a sincere and committed Christian, they accepted him as a church member. Surely many people looked at that young man, convinced that God would never use a person like that. They wrote off D.L. Moody as "a most unlikely evangelist," but God did not. By God's grace D.L. Moody was transformed into one of the most effective servants of God, a man whose impact is still with us.

WORSHIP HELPS

Call to Worship:
Praise the Lord, each tribe and nation,
Praise Him with a joyous heart;
Ye who know His full salvation,
Gather now from every part;
Let your voices glorify,
In His temple, God on high.
—*Johann Franck*

Scripture Medley:
He who continually goes forth weeping, bearing seed for sowing, shall doubtless come again with rejoicing, bringing his sheaves with him. (Ps. 126:6). The sower sows the word. Preach the word! Be ready in season and out of season. Convince, rebuke, exhort, with all longsuffering and teaching. Go into all the world and preach the gospel to every creature. You are the light of the world. A city that is set on a hill cannot be hidden. Nor do they light a lamp and put it under a basket, but on a lampstand, and it gives light to all who are in the house. Let your light so shine before men, that they may see your good works and glorify your Father in heaven. Look, here is seed for you. Blessed are you who sow.
(Ps. 126:6; Mark 5:14; 2 Tim. 4:2; Mark 15:14; Matt. 5:14–16; Gen. 47:23; Is. 32:20)

Offertory Quotes:
I have held many things in my hands and I have lost them all. But whatever I have placed in God's hands, that I still possess—*Martin Luther.*
He is no fool who gives what he cannot keep to gain what he cannot lose—*Jim Elliot.*

Benediction:
Now may the God of peace Himself sanctify you entirely; and may your spirit and soul and body be preserved complete, without blame at the coming of our Lord Jesus Christ (1 Thess. 5:23).

Additional Sermons and Lesson Ideas

Barnstorming the Bible
Date preached:

Based on an outline by W. H. Griffith Thomas

SCRIPTURE: Acts 20:27

INTRODUCTION: When aviator Charles Lindbergh was beginning his career, he'd drop in at county fairs and take wide-eyed farmers for hops in his barnstormer. These rural people were astounded to see their homes and villages from the air, for they'd never before seen the whole panorama at once. Perhaps it will help us to do that with the Bible.

1. Revelation (Genesis to Deuteronomy) Or, Introduction. This is where God introduces His World, His Word, and His Work.
2. Preparation (Joshua to Esther). The historical books set the stage for all that will come later.
3. Aspiration (Job to Song of Solomon). The poetical books express the cry of the human heart in suffering, in worship, and in relationship.
4. Expectation (Isaiah to Malachi). Dominated with predictions about the coming Messiah.
5. Manifestation (Matthew to John). The appearance of Christ.
6. Realization (Acts to Jude). How the followers of Christ are to live in this world.
7. Consummation (Revelation). This book tells us those things that will soon take place.

CONCLUSION: The Bible is a remarkably cohesive book, meeting all our needs. That's why we should preach "the whole counsel of God."

The Dependable Guide
Date preached:

SCRIPTURE: Jeremiah 23:1–8

INTRODUCTION: Good leaders are a rare breed. In Jeremiah's time, the Lord likened the political leaders to shepherds who were scattering the sheep. In other words, they were doing more harm than good. We have leaders like that today. But in contrast, there is one leader who is utterly dependable—the Good Shepherd. Here He is called:

1. A Branch of Righteousness (v. 5).
2. A King Who Will Reign and Prosper (v. 5).
3. The Lord Our Righteousness (v. 6).

CONCLUSION: The names of Christ, as given in this old prophecy, reassure our hearts when we need a Dependable Guide.

BAPTISM SERMON

The Pleasing Christian Life

Date preached:

By Joshua D. Rowe

Scripture: Mark 1:9–13, especially verse 11: Then a voice came from heaven, "You are My beloved Son, in whom I am well pleased."

Introduction: Many of us live our lives constantly trying to please others. We work hard to please our bosses, our parents, our boyfriend, girlfriend, or spouse. More than these, Scripture tells us to ". . . find out what pleases the Lord" (Eph. 5:10; NIV). In the first chapter of Mark's Gospel we have the ultimate example of the pleasing Christian life.

1. **Confession: Baptism (vv. 9–11).** Only eight verses into Mark's Gospel, we are presented with the major spiritual characters of Scripture: Jesus, the Holy Spirit, God the Father, angels, and Satan himself. Why such a scene? Jesus is about to give us a dynamic, audio-visual model of the Christian life which is pleasing to God. In Mark's Gospel, the dynamic beginning of Jesus' ministry was His baptism. Why was baptism important in Jesus' life, especially if He was sinless? A major purpose of John's baptism was to prepare the way for the coming Messiah (vv. 1–3), whose baptism would not be with water, but with the Holy Spirit (v. 8). So, here Jesus initiates what we know as New Testament baptism. Two main purposes of baptism are clear in this passage:

    A. **Profession of Purity.** Notice that John did not allow Pharisees and Sadducees to be baptized. Why? They put their faith in their ancestral roots, as Abraham's descendants, so John exhorted them towards true repentance (Matt. 3:7–9). The Jewish historian Josephus confirmed that John's baptism was for those who had already been inwardly cleansed. Is your faith in your heritage, or maybe in your church membership? These will never cleanse you! Have you been baptized, but you've never put your faith in Jesus Christ to cleanse you *inwardly* from sin? Baptism is an important act of obedience, but repentance from sin and faith in Jesus Christ are matters of spiritual life or death!

    B. **Association with the Trinity.** Jesus was not only professing His inward purity, but He was also publicly associating Himself with the Triune God of Scripture. John prophesied that Jesus would baptize with the Holy Spirit (Mark 1:8). The Spirit visually descended on Jesus like a dove (v. 10) and the Father audibly spoke, confirming Jesus as His Son, ascribing deity to Jesus (v. 11; see John 10:31–38). Later, Jesus commanded the apostles to baptize believers, " . . . in the name of the Father and of the Son and of the Holy Spirit" (Matt. 28:19). Baptism symbolizes a personal relationship with the Triune God of Scripture, based on the sacrifice of Christ (Rom.6:3–4). Do you think of baptism simply as a ritual? It's not just a ritual; it's an opportunity to confess Jesus as Lord, to publicly declare your personal relationship with the Triune, living God!

2. **Conflict: Temptation (vv. 12–13).** Undoubtedly, after we confess Jesus Christ as Lord and begin to follow the Triune God of Scripture, we will face conflict (John 16:33). Jesus, *immediately* after His baptism, faced temptation. Many translations read, "the Spirit *led*" or "*sent*" Jesus into the desert. The Greek word literally means "to drive out" or "to cast out." So the Holy Spirit *drove* Jesus into the desert to be tempted! What temptations are you driven to? How can you resist stealing from that cash drawer? How can you avoid lust or adultery, seeing that attractive co-worker daily? Jesus models perfectly how to deal with temptation.

3. **Comfort: God's Presence (vv. 12–13).** Do you think the Holy Spirit is only involved in your life when it's easy? The scene in these verses shows us otherwise; it is reminiscent of Adam and Eve's temptation in Genesis 3:1–7. What was the difference? Jesus, filled with the Spirit, in the face of Satan himself, chose to obey God's Word unlike Adam and Eve. The Spirit was there through Jesus' baptism *and* even through His incredible temptation. Imagine fasting 40 days and then trying to resist bread (Matt. 4:1–10)! It was so severe, in fact, that angels came to attend to Him afterward (Mark 1:13). He showed us that with the Spirit, we can resist! God may drive us into difficult circumstances, but He will never allow us to be tempted beyond what we can bear (1 Cor. 10:13). The God we confess will lead us through conflict and grant us His comforting presence.

Conclusion: It makes sense that God announced that He was "well pleased" (v. 11) with Jesus, for He gives us a perfect and dynamic model of the Christian life. Too often, Christians go through the motions; maybe that's what you're doing this morning. Perhaps you need to be baptized, to make public your relationship with the Holy Triune God. Perhaps you have never committed yourself to Jesus, allowing Him to cleanse you inwardly. Maybe you simply need to be reminded of God's presence in your trials. Respond to the Lord's conviction in your heart. A life filled with obedience to God's guiding presence is a life with which He is well pleased.

CLASSICS FOR THE PASTOR'S LIBRARY

E. M. Bounds

Many Christians have grown deeper in prayer by reading E. M. Bounds, but few of us know of the hardships that taught Bounds himself to pray.

Edward McKendree Bounds was born into a strong Christian family in Shelbyville, Missouri, in 1835. When his father, a businessman and politician, died from tuberculosis at age 44, Edward, 14, joined a wagon train and left for the California Gold Rush of '49. When he returned four years later, he was disillusioned, but ready to settle down. After studying law, he was licensed as the youngest attorney in Missouri. Still he was restless, and while attending a bush arbor meeting on the banks of the Mississippi River, Edward was so moved he resigned from the law and enrolled in Bible school. Two years later, on February 21, 1860, he was appointed a circuit-riding preacher by the Methodists for rural Missouri.

At the onset of the Civil War, Edward's name appeared on a list of men suspected as Confederate sympathizers, and he was taken into custody, eventually being imprisoned in Lynch's Slave Pit amid unspeakable filth and miserably overcrowded conditions. At length, he was banished from the North and given a pass through lines of war to secure a safe passage to the Southern states.

At age 28 Bounds joined the Confederate army as an army chaplain, and the next several years found him in the middle of the most terrible and tragic battles of the Civil War.

When the conflict ended, Bounds continued preaching and pastoring in Middle Tennessee until late 1871, when, at age 36, he moved to Eufaula, Alabama, to pastor a church. There he began his writing ministry by contributing a column to the local paper, the *Eufaula Times*. It was also in Eufaula that he fell in love with Emma Elizabeth Barnette.

By the late 1870s, Edward and Emma were married and engaged in church ministry in St. Louis. In 1883, Bounds was asked to become associate editor for *St. Louis Christian Advocate*, and his writing ministry took a more serious turn. At the same time Emma's health was failing, and she passed away on February 18, 1886, at age 30. They had been married nine years.

Some time later, Bounds resigned his position in St. Louis to move to Nashville, Tennessee, to become associate editor of the *Nashville*

Christian Advocate, but his work there was marred by controversies within his denomination.

In 1894, at age 59, discouraged and worn out by denominational politics, he left the *Advocate* and moved to Washington, Georgia, where he prayed, preached, and continued writing. Each morning he would rise at 4 A.M. and pray until breakfast at seven. Every afternoon he would go on a "prayer walk," in which he prayed for those in the houses he passed. Often the mid-morning hours would find him in the little prayer chamber he established on the second floor of his home, and here in the atmosphere of prayer he would scratch out on little scraps of paper his thoughts about prayer. An idea for a book burned in his heart and he began putting down his thoughts under the utilitarian title, *Preacher and Prayer.*

At the urging of Dr. G. Campbell Morgan, Bounds traveled to London in 1907 to present his manuscript to the editors of Marshall Brothers, who agreed to publish it. For several years, E. M. Bounds enjoyed his work, praying, preaching, and setting forth his thoughts about prayer. When he died on August 24, 1913, at age 78 at his home in Washington, Georgia, he was not particularly well-known or outwardly successful, but he had left behind in manuscripts and on miscellaneous scraps of paper some of history's richest ideas about the life of prayer. Dr. Homer Hodge assumed responsibility for crafting these writings into additional books. Thanks to him, E. M. Bounds is now remembered as one of Christianity's most prolific and eloquent writers on the subject of prayer.

I keep a copy of *Preacher and Prayer* (better known as *Power Through Prayer)* on the shelf above my desk and read a few paragraphs frequently. It never fails to spur me onward toward the Throne of Grace. It will improve your prayer life, too—by leaps and Bounds.

AUGUST 15, 2004

SUGGESTED SERMON

How to Live in the Last Days   *Date preached:*

By Woodrow Kroll

Scripture: Matthew 24:32–35, especially verse 33: So you also, when you see all these things, know that it is near—at the doors.

Introduction: Remember Chicken Little? When an acorn dropped on his head, he thought the sky was falling, and soon the whole barnyard was in an uproar. Many people feel like the sky is falling, but what does God's Word reveal about the future? Should we be in an uproar? What character should our lives take if Jesus is coming soon? Let me suggest four attitudes we ought to have:

1. **A Sense of Urgency.** If we're living in the end times, we need to have a sense that whatever we have to accomplish must be done quickly. If Jesus is coming soon, it should have a bearing on your lifestyle. There needs to be an urgency to your witness. You know that neighbor you've been thinking about witnessing to for years? This is the day. The Bible teacher F. B. Meyer asked D. L. Moody, "What's the secret of your success?" Moody replied, "For many years I have never given an address without the consciousness that the Lord may come back before I've finished."
   A. **Think of Noah in Hebrews 11:7:** "By faith Noah, being divinely warned of things not yet seen, moved with godly fear, prepared an ark for the saving of his household, by which he condemned the world and became heir of the righteousness which is according to faith." Noah had a sense of urgency, because the rain was on its way.
   B. **Think of Jonah.** When he finally got his heart straightened out and went to Nineveh, he preached an eight-word sermon: "Yet forty days, and Nineveh shall be overthrown." There was a time limit, and every passing day brought judgment closer. Jonah preached with urgency, and the city was saved.

2. **A Sense of Sinfulness.** As we draw closer to Christ's Coming, our sense of sinfulness should increase. By that, I mean we should sorrow over the

sin in our own lives and seek to turn from it; and we should groan over sin in our society and warn against it.
- A. **Think of John the Baptist.** In Matthew 3, he went out proclaiming, "Repent, for the kingdom of heaven is at hand!" He believed that God was about to do something very soon, that the coming of Christ was at hand. He urgently called people to repent, to take sin seriously and to deal with it.
- B. **Think of Isaiah.** In reading Isaiah 6, you clearly see that Isaiah's sense of urgency was tied to his sense of sinfulness. The nature of our culture is increasingly sinful; and when I recognize that we are sinful people in a generation of very sinful people, then we know that Jesus' Coming can't be far off.

3. **A Sense of Longing.** For generations, people have longed for Jesus to return. Nearly 500 years ago, Martin Luther wrote, "I hope that the day is near at hand when the advent of the great God will appear, for all things are everywhere boiling, burning, moving, falling, sinking, groaning."
   - A. **Think of Nicodemus.** He was a religious man with a deep longing for the Messiah. When Jesus appeared, Nicodemus recognized that if Jesus was indeed the Messiah, he had to have a relationship with Him.
   - B.. **Think of Zacchaeus.** He was a political man, but he so longed for the Messiah that he climbed a tree to get a glimpse of Jesus.

4. **A Sense of Exclusivity.** The world is doing its best to exclude Jesus from its future. But when Christ comes back, He will return as the only Savior and Messiah this world has ever known. We need to live exclusively for

>>> *sermon continued on following page*

APPROPRIATE HYMNS AND SONGS

Until Then, Stuart Hamblen; © 1958 Hamblen Music Company.

And He Shall Reign, Graham Kendrick; © 1991 Make Way Music, Admin. by Music Services.

God's Final Call, John W. Peterson; © 1961 John W. Peterson Music Company.

Lift Up Your Heads Ye Mighty Gates, George Weissel/Catherine Winkworth/Thomas Williams; Public Domain.

Rejoice the Lord Is King, Charles Wesley/John Darwell; Public Domain.

Christ, and to recognize that His is an exclusive message. We live in a world of pluralism, in which people say, "Hey, look, anybody who wants to get to God can get to Him any way they want." But that's not what the Bible says (see 1 Kin. 8:60; Is. 45:3–5; John 14:6.)

Conclusion: Are we living in the end times? Yes, we probably are. It looks like we are. World events are threatening on every side, but history is *His*-story, and He shall come again soon. Are you ready to meet Him? Are you prepared for the Lord to come today?

FOR THE BULLETIN

- On August 15, 1096, the First Crusade set out from Europe to "liberate" Jerusalem and the Holy Land from the Turks. ❋ On this day in 1534, Ignatius of Loyola, 43, pulled together a group of seven men who took an oath of poverty and dedicated themselves to doing the will of God, to reforming Catholicism, and to advancing evangelistic and educational work among the heathen. They were later known as the Jesuits, the "Society of Jesus." ❋ On August 15, 1549, the great Jesuit missionary, Francis Xavier, 43, disembarked in Japan, becoming the first Christian missionary in the history of that country. ❋ August 15, 1613, is the birthday of Jeremy Taylor, Anglican bishop and devotional writer. ❋ On August 15, 1620, the "Mayflower" set sail from Southampton, England, with 102 Pilgrims seeking freedom of religion in the New World. ❋ August 15, 1835, marks the birth of E. M. Bounds, Civil War pastor and the author of numerous books on prayer.

Kids Talk

Ask the children what kind of things they look forward to? What gets you excited when you think about it? What is something that you just cannot wait for? A birthday party? Opening presents on Christmas morning? Your dad or mom getting home from a business trip? A family vacation to the beach? Tell them that God wants us to have things to look forward to. He loves it when we're excited about something neat that's going to happen. That's why He has told us so much about the return of Jesus Christ to planet earth. Jesus is coming again! We can hardly wait.

STATS, STORIES AND MORE

"Today's world has reached a stage that if it had been described to preceding centuries, it would have called forth the cry, 'This is the apocalypse!'"
—Aleksandr Solzhenitsyn

"We must never speak to simple, excitable people about the Day without emphasizing again and again the utter impossibility of prediction. We must try to show them that the impossibility is an essential part of the doctrine. If you do not believe our Lord's words, then why do you believe in His return at all? And if you do not believe them, must you not put away from you utter and forever any hope of dating that return?"
—C. S. Lewis

"Many times when I go to bed at night I think to myself that before I awaken Christ may come."
—Billy Graham

A generation ago in Great Britain there was a bishop in the church who had a deep sense of longing for the Lord. Bishop Steed would get up every morning, go to his window, raise the shade, look out, and this is what he'd say: "Perhaps today. Perhaps today, Lord. I will be busy, but I will be ready." And then at night Bishop Steed would go to the window again before retiring and he would say, "Perhaps tonight, Lord. I will be asleep, but I will be ready. I will wake up when You come."

A tourist in Switzerland visited a beautiful mansion surrounded by well-kept gardens. "How long have you been the caretaker here?" he asked the gardener. The answer was twenty years. "How often does the owner of this property come here?" The answer was only four times in the twenty years. "And to think," said the guest, "you keep this property in superb shape just as though he might come tomorrow." The caretaker replied, "No, I look after these grounds as if I expected him to come today."

WORSHIP HELPS

Call to Worship:
How great are His signs, and how mighty His wonders! His kingdom is an everlasting kingdom, and His dominion is from generation to generation (Dan. 4:3)

Hymn Story:
One of the greatest hymns about the return of Christ and heaven is "Beyond the Sunset." Homer Rodeheaver lived in Winona Lake, Indiana, and built a nice home on Rainbow Point which became a center of fellowship for Christians traveling through the area. During the summer of 1936, "Rody" invited some friends to Rainbow Point for the evening. Among them were the musicians, Virgil Brock and his wife, Blanche Kerr Brock.

On this particular evening, the sunset was fabulous. As the friends discussed the splendor of the setting sun against the lake, one of them—a blind man named Horace Burr—exclaimed, "My, that sure is a wonderful sunset. Thanks so much for picturing it for me. I would have missed a lot if you folks hadn't been here to describe it."

When someone commented on Horace's "seeing," he replied, "I *can* see. I see through other people's eyes, and I think I often see more; I see beyond the sunset."

By and by the conversation shifted to the subject of heaven. Later, back in their own lodgings, Virgil and Blanche sat down together at an old piano and began putting together words and music of "Beyond the Sunset."

Additional Sermons and Lesson Ideas

The Sovereign Speaks
By Melvin Worthington

Date preached:

SCRIPTURE: Psalm 19

INTRODUCTION: Does the God who created all things communicate with finite man? Yes. God communicates in the following ways.

1. Through Creation (Ps. 19:1–6). This vital communication is *unique* (v.1), *unceasing* (v. 2), *understandable (v. 3) and universal* (vv. 4–6).
2. Through the Composition (Ps. 19:7–11). The Bible is God's divine revelation to mankind.
3. Through the Conscience (Ps. 19:12–14). God has placed inside every human being a conscience.
4. Through the Comforter (John 16:8). The Holy Spirit is to reprove the world of sin, righteousness, and judgment.
5. Through Christ (Heb. 1:2).
6. Through Circumstances (Acts 16:6–10). God uses circumstances to get our attention and communicate with us.
7. Through Christians (Acts 1:8). Christians are witnesses and ambassadors for the Lord Jesus Christ in this world.

CONCLUSION: Have you been attentive to the voice of the living God? Are you listening for and to His voice?

An Exhibition of His Work

Date preached:

SCRIPTURE: Psalm 111

INTRODUCTION: Any aspiring artist is thrilled when a museum, a gallery, or even a trendy coffee shop stages an exhibition of his or her works. God's artistry is on display every day in His creation. On a deeper level, His work is exhibited in our lives through grace. Psalm 111 is all about the works of the Lord.

1. His Work Should Be Studied (vv. 1–2).
2. His Work Should Be Remembered (vv. 3–6).
3. His Work Should Be Trusted (vv. 7–9).
4. His Work Should Make Us Fear His Name (v. 10).

CONCLUSION: Come, behold the works of the Lord.

AUGUST 22, 2004

SUGGESTED SERMON

Prayer: The Solid Foundation

Date preached:

By David Jackman

Scripture: Philippians 1:1–11, especially verse 9: And this I pray, that your love may abound still more and more in knowledge and all discernment.

Introduction: How do we as Christians react to uncertainties? Are you unsure about mortgage payments? Worried about how to afford college? How will you ever share your faith at school or at work to intimidating people? Paul was faced with an uncertain, unsettling situation. He was under house arrest in Rome awaiting a trial that would either vindicate him or sentence him to death. Even so, Paul began his letter to the believers at Philippi with the solid foundation of prayer, a model for us to follow. We must pray for one another during these difficult days. How should we pray?

1. **With Thanksgiving (vv. 3–8).** The phrase, "you all," occurs 4 times in verses 1–11. Paul is thankful for every last person. How do you feel about each individual in this congregation? With Paul, there are no exceptions and no preferential treatment. The church is one. A real New Testament church should reflect such unity that every individual matters. Paul is specifically thankful for the Philippians' partnership in the gospel (v. 5) and their partnership in grace (v. 7). It is . . .

   A. **Three-way Partnership.** The partnership involves God whose grace is the origin and content of the gospel, Paul the bondservant and messenger of the gospel, and the Philippians who are the participants of the gospel both by believing it and proclaiming it in their city. We need to ask ourselves, "How am I sharing in the partnership of the gospel? Praying? Giving? Serving?" If we are to be healthy Christians, we must be involved in gospel ministry, and that makes us want to pray for those who are serving side-by-side with us.

   B. **Three-dimensioned in Time (vv. 5–6).** Look at the time frame in these two verses: "He who began a good work . . . until now . . . will complete it until the day of Jesus Christ." The verb in verse 6 literally means, "to put the finishing touches on." That's an incredible thought! Paul was saying that the job was done when we first put our faith in Christ, that our hearts were changed and we were set free, and our future is certain. Between now and then, God is putting the finishing touches on us. Those finishing touches may be major life or attitude changes, but they are small in comparison to the change already made in our hearts if we have accepted Christ as our Savior and Lord.

2. **With Petition (vv. 9–11).** Paul was thankful for partnership in gospel grace, and now his prayer is for progress in gospel growth. These three verses are one complex sentence that needs careful unpacking.

    A. **What Paul Is Praying for (v. 9).** Paul is praying for love, for real love that abounds. If the love of Christ is in us, it is natural for it to show and to grow. Our model is God's love for us in Christ. A love like that is not motivated by duty but by personal concern. That kind of love is not feelings-oriented, but is a relational, intelligent love. It abounds in discernment and knowledge. Jesus always acted out His love. How do we love one another as partners in the gospel? If someone silently watched, would your love towards other Christians be obvious? Is your love growing more and more? Pray that our love for one another would be demonstrated and duplicated.

    B. **Why Paul Is Praying (vv. 10–11).** These are the results Paul anticipates. If believers are discerning, the natural conclusion is that a life in Christ is far superior to anything this life may offer (v. 10; see also Phil. 3:8). If Christians have genuine love, they will remain fruitful in ministry and blameless in integrity for the day of Christ's return (v. 11).

>>> *sermon continued on following page*

APPROPRIATE HYMNS AND SONGS

How Firm a Foundation, George Keith/Anne Steele/John Rippon/Joseph Funk; Public Domain.

Firm Foundation, Nancy Gordon/Jamie Harvill; © 1994 Integrity's Hosanna! Music/Integrity's Praise! Music.

If God Be For Us, Kirk Henderson; © 1993 Kirk Henderson, ASCAP.

Sure Foundation, Don Harris; © 1991 Integrity's Hosanna! Music.

The Church's One Foundation, Samuel J. Stone/Samuel S. Wesley; Public Domain.

Conclusion: God has dealt with all our needs to save us from sin and death, and He will bring that work to completion. Our part is to continue trusting, and to go on praying, both in thankfulness and petition. Even when life is uncertain, thank God for the certainties, and pray that His work will continue. The work of the gospel is corporate. We need one another. We are to demonstrate partnership in a congregation that loves, focusing on the grace of God in the gospel. Then, when Christ returns, the fruit flowing from our partnership and progress in the gospel will be an offering of praise and glory to God (v. 11).

FOR THE BULLETIN

❋ Columbia (born c. 521), was the son of an Ulster chief in a wild district of Donegal county, Ireland. He was hot-headed and violent, but after becoming a Christian, his zeal turned to evangelism, and he is remembered as one of history's foremost missionary advocates. On this day, August 22, A.D. 565, Columbia spied a monster in Scotland's Loch Ness, becoming the first recorded observer of the creature. ❋ Missionary to the American Indians, John Eliot, founded a church at Martha's Vineyard on this day in 1670, and placed two Native American Christians, Hiacoomes and Tackanash, in charge of preaching and teaching. ❋ During his twenties, George Frideric Handel was the talk of England and the best-paid composer on earth, but as he grew older, his music became outdated and he fell on hard times. The stress brought on a case of palsy that crippled some of his fingers, and people thought of him as a "has-been". One morning Handel received a script from Charles Jennens. It was a word-for-word collection of various biblical texts about Christ. On August 22, 1741, Handel shut the door of his London home and started composing music. Twenty-three days later, the world had *Messiah*. "Whether I was in the body or out of the body when I wrote it, I know not," Handel later said, trying to describe the experience. ❋ August 22, 1885, marks the death of medical doctor, William P. Mackay, author of the hymn "Revive Us Again."

STATS, STORIES AND MORE

How John Stott Prays

On the occasion of his 80th birthday, *Christianity Today* ran a profile of the British pastor, John Stott, pastor emeritus of All Soul's Church in London. The article was written by a former research assistant to Dr. Stott, who knew his daily habits intimately. He said that Dr. Stott begins every day at 5 a.m. He swings his legs over the side of the bed and starts the day with a version of this Trinitarian prayer:

Good morning, heavenly Father; good morning, Lord Jesus; good morning, Holy Spirit. Heavenly Father, I worship you as the Creator and Sustainer of the universe. Lord Jesus, I worship you, Savior and Lord of the world. Holy Spirit, I worship you, Sanctifier of the people of God. Glory to the Father, and to the Son, and to the Holy Spirit. As it was in the beginning, is now, and will be forever. Amen.

For decades, Stott has begun each day with a version of that Trinitarian prayer.

Then he has a small leather notebook, stuffed full of folded papers and held together with a rubber band. Each morning, having read three chapters of the Bible and meditated over them, he opens this prayer notebook and prays for families, friends, ministries, and even for strangers. He keeps a daily prayer list that is always under revision. Then he has a prayer calendar that lists missionary projects and people groups all over the world. He prays over these things without haste or hurry.

This is the way he begins each morning, and every one of us needs to develop a pattern of regular prayer in our lives. We may not do it just as John Stott does. After all, he is 80 years old, has never married, and perhaps has a quieter situation than most of us. But it is essential that we develop some sort of "quiet time" in our lives to pray for those with whom we're partners in the Lord's work.

WORSHIP HELPS

Call to Worship:
I will praise You, O Lord, among the peoples; I will sing to You among the nations. For Your mercy reaches unto the heavens, and Your truth unto the clouds (Ps. 57:9–10),

Readers' Theater (or Responsive Reading):

Reader 1: And this I pray, that your love may abound still more and more in knowledge and all discernment, that you may approve the things that are excellent, that you may be sincere and without offense till the day of Christ (Phil. 1:9–10).

Reader 2: I pray that out of His glorious riches He may strengthen you with power through his Spirit in your inner being, so that Christ may dwell in your hearts through faith. And I pray that you, being rooted and established in love, may have power, together with all the saints, to grasp how wide and long and high and deep is the love of Christ (Eph. 3:16–18, NIV).

Reader 1: Beloved, I pray that you may prosper in all things and be in health, just as your soul prospers (3 John 2).

Reader 2: I pray that God, who gives you hope, will keep you happy and full of peace as you believe in Him. May you overflow with hope through the power of the Holy Spirit (Rom. 15:13, NLT).

Reader 2: I pray also that the eyes of your heart may be enlightened in order that you may know the hope to which He has called you, the riches of His glorious inheritance in the saints (Eph. 1:18, NIV).

Both Readers: I pray that God, who gives peace, will be with all of you. Amen. (Rom. 15:33, CEV)

Benediction:
As we depart from this place, may the Word of God not depart from our hearts, nor the peace of God from our souls, nor the blessings of God from our lives. In Jesus' name, Amen.

Additional Sermons and Lesson Ideas

The Sin of Silence
By Denis Lyle

Date preached:

SCRIPTURE: 2 Kings 7:3–16

INTRODUCTION: The Good News is for sharing, but too often we keep it to ourselves. This story of four lepers encourages us to overcome the sin of silence.

1. The God They Abandoned (vv. 3–4). Leprosy is a symbol of sin in the Bible. These four lepers had been trapped between the enemy and the walls of the city, hopelessly left outside the city, separated from God and men (7:6).
2. The Gain They Acquired (vv. 5–8). As the lepers decided to surrender to the Syrians, they walked into a camp full of food and riches, so they plundered the deserted camp.
3. The Good They Accomplished (vv. 9–16). Despite their desperate situation, the lepers decided to repent of their selfishness. What good did they do?
4. They Refused to Be Silent. Because of the impact the Good News would have, they considered it sinful to withhold. What about the gospel? Are you keeping it to yourself?
5. They Resolved to Be Servants. Assuming it as their responsibility to tell the Good News, the lepers brought the message to the king.

CONCLUSION: We have been given the gospel, the ultimate Good News. Like these lepers, we should share responsibly and vocally!

I Have Loved You
By Peter Grainger

Date preached:

SCRIPTURE: Malachi 1:1–5

INTRODUCTION: The last book and the last prophet of the Old Covenant remind us of God's love despite our failure.

1. The People: Israel. Superficially, all seemed well to the people; they had land, a city, walls, a temple, and a sacrificial system. In reality, however, their worship was an outward sham (1:8–14; 3:8–12).
2. The Prophet: Malachi. Malachi was burdened with a message for the stubborn, rebellious people of Israel.
3. God: The Lord Almighty. God is referred to twenty times in Malachi as "The Lord of hosts," a majestic name of military leadership, yet His first words are, "I have loved you . . . ." He reminded them of His past actions (vv. 2–3) and offered them hope in the future (v. 5).

CONCLUSION: We live in the midst of rebellious people; many of us have rebelled in our own lives, but despite our surroundings or situations, God demonstrates His love for us through Jesus Christ (Rom. 5:8; 1 John 3:16, 19–20; 4:9–10).

AUGUST 29, 2004

SUGGESTED SERMON

One Thing I Know

Date preached:

Scripture: John 9, especially verse 25: He answered and said, "Whether He is a sinner or not I do not know. One thing I know: That though I was blind, now I see."

Introduction: This morning, I'm going to state the theme and thesis of my message at the very beginning: You don't have to be a famous evangelist or a great theologian to lead someone else to faith in Jesus Christ. You don't have to be a gifted soul-winner or a world-class missionary. You just have to be excited about the Lord, and willing for that excitement to overflow. You just have to say, "One thing I know: I once was blind, and now I see." Today, let's look at a man in the Bible who knew almost nothing about the Lord Jesus. He was an illiterate, thirty-year-old blind man. But his simple testimony confounded the greatest theologians of the Jewish state and witnesses to us to this day.

1. **Verses 1–3:** The Jewish people believed all misfortune was a direct result of specific sins. This isn't true (the Old Testament had devoted an entire book—the Book of Job—to debunking that theory), yet many people still feel that way. So the disciples, seeing the blind man, asked a theological question: What did this man or his parents do wrong? Jesus said, "Nothing." With that He lets us know that trials and tribulations in life are not necessarily God's punishments for specific sins. "Neither this man nor his parents sinned, but that the works of God should be revealed in him." God allowed this man to be blind because his blindness is going to present a great opportunity for God's work to be revealed and for God's glory to be seen. Our trials and tribulations become occasions for God's power and glory to be revealed. They provide an arena for His witnesses to testify.

2. **Verses 4–5:** Note the phrase, "Him who sent me." That's how Jesus repeatedly referred to His Father in John's Gospel, where the words *sent* and *send* occur 61 times. Jesus was sent as the Light of the World, and the implication is that as He leaves the world, you and I become the lights.

Christ is the sun, but we are the moon, reflecting His light. We're to let our light shine before men.

3. **Verses 6–7:** If you visit Jerusalem, you can still visit the Pool of Siloam. Not far from the Temple Mount in the Old City of Jerusalem is a hillside known as the City of David, the original spot where David established Jerusalem as the capital of Israel. It's covered with ancient ruins, and it slopes down into a valley to an Arab neighborhood known as Silwan. It's here that the water flows from Hezekiah's Tunnel into this pool. Why did Jesus send the man there? Why didn't He just heal him on the spot? John gives us a hint in verse 7: "And He said to him, 'Go, wash in the pool of Siloam' (which is translated Sent)." The word "Siloam" comes from a term meaning "sent" or "conducted." The waters of the Gihon Spring were sent or conducted into the Pool of Siloam, and thus the pool derived its name. The symbolism of this wasn't lost on Jesus. Just as the Father had sent Him to the world, now He was sending this man. He was sending him to the "Pool of Siloam" which means "sent." Verse 7 ends, "So he went and washed, and came back seeing." The Pool of Siloam represents the Lord Jesus Christ—the Sent One. We go to Him and wash and come back seeing.

4. **Verses 8–11:** Then what happens? We become His witnesses. The rest of this chapter shows us how, despite his ignorance and the newness of his experience, the former blinded man became a witness. What a simple testimony this man had: A Man called Jesus changed my life. A Man called

>>> sermon continued on following page

APPROPRIATE HYMNS AND SONGS

Amazing Grace, John Newton/Edwin Excell/John P. Rees; Public Domain.

All Because of God's Amazing Grace, Stephen R. Adams; © 1971 Pilot Point Music, Admin. by The Copyright Company.

Calvary Covers It All, Mrs. Walter G. Taylor; © 1934 Mrs. Walter G. Taylor. Renewed 1962 Word Music, Inc.

Touch of Grace, Ed Kerr/ George T. Searcy; © 1994 Integrity's Hosanna! Music/Integrity's Praise! Music.

Your Grace, Bill Batstone/Tommy Coomes; © 1995 Coomsietunes/Word Music, Inc., Admin. by Word Music Group, Inc.

Jesus healed my eyes. A Man called Jesus gave me sight. Could you and I not say something like that?

Conclusion: You don't have to be a great evangelist or a well-versed theologian. You just have to be willing to say: A Man called Jesus sent me to wash away my sins in His blood. I went and washed and came away seeing. I don't understand a lot about it, but one thing I know: I once was blind but now I see.

FOR THE BULLETIN

❉ This is the traditional date for the beheading of John the Baptist (August 29, A.D. 29). ❉ Diocletian became Emperor of Rome on August 29, A.D. 284. He was persuaded to unleash his armies against Christians in an attempt to totally destroy the church. The persecution spread over the entire empire. ❉ This day marks the death of Samuel Rutherford, Scottish theologian and Covenanter, who spent much of his ministry under persecution and in exile before dying a quiet death on August 29, 1661. ❉ John Dick, another Covenanter, was a godly Presbyterian who was attacked during the reign of Charles II. He lived a fugitive's life until betrayed by a poor woman who later lost her mind over the incident. John was brought before the Committee of Public Affairs on August 29, 1683, found guilty of treason, and sentenced to death. He escaped and wrote a 58-page book, *Testimony to the Doctrine, Worship, Discipline, and Government of the Church of Scotland*, before being recaptured and hanged. ❉ August 29, 1792, is the birthday of Charles Finney, one of the greatest evangelists in American history. As a young man Finney decided to study law. When he later came to Christ, he used his legal skills to present the gospel to audiences as if he were making a case to a jury. He is credited with winning a half million people to the Lord, either directly or indirectly, and with pioneering methods of evangelism which paved the way for the campaigns and crusades of evangelists like D. L. Moody and Billy Graham.

STATS, STORIES AND MORE

Fanny Crosby was born in 1820 in Putnam County, New York, about 60 miles from New York City. At age six weeks, something seemed wrong with her eyes. A man claiming to be a doctor was staying nearby, and he prescribed a hot poultice. As a result, Fanny was virtually blinded for life. But as a result of that, she developed a phenomenal memory. She memorized vast segments of the Scripture, and later said that whenever she wanted to read a portion, she turned a little button in her mind and the passage would flow through her brain like a recorded tape.

After she came to the Lord, that vast reservoir of memorized Scripture became the nurturing fountain for her hymns. She composed hymn after hymn in her brain and retained them with perfect memory, before going to her publishers to dictate them one after another. She was called the queen of American hymn writers and the mother of congregational singing in the United States. During her 94 years, she wrote about 9,000 hymns.

She often prayed that God would use her songs to bring people to Christ. She had a goal of winning a million men to Christ through the agency of her hymns, and she kept careful track of every story she heard of people being saved through her hymns.

Whenever anyone would sympathize with her over her blindness, she would say: "Don't blame the doctor. He is probably dead by this time, but if I could meet him, I would tell him that he unwittingly did me the greatest favor in the world."

She explained that although God does not order or ordain evil things, He sometimes permits them in order to bring good from them. About her own blindness, she said, "Now God did not order that," for, she said, the doctor who mistreated her eyes "broke a law of nature." Nevertheless God had used it in a marvelous way for His glory and for the saving of many souls.

WORSHIP HELPS

Call to Worship:
I will praise you, O Lord, with all my heart; I will tell of all your wonders. I will be glad and rejoice in you; I will sing praise to your name, O Most High (Ps. 9:1–2).

Offertory Comments:
The principle of stewardship reflects that fact that God is the owner of all we have, and we are simply the managers.
Psalm 24:1 says: The earth is the Lord's, and all its fullness, the world and those who dwell therein.
Haggai 2:8 says: "The silver is Mine, and the gold is Mine," says the Lord of hosts.
Deuteronomy 8:18 says: And you shall remember the Lord your God, for it is He who gives you power to get wealth.
1 Corinthians 6:20 says: For you were bought with a price; therefore glorify God in your body and in your spirit, which are God's.
The question isn't how much of our money we're going to give to God, but how much of His money we're going to spend on ourselves. As we give this morning, let's give as faithful stewards, not as self-sufficient owners.

Kids Talk

Travis got a job delivering the afternoon newspaper. There were fifty people in his neighborhood who subscribed to the paper, so he had to ride his bicycle up and down the street and throw the newspaper into fifty front yards. On the first day, Travis headed down the street, but when he started to throw out the newspaper, he spotted the headline and it looked very interesting. He decided to keep that newspaper for himself. At the next house, he decided to keep the second paper, too. In fact, Travis decided to keep all fifty newspapers for himself, and nobody on his street received their paper that day. He did the same thing the next day. Do you know what happened the next day? He was fired. You and I don't just have news—we have Good News. Have you been keeping it all to yourself?

Additional Sermons and Lesson Ideas

Two Ways of Life
By Peter Grainger

Date preached:

SCRIPTURE: Psalm 1

INTRODUCTION: Have you ever gone down a one-way street? There's a right way and a wrong way. Psalm 1 teaches that in life there are two paths, one leading to life and the other to destruction.

1. The Description of the Two Ways (vv. 1–2).
    A. The Way of the Wicked. The first verse reflects thinking, the behavior, and the allegiance.
    B. The Way of the Righteous. Notice the drastic difference from the wicked. The righteous delight in and meditate on the Law.
2. The Outcome of the Two Ways (vv. 3–4).
    A. The Righteous are Like Trees. Fruitful in season, they are able to withstand adversity.
    B. The Wicked are Like Chaff. Separated from the righteous, they have no value. Blown away by the wind, they're of no use.
3. The Parting of the Two Ways (vv. 5–6).
    A. The Wicked Perish. The wicked are condemned by the Lord's judgment and excluded from God's people.
    B. The Righteous Live. Righteous ones are known by God and included with His people.

CONCLUSION: Which of these descriptions characterizes you? In life, there's no middle ground; live righteously, according to God's Word.

And That Rock Was Christ

Date preached:

SCRIPTURE: Matthew 7:24; Luke 6:48

INTRODUCTION: Many homeowners have expensive foundation problems with their houses. Jesus said that when it comes to living, wise men and women build their lives on a Rock. Jesus is a solid foundation; He is:

1. The Rock (1 Cor. 10:4).
2. The Cornerstone (1 Pet. 2:6–7; Mark 11:10; Eph. 2:20).
3. A Precious Cornerstone (Is. 28:16).
4. The Stone Which the Builders Rejected (1 Pet. 2:7; Mark 11:10).
5. A Living Stone (1 Pet. 2:4).

6. A Stone for a Foundation (Is. 28:16).
7. A Tried Stone (Is. 28:16).
8. A Stone of Stumbling (Is. 8:14; 1 Pet. 1:8).
9. A Rock of Offense (Is. 8:14; 1 Pet. 1:8).
10. A Stone Cut without Hands (Dan. 2:34, 45).

CONCLUSION: "So build your life on the Lord Jesus Christ, and the blessings will come down."

CONVERSATIONS IN A PASTOR'S STUDY

The Pastor and His Reading
An "Interview" with Samuel Logan Brengle

How important is reading to a soul-winning pastor?

No man or woman need hope to be a permanently successful soul-winner who is not a diligent student of the truth, of the will and ways of God, of men, and of methods. A man cannot build a house, or write a poem, or govern a city, or manage a store without thoughtful study. A doctor must think and study, diligently and continuously; a lawyer must be a diligent student to win cases. How much more, then, should we study in order to understand the diseases of the soul, the ramifications of evil, the deceitfulness of the human heart, and the application of the great remedy God has provided to meet all the needs of the soul.

What books should the pastor read?

The first thing and the last thing to be studied is the Bible. The doctor may know all about law and art, history and theology, but if he is unacquainted with his medical books he will be a failure as a doctor. The lawyer may have devoured libraries, traveled the wide world over, and become a walking encyclopedia and dictionary, but if he is unacquainted with his law books, he will be a failure. So the worker for souls may read ten thousand books and be able to quote poetry by the yard, may be acquainted with all the facts of science and history, and may even be a profound theologian, but unless he is a diligent student of the Bible, he will not permanently succeed as a soul-winner. He must become full of the thoughts of God. He must eat the Word, and digest it, and turn it into spiritual blood and bone, and muscle and nerve and sinew, until he becomes, as someone has said, "a living Bible, eighteen inches wide by six feet long, bound in human skin."

Do you ever get tired of personal Bible study?

Personally for years I have given the best hour of the day to the Bible, and now I want it more than I want my food. Again and again I have read my Bible through on my knees, and it is ever new, and as David said, "sweeter than honey and the honeycomb." And like Job, I can say, "I have esteemed the words of His mouth more than my necessary food."

When do you read your Bible?

It should be read early in the day, before other things crowd in.

Do you find yourself looking for sermons when you spend personal time in Bible study?

We must not study it simply that we may preach it, but that we may live by it, be furnished, strengthened, enlightened, corrected, and made wise by it. It must pass through our own souls and become a part of our own spiritual life before we can preach it with power and apply it effectually to others.

What else should the pastor be reading?

Besides the Bible, the soul-winner ought to lay out a course of reading for himself, and stick to it, reading a few pages each day. Ten pages a day will mean from ten to fifteen books a year.

Anything else?

The soul-winner should study not only books, but people and methods. I know of no better and surer method of acquainting oneself with the human heart and the way the Holy Spirit works with people than by this close, personal, private conversation and inquiry about the religious experiences of the Christians around us. This is the scientific method applied to the study of the human heart, and it can be carried out wherever you can find a human soul to talk with you.

SEPTEMBER 5, 2004

SUGGESTED SERMON

A Book and a Blessing

Date preached:

By David Jeremiah

Scripture: Revelation 1:1–3

Introduction: Many of us are book lovers, and often we turn to the back cover of various books to find the ones we want to read. The title and author are usually listed on the front cover. On the back are endorsements and a biographical sketch of the writer. On the inside flap, we see a synopsis of what's in the book. The table of contents tells us what's in every chapter. We haven't read a word of the book yet, but we already know much about what the book is going to say. Well, the first verses of the Book of Revelation is the inside cover of the book, information to help us get excited about its contents and understand what it's all about. Verses 1–3 are particularly important because they serve as the title page, and verse three promises a special blessing to those who read and heed it. According to Revelation 1:1–3, this is:

1. **A Prophetic Book (v. 1).** The word "revelation" in the Greek is literally the "apocalypse" of Jesus Christ. When we hear this English word, we usually think of the end times, but the Greek term literally means "an uncovering, an unveiling, a setting forth, a manifestation." So the book itself is the revelation or the apocalypse or the uncovering of Jesus Christ. It is the making known of Jesus Christ. It's not just about the end times, nor is it primarily given to enable us to figure out how all these events fit together (though it will do that). The primary focus of Revelation is that we might come to know Jesus Christ and see Him disclosed in all of His glory. It was given to John to show His servants the things that must shortly take place. The words "shortly come to pass" are a translation of a Greek term "*en tachei*," from which we get our word "tachometer." It means something that will happen suddenly. In a car, a tachometer keeps track of the revolutions of the engine, but the Greek word means something that will happen suddenly. It doesn't mean it will happen tomorrow or the next day, but it means that once these things begin, they will happen very quickly.

2. **A Pictorial Book (v. 2).** This is not just a book that is written in words. It is written in pictures—John bore witness *to all the things that he saw.* This is a visible book that demonstrates in symbols and in images what's going to happen, and John translated it for us in words. Some of the pictures may seem confusing, but we learn best using pictures.

3. **A Profitable Book (v. 3).** This is the only book in the Bible that promises a special blessing for those who read and heed it.
   A. **It is profitable for personal application.** Many people don't read the book of Revelation. Sometimes we treat it like the priests and Levites treated the Samaritan. We pass by on the other side. I believe Satan hates this book and tries to turn us away from it. Do you think he wants people to learn that he himself is to be bound in the bottomless pit for 1,000 years and eventually be cast into the Lake of Fire? That his archenemy, Jesus Christ, is going to triumph?
   B. **It is profitable for public assembly.** "Blessed is he who reads and those who hear . . . " It has been a custom through church history, though now often neglected, to publicly read the Scripture at our open assemblies.
   C. **It is profitable for practical admonition.** Notice this phrase in verse 3: *. . . and keep those things that are written in it.* The book is read, heard, and followed. (Notice Rev. 2:7; 2:11; 2:29; 3:6; 3:13; 3:22; 13:9). This book isn't just for intellectually assimilation, but for practical admonition.
   D. **It is profitable for prophetic anticipation (v. 3).** Notice the phrase: " . . . for the time is near." A little boy came downstairs one day and heard the

>>> *sermon continued on following page*

APPROPRIATE HYMNS AND SONGS

Ancient of Days, Jamie Harvill/Gary Sadler; © 1992 Integrity's Hosanna! Music.

Standing On the Promises, R. Kelso Carter; Public Domain.

The Bible Stands, Haldor Lillenas; Public Domain.

Thy Word, Amy Grant/Michael W. Smith; © 1984 Meadowgreen Music/Word Music, Inc. Admin. by Word Music Group, Inc.

Thy Word Have I Hid In My Heart, Ernest O. Sellers; Public Domain.

clock begin to chime. It chimed thirteen times. "Mom," he said excitedly, "something's wrong. It's later than it's ever been!"

Conclusion: Nothing stands in the way of Christ coming at any moment, and it's never been more important to read and study the Book of Revelation. The days are urgent, and time is short. Come to Christ today and begin to anticipate the things that must soon take place.

FOR THE BULLETIN

❀ On September 5, 1661, John Eliot finished his translation of the New Testament for the Indians of New England. ❀ On September 5, 1847, Rev. Henry Francis Lyte left home for the last time, after writing the hymn, "Abide with Me." Henry, in his early 50s, contracted tuberculosis. On September 4, 1847, he preached his last sermon, planning to leave the next day for a therapeutic holiday in Italy. That afternoon he walked along the English coast in pensive prayer then retired to his private room, emerging an hour later with a written copy of "Abide with Me." He made it to the French Riviera and checked into the Hotel de Angleterre in Nice; there on November 20, 1847, he passed away. ❀ Allen Francis Gardiner left England for South America, hoping to plant a church among native South Americans, but his efforts were thwarted by inter-tribal fighting and governmental interference. He and his six companions all died of disease, starvation, and exposure on Picton Island. Gardiner's final journal entry is dated September 5, 1851: *Good and marvelous are the loving kindnesses of my gracious God unto me. He has preserved me hitherto and for four days, although without bodily food, without any feelings of hunger or thirst.* Gardiner died without seeing a single soul saved among those for whom he was most burdened. But his South American Missionary Society has been sending missionaries and saving souls for over 150 years. ❀ On one day, September 5, 1870, three Roman Catholic universities were founded in the United States: St. John's in New York City, Loyola in Chicago, and Canisius in Buffalo, New York. ❀ Today is the wedding anniversary of Billy and Nell Sunday, who were married in 1888. ❀ Baptist Bible College was founded in Springfield, Missouri, on September 5, 1950.

STATS, STORIES AND MORE

More from David Jeremiah

"Sometimes people say we shouldn't talk about the return of the Lord, that it's extraneous material. They say we should keep our mind on the here-and-now, not on the sweet by-and-by. Well, let me remind you that one out of every thirty verses in the Bible mentions the subject of Christ's return. Of the 216 chapters in the New Testament, there are well over three hundred references to the return of Christ. Only four of the twenty-seven books of the New Testament fail to mention it. That means that 1/20 of the entire New Testament is dedicated to the subject of our Lord's return."

An Illustration from W. A. Criswell

"I have read many times in history of those who went to bed in Galveston, Texas, in 1900, and the United States government weather bureau, had sent message after message after message to the citizens of Galveston saying, 'A great storm is headed your way. Get out. Get out.' And the citizens of Galveston had never seen a storm like that. And they scoffed at the warning of the weather bureau in Washington, D.C.

"At that time, there was an iron bridge connecting the island to the mainland. In the middle of the night, a wife awakened her husband saying, 'Husband, maybe you'd better close the window. The rain and the wind are beginning to fall.' And before the night was over, a great tidal wave washed over that entire island. That iron bridge was snapped asunder as though it were a matchstick, and they counted their dead by the thousands.

"I remember reading how the pastor of this church, Dr. (George) Truett, went down to Galveston to help bury the dead in that awesome and tragic disaster. Scoffers, walking after their own lusts saying, 'Since the world began, everything continues just as it is. And it will continue thus. There is no Second Coming of our Lord.' To that, the apostle Simon Peter addressed himself, and he said, 'Beloved, be not without knowledge of this one thing, that a day is with the Lord as a thousand years and a thousand years as a day. The Lord is not slack concerning His promise . . . .'"

WORSHIP HELPS

Call to Worship:
Blessing and honor and glory and power be to Him who sits on the throne, and to the Lamb forever and ever! (Rev. 5:13).

Pastoral Prayer:
Almighty God, We are immediate-thinkers instead of ultimate-thinkers, and we seldom see through the fog into the future. But You, O Lord, know the beginning from the end. Teach us to live our lives in the light of eternity, and to make our daily choices as those who possess everlasting life. Remind us that all that is in the world—the lust of the flesh, the lust of the eyes, and the pride of life—is not from You, but from the world which is passing away. Teach us, Lord, that even decisions about purchases, friends, habits, and hobbies may have eternal consequences. Make us ultimate-thinkers, O Lord, and may we eagerly await and hasten the coming of our Lord Jesus Christ, in whose name we pray. Amen.

A Word of Welcome:
The word "Welcome" comes from the little words, *well* and *come*. It's well that you've come. Or, to put it differently, coming here will make you well. Recent surveys have shown that people who attend church regularly are physically and emotionally healthier than those who don't. So a warm well-come to you all. Thanks for being with us today.

Appropriate Scripture Readings:
Daniel 2:20–23
Matthew 24:32–35
2 Peter 3:10–13

Benediction:
Even so, come, Lord Jesus! The grace of our Lord Jesus Christ be with you all (Rev. 22:20–21).

Additional Sermons and Lesson Ideas

Revelation Revealed
By David Jeremiah

Date preached:

SCRIPTURE: Revelation 1:4–7

INTRODUCTION: The key to unlocking the Book of Revelation is hanging on the front door—the first verses of chapter 1. We see:

1. The People Addressed in the Book (v. 4a). The seven churches in Asia. Paul sent seven letters to seven different churches, but John sent one letter to seven churches. The number seven in the Bible signifies completeness. This book is for everyone, all the churches.
2. The Publishers of the Book (vv. 4–8). This book is from Triune Publishers—God the Father (v. 4); God the Spirit (v. 4); and God the Son (v. 5), who is described as:
   A. The Faithful Witness
   B. The Firstborn from the Dead
   C. The Ruler of the Earth
3. The Personal Dedication of the Book (vv. 5b–6). John dedicated his book to Him who *loved* us and *loosed* us and *lifted* us.
4. The Purpose of the Book (vv. 7–8). These verses are a vignette of the whole book, giving us the *presentation* of the King (v. 7), and the *program* of the King (v. 8).

CONCLUSION: The message of Revelation is that Jesus is coming, and He is in charge. No wonder we get excited reading this book!

When Life Overwhelms Us
By Drew Wilkerson

Date preached:

SCRIPTURE: Mark 10:46–52

INTRODUCTION: When life overwhelms us, we should remember what a difference a day can make. In the story of Bartimaeus, we have three steps toward a miracle.

1. Speak Up (vv. 46–48). The crowds tried to silence Bartimaeus, but it was no use: "Son of David, have mercy on me!" If we want to see God's miracle we must cry out to Him.
2. Cheer Up (v. 49). To the crowd's surprise, Jesus stopped. The atmosphere changed dramatically. "Cheer up!" said the crowds. "Help is on its way!"
3. Rise Up (vv. 50–52). Immediately Bartimaeus rose up to meet Jesus, who asked, "What do you want me to do for you?" Bartimaeus replied, "I want to see." The answer came quickly: "Go, your faith has healed you."

CONCLUSION: If we want God's miracles, we must be willing to partner with Him and be willing to speak up, cheer up, and rise up. What a difference a day can make!

SEPTEMBER 12, 2004

SUGGESTED SERMON

Learning to Be Thankful Whatever Your Circumstances

Date preached:

By Ed Dobson

Scripture: Philippians 4:4–8, especially verse 4: Rejoice in the Lord always. I will say it again: Again I will say, rejoice!

Introduction: Our text today begins with a strong sentence: "Rejoice in the Lord always." It would be easier if the word "always" were not there. Surely it can't mean that we are to rejoice in the Lord all the time, no matter what! Paul almost reads our thoughts and responds: "Again I will say, rejoice!" Rejoice in the Lord in every situation, whatever the challenge—and again I say, rejoice! Have you noticed how many people offer you advice during adversity? Many times they are not facing troubles themselves, but will readily say "just pray" when you don't feel like praying, or "just take the next step" when you can barely walk. This advice is from Paul, who at this point was in prison, in chains, not planting churches or encouraging others, but falsely accused, confined, and limited. Yet he wrote a Book called Philippians, the theme of which was "joy." Does that get your attention? Paul gave us three practical steps to have joy regardless of circumstance.

1. **Don't Retreat (v. 5).** How can we rejoice always? Verse 5: "Let your gentleness be known to all men." Here are some synonyms for gentleness: big heartedness, kindness, charitableness, magnanimity, generosity. The natural human tendency is to withdraw, but here Paul tells us not to become reclusive in harboring hopelessness, but inclusive in displaying gentleness. Notice, he says to display gentleness "to all". Paul knows we need others around to keep us from focusing completely on our problems. How can we display gentleness when we're hopeless? This leads us to the next phrase: "The Lord is at hand." In studying the Bible, you will discover that whatever God asks of you, He will enable you to do through His power. So, when you face adversity, don't give up or isolate yourself. Keep others around and rely on God's empowering to display gentleness rather than despair.

2. **Pray (v. 6).** "Be anxious (worried) for nothing." The verb is present tense; we are not to live in a continual state of worry. There are times we ought to be concerned, but Paul is telling us not to live in a constant state of anxiety. This leads to the next phrase: "But in everything by prayer and supplication, with thanksgiving, let your requests be made known to God." Notice the phrase "with thanksgiving." When things fall apart in our lives, we tend to lose a thankful perspective. Paul tells us it's all right to bring our requests to God, but we should do it with thanksgiving. He uses a Greek word for thanksgiving which, in its root, means grace. Thanksgiving is an appropriate response to God's grace. Even during difficulty, we are recipients of the undeserved favor and blessings of God. We are to ask with thanksgiving.

3. **Stay Focused (v. 8).** "Finally, brethren, whatever things are true, whatever things are noble, whatever things are just, whatever things are pure, whatever things are lovely, whatever things are of good report, if there is any virtue and if there is anything praiseworthy—meditate on these things." The battle for joy takes place in the mind. We easily become self-centered, blaming ourselves, trying to figure out what we could have done differently. You may feel trapped in the past, overwhelmed by the present, or anxious about the future. The Bible encourages us to stay focused, but how and on what?

Second Peter 3 says, "... I now write to you ... that you may be mindful of the words which were spoken before by the holy prophets, and of the commandment

>>> *sermon continued on following page*

APPROPRIATE HYMNS AND SONGS

Rejoice and Be Exceedingly Glad, Nancy Gordon; © 1987 Integrity's Hosanna! Music.

Songs of Thankfulness and Praise, Christopher Wordsworth/George J. Elvey; © 1982 Hope Publishing Company.

Thank You Jesus, John C. Hallett/Ruth G. Hallett; © 1948. Renewed 1976 Word Music, Inc. Admin. by Word Music Group, Inc.

We Bring the Sacrifice of Praise, Kirk Dearman; © 1984 John T. Benson Publishing Company, Admin. by Brentwood/Benson Music Publishing Company, Inc.

We Give Thanks, Gerritt Gustafson/Don Moen; © 1989 Integrity's Hosanna! Music.

of us the apostles . . . " It isn't enough just to quote a verse of Scripture; it must be memorized, meditated on, or repeated, until it captivates our minds and grips our souls. We win the battle of joy in your mind by focusing on the Holy, wholesome Scriptures.

Conclusion: Paul, who understood difficult situations, told us to always rejoice. He said, "Don't retreat, but let your big heartedness be known to everyone. God is near to help. Pray with thanksgiving and stay focused, allowing wholesome thinking to dominate in your mind." The result? Verse 7: "and the peace of God, which surpasses all understanding, will guard your hearts and minds through Christ Jesus." God offers His peace, a peace which cannot be explained, which prevails in all circumstances. The same God who offers this peace offers His presence. Certainly we can say with Paul, "Rejoice in the Lord always. Again I will say, rejoice!"

FOR THE BULLETIN

❋ September 12, 1729, is the birthday of John Fletcher of Madeley, an early Methodist leader and close associate of John Wesley. ❋ Captain Thomas Webb helped build the "Mother Church of Methodism in America," the John Street Chapel in New York City. Webb, an early Methodist leader in America, wore a large, green patch over his left eye, the result of war wounds on September 12, 1759, during the Battle of Louisburg. It was described this way: *A ball hit him on the bone which guards the right eye, and taking an oblique direction, burst the eyeball, and passing through his palate into his mouth, he swallowed it. A comrade said, "He is dead enough." Webb replied, "No, I am not dead." In three months, he was able to rejoin his comrades.* ❋ Alexander Campbell, founder of the Disciples of Christ, was born in Ballymena, Antrim County, Ireland, on September 12, 1788. Coming to America in 1809, he preached the Word of God as an infallible all-sufficient standard for Christian life and conduct. His slogan: "Where the Scriptures speak, we speak; and where the Scriptures are silent, we are silent." ❋ A. W. Tozer, in his classic biography of A. B. Simpson, writes, "A. B. Simpson was no average man. So on September 11, he delivered his maiden sermon as the new pastor of Knox Church, Hamilton (Ontario). The next day (September 12, 1865), he . . . was ordained to the ministry by prayer and the laying on of hands. That same night he caught a train for Toronto, and the next day he was married!" Simpson later founded the Christian and Missionary Alliance. ❋ The Pocket Testament League was incorporated in Birmingham, England, on this day in 1908.

STATS, STORIES AND MORE

When one of her sons was living a wild and dangerous life, Ruth Bell Graham found herself torn apart by worry. While traveling abroad, she suddenly awoke in the middle of the night worrying about him. A current of worry surged through her like an electric shock. She lay in bed and tried to pray, but she suffered from galloping anxiety, one fear piling upon another. She looked at the clock and it was around three o'clock. She was exhausted, yet she knew she would be unable to go back to sleep. Suddenly the Lord seemed to say to her, "Quit studying the problems and start studying the promises." Turning on the light, she got out her Bible, and the first verses that came to her were these, Philippians 4:6–7. As she read those words, she suddenly realized that the missing ingredient in her prayers had been thanksgiving. " . . . in everything by prayer and petition, *with thanksgiving*, present your requests to God."

She put down her Bible and spent time worshiping God for who and what He is. She later wrote, "I began to thank God for giving me this one I loved so dearly in the first place. I even thanked Him for the difficult spots which had taught me so much. And you know what happened? It was as if someone turned on the light in my mind and heart, and the little fears and worries that had been nibbling away in the darkness like mice and cockroaches hurriedly scuttled for cover. That was when I learned that worship and worry cannot live in the same heart. They are mutually exclusive."

WORSHIP HELPS

Call to Worship:
Praise God, ye servants of the Lord,
O praise His Name with one accord;
Bless ye the Lord, His Name adore
From this time forth forevermore.
(from *The Psalter,* 1912)

Scripture Medley:
I am torn apart by worry and pain. . . . I have no peace or rest—only troubles and worries.

Don't give in to worry or anger; it only leads to trouble. Those who trust in the LORD will possess the land, but the wicked will be driven out. Abraham was worried about Ishmael. But God said, "Abraham, don't worry. . . ."

When God heard the boy crying, the angel of God called out to Hagar from heaven and said, "Hagar, why are you worried? Don't be afraid." Why do you look so worried today? You may be thinking, "How can we destroy these nations? They are more powerful than we are." But stop worrying! Just remember what the LORD your God did to Egypt and its king. You saw how the LORD used His tremendous power to work great miracles and bring you out of Egypt. And He will again work miracles for you . . . The LORD your God is great and fearsome, and He will fight at your side.

Give your worries to the Lord and He will take care of you.

Blessed is the man who trusts in the LORD, whose confidence is in Him. He will be like a tree planted by the water that sends out its roots by the stream. It does not fear when heat comes; its leaves are always green. It has no worries in a year of drought and never fails to bear fruit.

Therefore I say to you, do not worry about your life, what you will eat or what you will drink; nor about your body, what you will put on. Is not life more than food and the body more than clothing? Look at the birds of the air, for they neither sow nor reap nor gather into barns; yet your heavenly Father feeds them. Are you not of more value than they?

[Job 30:27 (TEV); Job 3:26 (CEV); Ps. 37:8–9 (TEV); Gen. 21:11 (CEV); Gen. 21:17 (CEV); Gen. 40:7 (NLT); Deut. 7:17–21 (CEV); Ps. 55:22 (NCV); Jer. 17:7–8 (NIV); Matt. 6:25–26 (NKJV)]

Additional Sermons and Lesson Ideas

Where to Find Christ
By W. Graham Scroggie

Date preached:

SCRIPTURE: Job 23:3

INTRODUCTION: Where in this disturbed and distressed world is Christ to be found? Job cried, "O, that I might know where to find Him!"

1. Christ in the Midst of Serious Inquiry (Matt. 2:1–2). The Magi asked where to find Him, and they asked not in vain, for He is in the midst of all serious inquiry. Those who really seek Him find Him.
2. Christ in the Midst of Religious Knowledge (Luke 2:46). The boy Jesus was sitting in the midst of the temple doctors.
3. Christ in the Midst of Spiritual Devotion (Matt. 18:20).
4. Christ in the Midst of Human Misery (John 19:18). Crucified between two thieves.
5. Christ in the Midst of Heart Bewilderment (Luke 24:36).
6. Christ in the Midst of Christian Testimony (Rev. 1:3).
7. Christ in the Midst of Eternal Glory (Rev. 5:6).

CONCLUSION: Is He in the midst of your life, your business, your home, your recreation, your friendships? If so, heaven is not a distant prospect but a present experience.

Unbroken Cords of Friendship
By Drew Wilkerson

Date preached:

SCRIPTURE: Ecclesiastes 4:9–12

INTRODUCTION: Pepper Rogers writes, "A few years back I was in the middle of a terrible season as football coach at UCLA. It even got so bad that it upset my home life. My dog was my only friend. So I told my wife that a man needs at least two friends, and she bought me another dog." God does not want us to be lonely. Hidden within these words in Ecclesiastes we find three unifying cords necessary to build a friendship that cannot be broken.

1. Cord #1: A friend is someone dedicated to you (vv. 9–10).
2. Cord #2: A friend is someone who you can depend on (v. 11).
3. Cord #3: A friend is someone who will defend you (v. 12).

CONCLUSION: Two friends are invaluable, but three are priceless. To have a friend we must be a friend, and nothing can compare to the joy and strength of the unbroken cords of friendship.

SEPTEMBER 19, 2004

SUGGESTED SERMON

The Forgotten Secret of Happiness
By Michael Easley

Date preached:

Scripture: Psalm 32, especially verse 1: Blessed is he whose transgression is forgiven, whose sin is covered.

Introduction: Some suffering in life is hard to explain, but much of it is self-inflicted. Could your misery be due to poor choices? Due to apathy or indifference? Could our suffering be due to sin? Psalm 32 shows God's blessings for those who are forgiven. This psalm gives us the forgotten secret of happiness, telling us that sin brings sorrow, but confession brings forgiveness and forgiveness brings joy.

1. **The Joy of Forgiveness (vv. 1–2).** Blessed is one of those religious words that's hard to translate into practical terms. Perhaps the closest we can come is "happiness." The psalmist says that the blessed person is the one who understands forgiveness. We can't understand the reality of forgiveness if we don't understand the concept of sin, so David uses three words to describe sin:

    Transgression—Rebellion against God.

    Sin—Missing the mark or falling short of a standard.

    Iniquity—Treachery, deceit.

    The psalmist was happy that . . .

    His transgression was forgiven (lifted, carried away).

    His sin was covered (hidden, concealed by removal).

    The Lord does not impute iniquity. This is an accounting term, as in reckoning to an account; it is not counted against us. A rough illustration is when you get pulled over for speeding and the kind officer tells you it will not go on your record. Now taken together, we have the comprehensive nature of our sins and the comprehensive nature of God's forgiveness. This is reason for joy!

2. **The Misery of Unconfessed Sin (vv. 3–4).** Notice the shift to a personal pronoun. David is giving us a personal illustration about the power of uncon-

fessed sin. When I kept silent, he said, unwilling to confess sin, my body wasted away and God dealt with me so severely that my vitality was drained like a man suffering in the summer heat. Do you recall a time when the summer's heat was so oppressive you found it difficult to even breathe? Unconfessed sin hunts us down, oppresses us, keeps us awake at night.

3. **Confession and Repentance (v. 5).** In this verse, David used the same three words he used in verses 1-2, saying that he had learned to acknowledge his sin, to expose his iniquity to the Lord, and to confess his transgressions.

4. **Instruction (vv. 6–7).** Now the psalmist is going to pass along the lesson he learned. He calls on us to turn to God as he did, and to find in Him relief, release, and protection. He depicts God's protection in three ways:
   A. A hiding place
   B. Preservation from trouble
   C. Surrounded by songs of deliverance.

5. **The Wisdom of God (vv. 8–10).** Now Psalm 32 shifts gears, warning the reader not to be like a horse or mule that requires a bit and bridle. Those who do not want God, who do not care about God, choose the hard way, the way of sin.

6. **The Glad Response (v. 11).** The one who groaned under the weight of sin (vv. 3–4) now rejoices and shouts for joy.

>>> *sermon continued on following page*

APPROPRIATE HYMNS AND SONGS

Bless the Lord My Soul, Danny Davis; © 1993 Wilde and Wooley Music.

Christ Receiveth Sinful Men, Erdmann Neumeister/James McGranahan; Public Domain.

Grace Greater Than Our Sins, Julia H. Johnston/Daniel Brink Towner; Public Domain.

He Set Me Free, Albert E. Brumley; © 1939. Renewed 1967 Stamps-Baxter Music, Admin. by Brentwood-Benson Music Publishing, Inc.

Shout to the Lord, Dennis Jernigan; © 1996 Shepherd's Heart Music, Admin. by Word Music Group, Inc.

Lessons:
We have a deficient view of repentance. Repentance isn't penance, reparation, or self-punishment. It isn't morbid introversion. True repentance involves contrition, sorrow, remorse, guilt, grief, and regret. But it is primarily a turning, a changing, a choice.

Forgiveness does not necessarily mean God removes the *consequences* of our sins.

The believer has assurance that God forgives sin. Forgiveness is the removal of sin. It is lifted. The debt is cancelled. All the debt of sin—impossible for us to pay off—is forgiven in Christ's work on the Cross. We can have full assurance of that.

When we understand forgiveness, we're thankful. This psalm has a thankful message. There is great joy in forgiveness.

The only real happiness is forgiveness from sin. Apart from forgiveness, there's no real joy. To live in sin is to live in grief. To live in sin is to lose joy. The only real happiness is being forgiven. Everything else is an artificial attempt to dull the pain.

Conclusion: Sin brings sorrow, confession brings forgiveness, and forgiveness brings joy. How many struggles in our lives are due to sin! Why not confess it? Why not admit to God what He already knows? Why not ask Him this minute? Why not come to the Cross of Jesus Christ?

FOR THE BULLETIN

✤ On September 19, 1853, J. Hudson Taylor sailed for China as a representative of the Chinese Evangelization Society. He later founded China Inland Mission (now Overseas Missionary Fellowship, or OMF). ✤ Dr. Joseph Parker, who had been pastoring in Manchester, England, accepted the call of London's Poultry Chapel; and on September 19, 1969, he began thirty-three phenomenal years there. Under his leadership the church relocated and changed its name to City Temple. Here he preached three times a week, year after year. His messages through the Bible were published in a 25-volume set called *The People's Bible*. ✤ E. M. Bounds married Emma Elizabeth Barnett, on September 19, 1876. He was a pastor and the writer of a popular set of books on prayer. ✤ As he strolled along Addison's Walk next to Magdalen College on September 19, 1931, C. S. Lewis had an important talk with J. R. R. Tolkien, and Hugo Dyson. The conversation led to Lewis' conversion to

FOR THE BULLETIN (CONTINUED)

Christianity. Shortly afterward, he wrote a friend, "I have passed from believing in God to definitely believing in Christ... My long night walk with Dyson and Tolkien had a great deal to do with it." ❋ As missionary aviator Nate Saint flew over the Ecuadorian jungle in his small plane, he spotted an Auca village for the first time on this day in 1955. This was the beginning of an effort to reach the Aucas that resulted in the deaths of five missionaries, but the eventual conversion of the tribe to Christ. ❋ On September 19, 1955, C. S. Lewis published his autobiography, *Surprised By Joy*. ❋ September 19, 1971, marks the death of William F. Albright, 80, noted Methodist archaeologist.

STATS, STORIES AND MORE

John Stott wrote about Marghanita Laski, one of England's best-known secular humanists and novelists. Just before she died in 1988, she said in a television interview, "What I envy most about you Christians is your forgiveness; I have nobody to forgive me."

In his book, *Healing for Damaged Emotions,* David Seamands writes about a young minister who once came to see him. He was having a lot of problems getting along with other people, especially his wife and family. He was continually criticizing her. He was sarcastic and demanding, and he was destroying their marriage. His attitude was also harsh toward members of his church. Finally in desperation, he came to see Dr. Seamands, and after a while, the painful root of the matter came to light. Seamands wrote:

"While he was in the armed forces in Korea, he had spent two weeks of R & R in Japan. During that leave, walking the streets of Tokyo, feeling empty, lonely, and terribly homesick, he fell into temptation and went three or four times to a prostitute.

"He had never been able to forgive himself. He had sought God's forgiveness, and with his head, believed he had it. But the guilt still plagued him and he hated himself. Every time he looked in the mirror, he couldn't stand what he was seeing.

"When he returned home to marry his fiancée, who had faithfully waited for him all those years, his emotional conflicts increased because he still could not accept complete forgiveness.... He felt he had no right to be happy.

"As A. W. Tozer put it, the young minister was living in 'the perpetual penance of regret.' "

WORSHIP HELPS

Call to Worship:
The LORD lives! Praise be to my Rock! Exalted be God, the Rock, my Savior! (2 Samuel 22:47 NIV)

Pastoral Prayer:
Our Father, we are very weak. Worst of all we are very wicked if left to ourselves, and we soon fall a prey to the enemy. Therefore help us. We confess that sometimes in prayer when we are nearest to You at that very time some evil thought comes in, some wicked desire. Oh! what poor simpletons we are. Lord, help us. We feel as if we would now come closer to You still and hide under the shadow of Your wings. We wish to be lost in God. Lord, visit our church. Oh! do not let any of us lose our first love. Lord revive us! Lord sanctify us. Oh! that Your spirit might come and saturate every faculty, subdue every passion, and use every power of our nature for obedience to God. In Jesus' name. Amen.—*Charles Haddon Spurgeon*

Appropriate Scripture Readings:
Psalm 51
John 8:1–11
Ephesians 1:3–7
1 John 1:7—2:2

Kids Talk

Have an erasable marker board with a red marking pen. Tell them about a time in your life when you were a child and did some things wrong (or, you can make up a story about a fictional child who threw a rock at a cat, stole some chewing gum, shouted at his or her mother, etc.). Write the wrong deeds on the marker board. Explain that God's love is like an eraser. When we confess our sins, He erases them forever.

Additional Sermons and Lesson Ideas

The Prince and the Paupers

Date preached:

SCRIPTURE: Daniel 9:25

INTRODUCTION: We think of the word "prince" as being the Son of the King. Jesus, being the almighty Son of God, is a prince. But the English word "prince" is related to the words "principality" and "principal," and "prime." It literally means the ruler of a principality. In that sense, too, Jesus is our Prince. He is called:

1. The Prince (Dan. 9:25).
2. The Prince of Peace (Is. 9:6).
3. The Prince of Life (Acts 3:15).
4. The Prince and Savior (Acts 5:31).
5. The Prince of the Host (Dan. 8:11).
6. The Prince of Princes (Dan. 8:25).

CONCLUSION: Do you remember Mark Twain's story about the prince who became an ordinary person and lived like a pauper? Our Prince has come to live among us, and while we are to enjoy His fellowship we're never to forget that He is the Prince of Peace, the Prince of Life, our Prince and Savior.

When You're Perplexed

Date preached:

SCRIPTURE: Daniel 9

INTRODUCTION: Daniel was an old man when the world turned upside down for him. His government was overthrown, and the stability of the world descended into chaos as the Medes superceded the Babylonians as the ruling world empire. Even worse, hope seemed to further fade for Daniel's people, the Jews. Chapter 9 tells us how he responded.

1. Perplexity (v. 1).
2. Promise (v. 2). Daniel went to the Scriptures, and in the writings of Jeremiah he found a powerful promise to claim.
3. Prayer (vv. 3:19). This is one of Scripture's greatest prayers of confession, coming from the lips of one of the few men in the Bible of whom virtually nothing bad is said. He is confessing the sins of his nation.
4. Prophecy (vv. 20–27). In response to Daniel's prolonged prayer, the angel Gabriel comes with assurances that God has a prophetic plan. This is one of Scripture's seminal prophecies regarding the end times.

CONCLUSION: Some perplexities, like a Gordian knot, can only be severed with the sword of prayer.

HEROES FOR THE PASTOR'S HEART

Isaac Watts

Perhaps you know that Isaac Watts is called the "Father of English Hymnody," and the author of such timeless hymns as "Alas, and Did My Savior Bleed," "I Sing the Mighty Power of God," "Jesus Shall Reign," and "Joy to the World." But do you know that that he wrote most of his best hymns when he was around 19 years old? And do you know that he was also a powerful preacher, a beloved pastor, a brilliant writer of collegiate textbooks? Furthermore, do you know that he was such an odd-looking fellow that one woman broke off her romance with him rather than look at him?

Isaac was born into a Dissenting family. His father, Isaac Watts Senior, was a clothier and a deacon in Above Bar Congregational Church in Southampton, England. The Watts were Non-Anglican—a treasonous offense in those days. They wanted to worship God apart from the state church. About the time Isaac Junior prematurely arrived, July 17, 1674, the elder Watts was arrested. Sarah reportedly nursed her newborn while seated on a stone outside the prison.

In time, Watts Senior was released, and the young couple soon discovered they had a precocious child. Young Isaac took to books almost from infancy. He learned Latin at age four, Greek at nine, and Hebrew at thirteen. He loved rhyme and verse. At age 7, he wrote this poem in childish script. Notice the acrostic—ISAAC:

> *I am a vile polluted lump of earth*
> *So I've continued ever since my birth*
> *Although Jehovah grace does give me*
> *As sure this monster Satan will deceive me*
> *Come, therefore, Lord, from Satan's claws relieve me.*

After Isaac graduated from grammar school in Southampton, a wealthy benefactor offered to send him to Oxford. But that would have required his becoming Anglican. Politely declining, Isaac enrolled in a college-level school for Dissenters in Stoke Newington, London, where he excelled.

After graduation, Isaac, about 19, returned to Southampton and spent two more years at home. One day he complained to his father about the dismal singing at church. Only versified arrangements of the

Psalms were used. Protestants in seventeenth-century Europe were divided about hymns. Though Martin Luther had taught his followers to sing hymns, John Calvin had allowed only the singing of Scriptures, and this was the general sentiment in England. But after a heated discussion, his father challenged Isaac to write a hymn for their church.

Drawing from Revelation 5, he did so. Shortly thereafter, the brave congregation of Above Bar Congregational Church sang, "Behold the Glories of the Lamb." This was the first of Isaac's 600-plus hymns. Published in 1707, it's been called the first English hymn designed for congregational use.

The church requested a new hymn each week, and Isaac, about 20, gladly complied. Those two years in Southampton became the richest hymn-writing period in Isaac Watts' life. Though barely out of school, he composed hymns that are still sung nearly three centuries later, earning him the title, "Father of English Hymnody."

Isaac then moved to London to tutor children in a wealthy family of Dissenters. While there he joined Mark Lane Independent Chapel. Soon he was asked to be a teacher in the church, and in 1698, he was hired as associate pastor. There on his twenty-fourth birthday he preached his first sermon. In 1702, he became senior pastor of the church, a position he retained the rest of his life. He was a brilliant Bible student, and his sermons brought the church to life.

In 1707, his *Hymns and Spiritual Songs* was published. Included was a hymn now considered the finest hymn ever written in the English language. It was based on Galatians 6:14: "But God forbid that I should boast except in the cross of our Lord Jesus Christ." Originally the first stanza said: *When I survey the wondrous cross / Where the young Prince of Glory died....* In an enlarged 1709 edition, Watts rewrote the lines to say:

When I survey the wondrous cross
On which the Prince of glory died,
My richest gain I count but loss,
And pour contempt on all my pride.

Also included in the 1707 hymnbook was "Heavenly Joy on Earth," better known today as, "Come, We That Love the Lord," or "We're Marching to Zion."

HEROES FOR THE PASTOR'S HEART — CONTINUED

As Isaac Watts quietly pastored Mark Lane Chapel in London, the growing popularity of his hymns was causing a tempest. "Christian congregations have shut out divinely inspired Psalms," one man complained, "and taken in Watts' flights of fancy." The issue of singing hymns versus Psalms split churches, including the one in Bedford, England, once pastored by John Bunyan.

The controversy jumped the Atlantic. In May, 1789, Rev. Adam Rankin told the General Assembly of the Presbyterian Church, meeting in Philadelphia: "I have ridden horseback all the way from my home in Kentucky to ask this body to refuse the great and pernicious error of adopting the use of Isaac Watts's hymns in public worship in preference to the Psalms of David."

We don't know Isaac's reactions. Dr. Samuel Johnson later reported "by his natural temper he was quick of resentment; but, by his established and habitual practice, he was gentle, modest, and inoffensive." But in 1712, Isaac suffered a breakdown from which he never fully recovered. He asked his church to discontinue his salary; but they raised it and hired a co-pastor who assumed the bulk of the pastoral duties. Watts remained as pastor the rest of his life, preaching whenever he could.

A wealthy couple in the church, Sir Thomas and Lady Abney, invited him to spend a week on their estate. Isaac accepted—and lived with them until his death 36 years later. He enjoyed the children in the home, and in 1715, he published *Divine and Moral Songs for Children.* It sold 80,000 copies in a year and has been selling ever since. In his preface, he said, "Children of high and low degree, of the Church of England or Dissenters, baptized in infancy or not, may all join together in these songs. And as I have endeavored to sink the language to the level of a child's understanding . . . to profit all, if possible, and offend none."

One hymn in this volume, intended for children, became popular with adults. Entitled, "Praise for Creation and Providence," it said:

> I sing the mighty power of God, that made the mountains rise,
>   That spread the flowing seas abroad, and built the lofty skies.
> I sing the wisdom that ordained the sun to rule the day;
>   The moon shines full at God's command, and all the stars obey.

While living on the Abney estate, Isaac devoted himself to a massive project, adapting the Book of Psalms for Christian worship. In 1719, *The Psalms of David Imitated in the Language of the New Testament* was published. In it, Watts worked his way through most of the 150 Psalms, paraphrasing them, injecting them with New Testament truth, and framing them in singing form.

He explained his approach with these words: "Where the Psalmist describes religion by the fear of God, I have often joined faith and love to it. Where he speaks of the pardon of sin through the mercies of God, I have added the merits of a Savior. Where he talks of sacrificing goats or bullocks, I rather choose to mention the sacrifice of Christ, the lamb of God. Where he promises abundance of wealth, honor, and long life, I have changed some of these typical blessings for grace, glory, and life eternal, which are brought to light by the Gospel, and promised in the New Testament."

Several of these have become favorites that have withstood the ages. His rendition of Psalm 72, for example, has been called the first missions hymn: "Jesus Shall Reign Where'er The Sun."

In appearance, Isaac Watts was . . . well, odd. Standing five feet in his stockings, he had an outsized head and prominent nose, and his skin was tallowy. One woman, Elizabeth Singer, having never met him, fell in love with him through his hymns and poems, but when she saw him face-to-face, she was unsettled. He fell in love with her, but she couldn't bring herself to marry him, later saying, "I only wish I could admire the casket (jewelry box) as much as I admire the jewel."

In 1739, Watts suffered a stroke that left him able to speak but unable to write. A secretary was provided to transcribe his dictated poems and books, but over the next several years he became increasingly weak and bedridden. He died on November 25, 1748, and is buried in Bunhill Fields in London.

In addition to his 600 hymns, he wrote 52 other works, including a book of logic widely used in the universities, and books on grammar, astronomy, philosophy, and geography. But it's his hymns—most of them written in his early twenties—for which we're most grateful.

SEPTEMBER 26, 2004

SUGGESTED SERMON
Shaking Off Discouragement
By Stuart Briscoe

Date preached:

Scripture: Haggai 2, especially verse 4: "Yet now be strong, Zerubbabel," says the LORD; "and be strong, Joshua, son of Jehozadak, the high priest; and be strong, all you people of the land," says the LORD, "and work; for I am with you," says the LORD of hosts.

Background: Haggai appeared on the scene in Jerusalem in 520 B.C. That was a critical time in the history of Jerusalem, because approximately 70 years earlier the city had been devastated, the temple had been destroyed, and the inhabitants had been in exile. Eventually through an edict of Cyrus, the Persian king, a Jewish remnant was allowed to return to Israel, intent on re-establishing the worship of Jehovah. They started off very well, but then ran into discouraging opposition; and for 18 years the work on restoring the temple and restoring the worship in the temple had ceased. That's when Haggai arrived. He reminded the people that whilst the temple of the Lord was being neglected, they had spent a lot of time on their own houses. He explained in chapter 1 that the hard times they were experiencing were directly related to the spiritually impoverished lives they were living. The people were very responsive, and they got to work, assured that the Lord was with them as they went about the work on His house. That is the essence of Haggai, chapter 1. Now, as we move into chapter 2, we find this dated very specifically (2:1)—October 17, 520 B.C. This is less than a month after they had set to work with a will, but their enthusiasm had drained away again, their energies had dissipated, and once again they were becoming discouraged. People *do* need an awful lot of encouragement. If we're not being continually renewed and refreshed and reminded, it's easy to slip into a low-grade attitude and to slide into a kind of spiritual depression. That's why it is so important that we constantly hear the Word of the Lord.

1. **The Debilitating Dynamic of Discouragement.** What happens to people when discouragement sets in? They become debilitated, their energy goes, and they begin to settle for considerably less than they should be settling for. Their reasons for discouragement:
   A. Repetitive problems with the authorities (Ezra 5:1–7).

B. Remembrance of former glory (Hag. 2:3).
C. **Recognition that their expectations may not be met.** The prophet Ezekiel had been talking about the future temple (Ezek. 40—48), and perhaps they realized that the temple they were going to be able to build was unlike anything Ezekiel had envisioned. Zechariah 4:10 reminded these people not to despise the day of small things. God usually begins things small and grows them.
D. **Realization that the problems are not going to be solved overnight.** It had been a time of famine. Even if God sent rains today, it would take awhile to see the results on the dinner table.

2. **The Empowering Effect of Encouragement (vv. 4–5).** Notice the six encouragements found in these two verses:
    A. **"Be strong."** Notice that three times Haggai told them to "Be strong" (v. 4).
    B. **"And work."** Haggai said, in effect, "There is something to do, and the thing to do is to get on doing it." R. A. Torrey used to say, "The best way to begin is to begin."
    C. **"For I am with you, says the LORD of hosts."** This is an oracle from God to be received and acted upon as unassailable truth.
    D. **"According to the word that I covenanted with you when you came out of Egypt . . ."** This harkened back to Exodus 19:4–6, and reminded the

>>> *sermon continued on following page*

APPROPRIATE HYMNS AND SONGS

All Your Anxiety, Edward Henry Joy; © 1953 Salvationist Publishing and Supplies, Admin. by The Copyright Company.

And That My Soul Knows Very Well, Darlene Zschech/Russell Fragar; © 1996 Darlene Zschech (Hillsong)/Russell Fragar (Hillsong), Admin. by Integrity Music, Inc.

God Will Take Care of You, Civilla D. Martin/Walter Stillman Martin; Public Domain.

Hope Set High, Amy Grant; © 1991 Age to Age Music, Inc.

Living For Jesus, Thomas O. Chisholm/C. Harold Lowdenl; Public Domain.

workers that they were a special people with whom God has made a special covenant.

E. **"My Spirit remains among you."** The same Holy Spirit who had assisted Israel's forefathers was with them now. The same Holy Spirit who inflamed Luther, Wesley, Whitefield remains with us here today.

F. **"Do not fear."**

3. **The Positive Power of Promise (2:6–9).** Notice the repetition of the phrase, "I will . . . " God gave the people some fantastic promises about the role of that temple in the future, and about the coming of their Messiah. God kept His promises to them, and He will keep His many promises to you.

Conclusion: What do you believe about the Lord's plan for your life? About His power? About His presence? About His promises? About the empowering that is available to you? Shake off discouragement. Be strong, and work, says the Lord, for I am with you.

FOR THE BULLETIN

❋ On September 26, 1460, Pope Pius II called European leaders together in Mantua to discuss his life's dream—a new crusade against the Turks. He preached three hours at the opening session, telling the princes they must emulate Stephen, Peter, and Andrew who were willing to lay down their lives in holy warfare. His message greatly stirred the assembly, and for a moment the princes appeared ready to rush from the room to undertake a new crusade. But the pope was followed by another preacher, Cardinal Bessarion, who spoke for another three hours. By the end of the day, the princes were so worn out by the preaching they had no passion for the cause. ❋ Sir Lancelot Andrews died on this day in 1626. He had been born in London in 1565, and became a powerful Anglican preacher and one of the translators of the Authorized (King James) Version of the Bible (he worked on the first twelve books of the Old Testament). He was deeply devoted to private prayer and personal devotions; and in the pulpit he was called "the star of preachers." Thomas Fuller said that he was "an inimitable preacher in his way; and such plagiarists as have stolen his sermons could never steal his preaching." Lancelot Andrews died at Winchester House, in Southwark, London, September 25th, 1626, aged sixty-one years. ❋ September 26, 1774, is the birthday of John Chapman, better known as "Johnny Appleseed." ❋ The Christian flag was conceived on this day in 1897.

STATS, STORIES AND MORE

More from Stuart Briscoe

Shortly after Haggai started preaching, Zechariah showed up in Jerusalem, too. So they had two prophets at the same time. One probably was a Baptist, and the other was a Presbyterian, and they prophesied on opposite sides of the street, but they had more or less the same ministry. As we read Zechariah 4:10, he tells the people not to despise the day of small things. You know why some people get discouraged? Because they have grandiose ideas. They've got fantastic plans, great projects, and very rarely do things happen like that. God usually starts small and builds from that. Remember how it all started as far as the Jewish nation was concerned? It started with Abraham, one man being called out of Ur of the Chaldees. Remember how the great story of Redemption started? With a baby being born of a virgin. Remember how the church was born? It was born as a result of twelve men being discipled by the Lord Jesus, one of them turning out no good. Do you know how Elmbrook Church started? With thirteen people. Do you know how our broadcast, "Telling the Truth," started, that now literally goes around the world every day? It started down in the basement of the old church with a little tape recorder that we put on the table.

For what it's worth, discouragement overcame some of the greatest heroes of the Bible. Elijah, Moses, and Jonah all grew so discouraged in the Lord's work they prayed for death. Jeremiah spent his whole life in the throes of depression. John the Baptist asked, "Are you really the Messiah or should we look of someone else?" David said, "Why art thou cast down, O my soul, and why art thou disquieted within me?" Even the apostle Paul said that he was once so weary and worried in ministry that he couldn't preach the gospel though a great door had opened to him.

WORSHIP HELPS

Call to Worship:
And He has on His robe and on His thigh a name written: King of kings and Lord of lords (Rev. 19:16).

Pastoral Prayer:
I suppose, Lord, the thing that encourages us more than anything else is knowing that You are God, and that You are with us, and that You are with us in our work here. Would you help anyone here today who is discouraged? If some here are going through times that are making them disconsolate and depressed, would you encourage them today? If some here are looking at the circumstances and feeling overwhelmed, would You help them to be encouraged in the Lord? May we carry on what You have told us to do, for there's so much that needs to be done. May today's service empower us for Your glory. We pray in Christ's name, Amen.
—*Stuart Briscoe*

The Christian Flag:
If you have a Christian flag in your auditorium or to project on your screen, this would be a good day to emphasize it. The Christian flag was conceived on this day in 1897. There was a planned Sunday school Rally at the Coney Island Chapel in New York, but the featured speaker never arrived. At the last moment, the church's Sunday school Superintendent, Charles C. Overton, rose to fill in. Having nothing prepared, he began talking about the large American flag that was draped over the pulpit, pointing out the heritage, symbolism, and significance of the flag. As he ad-libbed, a thought came to his mind. Why not have a Christian flag? He described what such a flag might look like and might mean. After the rally, the idea stayed with him so strongly that he made such a flag and later presented it to the church. The Christian flag is one of the oldest unchanged flags in the world. The traditional pledge to this flag says: "I pledge allegiance to the Christian flag and to the Savior, for whose kingdom it stands. One Savior, crucified, risen and coming again, with life and liberty for all who believe."

Additional Sermons and Lesson Ideas

Overcoming Legalism
By Peter Grainger

Date preached:

SCRIPTURE: Matthew 23

INTRODUCTION: The essence of legalism is found in answering the question: Are we slaves or sons?

1. The Appeal of Legalism. "Living by the rule book" provides a feeling of security and a sense of superiority that is especially attractive to religious people (e.g., the Pharisees).
2. The Attack on Legalism. The anger of Jesus was directed against "hypocrites," because they failed to practice what they preached (v. 3); enslaved others (v. 4); performed for an audience (vv. 5–12); barred the way into God's kingdom (vv. 13–15), distorted God's law (vv. 16–24), and hid their true nature (vv. 25–28).
3. The Antidote to Legalism. God's remedy is found in grace (Eph. 2:8–9; Rom. 8:3). This grace is for the sinner (such as the prodigal in Luke 15:17–25, and the Pharisee (in Luke 15:28–32), and for the "saint" (Gal. 5:1, 16–26).

CONCLUSION: Are we slaves to fear or sons of God (Rom. 8:14–16)?

What Think Ye of Christ
Adapted from a sermon by D. L. Moody

Date preached:

SCRIPTURE: Matthew 22:42

INTRODUCTION: It matters little what you think of the president, the queen, the prime minister, or of anyone else on earth. It matters little what you think of the Baptists, the Presbyterians, or the Established Church. It matters little what you think of me. But everything depends on what you think of Christ.

1. What do you think of Him as a man?
2. What do you think of Him as a physician?
3. What do you think of Him as a friend?
4. What do you think of Him as a teacher?
5. What do you think of Him as a Savior?

CONCLUSION: Will you not think well of Him as your own Savior and Lord? Will you not believe in Him? Will you not trust in Him with all your heart and mind? May God help us to glorify the Father by thinking well of His only-begotten Son.

OCTOBER 3, 2004

SUGGESTED SERMON

Nic at Night

Date preached:

By Dan Chun

Scripture: John 3:1–16, especially verse 3: Jesus answered and said to him, "Most assuredly, I say to you, unless one is born again, he cannot see the kingdom of God."

Introduction: We're often entertained by watching others face struggles or challenges. Some of the "reality shows" on television put people in challenging circumstances to see how they face the struggle. Our sporting events often pit athletes against one another in a struggle for victory. Struggles make for good entertainment. Humans, however, engage in a more important struggle to find purpose in life and to live life victoriously.

Background: In ancient Israel, a group of lay people called Pharisees took their Judaic faith very seriously indeed. During Jesus' time, there were around 7,000 of them. They became a major spiritual, intellectual, religious, and political power in Judaism. They obeyed a rigorous set of regulations that governed their lifestyle. One of these Pharisees named Nicodemus wanted to meet Jesus. His colleagues had been so critical of Jesus that "Nic" came to Jesus under the cloak of darkness. Their recorded conversation revolved around the most essential idea of the Christian life—the New Birth. From this story we learn that following Jesus Christ means:

1. **Death (vv. 1–3).** Nicodemus was spiritually dead when he came to Christ; yet he had to die in a different way in order to be born again. He had to die to his Pharisaic traditions as a basis for eternal salvation. Following Christ means dying to the world. From the time we accept Jesus and declare allegiance to Him, we die a spiritual death to this world (Rom. 6:3–7; Gal. 2:20; Col. 3:3).

2. **Rebirth (vv. 4–16).** Nicodemus, though an intellectual Pharisee, was quite confused about how He could be born a second time (v. 4). He was thinking in terms of physical birth rather than spiritual. Perhaps some of us are confused about the idea of being born again. Jesus explains that we must be born . . .

A. **Into God's Kingdom (v. 5).** When Jesus arrived and began His ministry He said that the kingdom of God is at hand (Mark 1:15). Joining this kingdom means having the strength, the weapons, the wisdom, and the know-how to fight the kingdom of this world and to live in the kingdom of God. God wants us to be part of His kingdom, to be citizens where we can live in love and joy.

B. **By the Holy Spirit (vv. 6–8).** Being born again means that the Holy Spirit enters into our hearts, and we start to change. It doesn't mean we talk about Jesus all the time. It means we want to be led by Him all the time. Instead of just having the human spirit, we now have the Holy Spirit. The word for "Spirit" in Greek literally means *wind*. We can't control God so we must allow God's wind to control us. Our job is to put up the sails. God blows and tells us how to turn our sails. It is good to be in "windy places" on a regular basis because the Spirit is there. Church services, Bible studies, prayer meetings, fellowship groups, small groups, and Sunday school are all examples of windy places.

C. **Through Faith in Jesus (vv. 9–16).** When Moses was leading the Israelites (Num. 21), they were attacked by deadly snakes because of their disobedience to God. God told Moses to set up a pole with the image of a poisonous snake on top of it. If the people would look at the snake on the pole, they would be saved and healed. Jesus gave new meaning to this familiar story. When Jesus was crucified on the Cross, for that one moment He had all of the sin of the world on Him. But

>>> *sermon continued on following page*

APPROPRIATE HYMNS AND SONGS

Ye Must Be Born Again, William T. Sleeper/George C. Stebbins; Public Domain.

Behold the Lamb, Dottie Rambo; © 1979 John T. Benson Publishing Company, Admin. by Brentwood-Benson Music Publishing, Inc.

Blessed Redeemer, Avis B. Christiansen/Harry Dixon Loes; © 1921. Renewed 1949 Harry Dixon Loes, Admin. by Brentwood-Benson Music Publishing, Inc.

Bring Them In, Alexcenah Thomas/William A. Ogden; Public Domain.

Come Just As You Are, Joseph Sabolick; © 1993 Maranatha Praise, Inc., Admin. by The Copyright Company.

later, as the resurrected Jesus, this sin was defeated. Through His death all of *our* sin can be removed if we look to Jesus to be saved from sin's deadly poison. Have you looked to Him for this salvation?

Conclusion: Like Nicodemus, we attempt to find our purpose and fulfillment by our own strength, using our own resources. We're often ashamed to come to Jesus for fear of being looked down upon. We have to realize that Jesus doesn't want to just be a friend or a helper, but to give us new life through His Spirit! He wants to save us from the sin that condemns us to bring us into His kingdom for eternity. Won't you accept His invitation today?

FOR THE BULLETIN

● On October 3, 1683, the Scottish Worthy, James Renwick, was called into the ministry. He was later martyred, the last of the Scottish Covenanters to die for his faith. ● One October 3, 1692, Increase Mather published his *Cases of Conscience Concerning Evil Spirits*. This book effectively ended the era of the Salem Witch Trials. ● October 3, 1809 marks the birthday of Robert Gray, Anglican missionary to South Africa, and first Anglican Bishop of Capetown. ● Karolina (Lina) Sandell-Berg was born on this day in 1832 in Fröderyd, Sweden. She was the daughter of the pastor of the village's Lutheran church. When she was twenty-six, she and her father were enjoying a boat trip near Gothenburg when Rev. Sandell pitched overboard and drowned. Returning home alone, Lina began processing her grief through the Scriptures and expressing her faith in poetry. Fourteen poems were published that year, 1858, one of which is sung to this day: *Children of the heavenly Father* . . . Seven years later, her best-known hymn, "Day by Day," was published. She is known as the "Fanny Crosby of Sweden." ● On this day, October 3, 1852, Thomas Gallaudet held the world's first church service for the deaf in the little Washington Square chapel of New York University. ● Throughout early American history, the observance of Thanksgiving was an on-again, off-again affair until magazine editor Sarah Hale launched a crusade to establish Thanksgiving as a holiday. She wrote stirring editorials about it, and November issues featured Thanksgiving poetry, stories, and turkey recipes. On October 3, 1863, President Lincoln established Thanksgiving as a national holiday for the last Thursday of November.

STATS, STORIES AND MORE

Death before Rebirth
In Argentina, they sometimes have a different way of baptizing people. Instead of baptizing them in the name of the Father, of the Son, and of the Holy Spirit, they say, "I KILL you in the name of the Father and of the Son and of the Holy Spirit and I make you born into the Kingdom of God to serve Him and to please Him."

Dying to Self
When James Calvert went out as a missionary to the cannibals of the Fiji Islands, the captain of the ship sought to turn him back. "You will lose your life and the lives of those with you if you go among such savages," he cried. Calvert only replied, "We died before we came here."—*David Augsburger*

"There came a day when George Mueller died, utterly died! No longer did his own desires, preferences, and tastes come first. He knew that from then on Christ must be all in all."—*George Mueller, when asked the secret of his victorious Christian life.*

"We dye to live, we live to dye; the more we dye, the more we live; and the more we live, the more we dye."—*sign in the window of a dry-cleaning and dyeing business.*

The Kingdom of this World
The Bible says that this world is the world of the Prince of Darkness; it is ruled by Satan.

It is like the movie trilogy based on the books by J.R. R. Tolken called *The Lord of the Rings*. Prince Aragorn and other "good guys" are way outnumbered in fighting against thousands and thousands of evil creatures led by the dominant, demonic ruler of Middle Earth. It's a good thing Jesus offers us the kingdom of God!

Necessity of Rebirth
Juan Carlos Ortiz says, "The Kingdom of God does not accept immigrants. You have to be born into the Kingdom of God. It does not accept naturalized citizens."

The Spirit's New Control
There's a place called the Pali lookout located between Honolulu and Kaneohe, where the wind is so strong, you bend in its direction. The Holy Spirit wants us to come into the presence of God for this purpose, so that we might be surrendered to Him and empowered by Him, bending in His direction.

WORSHIP HELPS

Call to Worship:

It is good to give thanks to the Lord, and to sing praises to Your name, O Most High; to declare Your lovingkindness in the morning, and Your faithfulness every night, on an instrument of ten strings, on the lute, and on the harp, with harmonious sound. For You, Lord, have made me glad through Your work; I will triumph in the works of Your hands.

Lord, how great are Your works! Your thoughts are very deep (Ps. 92:1–5).

Pastoral Prayer:

Lord, for some of us, we have been far away from you for a long time. But due to circumstances we have seen so clearly that we can't control our own lives and that the evil in the world is so overwhelming. We need You. And so, Lord, for some of us, we have also realized that much of the struggle in our lives is due to sin in our own lives. We come to You today to ask for Your forgiveness. Thank You for dying for us. Thank You for loving us. Thank You for being on the side of sinners, of the weak, the oppressed, and those who need help. From the bottom of our hearts we thank You. Amen.

Kids Talk

Have you ever done anything at school you shouldn't have done? Once there were students in a class who were allowed to decide their own rules and punishments. They decided that if anyone stole, he should have to sit in the "time out chair" during recess every day. One of the boys named Jim was poor and hungry, so he stole a sandwich from an older boy named Tom. When Jim was caught, he was punished. Tom felt sorry for him and asked the teacher if he could sit in the chair and let Jim play. For the rest of the year, Jim couldn't help but look at that chair and remember how Tom took his punishment. Did you know Jesus took our punishment? He died to pay the consequence of our sins. Every time we see a cross, we can remember how Jesus took our punishment and thank Him for it. Let's pray and thank Him now.

Additional Sermons and Lesson Ideas

The Love Life
Date preached:

Based on an Outline by W. Graham Scroggie

SCRIPTURE: 1 Corinthians 13:1–13

INTRODUCTION: Of all the commandments in Scripture, none is more important than to love (Mark 12:28–31). Paul, in these often-quoted verses, explains the supremacy of love in the Christian life.

1. The Preeminence of Love (vv. 1–3).
2. The Prerogatives of Love (vv. 4–7).
3. The Perseverance of Love (vv. 8–13).

CONCLUSION: One of the most basic human needs and desires is love, meant to be met first in the Lord and secondly in others. Are you living the true Scriptural love life?

Close Down the Temple
Date preached:

By Peter Grainger

SCRIPTURE: Malachi 1:6–14

INTRODUCTION: Malachi prophesied to God's people who were living privileged lives and yet neglected true worship. We should be warned against false worship.

1. Privileged Relationships.
   A. Father and Sons (Hos. 1:1–4; 1 John 3:1).
   B. Master and Servants (Is. 44:21; 1 Cor. 4:1).
   C. Priests and People (v. 6).
2. Unacceptable Worship.
   A. Actions (v. 8).
   B. Attitudes (vv. 12–14).
3. Inevitable Consequences.
   A. God Will Not Accept Their Offerings (v. 10).
   B. God Will Not Accept Them (v. 8).

CONCLUSION: God would sooner close down the temple than let it continue to dishonor His name (v. 10). This prophecy was fulfilled in A.D. 70 after 500 years of patience. Is it possible we are dishonoring God with our lives? We are to worship God His way, in Spirit and in truth!

OCTOBER 10, 2004

SUGGESTED SERMON
Playing Favorites
By Timothy Beougher

Date preached:

Scripture: James 2:1–7, especially verse 1: *My brethren, do not hold the faith of our Lord Jesus Christ, the Lord of glory, with partiality.*

Introduction: We live in a world that tends to judge people based on externals. Our culture says that your worth is determined by the kind of job you have, the kind of car you drive, the kind of house you live in, and the kind of clothes you wear. But the Bible tells us a person's value is not determined by the amount of their valuables. James makes clear in our passage for today that while prejudice and favoritism may be commonplace in the world, they have no place in the church.

1. **The Prohibition of Favoritism (v. 1).** Notice James' reference to "the Lord of glory." He reminds us of the basis for our fellowship with one another. If God brought about our fellowship, we as believers should not break our relationships because of prejudice. The term "favoritism" or "partiality" comes from a word that means "face." Favoritism is judging others based on appearance, or in other words, at face value. Partiality, judging on the basis of appearance instead of on the basis of the heart, is directly contradictory to the character of God (see 2 Cor. 5:16). When we see a fellow believer in sin, we care enough about him to approach him in love and point him back to God; that is judging with proper motives. The kind of judging James warns against is sin: judging with the wrong motive. In this case, we do not have the other person's interests at heart, but our own bias and selfish interests.

2. **A Picture of Favoritism (vv. 2–4).** Lest anyone think that this is a sin that only *others* struggle with, James illustrates a situation that each of us can immediately identify with. In the context of a worship service, two different people enter. These individuals are judged on the basis of appearance alone. In ancient times, it was a sign of great wealth and social aristocracy to wear many rings. The culture of that day so valued rings that you could

go to stores and rent a ring or two for a special occasion to impress others. Notice the response of the church member, "Here's a good seat for you." Taking the rich man down to the "chief seats" was an attempt to flatter him in hopes of getting something from him (see Matt. 23:6). A second person enters, this time described as a poor man in shabby clothes. The church member is also quick to direct this man, to make him stand or sit on the floor. This "church member" or "usher" is communicating that this person is really not welcome. I wonder if any of us secretly consider ourselves "above" others. Do we turn away from someone of seeming "lesser importance" to seek the favor of someone "more important?" James concludes his illustration in response to this behavior, "Have you not shown partiality among yourselves, and become judges with evil thoughts?"

3. **The Presumption of Favoritism (vv. 5–7).** Favoritism is to believe that God thinks the same way we think, that God values the same things that we value. First, James tells us that while we may think it is noble to show favoritism, God does not show favoritism on the basis of outward appearance (see Mark 12:14). The believers in James' day needed to hear the message that to follow Christ means to judge on His standards, not on human standards. They needed to be reminded (and so do we) that God chooses the poor in the eyes of the world (see 1 Cor. 1:26–29). The presumption of favoritism is that *this life* is all that matters. If the rich really are in charge,

>>> *sermon continued on following page*

APPROPRIATE HYMNS AND SONGS

Rise Up, O Men of God, William P. Merrill/William H. Walter; Public Domain.

Rise Up, O Men of God, William P. Merrill/William H. Walter/Bill Batstone/Owens; © 1994 Maranatha Praise, Inc., Admin. by The Copyright Company.

Come, Let Us Worship Jesus, Graham Kendrick; © 1992 Make Way Music, Admin. by Music Services.

Glory to God, Jim Cowan; © 1997 Integrity's Hosanna! Music.

Holy, Holy, Holy, Gary Oliver; © 1991 CMI-HP Publishing, Admin. by Word Music Group, Inc.

then we would be wise to cater to their every whim. But if Christ is truly the King of kings, the Glorious Lord of the world (and He is), then He, not the rich, deserves our service, our allegiance, and our loyalty. The one who claims to be a follower of the glorious Lord Jesus but who then shows favoritism is guilty of having a divided heart, a double mind.

Conclusion: Let's search our hearts for attitudes that don't belong there, attitudes of favoritism or attitudes of prejudice. If we find them there, let's repent of them. Let's ask God to take them away, and to replace them with attitudes of love and compassion. I wonder if people come to mind whom we have not treated properly. We need to resolve, with God's help, to treat these people differently.

FOR THE BULLETIN

● On October 10, 1414, on the eve of his departure for Council of Constance where he would be condemned, John Hus wrote to his friends that he was going to face more foes than the Redeemer Himself had to face. He prayed that if his death would contribute to God's glory he might be enabled to meet it without fear. ● Martin Luther received Pope Leo's famous pronouncement, "*Expurge Domini*," on this day in 1520. It began with the words, "Rise up, Lord, rise up . . . for a wild boar has invaded your vineyard." Luther was given sixty days to recant. ● On October 10, 1533, Nicolas Cop was elected Rector of the University of Paris and his inaugural address, prepared by a 24-year-old firebrand named John Calvin, was a declaration of war on the Catholic Church. The speech demanded reformation on the basis of the New Testament and attacked the theologians of the church who "teach nothing of faith, nothing of the love of God, nothing of remission of sins, nothing of grace, nothing of justification." The speech so inflamed Paris that Cop fled to Basel, and Calvin reportedly escaped his room from a window by means of sheets, fleeing disguised as a vine-dresser with a hoe on his shoulder. ● October 10, 1560, is the birthday of Dutch theologian, Jacob Arminius. ● Charles Finney was converted on this day in 1821. (See the account of his conversion elsewhere in this volume). ● On October 10, 1886, the body of Joseph Scriven, 66, was found in a small stream of water in Lake Rice, Canada. He is the author of "What a Friend We Have in Jesus."

STATS, STORIES AND MORE

Million Dollar Mistake
Elisa Tinsley, in *USA Today*, described how a Spokane, Washington bank lost one of its best customers, a construction company owner named John Barrier. John Barrier had just come from a construction site and his clothes were dirty. He went to the bank to cash a $100 check. When he tried to get his parking slip validated, the teller refused, saying he hadn't conducted a transaction. "You have to make a deposit to get your parking slip validated," she insisted. John Barrier told the teller he was a *substantial* depositor but she was obviously doubtful. He asked to see the manager, who also refused to validate the parking slip. The next day, John Barrier went back to the bank and withdrew a rather large sum of money, one million dollars to be exact.

Wrong Motives
Someone once penned a clever rhyme to illustrate the problem of favoritism:
. . . many people go to church,
As everyone knows;
Some go to close their eyes,
And some to eye their clothes.

Favoritism Challenged
Muretus, a wandering scholar in the Middle Ages was very learned but very poor. In his wanderings he fell ill, and he was taken to the place where the destitute were kept. The people who cared for him did not know that he was a scholar and that he understood Latin. The doctors were discussing his case in Latin, saying that he was a poor creature of value to no one and that it was hopeless and unnecessary to expend care and money on attention to such a worthless individual. Muretus looked up and answered in their own Latin, "Call no man worthless for whom Christ died."

WORSHIP HELPS

Call to Worship:
Many, O Lord my God, are Your wonderful works which You have done; and Your thoughts toward us cannot be recounted to You in order; if I would declare and speak of them, they are more than can be numbered. Let all those who seek You rejoice and be glad in You; let such as love Your salvation say continually, "?The Lord be magnified!?" *(Ps. 40:5, 16).*

Scripture Reading:
For you see your calling, brethren, that not many wise according to the flesh, not many mighty, not many noble, are called. But ??God has chosen the foolish things of the world to put to shame the wise, and God has chosen the weak things of the world to put to shame the things which are mighty; and the ??base things of the world and the things which are despised God has chosen, and the things which are not, to bring to nothing the things that are, that no flesh should glory in His presence *(1 Cor. 1:26–29).*

Pastoral Prayer:
Heavenly Father, You are the holy and just Judge. Thank You for saving us from the penalty of eternal death through the sacrifice of Jesus Christ. Thank You that our eternal security doesn't depend on our bank accounts. You have chosen to change poor fools like us into Your people to take Your gospel to the world. Help us to carry out this great commission without prejudice or favoritism so that we may one day join hands with people from every tribe and nation around the glorious throne of the Lamb and sing Your praises throughout eternity. In Jesus' name we ask these things, Amen.

Additional Sermons and Lesson Ideas

The Discipline of Distress
By Denis Lyle

Date preached:

SCRIPTURE: Exodus 14:1–30

INTRODUCTION: In our lives, difficulties and distress are often what shape and grow us the most. We can learn from the Israelites' situation at the shore of the Red Sea, the "discipline of distress."

1. The Situation of the People (vv. 2–3, 9). Three enemies surrounded them at the same time and it's difficult to say which of them was the cruelest. Pharaoh (v. 9) the sea: (v. 2) or the inaccessible rocks and wilderness (v. 3). Before them broke the thunder of the angry sea, beside them rose inaccessible mountains, behind them came Pharaoh and his army.
2. The Salutation of the Leader (14:13, 15). Moses spoke words of comfort, "Do not be afraid," composure, "Stand still," and challenge, "Go forward."
3. The Salvation of the Lord (14:21–30). The sea was divided (v. 21), the enemy was destroyed (vv. 26–28), and the people were delivered (v. 30).

CONCLUSION: If you're facing incredible distress, simply obey the Lord one step at a time; He will show you His salvation (Ps. 98:2).

The Believer's Badge
By Melvin Worthington

Date preached:

SCRIPTURE: John 13:35

INTRODUCTION: The most distinctive and effective characteristic of God's children is love. On the night of His Crucifixion, Jesus stated this idea clearly, "By this all will know that you are My disciples, if you have love for one another" (John 13:35).

1. The Source of Love (1 John 4:16). This divine love comes from God and is imparted by the Holy Spirit. Those who do not love have no true acquaintance with God, for God is love.
2. The Sample of Love (John 13:34). Jesus, in a "new commandment," instructs the disciples to love one another as He had loved them. His love was *unselfish, universal, untiring, undeserved,* and *unique.*
3. The Sign of Love (John 13:35). Believers' love one for the other is the decisive evidence that they are disciples of Christ. It is that which identifies them as followers of Christ.

CONCLUSION: There is nothing that the world understands and values more than true love.

OCTOBER 17, 2004

SUGGESTED SERMON

You Are What You Eat

Date preached:

By Todd Kinde

Scripture: Matthew 5:6: Blessed are those who hunger and thirst for righteousness, for they shall be filled.

Introduction: Nutritionist and health experts say, "You are what you eat." Maybe you've read the book entitled *Charlie and the Chocolate Factory* or perhaps you have seen the movie *Willie Wonka and the Chocolate Factory*. In this story one spoiled girl who must have everything at once takes a piece of gum, which has the flavors of a full meal, and she begins chewing. When it comes to the dessert flavor, blueberry cobbler, she begins to turn blue and rather plump like a blueberry. This story demonstrates that our appetites can get the best of us and what we hunger for will change us. In teaching the values of His kingdom, Jesus explains the equal reality, that in our spirit we are what we eat. What our spirit hungers for will change us. That for which we hunger will shape us into its image and likeness.

1. **Our Need for Righteousness.** We need righteousness to get into the kingdom and to live in the kingdom. The word "righteous" simply means, "characterized by what is right." We do well and we do right. We teach our children to do what is right. We must learn to discern between right and wrong. This implies that there is a standard for what is right. The standard for rightness is the will of God. Yes, we do right things, we think right things, and we say right things. But all our rightness is like filthy rags (Is. 64:5–7). Jesus says in Matthew 5:20, "For I say to you, that unless your righteousness exceeds the righteousness of the scribes and Pharisees, you will by no means enter the kingdom of heaven." Paul realized that he needed a righteousness that surpassed that of the Pharisee that he was (Phil. 3:7–9). We, too, should seek righteousness based not on the world's standards, but on God's.

2. **Our Craving for Righteousness.** C. S. Lewis observed that the problem is not that our cravings are too big but that our cravings are much too small

and too easily satisfied with lesser things. We assume that we must get a control on our cravings and subdue them if not eradicate them. The reality of satisfaction is not in the denial of our cravings, but in redirecting them from small things to the One Great Thing. Our cravings tend to favor things like food, drink, and clothing (Matt. 6:25–34). We crave power, pleasure, prestige and possessions. Our cravings are far too small. The Lord teaches us that those who crave the righteousness of God and His kingdom are blessed. The form of the verb here denotes a present continuous action, "Those who are now hungering and thirsting." What do you crave? We should find righteousness to be more necessary than food and drink. The psalmist declares that the Word of the Lord is sweeter than honey (Ps. 19:10; 119:103). Psalm 34:8–9 speaks of righteousness that is satisfied only by tasting of the Lord, "Oh, taste and see that the Lord is good; blessed is the man who trusts in Him! Oh, fear the Lord, you His saints! There is no want to those who fear Him."

3. **Our Satisfaction with Righteousness.** The satisfaction of our cravings is found only in the righteousness of Jesus Christ. Here is the promise, "They shall be filled" (Matt. 5:6b). They will be satisfied! Jesus says in John 6:35, "I am the bread of life. He who comes to me will never go hungry, and he who believes in me will never be thirsty" (NIV). The words of this poem called *Satisfied*, written by Clara T. Williams (1858—1937), beautifully illustrate this concept:

>>> *sermon continued on following page*

APPROPRIATE HYMNS AND SONGS

Springs of Living Water, John W. Peterson; © 1950. Renewed 1978 John W. Peterson Music Company.

Arise, John Barnett; © 1995 Mercy/Vineyard Publishing.

Nothing But the Blood, Robert Lowry; Public Domain.

Righteous One, Bruce Muller; © 1991 Maranatha Praise, Inc., Admin. by The Copyright Company.

We Will Glorify, Twila Paris; © 1982 Singspiration Music, Admin. by Brentwood-Benson Music Publishing, Inc.

All my life long I had panted For a drink from some cool spring
That I hoped would quench the burning Of the thirst I felt within.
Feeding on the husks around me Till my strength was almost gone,
Longed my soul for something better, Only still to hunger on.
Poor I was, and sought for riches, Something that would satisfy;
But the dust I gathered round me Only mocked my soul's sad cry.
Well of water, ever springing, Bread of life, so rich and free.
Untold wealth that never faileth, My Redeemer is to me.
Hallelujah! I have found Him Whom my soul so long has craved!
Jesus satisfies my longings; Through His blood I now am saved.

Conclusion: Be satisfied with nothing less than Jesus' blood and righteousness. Let the hunger and thirst for righteousness shape you into the image and likeness of Christ. You are what you eat!

FOR THE BULLETIN

❈ Ignatius, disciple of the apostle John, was bishop of the church in Antioch for 40 years. When persecution arose he was arrested and sent to Rome. He died, reportedly on October 17, 108, killed by lions or tigers as entertainment for Emperor Trajan. ❈ October 17 is the birthday of two famous American evangelists, Sam Jones (1847) and Vance Havner (1901). ❈ As Billy Graham's three-week Los Angeles evangelistic campaign neared its end, local crusade organizers wanted to extend the meetings. Billy was hesitant, and he asked God for a sign. The next morning, October 17, 1949, at 4:30, he was awakened by a phone call. It was cowboy entertainer, Stuart Hamblen, in tears. He drove to Billy's hotel and confessed Christ as Savior. That was the sign Billy needed to extend the meetings. Stuart excitedly told the story of his conversion on his radio show, and the local newspapers picked up the story. Soon all Los Angeles was buzzing about the Billy Graham meetings. The resulting publicity launched a half-century of mass evangelism virtually unparalleled in Christian history. ❈ On September 10, 1952, missionary Walter Erickson and his partner, Edward R. Tritt, set out on foot with five native carriers for remote regions of New Guinea. On October 17, 1952, their mutilated bodies were found near the Ainim River. The carriers later confessed to the murder. They had been afraid to press further into the jungle, and had killed the missionaries with machetes. The martyrdom of the two men sparked a host of new applications for missions to this area, and by 1965 there were forty-seven missionaries working in this area; by 1969, there had been 4,280 baptisms.

STATS, STORIES AND MORE

Statistics
A study on teens and junk food from the Pacific Health Education Center in Bakersfield, California, highlighted the following problems: 80% of the adolescent junk-food eaters in the study were consuming more than the recommended amount of fat; 49% were taking in more than the recommended amount of cholesterol; and almost 33% were likely to develop high blood pressure and clogged arteries. If the effects are so severe in our physical bodies, how much more detrimental to our spiritual life if we are not being spiritually fed (1 Tim. 4:8)!

You Are What You Eat
The common expression, "You are what you eat," is quite literal in the case of one type of sea slug, called the *nudibranch*. This ocean-dwelling creature may eat sea anemone stingers or poisonous sponges and use these poisons as its own defense mechanism. If you need to get rid of moles in your back yard, you may witness a similar phenomenon. Simply spread grub-worm-killing pellets on your lawn. The grub worms will eat the pellets, which contain a toxic poison. In turn, the moles which feed off of grub worms will meet their fate when they dine on the now toxic worm. You are what you eat!

Righteousness of the World
Our righteousness can be compared to salt water; if drunk it simply increases your thirst and dehydrates you, making you unable to reason and slowly kills you. It wets your dry lips and throat but it does not truly satisfy the needs of your body.—*Todd Kinde*

WORSHIP HELPS

Call to Worship:
Let the peoples praise You, O God; let all the peoples praise You. Oh, let the nations be glad and sing for joy! For You shall judge the people righteously, and govern the nations on earth (Ps. 67:3–4).

Readers' Theater (or Responsive Reading):

Reader 1: Blessed are those who hunger and thirst for righteousness, for they shall be filled.

Reader 2: And if Christ is in you, the body is dead because of sin, but the Spirit is life because of righteousness.

Reader 1: Blessed are those who are persecuted for righteousness' sake, for theirs is the kingdom of heaven.

Reader 2: For I am not ashamed of the gospel of Christ, for it is the power of God to salvation for everyone who believes, for the Jew first and also for the Greek. For in it the righteousness of God is revealed. . .

Reader 1: But seek first the kingdom of God and His righteousness, and all these things shall be added to you.

Reader 2: Nevertheless we, according to His promise, look for new heavens and a new earth in which righteousness dwells.

(Matt. 5:6, 10; 6:33; Rom. 1:16–17; 8:10; 2 Pet. 3:13)

Benediction:
Fill my Cup, Lord, I lift it up Lord!
Come and quench this thirsting of my soul;
Bread of heaven, feed me till I want no more,
Fill my cup, fill it up and make me whole!
(*Fill my Cup, Lord*, Richard Blanchard, 1959)

Additional Sermons and Lesson Ideas

I Saw the Lord
By Peter Granger

Date preached:

SCRIPTURE: Isaiah 2:1–22

INTRODUCTION: Most of us live our lives in light of the probable future. If we knew the future with absolute unerring certainty, we would be fools to live our lives regardless of what we know. God has revealed the future with absolute certainty, and we should live our lives in light of the Day of the Lord (when He returns).

1. Exaltation: *The Mountain of the Lord* (vv. 2–5). These images of worship and peace exhort not only Israel but us to "walk in the light of the Lord" (v. 5).
2. Humiliation: *The Pride of Mankind* (vv. 6–22). When the Lord returns, He will judge mankind according to their deeds. One warning is that many will be influenced by other nations to worship idols. A second warning is against self-reliance: some will seek financial gain, military potential, and natural resources for security. But for these, the Day of the Lord will be disastrous.

CONCLUSION: Are you living your life in the light of the Lord (1 John 1:7) or in idolatry or self-reliance (Rev. 6:12–17; Heb. 2:1–4; 12:25–28)?

Disobedient Children
By Richard S. Sharp, Jr.

Date preached:

SCRIPTURE: Isaiah 30:18

INTRODUCTION: Children often say to their parents, "No, let me do it!" We often want to do things our way rather than God's. The Israelites wanted to ask Egypt for help against the Syrians rather than God. Regardless of their behavior, God's loving character shows through to His children.

1. The LORD Waits. God allows us to face the consequences of our disobedience, but He never leaves us. He waits in order to be gracious to us.
2. The LORD Exalted. Because of God's patient, merciful character, He will be exalted! Are you aware of His character? Do you worship Him for it?
3. The LORD Is Just. God disciplines His children justly; He is in control and never makes a wrong decision. Do you respect His discipline, or complain about it?
4. The LORD Calls His Children to Patience. The last part of our verse exhorts us to be patient despite our circumstances, "Blessed are all those who wait on Him."

CONCLUSION: Israel saw God's power over and over; don't we? And yet we, too, are so often disobedient children. Respect the Lord's discipline and allow Him control of your life completely; be patient and trust in the Lord.

TECHNIQUES FOR THE PASTOR'S DELIVERY

The Public Reading of Scripture

The following quotes regarding the public reading of Scripture are found in an old book entitled, *Precepts for Preachers in the Pulpit and Out of It*, published in London in 1884:

Dr. Joseph Parker:

Few men read the Scriptures intelligently and expressively. Some read in a tame and deadening tone, as if they had mistaken insipidity for veneration; others read it with a theatrical rant, which is shockingly impious; others again read it in a slovenly manner, as if the exercise was hardly worth attending to, in comparison, as Mr. Binney truly says, "with their grand intellectual sermon." What is the remedy? We must, first of all, feel that the Word of God itself is actually before us, and our elocution will then be dictated by our veneration.

In the next place we must, by private study, prepare ourselves for the public reading of the Scriptures. I doubt whether it is not profane to read in the pulpit a chapter to which no attention has been paid in private. How can the adventurer who does so know anything of the sentiment of the chapter? How can he remember the punctuation? How can he be prepared for change of subject, or for parenthetic modification? He cannot *read* the chapter: he can only pronounce the words, and flounder through the meaning. The indispensable requisite for good reading is an intelligent and sympathetic conception of the author's meaning; I say not only intelligent, but sympathetic, because appreciation always suggests the best expression.

It is said of a celebrated novelist, who occasionally reads his own compositions in public, that in anticipation of a public reading he will spend not less than six hours a day in studying the most appropriate accent, cadence, and force; if he does this for a corruptible crown, what shall *we* do for a crown that is incorruptible? Surely we should at least read over in secret the portion of Scripture we intend to read in public.

Dr. John Broadus:

It is particularly important that the Scriptures should be well read. Good reading has an exegetical value, helping to make plain the sense. It also brings out the full interest and impressiveness of the passage read. There are passages which have had a new meaning for us, and an added sweetness, ever since we once heard them read, it may be long ago, by a good reader.

Dr. R.W. Dale:

I have heard several men who read the Bible well; I never heard but one who read it supremely well. This was the late Mr. Dawson, of Birmingham. His was genuine reading, not dramatic recitation; the dramatic recitation of the Bible is irreverent and offensive. But if he was reading a narrative, he read it, not indeed as if he were telling the story himself, but as if he, too, had seen what he was reading about, and as if, while he read, the whole story lived again in his imagination and in his heart. If he was reading a psalm, he read it, not as some read a psalm, as though they had written it, which is the dramatic style, and which seems to me false in art and morally presumptuous; but while he was reading, you felt as if the words of the psalmist recalled to him the brightest and the saddest passages in his own history, and as if these personal experiences naturally led him to read with a tone and an emphasis which were in perfect sympathy with the psalmist's thought and feeling. To read in this way is not possible to most of us. It requires a rare combination of powers. But we should try to do our best.

If we master the meaning of the passages we intend to read in public; if we so fully enter into the spirit of what we are reading that the printed book vanishes, and the story it tells come to us fresh from the man that wrote it; if we read a psalm as though we ourselves had heard it from the lips of David, and as if the broken tones in which he confessed his sin, or the triumphant joy in which he spoke of the goodness of God, were still lingering in our ears; if we read a prophecy of Isaiah's with the feeling which the words would excite if we ourselves had listened to him while he was denouncing the crimes of his contemporaries, and predicting the glories of the future kingdom of God; and if we read a passage from St. Paul's Epistle to the Galatians with that perfect sympathy with the sorrow and anger of the apostle which will be created by a vivid realization of his fierce conflict with the Judaizers; if, in short, by a vigorous imaginative effort we place ourselves by the very side of the men who wrote the Bible, see what they saw and feel what they felt, our mere reading of the Scriptures will throw an intense light on every passage that the people understood before, and will often bring out the meaning of passages which they had been accustomed to pass over as being quite unintelligible.

OCTOBER 24, 2004

SUGGESTED SERMON

The Marks of Maturity

Date preached:

By Melvin Worthington

Scripture: 1 Corinthians 3:2: I fed you with milk and not with solid food; for until now you were not able to receive it, and even now you are still not able.

Introduction: One of the most significant issues the church faces today is the question of spiritual maturity. We should each take time to evaluate ourselves as to our own level of spiritual growth. Some believe that critical self-examination is a waste of time, but nothing could be further from the truth. Spiritual maturity is measured on the basis of our striving to reach the fullness of Christ. Mature Christians imitate Christ in their thinking, talking, and toiling.

1. **Spiritual Maturity Is Marked by Diet (1 Cor. 3:2).** Paul declares in 1 Corinthians 3:2 that he had fed them with milk rather than meat because of their immaturity. The writer of Hebrews declares that milk belongs to babes, while meat belongs to those who are of full age (Heb. 5:13–14). The mature Christian has progressed from milk to meat. He is informed. He knows the Word. He acquires facts, analyzes the issues, and applies his knowledge to his circumstances.

2. **Spiritual Maturity Is Marked by Discernment (Phil. 1:9).** This means that one is able to distinguish between that which is important and that which is injurious in religious instruction. By long experience, Christians develop the ability to understand the more elevated doctrines of Christianity. They see their beauty and are carefully and accurately able to detect the truth from error. They have insight and display wisdom. Albert Barnes aptly notes, "They will appreciate and understand that which is true. They will reject that which is false."

3. **Spiritual Maturity Is Marked by Deeds or Duty (Eph. 2:10).** Mature Christians are zealous of good works. They fulfill their duty. Maturity brings a heightened sense of responsibility. With maturity must come work that matches it (Luke 12:48). The mature Christian is a worker. He is industrious (see 2 Thess. 3:10).

4. **Spiritual Maturity Is Marked by Discipline (1 Cor. 9:24–27).** Spiritual maturity manifests itself in discipline. Daniel displayed this in Babylon (Dan. 1:8); the three Hebrew children displayed it in Babylon (Dan. 3), Joseph displayed it in Egypt (Gen. 39), and Paul declared it in 1 Corinthians 9:24–27. The mature Christian practically integrates the Word of God into life experiences. He knows about victory over the world, the flesh, and the devil through the grace of God. While "spiritual children" are unstable, the mature Christian is firm in the faith. He is a warrior.

5. **Spiritual Maturity Is Marked By Devotion (Titus 3:8, 14; Col. 4:2, NIV).** There is present in the mature Christian the proper devotion to the Word of God, will of God, worship of God, and work of God. Spiritual maturity is not achieved in a short period of time. Although we aspire to be mature and advance toward perfection, full achievement will only come through eternal life. Spiritual maturity should be the goal of all Christians. All should desire to be like Jesus Christ, to be conformed to His image, to reach the measure of His fullness (Rom. 8:29).

6. **Spiritual Maturity Is Marked by Development (2 Pet. 1:1–11).** Peter reminds his readers that God has make ample provision for their spiritual development. His power and promises were available to them. God expected them to make spiritual progress. They were to diligently add into their faith virtue; and to virtue, knowledge; and to knowledge, self-control; and to self-control, perseverance; and to perseverance, godliness; and to godliness, brotherly kindness; and to brotherly kindness, love (vv. 5–7). Spiritual growth is a continual process. Paul addresses this process when

>>> *sermon continued on following page*

APPROPRIATE HYMNS AND SONGS

Another Drink, Scott Underwood; © 1995 Mercy/Vineyard Publishing.

Deeper, Deeper, Charles P. Jones; Public Domain.

I Throw My Heart to the Wind, Dennis Jernigan; © 1995 Shepherd's Heart Music, Admin. by Word Music Group, Inc.

Soldiers of Christ Arise, Charles Wesley/George J. Elvey; Public Domain.

We Have the Spirit of David, David Binion; © 1985 Word Music, Inc., Admin. by Word Music Group, Inc.

he says, "Not that I have already attained, or am already perfected; but I press on, that I may lay hold of that for which Christ Jesus has also laid hold of me. Brethren, I do not count myself to have apprehended; but one thing I do, forgetting those things which are behind and reaching forward to those things which are ahead, I press toward the goal for the prize of the upward call of God in Christ Jesus" (Phil. 3:12–14).

Conclusion: Where are you in your spiritual development? Are you still feeding on milk or have you progressed to the place you are feeding on meat? Spiritual maturity is not reached overnight; it's the result of a disciplined effort. It does not just happen. Each of us should evaluate ourselves, and make a deliberate and diligent effort to be conformed to the very image of Christ in all His fullness.

FOR THE BULLETIN

✦ The Thirty Years' War began when the Austrian Habsburgs tried to impose Roman Catholicism on Protestants in Bohemia. Though largely fought on German soil, it involved armies from all over Europe. It ended at 2 p.m. on Saturday afternoon, October 24, 1648, in the Treaty of Westphalia in which prospects of a Roman Catholic conquest over Protestant Europe ended. ✦ On October 24, 1685, the Edict of Nantes, giving French Protestants freedom from persecution, was revoked by Louis XIV. ✦ Missionary Henry Martyn in India was lonely and lovesick for his beloved Lydia, who he hoped to marry. But she sent a letter refusing his proposal. His journal entry says: *October 24, 1807. An unhappy day; received at last a letter from Lydia in which she refuses to come because her mother will not consent to it.* As his health began to fail, he poured himself into Bible translation. By 1812, he had grown so weak that an overland trip to England seemed the only solution. He died en route at age 31. When his journal was opened, the name Lydia was found on almost every page. But Martyn had fulfilled his objective in coming to India, having translated the New Testament into Hindustani and Persian. ✦ October 24, 1867, marks the birth of Charles M. Alexander, evangelistic gospel song leader and personal evangelist. ✦ On October 24, 1869, nearly 11 years after his arrival in the New Hebrides, Scottish missionary John Paton led his first communion service. Twelve converted cannibals partook of the Lord's Supper. "As I put the bread and wine into those hands once stained with the blood of cannibalism, now stretched out to receive and partake the emblems of the Redeemer's love," he wrote, "I had a foretaste of the joy of Glory that well nigh broke my heart to pieces."

STATS, STORIES AND MORE

Twenty Years?

A teacher with twenty years' experience was passed over for a promotion. Going to the administrator, she demanded, "Why did you choose that new young man who only had four years of experience at this job, when I have twenty years of experience?" The man answered, "Because you do not have twenty years of experience. You have one year of experience twenty times. You're still teaching the same things in the same way as you did when you were first hired. You haven't grown in the job."

Someone Once Said . . .

"The knowledge of Christ's love for us should cause us to love Him in such a way that it is demonstrated in our attitude, conduct, and commitment to serve God. Spiritual maturity is marked by spiritual knowledge being put into action."
—*Edward Bedore*

"To know the mechanics does not mean that we are practicing the Disciplines. The Spiritual Disciplines are an inward and spiritual reality, and the inner attitude of the heart is far more crucial than the mechanics for coming into the reality of the spiritual life."
—*Richard Foster*

"Those who know God the best are the richest and most powerful in prayer. Little acquaintance with God, and strangeness and coldness to Him, make prayer a rare and feeble thing."
—*E.M. Bounds*

"Self-respect is the fruit of discipline: the sense of dignity grows with the ability to say no to oneself."
—*Abraham J. Heschel*

"I never had a close relationship with God through prayer and the usual disciplines. That worried me. At the end of life, I find He's been a part of my life, very clear; and it's OK. He reached out; I didn't."
—*Reuel Howe*

The work of Japanese painter Hokusai spanned many years before his death in 1849 at age 89. But toward the end of his life, the artist dismissed as nothing all the work he had done before age 50. It was only after he reached 70 that he felt he was turning out anything worthy of note. On his deathbed Hokusai lamented, "If heaven had granted me five more years, I could have become a real painter."—*Today in the Word.*

WORSHIP HELPS

Call to Worship:
Praise be to the God and Father of our Lord Jesus Christ! In his great mercy he has given us new birth into a living hope through the resurrection of Jesus Christ from the dead (1 Pet. 1:3, NIV)

Offertory Prayer:
Lord, as we worship, we want to thank You for the way You grow us. Thank You for putting us through tests, for guiding us through every decision, and for teaching us as we walk with You. Would You help us to become cheerful givers, being good stewards of Your provisions to us? Accept our worship today, Lord, and accept our offerings. We pray in Jesus' name, Amen.

Suggested Scripture Readings:
2 Peter 1:1–11
1 Corinthians 9:24–27
Hebrews 5:11–14

Benediction:
Finally, brethren, whatever things are true, whatever things are noble, whatever things are just, whatever things are pure, whatever things are lovely, whatever things are of good report, if there is any virtue and if there is anything praiseworthy—meditate on these things. The things which you learned and received and heard and saw in me, these do, and the God of peace will be with you (Phil. 4:8–9).

Additional Sermons and Lesson Ideas

Daniel's Prayer
By Dennis Lyle

Date preached:

SCRIPTURE: Daniel 2:18–23

INTRODUCTION: We can be challenged and guided in our prayer life through study of Biblical prayers of the Lord's people. In the face of trials, Daniel and his three companions give us an excellent model.

1. They Prayed in Unity (v. 18).
2. They Prayed Specifically (v. 19).
3. They Prayed Effectively (v. 19).
4. They Prayed Thankfully (vv. 20–24).

CONCLUSION: Are you facing trials? Join or start a prayer group; pray in unity. Pray specifically and effectively for the situation, and remember to always give thanks!

The Royal Bounty
By Frances Ridley Havergal

Date preached:

SCRIPTURE: 1 Kings 10:13

INTRODUCTION: When God answers our prayers, we are greatly humbled and we cry out, "Who am I, O Lord, that You have so wonderfully answered my prayer." But it is more humbling still when we stand face to face with great things which the Lord has done for us and given us, for which we never asked at all, nor even thought of asking—Royal Bounty. Let us give things today for the overwhelming mercies for which we never asked.

1. We did not ask Him to choose us in Christ Jesus before the world began (Eph. 1:4).
2. We did not ask Him to call us by His grace (2 Tim. 1:9).
3. We did not ask to be taught to pray. Jesus put into our sinful hearts the thought of asking Him for that which we need (Job 37:19).

CONCLUSION: In addition to granting her requests, King Solomon gave the Queen of Sheba from his "royal bounty." Psalm 68:19 says: "Blessed be the LORD, who daily loads us with benefits."

OCTOBER 31, 2004

SUGGESTED SERMON
Faith Alone

Date preached:

Scripture: Ephesians 2:1–9, especially verse 8: For by grace you have been saved through faith, and that not of yourselves; it is the gift of God.

Introduction: Today is Reformation Sunday. It was on this day in 1518 that Martin Luther took a stand against excesses in the church of his day, listing 95 objections to the theology and morality of the clergy. In nailing his document to the church door in Wittenberg, he sparked the Protestant Reformation, the great cries of which were *Sola Gratia, Sola Fide, Sola Scriptura, Solus Christus* — Grace alone, Faith alone, Scripture alone, Christ alone. That's not only the great theme of the Reformation; it is the theme of this passage in Ephesians 2. Paul discusses the richness of salvation, and he explains it this way:

1. **Human Condition (vv. 1–3).** The first thing we notice in verses 1–3 is the hopelessness of our human condition. In these three verses, Paul describes our condition without Christ in six different ways.
    A. **We are dead in our transgressions and sins (v. 1).** The word in the Greek for *transgressions* comes from two smaller words: a preposition meaning *beside,* and a stem word meaning *to fall.* The word *transgression* literally means *to fall beside the road.* Have you ever tried to climb up a steep path, lost your footing, and slid back down? Have you ever taken a false step? That's the idea here. The word *sin* means *to miss the target.* No matter how hard we aim at perfection, we keep missing the mark.
    B. **We follow the ways of the world (v. 2).** Jesus said there are two pathways. One is wide and bright and crooked, leading to destruction. The other is straight and narrow, but it leads to life.
    C. **We follow the ways of the ruler of the kingdom of the air (v. 2).** This is a clear reference to Satan.
    D. **We follow the spirit who works in those who are disobedient (v. 2).** Another reference to Satan, who is prominently mentioned in Ephesians.
    E. **We gratify the craving of our sinful nature (v. 3).**

F. We are by nature children of wrath (v. 3).

2. **Divine Motivation (v. 4).** According to this verse, God has two great motivations for wanting to save us from judgment. The first is: His great love (see John 3:16; Jer. 31:3; Rom. 5:8; 1 John 4:19). The second is: His rich mercy. Mercy is a feeling compassion that makes one person want to save or rescue someone else. And God's great love and His rich mercy combined to send Him to this earth for the express purpose of being nailed hand-and-foot to an upright post, the blood flowing from His forehead where the thorns had been, the blood flowing from His back where the scourge fell, the blood flowing from His hands and feet where the nails were, the blood flowing from His wounded side, pierced by the soldier's lance. And the Bible says there is something about the blood of Jesus Christ that satisfies the wrath of God (Rom. 5:9).

3. **Eternal Salvation (vv. 5–9).** God does three things for us: He makes us alive in Christ (v. 5), seats us with Christ in the heavenly realms (v. 6), and promises to one day show us plainly the full riches of his incomparable grace (v. 7).

Conclusion: This passage ends by giving us the governing principles for God's plan of salvation—it is by grace through faith (vv. 8–9). In other words, we can't do anything good enough to earn heaven. We are forgiven of our sins, reconciled with God, and given eternal life in spite of ourselves because of His love and grace which we receive by trusting Him, by faith alone.

>>> *sermon continued on following page*

APPROPRIATE HYMNS AND SONGS

A Mighty Fortress Is Our God, Martin Luther; Public Domain.

I Love to Tell the Story, Catherine A. Hankey/William G. Fischer; Public Domain.

We Believe, Rick Founds; © 1989 Maranatha Praise, Inc., Admin. by The Copyright Company.

Some Trust in Chariots, Dennis Jernigan; © 1989 Shepherd's Heart Music, Admin. by Word Music Group, Inc.

My Faith Has Found a Resting Place, Lidi H. Edmunds/Andre Gretry; Public Domain.

Perhaps today you need to be rescued, you need to be saved. Perhaps today you are dead in your sins, following the ways of the world, following the ruler of the kingdom of the air, following the spirit that now works in those who are disobedient, gratifying the cravings of your sinful nature, an object of wrath. But God in His great love and rich mercy loves you. He wants to raise you from the dead, seat you with Himself in the heavenly realms, and show you the incomparable riches of His grace in Christ Jesus. And by grace you can be saved through faith, not of yourself—it is the gift of God. Will you come to Him today?

FOR THE BULLETIN

* On October 31, 1517, a 31-year-old German Augustinian monk named Martin Luther nailed to the door of the castle church in Wittenberg a list of 95 theological points he wished to debate, touching off the Protestant Reformation. * Scottish Missionary Robert Moffat, a gardener by profession, sailed off on this day, October 31, 1816, sent by the London Missionary Society to South Africa. He boldly began evangelizing dangerous, savage, and cannibalistic tribes, winning to Christ a man named Afrikaner, the most notorious outlaw in the south of Africa. Robert and Mary Moffat had a remarkable missionary career, and it was their ministry that inspired David Livingstone. * George Muller, a German whose youthfulness was spent in careless crime, was converted to Christ on this day in 1852. He went on to become one of the most effective humanitarians and evangelists of the nineteenth century. He is especially noted for his ministry to orphans in Bristol, England. His biography by A. T. Pierson is a classic. * October 31, 1896, marks the birthday of Ethel Waters who overcame incredible odds to become one of the most popular African-American jazz singers in the United States. She is best remembered, however, for her conversion to Christ and her signature song at Billy Graham's Crusades, "His Eye Is on the Sparrow." * On October 31, 1992, Pope John Paul II formally admitted the Roman Catholic Church's error in condemning Galileo Galilei in 1633 for believing the sun, not the earth, was the center of the universe.

STATS, STORIES AND MORE

Charles Haddon Spurgeon, who preached and pastored in London 100 years ago, is called the "Prince of Preachers." There are many stories about him, but one of the best has to do with an experience he had when he was just learning to preach. Almost from the beginning he possessed unusual power and eloquence in the pulpit. As a "boy preacher," he had been invited to speak one evening in Suffolk, but he was late in arriving. His grandfather, also a preacher, finally began the service by reading Ephesians 2. He began preaching on the theme, "For by grace are ye saved through faith. . . ." He had gotten some way into his discourse when there was a little commotion at the back door and in walked his grandson, arriving late. "Here comes my grandson," exclaimed the old man. "He can preach the gospel better than I can, but you cannot preach a better gospel, can you, Charles?"

Charles, walking up the aisle, said, "You can preach better than I can. Please go on." The grandfather refused, but he told him his text and explained that he had already shown the people the source of salvation—grace—and was now speaking about the channel—faith. The younger preacher stepped into the pulpit and took over just where his grandfather had left off.

After a few minutes, the grandfather interrupted, wanting to preach a little more of the sermon. Then he sat down, and Charles resumed preaching, with the grandfather sitting behind him, saying, "Good! Good! Tell them that again, Charles. Tell them that again."

Ever after that, Charles Spurgeon said that whenever he preached from Ephesians 2, he could hear his old grandfather saying, "Tell them that again, Charles. Tell them that again."

I love to tell the story, for those who know it best
Seem hungering and thirsting to hear it like the rest . . .

WORSHIP HELPS

Call to Worship:
For I am not ashamed of the gospel of Christ, for it is the power of God to salvation for everyone who believes.... For in it the righteousness of God is revealed from faith to faith, as it is written, "The just shall live by faith." (Rom. 1:16–17).

Hymn Story:
Martin Luther was not only a great reformer, Bible translator, political leader, fiery preacher and theologian—he was also a musician, having been born in an area of Germany known for its music. There in his little Thuringian village young Martin grew up listening to his mother sing. He himself joined a boys' choir that sang at weddings and funerals. He became proficient with the flute (recorder), and his volcanic emotions often erupted in song.

When the Protestant Reformation began, Luther determined to restore worship to the German church. He worked with skilled musicians to create new music for Christians, to be sung in the vernacular. He helped revive congregational singing and wrote a number of hymns.

Luther once wrote: "Next to the Word of God, the noble art of music is the greatest treasure in the world. It controls our thoughts, minds, hearts, and spirits.... A person who... does not regard music as a marvelous creation of God... does not deserve to be called a human being; he should be permitted to hear nothing but the braying of asses and the grunting of hogs."

Luther's most famous hymn is "*Ein' feste Burg ist unser Gott*,"—"A Mighty Fortress Is Our God." Based on Psalm 46, it reflects Luther's awareness of our intense struggle with Satan. In difficulty and danger, Luther would often resort to this song, saying to his associate, "Come, Philipp, let us sing the 46th Psalm."

Additional Sermons and Lesson Ideas

Profile of a Priest
By Peter Grainger

Date preached:

SCRIPTURE: Malachi 2:1–9

INTRODUCTION: Malachi was to preach against the corrupt priests of his day. We can learn from these verses what a godly priest should have:

1. Ears: *To Listen to the Voice of the Lord* (v. 1).
2. Mouth and Lips: *To Teach the Word of the Lord* (v. 7).
3. Feet: *To Walk in the Ways of the Lord* (v. 6).
4. Hearts: *Set to Glorify the Name of the Lord* (v. 1).

CONCLUSION: The Levites that Malachi prophesied to didn't listen (v. 1) and were judged, given barrenness (v. 2) and public disgrace (v. 3). Since we are a royal priesthood (1 Pet. 2:9), we are to offer our bodies as living sacrifices (Rom. 12:1; Heb. 13:15).

Hang In There
By Dan Chun

Date preached:

SCRIPTURE: Matthew 26:47–56

INTRODUCTION: This scene from Jesus' last days before the Crucifixion takes place in the darkness of night in the Garden of Gethsemane, now faintly lit by a thin line of torches and lanterns with the silhouettes of clubs and swords against it. How did this happen to the Messiah?

1. Betrayal Is a Part of Life. Many believe that people are basically good. It's true that we are made in God's image, but we as sinful humans have a tremendous capacity for evil. Has anyone close to you lied or deceived you? Whether it's a little white lie or a broken marriage vow, it hurts.
2. God Is in Control. Jesus was confronted by a mob of armed men, yet he kept cool. He even healed one of his captors (vv. 51–52). Jesus taught His disciples that He was in control of even this situation (v. 53) and chose obedience to the Father's will (vv. 54, 56).

CONCLUSION: Matthew concludes the account by admitting that "all the disciples forsook Him and fled. "Let us keep our focus on Christ as our model in every circumstance.

NOVEMBER 7, 2004

SUGGESTED SERMON

The True Lifeline

Date preached:

By Richard Sharpe, Jr.

Scripture: Isaiah 6:1–10, especially verse 8: Also I heard the voice of the Lord, saying: "Whom shall I send, and who will go for Us?" Then I said, "Here am I! Send me."

Introduction: D. L. Moody grew up in church. He was surrounded by loving people who showed compassion and concern in his life. One might assume that he was a "nice Christian young man." Moody, however, grew up in a Unitarian church. He didn't know the first thing about the gospel of Jesus Christ. It took an alert Sunday school teacher to realize that although Moody's background was full of church, he didn't really understand the gospel. Moody was led to Christ by this Sunday school teacher and became one of the greatest American evangelists of all times. As we walk with the Lord, we are often prompted by the Word of God to share the gospel with people we know, perhaps with co-workers or neighbors. But how often do we share Christ with people who go to church? To people in this congregation? This is often the most difficult ministry, to share with those who think they already know! Isaiah was called to preach to Israel, people who should have been intimately seeking God, but were instead rebellious and ignorant. God is calling us to preach to our generation of "nominal" Christians in the same way.

1. **The First Hook: Seeing (v. 1).** Isaiah saw the Lord, high and exalted, in an array of kingly splendor with angels surrounding Him. Imagine, God Himself who is so high and exalted, so glorious, so perfect, descending to confront a man. Isaiah was not asking God to visibly show up, but God came seeking someone to go to His people. How often do we see the incredible work of God in our lives? His majesty and splendor are evident in all of creation (Ps. 19; Rom. 1:20). God again came in the form of Jesus Christ to die for our sins and to commission us to share His gospel; He promised us His eternal presence to accomplish this task (Matt. 28:19–20). We must react like Isaiah—in worship and obedience, sharing the gospel of our majestic creator who humbled Himself to save us from sin.

2. **The Second Hook: Hearing (vv. 3, 7, 8).** Isaiah heard the angels proclaiming the holiness of God (v. 3). His reaction was to confess that he, like his people, was unclean (v. 5). Next he heard the angel who put a coal to his lips, saying, "Your sin is purged." (v. 7). Then he heard the voice of God asking, "Whom shall I send?" (v. 8). Isaiah quickly volunteered (v. 8). Isaiah would preach not to an easy crowd, but to stubborn and rebellious people. Have you ever tried to share Christ with someone who thought they were "just fine?" It's a difficult and often uncomfortable ministry. However, when people hear sermons or read Scripture that portrays God's holiness, they often feel convicted and repent of sin like Isaiah. Do you hear God's voice? Convicting you of sin? Calling you to His service?

3. **The Third Hook: Understanding (vv. 9–10).** An interesting parallel is drawn here: Isaiah just saw the glory of God, heard His forgiveness and His call, then understood as he responded. He was to preach this to people, "Keep on hearing, but do not understand; keep on seeing, but do not perceive?" (v. 9). The Lord told Isaiah that if the people did believe and understand, they would be healed (v. 10). Sometimes we are called to difficult ministry to difficult people. The message is powerful, able to save all who believe (Rom. 1:16).

Conclusion: As people who have seen, heard, and understood the gospel of Jesus Christ, we have the responsibility of sharing this message of salvation, often to people who believe they are Christians but are not. We can show people

>>> *sermon continued on following page*

APPROPRIATE HYMNS AND SONGS

Holy, Holy, Holy, John B. Dykes/Reginald Heber; Public Domain.

I Saw the Lord, Dallas Holm; © 1981 Dimension Music, Admin. by Brentwood-Benson Music Publishing, Inc.

Holy Is the Lord, Bill Batstone/Phil Kristianson; © 1994 Maranathan Praise, Inc., Admin. by The Copyright Company.

O Zion Haste, Mary A. Thomson; Public Domain.

Go Forth and Tell, James E. Seddon/Michael Baughen; © 1964 Hope Publishing Company.

Christ in our lives visibly and audibly, but we must trust the Lord to help them understand and comprehend the gospel. Because of God's holiness and mercy, we are to respond like Isaiah, saying in essence, "Lord, here I am. I know ministry may be difficult; I know people often think they understand but do not. They will laugh at me, reject me, and maybe even physically hurt me, but your message is powerful and it must be preached, so send me."

FOR THE BULLETIN

❋ The Scottish Reformation cost the lives of many staunch Protestants, including John Nisbet, whose 16-year-old son later penned this account: "On the 7th of November, 1685, my father . . . (was) seized by forty of the enemy. The night before, I had gone to the Earl of Loudon's house; and in my sleep I dreamed of all the passages of trouble my father was in. I awoke with much sorrow of spirit, and immediately rose and essayed prayer. But alas, alas, I was . . . overwhelmed with such a flood of sorrow that I could do nothing all that day but sigh to the breaking of my heart. . . . But kind Providence ordered the matter so, that though very dark, I met an eminent Christian, William Woodburn, my father's friend, who counseled me to acquiesce in and submit to the sovereign will of God who is a father to the fatherless. Upon this blessed advice and seasonable counsel, the weight of my burden was much taken off, my sorrow alleviated, and all fretting at the dispensation prevented. I spent this night looking to the Lord, that my father might be strengthened to be faithful unto the death." ❋ On November 7, 1793, Christianity was "abolished" by the leaders of the French Revolution, and 2,000 churches were afterward destroyed throughout France. ❋ November 7, 1835, is the birthday of Scottish divine Robert Murray McCheyne (1835) and hymnist Will Thompson, author of "Jesus Is All the World to Me," and "Softly and Tenderly."

STATS, STORIES AND MORE

Holy, Holy, Holy

The Hebrew language paints a beautiful picture in Isaiah 6:1–8. There were "seraphim" surrounding the King, covering His face and feet. The Hebrew root *saraph* means "to burn." Thus *seraphim* translates into something like "burning ones." Since God's glory or holiness is often represented by light (John 1; 1 John 1:5–7; Rev. 22:5), perhaps the closest representation of His glory and holiness is through incredible brightness (Ex. 34:29–35), in this case alluding to fire (also see Ex. 3:2–4). These "burning ones" were bright as fire, yet they hid the full glory of God, for seeing it would cause death (Ex. 33:20). Not only did they represent God's incredible glory, but they proclaimed His holiness. The Hebrew word for "holy" in Isaiah 6:3 is *kadosh*. Hebrew adjectives function differently than English adjectives. Repetition of adjectives in Hebrew adds emphasis. It's as if these radiant angels were saying "incredibly, magnificently holy is the LORD." Arthur Pink comments, "It has been well said that 'true worship is based upon recognized greatness . . . In the presence of the Divine King upon His throne even the seraphim 'veil their faces.'"

The Cleansing Touch

"We see how God condescends to meet the weakness of human sense. He puts the tongs into the hand of a seraph, that by means of it he may take a coal from the altar and apply it to the Prophet's mouth . . . There is no reason to believe that the coal possessed any virtue, as superstitious persons imagine that in the magical arts there is some hidden power. Nothing of this sort is to be found here; for it is God alone who can cleanse our pollution, in whatever part it exists."
—*John Calvin*

WORSHIP HELPS

Call to Worship:

Holy, holy, holy! Lord God Almighty!
Early in the morning our song shall rise to Thee;
Holy, holy, holy, merciful and mighty!
God in three persons, blessed Trinity!

Scripture Reading:

The four living creatures, each having six wings, were full of eyes around and within. And they do not rest day or night, saying: "Holy, holy, holy, Lord God Almighty,
Who was and is and is to come!" Whenever the living creatures give glory and honor and thanks to Him who sits on the throne, who lives forever and ever, the twenty-four elders fall down before Him who sits on the throne and worship Him who lives forever and ever, and cast their crowns before the throne, saying: "?You ?are worthy, O Lord, to receive glory and honor and power; for You created all things, and by Your will they exist and were created" *(Rev. 4:8–11)*.

Hymn Story:

Reginald Heber, the author of this hymn, wrote it for Trinity Sunday while he was Vicar of Hodnet, England. Heber desired to take the gospel to India and finally did so in 1822. As Bishop of Calcutta, India, Heber was surrounded by the worship of false gods, but continued his ministry nonetheless. The tune to this song is called "Nicaea," named after the church council that met in A.D. 325, which affirmed the doctrine of the Trinity. This hymn was found after Heber's death in 1826, and deemed by Alfred Lord Tennyson as the world's greatest hymn.

Additional Sermons and Lesson Ideas

Praise the Lord!

Date preached:

SCRIPTURE: Psalm 113

INTRODUCTION: What would you think of a man who never got an ounce of exercise? Never lifted a finger, flexed a muscle, or took a step. It's impossible to be in glowing health without exercise. Our bodies need exercise. In the same way, our souls need to praise God. We need the psychological health that comes from flexing our praise muscles, of knowing and acknowledging our great Lord. This is the theme of Psalm 113.

1. Who should praise the Lord? (v. 1). The servants of the Most High.
2. When should we praise the Lord? (v. 2). From this time forth and forever.
3. Where should we praise the Lord? (v. 3). From the rising of the sun to the place where it sets.
4. Why should we praise the Lord? (vv. 4–9).
5. He is a high God (vv. 4–5).
6. He is a humble God (v. 6).
7. He is a helping God (vv. 7–9).

CONCLUSION: Praise the Lord!

The Light of the World
By Peter Grainger

Date preached:

SCRIPTURE: Isaiah 9:1–7

INTRODUCTION: Have you ever seen a faithful church look like it's going under? So often, the Lord restores and revives His people despite how desperate the situation seems. In Isaiah's time, the people of Israel seemed to be "going under," but there was reason to hope; a light was coming.

1. Illumination (vv. 2–3): *The Light Dawns.*
   A. For the People Who Walked in Darkness.
   B. For Those Who Dwelt in the Land of the Shadow of Death.
   C. The Fulfillment (Matt. 4:12–17; 2 Cor. 4:3–6).
2. Liberation (vv. 3–4): *The Light Shines.*
   A. The End of Oppression (see Judg. 6—7).
   B. The End of War (v. 4; see Ps. 46:9).
   C. The Fulfillment (Luke 4:16–21; Heb. 2:14–16).
3. Incarnation (vv. 6–7): *The Light Spreads.*
   A. Through the Government of the Son.
   B. Through the Zeal of the Lord of Hosts.
   C. The Fulfillment: (1 Cor. 15:20–28; Rev. 11:15).

CONCLUSION: Don't be overwhelmed by the dark world around you; live in the light (1 John 1:7).

CLASSICS FOR THE PASTOR'S LIBRARY

Two Classics on Ephesians

Millions of us read the *Wall Street Journal* or the business section of our local newspaper. We subscribe to *Money Magazine, Forbes,* or *Kiplinger's,* and watch Louis Rukeyser on *Wall Street Week.* We study our investment portfolios like misers counting coins. But how long since we've poured over the reports of our spiritual investments?

The Book of Ephesians—the Bible's counterpart to *Forbes* and *Kiplinger's*—describes our wealth from God, who is "rich in mercy" (Eph. 2:4). Reading Ephesians is like taking an inventory of our heavenly vaults. In Ephesians, we read of:

- The **riches** of His grace (1:7)
- The **riches** of the glory of His inheritance (1:18)
- The exceeding **riches** of His grace (2:7)
- The unsearchable **riches** of Christ (3:8)
- The **riches** of His glory (3:16)

Many wonderful commentaries have been written on Ephesians, some scholarly in nature, and others lay-oriented. I have a 1,500-page tome called *Puritan Exposition of Ephesians*, which I haven't read; I can't even lift it off the shelf. But my favorite works on Ephesians are two short devotional commentaries that grew out of God's work in China.

Sit, Walk, and Stand

Sit, Walk, and Stand was compiled from a series of lectures given by the Chinese Christian, Nee To-sheng, better known as Watchman Nee. At age 16, Nee was converted to Christ under the influence of his mother and a woman evangelist named Dora Yu. Shortly thereafter, he began preaching and leading evangelistic teams into Chinese villages. During the 1930s he was involved in planting hundreds of churches across China. When the Communists took over, Nee was imprisoned under harsh conditions. He died in 1972, but his writings made him the best-known Chinese Christian of the twentieth century.

In his lectures on Ephesians, Watchman Nee divided the epistle into three sections. Chapters 1—3, doctrinal in nature, describe the Christian's position in Christ: "God . . . raised us up together, and made us sit together in the heavenly places in Christ Jesus" (2:4–6). Hence the word, "Sit."

The last half of Ephesians (chs. 4—6) is practical in nature, and the bulk of this section deals with our daily walk. "Walk worthy of the calling which you have received" (4:1); "No longer walk as the rest of the Gentiles walk" (4:17); "walk in love" (5:2); "walk as children of light" (5:8); "walk circumspectly" (5:15).

The final portion of the book, Ephesians 6:10–24, tells us to "stand against the wiles of the devil . . . and having done all, to stand" (Eph. 6:11). Watchman Nee's analysis of Ephesians, then, revolves around this outline:

Our Position in Christ—"Sit" (chs. 1—3)
Our Life in the World—"Walk" (chs. 4–6a)
Our Attitude to the Enemy—"Stand" (ch. 6b)

Wealth, Walk, and Warfare

Ruth Paxson uses the same outline but different words in her book, *The Wealth, Walk, and Warfare of the Christian.* According to Paxson, Ephesians 1—3 describes our wealth in Christ. In chapters 3—6a, we're instructed to walk in unity, holiness, love, light, wisdom, praise, and harmony. Finally, Ephesians 6:10–18 describes our warfare against Satan.

Paxson was born in the American Midwest, but little is known of her childhood or upbringing. As a young woman, she was active in the Student Volunteer Movement and served with the YWCA as an evangelist to colleges on the East Coast. At age 35, she felt called to China. Once there, she helped establish missionary schools for girls. Later she became a popular advocate of the "deeper" Christian life. Her book, *Life on the Highest Plane,* is still in print.

My friend Jim Weaver, editor of scholarly books, told me that shortly after he was saved, he read *The Wealth, Walk, and Warfare of the Christian.* "It was delightful to read then, and still remains one of the best commentaries on Ephesians. It excels in not only explaining the text, but in applying it to the believer's life."

Featured in the back of the book is Paxson's chart of Ephesians that is unbeatable. *Wealth, Walk, and Warfare* is not currently in print, but due to its former popularity, it's available in used bookstores, and it's worth the search.

Why not lay aside the current issue of *Online Investing* for a moment, and invest some time working on your Christian posture, sitting with Christ in the heavenly realms, walking worthy of your calling, and taking your stand against the wiles of the devil? Our greatest assets are bound up with our wealth, walk, and warfare as believers in Christ.

Quotes for the Pastor's Wall

> A truly evangelical sermon must be like offering a child a beautiful red apple or holding out a glass of water to a thirsty man and asking, "Wouldn't you like it?"
>
> —Dietrich Bonhoeffer

HEROES FOR THE PASTOR'S HEART

Anskar

In the evangelization of Europe, the Scandinavians were the last Teutonic peoples to accept Christianity. These Vikings from the North threatened Western Christendom, and their raids terrorized Britain and Western Europe.

One man wanted to reach them, and his desire for a martyr's crown gave him courage to try.

Anskar, born in France in 801, was schooled from age five at the monastery of Corbey founded by Columba, and he possessed a tender heart. As a young man he was recruited to help establish a new monastery, New Corbey, in Germany.

While there, Anskar heard of a Scandinavian politician, Harald, who was asking for military assistance. The resulting discussions opened a door, albeit dangerous, for a missionary to go to the Danes. Anskar volunteered. His friends tried to dissuade him, but he was ready, he told them, to perish if need be. He didn't die, but little is known of Anskar's resulting trip to Denmark, and when Harald fell from power, Anskar was expelled.

Swedish envoys soon requested missionaries, and Anskar again headed north. This time pirates attacked his ship, and he lost his possessions but not his life. Reaching Sweden, he was warmly welcomed by King Bjorn. But his preaching produced few converts.

Meanwhile, German Emperor Louis the Pious, seeing Anskar's work, conceived an ambitious plan for Christianizing the North. He had Anskar appointed Archbishop, gave him money, and established a monastery in Flanders as headquarters for the Scandinavian thrust. Anskar did his best, but headway was difficult. Pirates raided his monastery. He lived in hiding. His missionaries were driven from Sweden. Many of his converts reverted to paganism.

But Anskar prayed and fasted and worked until February 3, 865, when he felt the life draining from his body. He gave urgent instructions to his associates, then died peacefully—without gaining his coveted martyr's crown. His efforts failed to establish a permanent Scandinavian base for Christianity, but the seed was planted, and in the tenth century the church there gained a sure foothold. For this reason, Anskar is known in church history as the "Apostle to the North."*

Excerpted from the author's book, *On This Day* (Nashville, Thomas Nelson Publishers, 1997), entry for February 3.

NOVEMBER 14, 2004

SUGGESTED SERMON
Mourning Has Broken: The Gift of Tears
By Todd Kinde   Date preached:

Scripture: Matthew 5:4: Blessed are those who mourn, for they shall be comforted.

Introduction: We identify mourning with tragic events such as death or severe loss. Mourning and grief are not emotions that we particularly want to experience. In fact, at times of tragedy we will often refrain from mourning in order to "be strong." In a culture that has as part of its credo the "Pursuit of life, liberty and happiness," we simply do not have much room for mourning in our value system. The world in which we live likes to laugh and be happy. But the Lord stops us in our pursuits of happiness and says quite the contrary, "Blessed are those who mourn." What kind of mourning brings God's favor? We should understand mourning in light of the previous verse. Spiritual poverty is recognition of having nothing to give to God, having no resources to redeem ourselves or to buy ourselves out of slavery to sin. Mourning is the emotional counterpart of this. Being poor in spirit is the intellectual side of admitting our spiritual poverty. Mourning is the emotional response, the feeling of our fallen sinful condition before God.

1. **Mourning Over Personal Sin.** Mourning is the experience of the person who increasingly recognizes the blackness of sin as a result of being exposed to the purity of God. Isaiah experienced this sense of spiritual grief as the angels cried out, "Holy, Holy, Holy." His response was, "Woe to me . . . I am ruined! For I am a man of unclean lips, and I live among a people of unclean lips, and my eyes have seen the King, the LORD Almighty" (Is. 6:5, NIV). Paul cried out, "O wretched man that I am! Who will deliver me from this body of death?" (Rom. 7:24).

2. **Mourning Over Others' Sin.** The sin of others should also cause us to mourn. 1 Corinthians 5:2–3 states, "Shouldn't you rather have been filled with grief and have put out of your fellowship the man who did this?" (NIV). We may be quick to judge and even condemn the sin of others. But notice in 1 Corinthians that grief causes us to react with church discipline.

Jeremiah is known as "the weeping prophet" lamenting over the sin of Israel. "Oh, that my head were waters, and my eyes a fountain of tears, that I might weep day and night for the slain of the daughter of my people!" (Jer. 9:1). Jesus, the only sinless One who is able to rightfully judge and condemn, wept over the very city that rejected Him (Luke 19:41). When have you last wept over sin? When have you last wept over the coming Judgment that will result in many souls condemned to hell? When have you last wept over the rampant death in our society through the practice of abortion? Oh, that God would give us a mourning heart and the gift of tears as we grieve the sin of our own hearts, the sin of the world around us, for the souls who will be condemned to an eternity apart from the blessing of God.

3. **Mourners Will Be Comforted.** The Old Testament prophets anticipated the Comforter in the coming Messiah. "The Spirit of the Lord God is upon Me, because the Lord has anointed Me to preach good tidings to the poor; He has sent Me to heal the brokenhearted, to proclaim liberty to the captives, and the opening of the prison to those who are bound; to proclaim the acceptable year of the Lord, and the day of vengeance of our God; to comfort all who mourn" (Is. 61:1–2). As the hymn writer says, "*The Comforter has Come!*" (Frank Bottome, 1823–1894). We are comforted now in the forgiveness of sin; we are comforted today by the presence of

>>> *sermon continued on following page*

APPROPRIATE HYMNS AND SONGS

Comfort, Comfort Now My People, Johannes Oleaarius/Louis Bourgeois/Catherine Winkworth; Public Domain.

A Shelter in the Time of Storm, Vernon J. Charlesworth/Ira D. Sankey; Public Domain.

Does Jesus Care?, Frank E. Graeff/J. Lincoln Hall; Public Domain.

Father Me, Graham Kendrick; © 1992 Make Way Music, Admin. by Music Services.

Hold Me, Joan Ewing; © 1982 John T. Benson Publishing Company, Admin. by Brentwood-Benson Music Publishing, Inc.

the Holy Spirit indwelling our lives, which produces the spiritual fruit of joy! To be a spiritual mourner is to enjoy God's comfort now.

Conclusion: Nothing less than the forgiveness of God will comfort those who weep and mourn in this fashion over personal sin and the sin of others. We anticipate the day of His appearing when ". . . God will wipe away every tear from (our) eyes; there shall be no more death, nor sorrow, nor crying. There shall be no more pain, for the former things have passed away" (Rev. 21:4).

FOR THE BULLETIN

* Today marks the death of the Roman Emperor Justinian, who died in 565 at age 82. He is primarily remembered for the Justinian Code, which influenced the development of canon law in the Middle Ages. * November 14, 1731, is the wedding anniversary of evangelist George Whitefield to Elizabeth Burnell. * Andrew Murray, later to become a prominent South African pastor and devotional writer, wrote to his parents on November 14, 1845, telling them of his conversion to Christ: "My dear Parents, It was with very great pleasure that I today received your letter of August 15, containing the announcement of the birth of another brother. And equal, I am sure, will be your delight when I tell you that I can communicate to you far gladder tidings, over which angels have rejoiced, that your son has been born again. . . . When I look back to see how I have been brought to where I now am, I must acknowledge that I see nothing. "He hath brought the blind by a way that he knew not, and led him in a path that he hath not known." For the last two or three years there has been a process going on. . . . And though I cannot yet say that I have had anything of that deep special sight into the guiltiness of sin which many people appear to have, yet I trust, and at present I feel as if I could say, I am confident that as a sinner I have been led to cast myself on Christ. * November 14, 1915, marks the death of Booker T. Washington at age 59. * On November 14, 1941, Intervarsity Christian Fellowship was founded in Chicago.

STATS, STORIES AND MORE

The Gift of Tears
Humans are the only animals that are known to cry based on emotions. Often, we feel much better after we cry. This phenomenon was researched by a University of Minnesota biochemist named William Frey. He discovered that the makeup of tears is different depending on the stimulus. The chemicals found in tears induced by slicing onions are very different than those induced by emotional stimuli. Emotional tears release both endorphins and a primary hormone usually emitted during stressful situations. This evidence suggests that tears are our bodies' way of alleviating stress and releasing toxins.

Mourning for the Lost
Dr. George Murray, president of Columbia International University, once sat around a dinner table with the late Francis Schaeffer, one of the most influential apologist-philosophers in American history. Murray remembers that Schaeffer enjoyed being challenged with the most difficult questions one could ponder. One student sitting at the table asked Schaeffer about un-evangelized people, whether or not they would be saved if they never heard the gospel. His countenance quickly changed and he began to weep, unable to answer. This was the only answer Murray needed.

Mourners Shall Be Comforted
The hymn writer, Johannes G. Olearius (1671) sings in "Comfort, Comfort Now My People":

Comfort, comfort now my people; tell of peace so says our God;
Comfort those who sit in darkness mourning under sorrow's load;
For the herald's voice is crying in the desert far and near,
Calling us to true repentance since the Kingdom now is here.

WORSHIP HELPS

Call to Worship:
I will love You, O Lord, my strength. The Lord is my rock and my fortress and my deliverer; my God, my strength, in whom I will trust; my shield and the horn of my salvation, my stronghold. I will call upon the Lord, who is worthy to be praised . . . (Ps. 18:1–3).

Benediction:
Those who sow in tears shall reap in joy. He, who continually goes forth weeping, bearing seed for sowing, shall doubtless come again with rejoicing, bringing his sheaves with him (Ps. 126:5–6).

Kids Talk

Brad loved to play soccer. He practiced in his back yard with his brother, Paul, every day after school. Finally it was time for his first game and Brad was determined to win. He played well the whole game, scoring two goals for his team, but in the end it just wasn't enough. They lost by one goal. As Brad walked off the field, he began to cry in front of his whole team, his whole family, and all the fans; even Paul was watching. When he got home he was so angry at himself for "being such a baby" that he threw off his cleats, jumped into bed, and buried his head in his pillow. Then he picked up his Bible, hoping he would read something that would cheer him up. He read these words from John 11:35, "Jesus wept." You see, all of us get sad or upset. Whether our pet fish died, or our best friend hurt our feelings, we can remember that Jesus cried, and it's okay for us to cry, too.

Additional Sermons and Lesson Ideas

Two Kinds of Talkers
By Peter Grainger

Date preached:

SCRIPTURE: Malachi 3:13–18

INTRODUCTION: Luke 6:45 tells us that our words reflect our character. In Israel, the Lord drew a distinction between two kinds of talkers:

1. Those Who Show Contempt for the Lord (vv. 13–15).
    A. Their Premise: *It is useless to serve God* (v. 14).
    B. Their Priority: *What profit is it that we have kept His ordinance?* (v. 14).
    C. Their Profile: *We have walked as mourners* (v. 14).
    D. Their Presumption: *So now we call the proud blessed* (v. 15).
2. Those Who Serve the Lord (v. 16).
    A. They Feared the Lord and Honored His Name.
    B. They Talked with Each Other (see Deut. 6:6–7).
3. The Lord's Response (vv. 16–18).
    A. He Listened and Heard (v. 16).
    B. He Remembered and Recorded (v. 16).
    C. He Made Them His Jewels (v. 17).
    D. He Counted Them as His Children (v. 17).

CONCLUSION: Choose which type of talker you will be carefully, for one day we, too, will see the distinction (Rom. 8:18–19).

The Marks of Discipleship
Based on a Sermon by J. J. Luce

Date preached:

SCRIPTURE: Matthew 26:69–73; Luke 14:26–27

INTRODUCTION: Do people at your workplace or school know that you follow Jesus? A disciple of Christ should have two main characteristics:

1. Companionship with Christ (Matt. 26:69–73). These verses are often used to show Peter's failure. They also show us his faithfulness. Even when he denied being a follower of Christ, the servant girl didn't believe him. He was with Jesus (v. 69) and even his accent gave him away (v. 73)! Do people know without a doubt that we follow Christ? Is our life so centered around following Him that our companionship with Him is unmistakable?
2. Conformity to Christ (Luke 14:26–27). Jesus made the ultimate sacrifice for us on the Cross. Our lives should be marked by sacrifice for the gospel, by giving up our sinful desires to follow Christ, and by allowing the Holy Spirit to live in us and control us completely.

CONCLUSION: Draw near to Jesus and allow Him to conform you into His image.

NOVEMBER 21, 2004

SUGGESTED SERMON
Solomon's Legacy
Date preached:

By David Jeremiah

Scripture: 1 Kings 2:1–9, especially verse 2: *Be strong, therefore, and prove yourself a man.*

Introduction: Several years ago, an airplane crash in Japan killed over 500 people. Four survivors told about the last half hour of the flight. The plane was without a rear tail stabilizer and its erratic descent caused some passengers to lose control. But one middle-aged man, Hirotsugo Kawaguchi, wrote this note to his family: "I'm very sad, but I'm sure I won't make it. The plane is rolling around and descending rapidly . . . Uoshi, I'm counting on you. You and the other children to be good to each other and work hard. Remember to help your mother. . . . Keiko, please take good care of yourself and the children. To think our dinner last night was our last. I am grateful for the truly happy life I have enjoyed. . . . " Most of us will not have a chance to write a note like that, but we all pass on a legacy to our families. By the words and deeds, we leave a clear path for them to follow. In this passage, David is preparing to pass the throne to Prince Solomon, and he gives him this legacy:

1. **The Legacy of Hope (vv. 1–4).** These verses contain several interesting elements:
    A. **Courage (v. 2).** *Be strong . . . prove yourself a man.* This is a call to moral, mental, and physical strength. This transition from David to Solomon was during a time of intrigue and danger. Whoever would lead must have courage. Strength of character is an absolute requirement for those who would serve God in any way.
    B. **Conviction (v. 3).** *Keep the charge of the Lord your God.* David told Solomon to be a man of the Book. The law of God was to ever be before him. His courage was to be based upon the conviction that God has spoken.
    C. **Conduct (v. 3).** *Keep His statutes.* A godly legacy starts with courage, it's built from conviction, and it expresses itself in conduct. The *hope* part of the message is in verse 4, as God promises Solomon *prosperity and posterity.* What a legacy to leave to your people!

2. **The Legacy of Hatred (vv. 5–6).** But now David passes on to Solomon a legacy of hatred involving a man named Joab. (see 2 Sam. 3 and 20, and also Joab's role in killing Uriah and covering up David's sin with Bathsheba.) How often it happens that the enemies we have in life are passed on to our children. The problems that we haven't been able to work out with others, our kids inherit.

3. **The Legacy of Hospitality (v. 7).** David told Solomon to show kindness to the sons of Barzillai the Gileadite. Barzillai was an 80-year-old man who appeared at a critical time in David's life, during the rebellion of Absalom. It's hard enough when one of your children forsakes the Lord; but when he makes you his enemy, too, it is pain beyond description. In 2 Samuel 17, pursued by Absalom's armies, David was cared for by Barzillai. In chapter 19, after the war, Barzillai took David back across the Jordon, but declined the royal honors David offered. Now, nearing death, David thought of Barzillai and wanted Solomon to repay the hospitality. It's good to remember people who have been good to you, and to make sure our children know about those who have blessed us.

4. **The Legacy of Humiliation (vv. 8–9).** David's final words were about Shimei, who had humiliated David during the flight from Absalom (see 2 Sam. 16:5). On his deathbed, David thought of this event and told Solomon to kill Shimei. The next chapter tells us how it was carried out. David set the agenda for his son's first years on the throne. Here is

>>> *sermon continued on following page*

APPROPRIATE HYMNS AND SONGS

God We Praise You, Christopher Idle/C. Hubert H. Parry; © 1982 Hope Publishing Company.

God You Are My God, Andy Park; © 1990 Mercy/Vineyard Publishing.

Here We Are Once Again, Jack Hayford; © 1981 Rocksmith Music, Admin. by Madina/Rocksmith Music.

How Great Thou Art, Stuart Hine; © 1941, 1953, 1955, Stuart K. Hine. Renewed 1981 Manna Music, Inc.

Let Us Proclaim His Majesty, Robert Gay; © 1988 Integrity's Hosanna! Music.

Solomon—his name meant peaceful—beginning his kingdom with bloodshed left him by his father.

Conclusion: There are several lessons here for us:

The matter with Joab (especially his role with Uriah) teaches us the power of a clear conscience. May God help us to live our lives in such a way that we have no skeletons in our closet.

The matter with Barzillai teaches that it's possible to make a difference in someone's life. This 80-year-old man had stepped into David's life and left a blessing that David never forgot.

The matter with Shimei teaches us the potential of one negative experience that isn't forgiven or forgotten.

The opening verses teach us that the purpose of a legacy is to give hope to our children. If David had just stopped with verse 4, how much better it would have been for Solomon. What kind of legacy are we leaving for those who follow?

FOR THE BULLETIN

❋ Columbanus, who was born in Ireland in 543, was so strikingly handsome that many women desired him, and he struggled greatly with temptation. At last, he sought the advice of a godly woman who warned him about following in the footsteps of Samson, David, and Solomon. Deeply moved, Columbanus committed himself to celibacy and entered a monastery to study the Scriptures. At age 40, he felt God calling him to take the gospel to Central Europe where he spent the rest of his life as a missionary before dying on this day in 615, in Italy. ❋ November 21, 1768, marks the birth of Friedrich E. D. Schleiermacher, German theologian and philosopher, in Breslau, Germany. He was the son of an army chaplain, and is considered the father of modern theological liberalism. ❋ On this day in 1818, the Russian Czar Alexander I petitioned for a Jewish state in Palestine. ❋ November 21, 1847, is the birthday of John Henry Yates, Freewill Baptist preacher and author of the hymn "Faith Is the Victory." Prior to his years in ministry, he was a salesman, newspaper editor, and the manager of a hardware store. His other popular hymn said: "The old Book stands! O yes, it stands! / Firm as a rock 'mid shifting sands! / Billows may run high, tempests sweep the sky; / Firmly the old Book stands!"

STATS, STORIES AND MORE

More from David Jeremiah

"Bubs" Russell was seventeen on that Sunday morning in 1941 when Pearl Harbor was bombed. He was called into the Army and ended up serving in the Army Air Corps, as a radio operator in a B-29 bomber. In only a few months he was stationed on the island of Saipan in the western Pacific. From this tiny island, B-29s were making bomber runs on Japan. The work was dangerous and deadly. On the morning of December 13, 1944, eighteen bombers soared out over the Pacific to make a bomb run on factories at Nagoya, Japan. Four of those planes never returned, and Bubs Russell's plane was among them.

The official word came from the War Department saying their son had been killed in action. A long telegram arrived, and a small white flag, bordered with red and trimmed with blue and gold. The flag had one small star in the middle which was the symbol of a son who had fallen in battle.

About a month later, the Russells received a letter that Bubs had placed on his pillow just before his last mission. It said: "Dear Folks: I have left this with instructions to send it on to you if anything ever happens to me. I send you my love and my blessings. My life has been a full life. I have been loved like very few people have ever been loved. And I love you all with the best that is in me. It hasn't been hard for me at all, knowing that you believe in me, that you trust me, and that you stand behind me no matter what. Knowing this has made me strong." And he signed his name.

If we want our children to be able to write letters like that to us, we had better be concerned about the legacy we are leaving them. And you know, it is never too late, never.

WORSHIP HELPS

Call to Worship:
But when the kindness and the love of God our Savior toward man appeared, not by works of righteousness which we have done, but according to His mercy He saved us, through the washing of regeneration and renewing of the Holy Spirit, whom He poured out on us abundantly through Jesus Christ our Savior, that having been justified by His grace we should become heirs according to the hope of eternal life (Titus 3:5–7).

Offertory Comments:
Often, when the offering plate is passed around, sometimes we put in our gift, feeling as if we've paid our dues. Some compare their offering to paying rent for using the church's space. Nothing could be further from the truth. A pastor once decided to give the congregation a glimpse of what their offering does for others. He announced that he had a burden that all those who had been financially blessed that week should give according to how the Lord provided for them in abundance; he asked them to put their money on the altar instead of in a plate. Then, he asked that everyone who was financially struggling that week come and take as much money as they needed. Reluctantly, then joyfully, those who had dire need of funds took from the offering with tears in their eyes. I'm sure no one in that congregation ever forgot that day. They must have realized, as we all should, that our offerings are used to help real people: to feed the poor, to fund life-changing events, and most importantly to preach the gospel of Jesus Christ to lost souls. Don't give out of obligation this morning. Trust the Lord to bless and multiply your offering for someone who really needs it; and He will bless you, too!

fear in life (vv. 2–3). He speaks of God as his hiding place (v. 5). There was a popular movie some time ago entitled "Panic Room" about the special, secure room built into some houses. This is one of the newest fads in home design. Some homeowners are building a high-tech bunker into their homes, capable of withstanding an onslaught. There you can feel safe until help arrives. All of us need a hiding place. We need a place secure from all alarms, a place where we can rest, knowing that everything is going to be all right because our Lord is in control. Colossians 3:2–3 says: *Set your mind on things above, not on things on the earth. For you died, and your life is hidden with Christ in God.*

2. **My Closeness to the Lord (vv. 4–6).** That brings us to the next division of Psalm 27. Our confidence in the Lord is based on our closeness to the Lord. This was written before the construction of the temple in Jerusalem, so the primary place of worship was at the ancient tabernacle in Gibeon. The tabernacle represented the presence of God among His people, and here David refers to the Tabernacle as: (1) The house of the Lord; (2) the temple; (3) His pavilion; (4) His tabernacle. He is saying: "If I could only do one thing in life, I'd just move to Gibeon and live there near the tabernacle and fellowship with God all day and all night." In other words, "Lord, I want to dwell with You, to live in Your presence, to be hidden in Your care day and night." There was a native Indian of high caste, the daughter of an Indian clergyman, named Ellen Goreh. Her mother died when she was young, and she eventually came under the care of British

>>> *sermon continued on following page*

APPROPRIATE HYMNS AND SONGS

Like a River Glorious, Frances R. Havergal/James Mountain; Public Domain.

Come, Ye Thankful People Come, Henry Alford/George J. Elvey; Public Domain.

Enter Into His Gates With Thanksgiving, Jack Hayford; © 1987 Annamarie Music/Rocksmith Music, Admin. by Madina/Rocksmith Music.

How Rich Am I, John W. Peterson; © 1956. Renewed 1984 John W. Peterson Music Company.

In Thanksgiving Let Us Praise Him, Claire Cloninger/Franz Joseph Haydn; © 1986 Word Music, Inc., Admin. by Word Music Group, Inc.

missionaries who took her to England and raised her. In time, she returned to India as a soul-winner herself. She's best-known for her hymns, one of which fits this theme:

> *In the secret of His presence how my soul delights to hide!*
> *Oh, how precious are the lessons which I learn at Jesus' side!*
> *Earthly cares can never vex me, neither trials lay me low;*
> *For when Satan comes to tempt me, to the secret place I go.*

3. **My Cry before the Lord (vv. 7–12).** But now we come to the third section of this Psalm, and the tone changes. Up to this point, David has been talking about the Lord; now he addresses the Lord personally in prayer: In the first part of this Psalm, David speaks with unbridled confidence. Now he is pleading with God not to leave him or forsake him. First he talks of his confidence in the Lord, then of his closeness to the Lord. But as he thinks about that, he begins to feel unworthy. So he comes to confess his sins and to reassure himself that God is a God of mercy and forgiveness. He asks God to teach him to be a healthier, holier, more righteous person (v. 11).

4. **My Counsel from the Lord (vv. 13–14).** He ends his psalm with a little sermon giving us the benefit of his counsel: *I would have lost heart, unless I had believed that I would see the goodness of the Lord in the land of the living.* We sometimes face staggering problems. The Christian has two options at every point along the way. We can despair or we can depend. We can worry or we can worship. We can give up or we can look up. We can bear it ourselves or we can cast our cares on the Lord. So take heart and wait on the Lord.

Conclusion: What does all this mean to us?

Regarding your confidence in the Lord, make up your mind to cast out depression and discouragement and to launch into every day with a thankful attitude.

Regarding your closeness to the Lord, make it a priority every day to spend time in personal Bible study and prayer.

Regarding your cry before the Lord, become more sensitive to sin in your life. Confess your sins daily and ask God to help you grow in holiness.

Regarding your counsel from the Lord, cast your cares on the Lord, waiting on Him with thanksgiving and trusting Him to do what only He can do in His own timing and in His own way.

FOR THE BULLETIN

✦ November 28, 1628 is the birthday of John Bunyan. He was a foul-mouthed youth who came to Christ after hearing a group of ladies talking about spiritual things. Later as a Baptist preacher, he was imprisoned for his faith. While in prison, he wrote Christian classics such as *Pilgrim's Progress*. ✦ Hugh MacKail, a Presbyterian in Scotland, was licensed to preach at 20 and preached his last message at 21. He was captured for his faith, and his trial occurred on November 28, 1666. When he refused to recant, he was tortured and taken to the scaffold. As he ascended, he told the crowd, "Every step is a degree nearer heaven." At the top, he took out his pocket Bible, read from its last chapter, and spoke of Christ before being hanged. ✦ On November 28, 1863, Thanksgiving was observed for the first time as a regular, official American holiday, having been declared the previous month by President Abraham Lincoln. ✦ November 28, 1902, marks the death of Joseph Parker (1830–1902), one of London's most popular preachers who pastored The City Temple from 1869 to his passing. His sermons through the Bible were published in a popular set of books. ✦ On November 28, 1904, Jeremiah E. Rankin, 76, died. He was the author of the hymns, "Tell It To Jesus" and "God Be With You Till We Meet Again." ✦ The funeral of missionary doctor Paul Carlson, a Covenant medical missionary murdered by Congo rebels in 1964, was held on November 28, 1964. *Time Magazine* featured Dr. Carlson on its cover, making his martyrdom a matter of worldwide attention.

STATS, STORIES AND MORE

There is a great debate in our day as scientists and scholars argue among themselves whether there is a God and whether or not the universe has meaning Steven Weinberg, who won the Nobel Prize for Physics in 1979, is one of the most famous scientists on earth. But he is perhaps most famous for having written one sentence that's been widely quoted, a quote based on an earlier observation by Albert Einstein. Einstein had said, "The only incomprehensible thing about the universe is that it is comprehensible." Steven Weinberg said, "The more the universe seems comprehensible, the more it also seems pointless."

I read of a debate that took place between two great scientists at Franklin and Marshall College in Lancaster, Pennsylvania. One of the scientists presented evidence that the universe appears to be created by an intelligent designer and that there is purpose and meaning in the universe. The other argued that there is no supernatural element to the universe, and no purpose to it. Therefore there is no real purpose to life itself. Everything is ultimately pointless, he said.

But the psalmist said, "The Lord is . . . Jehovah is. . . . God exists." And if there is God there must be, somehow and somewhere, meaning and purpose to the universe. And if there is meaning and purpose to the universe, there must be, somehow and somewhere, meaning and purpose to life. And if there is meaning and purpose to life, there must be, somehow and somewhere, meaning and purpose to my life, and to yours.

Hidden in the hollow of His blessed hand,
Never foe can follow, never traitor stand;
Not a surge of worry, not a shade of care,
Not a blast of hurry touch the spirit there.

Stayed upon Jehovah, hearts are fully blest,
Finding as He promised perfect peace and rest.

WORSHIP HELPS

Call to Worship:
Oh, give thanks to the Lord! Call upon His name; make known His deeds among the peoples! (1 Chr. 16:8).

Readers' Theater (or Responsive Reading):

Reader 1: We are bound to give thanks to God.

Reader 2: But fornication and all uncleanness or covetousness, let it not even be named among you, as is fitting for saints; neither filthiness, nor foolish talking, nor coarse jesting, which are not fitting, but rather giving of thanks.

Reader 1: Oh, give thanks to the Lord! Call upon His name; make known His deeds among the peoples! Sing to Him, sing psalms to Him; talk of all His wondrous works! Glory in His holy name; let the hearts of those rejoice who seek the Lord!

Reader 2: Oh, give thanks to the Lord, for He is good!

Reader 1: At midnight I will rise to give thanks to You, because of Your righteous judgments.

Reader 2: Giving thanks always for all things to God the Father in the name of our Lord Jesus Christ.

Reader 1: Giving thanks to the Father who has qualified us to be partakers of the inheritance of the saints in the light.

Reader 2: Rejoice always, pray without ceasing, in everything give thanks; for this is the will of God in Christ Jesus for you.

Reader 1: Oh, that men would give thanks to the Lord for His goodness, and for His wonderful works to the children of men!

(2 Thess. 2:13; Eph. 5:3–4; 1 Chr. 16:8–10; 1 Chr. 16:34; Ps. 119:36; Eph. 5:20; Col. 1:12; 1 Thess. 5:16–18; Ps. 107:2)

Kids Talk

For today's children's sermon, take a microphone and ask the children to name some things for which they are thankful.

Additional Sermons and Lesson Ideas

The Lord Is My . . .
By Joshua Rowe

Date preached:

SCRIPTURE: Various

INTRODUCTION: Often we view ourselves as the Lord's people, His servants, His messengers, and rightly so. I wonder how often, though, we remember what the Lord is to us.

1. The Lord Is My Rock and My Fortress (2 Sam. 22:2; Ps. 18:2).
2. The Lord Is My Light (Ps. 27:1).
3. The Lord Is My Strength (Ex. 15:2; Ps. 28:7; 118:14).
4. The Lord Is My Shield (Ps. 28:7).
5. The Lord Is My Song (Ex. 15:2; Ps. 118:14).
6. The Lord Is My Portion (Lam. 3:24).
7. The Lord Is My Helper (Heb. 13:6).
8. The Lord Is My Salvation (Ex. 15:2; Ps. 27:1).

CONCLUSION: May these verses encourage us to have closer intimacy with God and exhort us to daily crown Him as our Lord.

Stay Awake
By Dan Chun

Date preached:

SCRIPTURE: Mark 14:32–37; Luke 22:43

INTRODUCTION: Can you remember the most desperate time in your life? Perhaps a loved one died; maybe you faced a life-threatening illness. Jesus faced a time like this in the Garden of Gethsemane, but had three sources of strength, as do we:

1. Other People (v. 32). The Lord brought Peter, James, and John with Him. The Lord gives us a fellowship of believers who are committed to helping us in our Christian walk.
2. Prayer (vv. 32–37). Jesus asked the disciples to pray, but instead they slept. Prayer is our way of "staying awake." We should ask others to pray for us in our times of need, and pray for others during theirs.
3. Angels (Luke 22:43). In writing the Gethsemane scene, Luke mentions something that the other gospel writers do not---that an angel strengthened Jesus. In Jesus' greatest time of need, He asked for help from His friends, but they fell asleep. He must have felt so alone that God sent a messenger to help.

CONCLUSION: We have such a loving God, that He will do all He can to comfort us, give us strength and bring us to safety. Stay awake and keep on praying!

PRAYERS FOR A PASTORS CLOSET

Lord, Speak to Me

Lord, speak to me that I may speak
    In living echoes of Thy tone;
    As Thou has sought, so let me seek
    Thine erring children lost and lone.
O lead me, Lord, that I may lead
    The wandering and the wavering feet;
    O feed me, Lord, that I may feed
    Thy hungering ones with manna sweet.
O strengthen me, that while I stand
    Firm on the rock, and strong in Thee,
    I may stretch out a loving hand
    To wrestlers with the troubled sea.
O teach me, Lord, that I may teach
    The precious things Thou dost impart;
    And wing my words, that they may reach
    The hidden depths of many a heart.
O give Thine own sweet rest to me,
    That I may speak with soothing power
    A word in season, as from Thee,
    To weary ones in needful hour.
O fill me with Thy fullness, Lord,
    Until my very heart o'erflow
    In kindling thought and glowing word,
    Thy love to tell, Thy praise to show.
O use me, Lord, use even me,
    Just as Thou wilt, and when, and where,
    Until Thy blessèd face I see,
    Thy rest, Thy joy, Thy glory share.
              —Frances Ridley Havergal (1836–1879)

DECEMBER 5, 2004

SUGGESTED SERMON
Who Is He in Yonder Stall?

Date preached:

By Morris Proctor

Scripture: Matthew 1:18–25, especially verse 21: And she will bring forth a Son, and you shall call His name Jesus, for He will save His people from their sins.

Introduction: An old hymn asks, "Who is He in yonder stall at whose feet the shepherds fall?" That question and its answer are critical. If we answer incorrectly, we miss our Messiah. We can be mistaken about many things and still enter heaven, but we mustn't be wrong about the Baby in the manger. He is the God-Man, both human and divine, two complete natures combining in one Person. Let's investigate Jesus' deity as discussed in Matthew's account of the Christmas story. Mathew would make a good Sgt. Joe Friday of *Dragnet* because he gives "just the facts" without a lot of commentary (v. 18).

1. **The Virgin Birth Reveals Jesus' Deity (v. 18).** Matthew states that Mary and Joseph were betrothed. In the ancient culture, parents arranged marriages for their children. When the "engaged" children reached mid-teens, they entered a betrothal period, and it was during this time that Mary became pregnant. There were only two options: either she was a virgin or she was not. Let's assume she was not a virgin. Now we have two more options. Either she had relations with Joseph or with some other man. Nothing we know of Mary indicates unfaithfulness to Joseph, and nothing we know of Joseph indicates he would disclaim responsibility if it were his. If Mary had not been with a man, then she was, in fact, a virgin. How is that possible? When Mary asked that question Luke 1:34, the angel said: "The Holy Spirit will come upon you, and the power of the Highest will overshadow you; therefore, also, that Holy One who is to be born will be called the Son of God." Son of God is a Hebrew idiom meaning possessing the nature of God. Without His deity there is no explanation for the virgin conception and birth.

2. **The Angel's Words Announce Jesus' Deity (vv. 19–20).** On learning of Mary's pregnancy, Joseph was crushed. But an angel appeared to him saying: ". . . that which is conceived in her is of the Holy Spirit." Literally, it is: ". . . out of the Holy Spirit," implying source and substance. The substance or essence of this child is God Himself.

3. **Jesus' Mission Demands His Deity (v. 21).** The angel continued: "You shall call His name Jesus, for He will save His people from their sins." The name "Jesus" means "God saves." Jesus' name and mission reveal His deity. Do you recall from algebra class a formula that states, "If A = B and B = C, then A = C"? God saves. Jesus saves. Hence, Jesus is God. Why must Jesus be God in order to save us? Sin created a penalty—"the penalty of eternal destruction, away from the presence of the Lord and from the glory of His power" (2 Thess. 1:9, NASV). The penalty for sin is an eternal penalty. If our Savior were a mere man how long would he be paying the penalty? Forever. We'd never be saved because the penalty would never be paid. If we're to be saved we have to have a Savior who can pay an eternal penalty without taking eternity to do it. Only God Himself can do that (see Is. 43:11).

4. **Isaiah Predicts Jesus' Deity (vv. 22–23).** Matthew refers to Isaiah 7:14, in which armies attacked the kingdom of Judah led by King Ahaz. Fear gripped Ahaz, and God instructed Isaiah to calm him by allowing him to ask for a sign. When Ahaz refused, Isaiah said, "The Lord Himself will give you a sign. Behold, the virgin shall conceive and bear a Son, and shall call His name Immanuel." God's promise was that a young woman who currently hadn't known a man would bear a son. Before the boy was old enough to know the difference between good and evil, God would rid Judah of these invaders. The promise was, "Ahaz, when you're afraid, relax and look at the boy, Immanuel. He is a sign that God is with you."

>>> *sermon continued on following page*

APPROPRIATE HYMNS AND SONGS

Who Is He In Yonder Stall?, Benjamin Hanby; Public Domain.

Advent Canticle, Mark Hayes; © 1983 Sound III, Inc./Universal-MCA Music Publishing, Admin. by Universal-MCA Music Publishing.

Jesus is Born, Gerald S. Henderson; © 1986 Word Music, Inc., Admin. by Word Music Group, Inc.

O Come, O Come Emmanuel, John M. Neale/Henry S. Coffin/Thomas Helmore; Public Domain.

Celebrate the Child, Michael Card; © 1989 Birdwing Music/Mole End Music, Admin. by EMI Christian Music Publishing.

Matthew explained that the ultimate fulfillment of Isaiah 7:14 is Jesus Himself. He is a sign God will deliver His people. He is "God with us."

5. **Joseph's Faith Embraced Jesus' Deity (vv. 24–25).** Hearing the angel, Joseph awakened and obeyed. What faith! It overcame crushed emotions and public ridicule. It overcame physical desire, keeping Mary a virgin until after Christ was born. What could fuel such faith? The fact that this was no ordinary conception. This was miraculous. This was God Himself.

Conclusion: How should we respond to Matthew's Christmas story? Just as Joseph did. In this day of political correctness where Jesus is not to be mentioned, let alone declared to be God, we are ready to declare our Savior's name. Who is that in yonder stall? He is Jesus, Immanuel, God with Us. My God is in yonder stall.

FOR THE BULLETIN

❋ This is the traditional date for the death of the church father, Clement of Alexandria (c. 150–215). He is called the father of the Eastern Church. He is also the author of the oldest Christian hymn that has come down to us, "Shepherd of Tender Youth." ❋ On December 5, 1482, Pope Innocent VIII issued a document ordering an inquisition to discover and punish witches throughout Europe. This led to the witch hunts that spread even to the American colonies two centuries later. ❋ On December 5, 1823, Robert Morrison, first Protestant missionary to China, left China to return to England, taking his first furlough since arriving there in 1807. Back in London, he presented a copy of his Chinese Bible to King George IV and was elected a Fellow of the Royal Society. He spent many months traveling across the British Isles promoting the cause of Chinese evangelism. Returning to China in 1826, he remained there until his death in 1834. During the course of his twenty-seven years among the Chinese, he saw only three or four converts, but he laid the foundation for all subsequent missionary work in that great land. ❋ December 5, 1878 marks the death of "Uncle" John Vassar, famous preacher and personal evangelist. His family had gathered around him and his last words were "Farewell . . . farewell . . . Hallelujah!" ❋ Prohibition ended in the United States on this day in 1933. ❋ December 5, 1934, was the last full day missionaries John and Betty Stam spent together in their home in China. The next day, their city of Tsingteh was captured by Communist troops. John and Betty were seized and forced to leave their little baby, Helen Priscilla, in a blanket on the bed. On the morning of December 8, 1934, the Stams were beheaded for their faith in Christ. Little Helen was miraculously found by national Christians and smuggled out of the country.

STATS, STORIES AND MORE

Attributed to John Chrysostom (ca. A.D. 347–407), Bishop of Constantinople:

"I do not think of Christ as God alone, or man alone, but both together. For I know He was hungry, and I know that with five loaves He fed five thousand. I know He was thirsty, and I know that He turned the water into wine. I know he was carried in a ship, and I know that He walked on the sea. I know that He died, and I know that He raised the dead. I know that He was set before Pilate, and I know that He sits with the Father on His throne. I know that He was worshipped by angels, and I know that He was stoned by the Jews. And truly some of these I ascribe to the human, and others to the divine nature. For by reason of this He is said to have been both God and man."

Quotes for the Pastor's Wall

❝ It is not necessary for a preacher to express all his thoughts in one sermon. A preacher should have three principles: first, to make a good beginning, and not spend time with many words before coming to the point; secondly, to say that which belongs to the subject in chief, and avoid strange and foreign thoughts; thirdly, to stop at the proper time. ❞

—Martin Luther

WORSHIP HELPS

Call to Worship:
Christians, awake, salute the happy morn
Whereon the Savior of the world was born.
—*John Byrom* in 1745

Advent Reading:
A Forgotten Christmas Carol
John Byrom was a shorthand teacher (he invented his own system) and an aristocrat in England in the 1700s. In December 1745, after playing with his daughter, Dolly, he promised to write a Christmas poem just for her. On Christmas morning, she found it in an envelope among her other gifts. It was published in 1746, and was at one time quite popular, and though now seldom sung, it deserves to be rediscovered:

Christians, awake, salute the happy morn
Whereon the Savior of the world was born.
Rise to adore the mystery of love
Which hosts of angels chanted from above,
With them the joyful tidings first begun
Of God incarnate and the virgin's Son.

Like Mary let us ponder in our mind
God's wondrous love in saving lost mankind!
Trace we the Babe, who hath retrieved our loss,
From His poor manger to His bitter cross,
Tread in His steps, assisted by His grace,
Till man's first heav'nly state again takes place.

Then may we hope, th'angelic hosts among,
To sing, redeemed, a glad triumphal song.
He that was born upon this joyful day
Around us all His glory shall display.

Additional Sermons and Lesson Ideas

Her Firstborn Son

Date preached:

SCRIPTURE: Matthew 1:25

INTRODUCTION: The word "firstborn" in the Bible can mean "first in birth order," but also "first in sequence" or "first in rank." Matthew 1:25 says that Mary brought forth her firstborn Son and laid Him in a manager. But Jesus is the "firstborn" in other ways, too:

1. He Is God's Firstborn (Heb. 1:6; Ps. 89:27).
2. His Is Firstborn Over All Creation (Col. 1:15).
3. He Is the Firstborn from the Dead (Col. 1:18; Rev. 1:5).
4. The Firstborn Among Many Brethren (Rom. 8:29).

CONCLUSION: God, Thine own God, has richly shed / His oil of gladness on Thy head, / And with His sacred Spirit blest / His firstborn Son above the rest.—*Isaac Watts*

Healing for the Wounded
By Charles Haddon Spurgeon

Date preached:

SCRIPTURE: Psalm 147:3

INTRODUCTION: Psalm 147:4 tells how God counts the stars and calls them by name. This verse, verse 3, tells of how He heals the brokenhearted. The Psalmist places two facts side by side: The same God who guides the stars heals the wounded.

1. A Great Ill. Both body and soul can receive injury and hurt. The wounds of the body are painful, but the wounds to our inner person are worse, especially when we are:
   A. Broken by desertion
   B. Broken by bereavement
   C. Broken by poverty and need
   D. Broken by discouragement and defeat
   E. Broken by sin and guilt
2. A Great Mercy.
   A. God can heal the broken heart. He has the healing power.
   B. God will heal the broken heart. Our Great Physician longs to treat our wounds.

CONCLUSION: The queen has visited the hospitals of our soldiers to cheer, by her royal words, her loyal defenders; but when the infinite Creator stoops to become a servant to His own creatures, can you conceive the majestic condescension, which bows itself in mercy over the miserable heart. Oh, sin-sick sinner! The King of heaven will not despise you, but you, too, will find Him your Comforter who heals your broken heart.

DECEMBER 12, 2004

SUGGESTED SERMON
The Bible and the Babe
Date preached:

By Melvin Worthington

Scripture: 2 Corinthians 9:15: Thanks be to God for His indescribable gift!

Introduction: Benjamin P. Browne suggests that the millions who have no concept of its spiritual significance are "Christmas Christians." He writes: "Christmas Christians are limited Christians. It might seem safe to try to keep Christ wrapped as a baby and limited to a manger, a cradle, or a crèche, but too much is lost. It is in the context of His life and ministry—and, we should add, His death—that Bethlehem has meaning." Those who properly celebrate this season want to shout with Paul, "Thanks be to God for His unspeakable gift" (2 Cor. 9:15). God's gift is the gift of Himself in His Son. Here is the source of all His grace, blessings, and love. The gift of God's Son reveals God's plan, purpose, passion, presence, and provision. He knew what was best for us, and at the precise moment He interjected His Son into the world. When we look around and see the apparent collapse of what is right, we are tempted to doubt. But faith has always had to rise above the tangled fears that seek to drag it down. God's gift of His Son is His constant reminder that there is hope. He doesn't forget His promises, for He works His will as surely as day follows night. The traditional Christmas scene is but one of six stages of the total Christmas story.

1. **His Virgin Birth.** Isaiah predicted the Virgin Birth 700 years before the event startled the Roman world and divided time (Is. 7:14). Matthew 1:22–23 declared the fulfillment of Isaiah's sparkling prophecy. When Jesus was born, He had a human mother but no human father (Matt. 1:20). He was the God-Man, the Virgin Birth being the essential vehicle to the mysterious, unexplainable union of the divine and the human which took place when Jesus was conceived by the Holy Ghost in the womb of Mary. The Lord needed a human body and a sinless nature, thus He was "made of woman" (Gal. 4:4), born of a virgin.

2. **His Virtuous Life.** Jesus lived a perfect life while here on earth, a record never once flawed by sin. That sinless life was one of the qualifications for

Him to be the Redeemer for mankind. This Christmas season may we be keenly conscious of the price He paid to live that virtuous life.

3. **His Vicarious Death.** Jesus Christ, God's Gift, became a vicarious offering and died in the stead of sinners. The heart of the gospel is the truth that "Christ gave Himself" for our sins. He died as our substitute, bearing God's wrath for our sins, the Sinless One in the place of sinful ones. Albert Barnes refutes the error of those who would see Christ's death as a horrible accident of history, writing, "The whole plan originated in the divine purpose, and has been executed in accordance with the divine will. If in accordance with His will, it is good, and is worthy of universal acceptance."

4. **His Victorious Resurrection.** Christ's death and Resurrection are bedrock doctrines of Christianity. Paul declares that Jesus Christ was delivered for our offenses and raised for our justification (Rom. 4:25). He hurls to any hesitant believer the truth that "if Christ be not raised, your faith is vain (1 Cor. 15:17). The gospel Paul preached consisted of the death, burial and Resurrection of Jesus Christ, according to the Scriptures (1 Cor. 15:3, 4).

5. **His Visible Ascension.** Acts 1 records the Ascension of Christ. As the disciples watched, Christ ascended and a cloud received Him from their sight. Angelic messengers announced the Second Coming of Christ to them as they returned to Jerusalem.

>>> *sermon continued on following page*

APPROPRIATE HYMNS AND SONGS

Come, Thou Long Expected Jesus, Charles Wesley/Rowland H. Prichard; Public Domain.

Joy to the World, Isaac Watts/ George F. Handel; Public Domain.

A King Is Born, Sy Gorieb/Tim Hosman; © 1993 Integrity's Praise! Music/Integrity's Hosanna! Music, Admin. by Integrity Music, Inc.

All Is Well, Wayne Kirkpatrick/Michael W. Smith; © 1989 Careers/BMG Music Publishing, Inc./Milene Music, Inc., Admin. by Acuff-Rose Music Publishing, Inc.

Angels from the Realms of Glory, James Montgomery/Henry T. Smart; Public Domain.

6. His Vital Intercession. John 17 and Romans 8 clearly set forth the truth that Christ is praying for us. Hebrews 9:24 states that Christ now appears in the presence of God interceding on our behalf. What a comforting thought that Christ is our High Priest. He is interested in us; He intercedes for us; He intervenes on our behalf; and He interprets the deepest desires of our hearts as He and we await His return.

Conclusion: Christmas is not an isolated event that is over in one day, but it is one in a series of glorious days that involves God's redemptive plan, purpose, power, provision, and people. Christmas belongs to Christians. But let us not be a Scrooge about this truth. Spread the good cheer that He came once and will some day come again.

FOR THE BULLETIN

❉ The Bible Society of Philadelphia was organized on this day in December 12, 1808, the first Bible Society in America. ❉ Today is the birthday of Lottie Moon (1840), Southern Baptist missionary from Virginia who labored for forty years in North China. At her birth, she was named Charlotte Diggs Moon, but her first name was later shortened to Lottie. Her desire to be a missionary was sparked by reading *The Lives of the Three Mrs. Judsons*. After years in China, she passed away in 1912, aboard a ship heading back home to America. She had virtually starved herself in feeding her Chinese friends during a time of famine. Today she is best known for the Christmas offering she began in 1888 in the Women's Missionary Union of the Southern Baptists and which now raises millions of dollars every year for the expansion of Christianity in the world. ❉ The Spanish general, Fernando Alvarez de Toledo, the Duke of Alba, served at the pleasure of Philip II of Spain, who wanted to destroy the Protestants of Europe. The Duke of Alba had been sent with 10,000 troops into the Netherlands to quell the Reformation. Over the next six years, 6,000 Lowlanders were sentenced to death in the Duke's "Council of Blood." Some estimates put the total number of martyrs at 100,000, including women and children. One historian claims that more Christians lost their lives during this bloodletting than during all the Roman persecutions of the first 300 years of church history. In 1580, Alba was sent against Portugal. He was victorious, but on the way back, a fever developed and he died in misery on December 12, 1582. ❉ Boys' Town was opened by a compassionate Irish Roman Catholic priest named Father Edward Flanagan in Omaha, Nebraska, on December 12, 1917.

STATS, STORIES AND MORE

The Unspeakable Gift

According to an old legend, a wise and good king once ruled ancient Persia. He loved his people; but feeling separated from them, he determined to learn how they lived and about their hardships. From time to time, he would dress in tattered clothes and walk through the streets, a turban around his head to aid his disguise. He drifted in and out of their homes and received their hospitality and listened to their problems. No one knew he was their ruler. One time he visited a very poor man who lived in a cellar. He ate the poor man's food and spoke kind words to him. Imagine the poor man's shock when he later learned that his new, compassionate friend was the king himself. "You left your palace and your glory to visit me in this dark, dreary place," he said. "You ate the coarse food I ate. You brought gladness to my heart! To others you have given your rich gifts. To me you have given yourself! I desire nothing more."

Who is Jesus?

He began His ministry by being hungry, yet He is the Bread of Life.
Jesus ended His earthly ministry by being thirsty, yet He is the Living Water.
Jesus was weary, yet He is our rest.
Jesus paid tribute, yet He is the King.
Jesus was accused of having a demon, yet He cast out demons.
Jesus wept, yet He wipes away our tears.
Jesus was sold for thirty pieces of silver, yet He redeemed the world.
Jesus was brought as a lamb to the slaughter, yet He is the Good Shepherd.
Jesus died, yet by His death He destroyed the power of death.
—Gregory of Nazianzus, A.D. 381

WORSHIP HELPS

Call to Worship:

Jehovah enjoys his people; He will save the humble. Let His people rejoice in this honor. Let them sing for joy . . . . Adore him, O his people! (Ps. 149:4–7, TLB).

Advent Reading:

A Forgotten Christmas Carol

William How, an attorney's son, was ordained an Anglican minister in 1846, and spent many years as the rector of the church in Whittington, Shropshire, near the Welsh border. He had a great concern for poor and working class peoples, and a great love for writing hymns, many of which are all about the Lord Jesus. This Christmas hymn was written while he was ministering at Whittington and was published in a British hymnal in 1867:

Who is this so weak and helpless, Child of lowly Hebrew maid,
Rudely in a stable sheltered, coldly in a manger laid?
'Tis the Lord of all creation, Who this wondrous path hath trod;
He is God from everlasting, and to everlasting God.

Who is this, a Man of sorrows, walking sadly life's hard way,
Homeless, weary, sighing, weeping, over sin and Satan's sway?
'Tis our God, our glorious Savior, Who above the starry sky
Now for us a place prepareth, where no tear can dim the eye.

Who is this? Behold Him shedding drops of blood upon the ground!
Who is this, despised, rejected, mocked, insulted, beaten, bound?
'Tis our God, Who gifts and graces on His church now poureth down;
Who shall smite in righteous judgment all His foes beneath His throne.

Who is this that hangeth dying while the rude world scoffs and scorns,
Numbered with the malefactors, torn with nails, and crowned with thorns?
'Tis the God Who ever liveth, 'mid the shining ones on high,
In the glorious golden city, reigning everlastingly.

Additional Sermons and Lesson Ideas

King of Kings

Date preached:

SCRIPTURE: Matthew 2:2

INTRODUCTION: A king is someone who rules for life, a perpetual ruler. The Bible repeatedly refers to Christ in royal terms. He is called:

1. A King (John 18:37).
2. Another King (Acts 16:7).
3. King of the Jews (Matt. 2:2; Matt. 27:11, 29, 37; John 18:33, 39; 19:3, 19)
4. King of Israel (Matt. 27:42; John 1:49).
5. King of Kings (Rev. 17:14; 19:16).
6. King of Righteousness (Heb. 7:2).
7. King of Salem (Peace) (Heb. 7:2).

CONCLUSION: Is He the perpetual ruler—the King—of your life and family?

The Babe

Date preached:

SCRIPTURE: Luke 2:16

INTRODUCTION: Christmas affords a great opportunity to focus our attention on Christ, the Babe in the manger. The Bible presents Him as:

1. The Babe Lying in the Manger (Luke 2:16).
2. The Bright and Morning Star (Rev. 22:16).
3. The Bread of Life (John 6:35).
4. The Beginning and The End (Rev. 1:8).
5. The Bondservant (Phil. 2:7).
6. The Bridegroom (Matt. 25:1).
7. The Beloved Son (Matt. 3:17).
8. Our Beloved (Eph. 1:6).

CONCLUSION: "Infant holy, infant lowly, for His bed a cattle stall / Oxen lowing, little knowing, Christ the Babe is Lord of all."

DECEMBER 19, 2004

SUGGESTED SERMON
The Peace of Christmas *Date preached:*
By Kevin Riggs

Scripture: Micah 5:1–5

Introduction: Can there really be peace on earth? Since the beginning of recorded history the world has been entirely at peace only 8% of the time. In other words, in over 3,100 years of recorded history, only 286 have been warless. During that same period of time, 8,000 treatises have been broken as well. And what about personal peace? Peace at home? Peace at work? Financial peace? In the midst of national uncertainty and personal turmoil, can the hope of Christmas still deliver peace? The prophet Micah lived between 725–710 B.C. He came from the poorer class of Israel and was acutely aware of the injustices of the rich. Micah explained that because of the sins of Israel, God had sent the Assyrians as His arm of punishment. However, the people were not to lose hope. Following God's discipline would come a time of tremendous blessings, blessings connected with the coming of the Messiah. At some time in the future, he predicted, a woman will give birth to a child in Bethlehem. This child, proclaimed the prophet, "will be their peace" (v. 5). Isaiah likewise called Him the "Prince of Peace" (Is. 9:6). Some 700 years later, in a cave on the outskirts of Bethlehem, a virgin by the name of Mary gave birth to this promised Messiah who brought peace.

1. **Peace Through Forgiveness.** What type of peace does Jesus bring? Jerome, an early church father, had a dream one night in which Jesus visited him. In the dream, Jerome collected all his money and offered it to Jesus as a gift. Jesus said, "I don't want your money." So Jerome rounded up all his possessions and tried to give them to Jesus. Jesus responded, "I don't want your possessions." Jerome then turned to Christ and asked, "What can I give you? What do you want?" Jesus simply replied, "Give me your sins. That's what I came for; I came to take away your sins." Forgiveness of sins! That is the essence of the peace Christ gives. Without that forgiveness you and I cannot experience true peace. Once we accept Christ's forgiveness, then we can experience His peace. His peace is characterized by three truths.

2. **The Peace Christ Gives Is Above Circumstances.** Happiness is dependent on circumstances. Peace is the result of Christ living in my heart. Peace is the assurance I am safe in His hands, no matter what may be going on around me. Peace is trust in the midst of turmoil. The peace of Christ gives you the confidence to say, "And we know that in all things God works for the good of those who love Him, who have been called according to His purpose . . . For I am convinced that neither death nor life, neither angels nor demons, neither the present nor the future, nor any powers, neither height nor depth, nor anything else in all creation, will be able to separate us from the love of God that is in Christ Jesus our Lord" (Rom. 8:28, 38–39).

3. **The Peace Christ Gives Is Beyond Understanding.** How can a Christian lose his job and not worry? How can a believer look cancer in the face and not flinch? How can a Christian keep going after the loss of a loved one, or a child, or some other tragedy? How can a believer give his life up to the flames instead of denying Christ? It is because of the peace Jesus gives when you place your faith in Him. A peace that "transcends all understanding" (Phil. 4:7).

4. **The Peace Christ Gives Is Always Available.** Before Jesus left His disciples He promised after He was gone the Holy Spirit would come and be with them, comforting, teaching, encouraging them. In Acts 2, the Holy Spirit did come. Now His comforting, teaching, and encouraging is available to all who believe in Jesus. There is never a moment in which we are away

>>> *sermon continued on following page*

APPROPRIATE HYMNS AND SONGS

Emmanuel Has Come, Don Moen; © 1996 Integrity's Hosanna! Music, Admin. by Integrity Music, Inc.

Let There Be Peace On Earth, Sy Miller/Jill Jackson; © 1955. Renewed 1983 Jan-Lee Music.

As With Gladness Men Of Old, William Chatterton Dix/Conrad Kocher; Public Domain.

Go Tell It On the Mountain, John W. Work, Jr.; Public Domain.

Immanuel, Andy Park; © 1990 Mercy/Vineyard Publishing.

from Christ's peace. There is never a second when we need to worry, or need to be afraid. The peace that comes from Christ is available 24 hours a day, 7 days a week.

Conclusion: Are you in need of this type of peace? Is your life characterized by anything but peace? Today Jesus is waiting to give you His peace. He came into the world to be your peace. He is the Prince of Peace.

FOR THE BULLETIN

* December 19, 1498, is the birthday of Andreas Osiander, a German theologian who was ordained in the Catholic Church at about the time Luther was sparking the Reformation. Osiander joined the Lutheran movement in 1522, and developed a reputation for being strong-willed, opinionated, impulsive, contentious, and sometimes arrogant. He became the professor of theology at the newly founded Protestant University at Konigsberg. * December 19, 1808, is the birthday of Horatius Bonar, one of Scotland's most famous pulpiteers. He began writing hymns when hymns were unpopular in the Scottish church, which believed in singing only the Psalms. Bonar therefore wrote most of his hymns for children. Among them was "I Heard the Voice of Jesus Say," written for his Sunday school children in 1846. On the page containing the words, he doodled four faces and the head of a man wearing a hat.
* December 19, 1860, is the birthday of Rev. Frank Graeff, the Methodist minister who wrote "Does Jesus Care?" Frank was dubbed the "Sunshine Minister" because of his radiant personality. When a series of heartbreaks shattered his spirits, he found comfort in Joseph Scriven's old hymn, "What a Friend We Have in Jesus," and out of that experience he wrote, "Does Jesus Care?" * December 19, 1909, is the birthday of Dr. W. A. Criswell, inimitable preacher and longtime pastor of the First Baptist Church of Dallas, Texas.

STATS, STORIES AND MORE

This story has been told in a variety of ways, but this is the researched version that appeared in newspapers nationwide on December 25, 1994 from the Associated Press, dateline London: Eighty years ago, on the first Christmas Day of World War I, British and German troops put down their guns and celebrated peacefully together in the no-man's land between the trenches. The war, briefly, came to a halt. In some places, festivities began when German troops lit candles on Christmas trees on their parapets so the British sentries a few hundred yards away could see them. Elsewhere, the British acted first, starting bonfires and letting off rockets.

Pvt. Oswald Tilley of the London Rifle Brigade wrote to his parents: "Just you think that while you were eating your turkey, etc., I was out talking and shaking hands with the very men I had been trying to kill a few hours before!! It was astounding."

Both armies had received lots of comforts from home and felt generous and well-disposed toward their enemies in the first winter of the war, before the vast battles of attrition began in 1915, eventually claiming 10 million lives. All along the line that Christmas Day, soldiers found their enemies were much like them and began asking why they should be trying to kill each other. The generals were shocked. High Command diaries and statements express anxiety that if that sort of thing spread it could sap the troops' will to fight. The soldiers in khaki and gray sang carols to each other, exchanged gifts of tobacco, jam, sausage, chocolate, and liquor, traded names and addresses and played soccer between the shell holes and barbed wire. They even paid mutual trench visits. This day is called "the most famous truce in military history" by British television producer Malcolm Brown and researcher Shirley Seaton in their book "Christmas Truce," published in 1984.

WORSHIP HELPS

Call to Worship:
Behold, I bring you good tidings of great joy which will be to all people. For there is born to you this day in the city of David a Savior, who is Christ the Lord (Luke 2:10–11).

Advent Reading:
A Forgotten Christmas Carol
This sprightly, simple hymn comes from the German church, written by Paul Gerhardt and published in 1667. Gerhardt was a seventeenth century Lutheran pastor who spent most of his ministry serving in Berlin and who wrote a number of beautiful hymns. This carol is called *"Come, and Christ the Lord Be Praising."*

Come, and Christ the Lord be praising,
Heart and mind to Him be raising,
Celebrate His love amazing,
Worthy folk of Christendom.

See what God for us provideth,
Life that in His Son abideth,
And our weary steps He guideth
From earth's woe to heav'nly joy.

Jacob's star His advent maketh,
Soothes the longing heart that acheth,
And the serpent's head He breaketh,
Scattering the powers of hell.

Beauteous Infant in the manger,
O befriend us! beyond danger
Bring us where is turned God's anger
Where with angel hosts we'll praise.

Additional Sermons and Lesson Ideas

The Journey of a Lifetime
By Peter Grainger

Date preached:

SCRIPTURE: Matthew 2:1–18

INTRODUCTION: Why does Matthew include the story of the Magi in his Gospel? It tells us four things about the birth of Jesus.

1. Jew and Gentile. The first to hear of the Babe were Jewish shepherds, but the Good News wasn't just for the Jews. Those Magi were the first of many to come from the ends of the earth to worship the Lord Jesus.
2. Star and Scripture. The star pointed the Magi in the right direction, but they had to go to the Scriptures to get specific information about finding the Messiah.
3. Baby and King. For many, the Christmas story is limited to a baby in a manger, but babies don't stay in mangers forever. They grow up, and it is what they grow up to become that is important.
4. Joy and Sorrow. The Magi were filled with joy, but Bethlehem was soon filled with sorrow as Herod sought to kill the innocents. Similarly, this baby grew up to be a man of sorrows and acquainted with grief, yet the Giver of joy.

CONCLUSION: The Magi returned home, changed forever. This Christmas could make for you an end to all your searching, and the beginning of a new life, eternal life, in Christ.

Why Did He Come?
By Timothy Beougher

Date preached:

SCRIPTURE: Hebrews 2:14–18

INTRODUCTION: Jesus did not enter the world just to be here; He had a mission to fulfill.

1. He came to deliver us from the fear of death (vv. 14–15). George Bernard Shaw said, "The ultimate statistic is this: 1 out of 1 dies." Jesus came to deliver us from death and its terrors.
2. He came to deliver us from the fury of judgment (vv. 16–17). He has made propitiation for our sins.
3. He came to deliver us from the force of temptation (v. 18). This remarkable verse tells us that Christ identifies with our temptation; He can overcome.

CONCLUSION: He has come for us; now He invites us to come to Him.

DECEMBER 26, 2004

SUGGESTED SERMON

Delayed Re-entry: Why Christ Hasn't Returned Yet

Date preached:

Scripture: 2 Peter 3:1–12a, especially verse 10: But the day of the Lord will come as a thief in the night.

Introduction (vv. 1–2): Many of us undoubtedly have mixed emotions now that Christmas is over. Some of us are exhausted. Some are disappointed with the gifts we gave or received. Some of us are worried about having spent too much money during the holiday, and we dread seeing our credit card bills coming in the mail. Some of us have a happy glow due to being with family and friends, and for many of us, this season has been a wonderful experience of revisiting the wonder of the Savior's birth. On this day after Christmas, may I suggest that the most logical thing for us to do is shift our focus from His First Coming to His Second Coming. He showed up the first time, in the fullness of time and according to prophecy. He will do so again. In 2 Peter 3:1–12, Peter deals with this subject, discussing in some detail the return of Christ to this planet, warning us of a skeptical question and providing a Scriptural answer. Let's end the year with this forward-looking passage.

1. **A Skeptical Question (vv. 3–7).** Here Peter says that in the last days, scoffers are going to challenge Christians with an awkward question. The Greek word for "last" days here is *eskatos* from which we get our English term "eschatology." This is a phrase that occurs five times in the New Testament, and it seems to refer to this present age—to the age of grace, the age of the church, the years between the Day of Pentecost when the church was born, and the coming of Christ. Now, Peter says that we can be sure of one thing about these last days—that there will be skeptics who belittle and ridicule and seek to marginalize the teachings of God's Word. And they will be asking, "Where is His coming? Why hasn't Christ come back? Why haven't your predictions come true? Where is He?"

Peter goes on to explain in verse 5 that these scoffers are deliberately rejecting the biblical warnings of the flood of Noah. During those days, people forgot about God. They started thinking about immoral sex all day long and all night long, and their society became very sensual and degraded and violent. If they had had TVs in that day, they would probably have invented some of the programming we're getting on our televisions today. There was dishonesty and thievery and an overall lack of the fear of God in their culture. For many years, while he was building the ark, Noah preached a message of warning, but nobody listened; nobody responded. Not one. Then the day came, Noah and his family entered the ark, and God closed the door. The game was up. Time was gone. The rain began to fall, the floods came, the ark rose, the people scratched at the door trying to get in, but it was too late. They had passed the redemption point.

Right now is a season of preaching and pleading and warning. Be born again! Get right with God! Come to Christ! Change the way you're living! Let Jesus Christ be your Savior and Lord! But one day soon, any day now, the door will be closed and judgment will fall. Peter tells us that right up until the moment of His return, scoffers will be asking, "Where is this coming He predicted?"

2. **A Scriptural Answer (vv. 8–9).** Here Peter provides two answers to the question: "Why hasn't Christ come back?"
   A. **God does not calculate time the way we do (v. 8).** We view time from the context of time, but God views time from the context of eternity and from that context there isn't much difference between a day and

>>> *sermon continued on following page*

APPROPRIATE HYMNS AND SONGS

O Come All Ye Faithful, John Frances Wade/Frederick Oakeley; Public Domain.

Tell Me the Story of Jesus, Fanny J. Crosby/John R. Sweney; Public Domain.

O Lord the Clouds Are Gathering, Graham Kendrick; © 1987 Make Way Music, Admin. by Music Services.

Prepare Ye the Way, Dominic Reichel/Bruce McGrail; © 1972 Scripture in Song, Admin. by Integrity Music, Inc.

All Hail King Jesus, Dave Moody; © 1981 Dayspring Music, Inc., Admin. by Word Music Group, Inc.

a millennium. To God, the 2,000 years of Christian history—this age of grace—has only lasted a couple of days.

B. **He is giving you and me time to repent (v. 9).** God is waiting for you to be saved. He is delaying His coming in order to give some people a little more time to come to Jesus.

Conclusion: This passage in 2 Peter 3 is remarkable, because it tells us that Jesus Christ is delaying His return to this earth just a little longer in order to give you a few extra moments to repent of your sins and confess Him as Lord. But verse 10 warns that the delay is only temporary, and that at any moment Christ may suddenly return like a thief in the night. Since all of this is soon to take place and since this planet will soon face the fires of judgment, what sort of person ought you to be?

FOR THE BULLETIN

✹ London's Westminster Abby was dedicated on this day in 1065. ✹ The Pilgrims disembarked at Plymouth on this day in 1620. ✹ December 26, 1822, is the birthday of Richard Weymouth, translator of *The New Testament in Modern English*. ✹ In 1899, evangelist D. L. Moody grew ill in Kansas City, canceled his engagements, and returned home to Northfield, Massachusetts. He lugged himself up to his bedroom to dress for dinner, but felt so exhausted that he took to bed. On December 22, he suddenly opened his eyes and spoke clearly: "Earth recedes! Heaven opens before me." His son, sitting near him, suggested he was dreaming. "This is no dream, Will," Moody replied. "It is beautiful! It is like a trance! If this is death, it is sweet! God is calling me, and I must go!" The family gathered around. "This is my triumph!" said Moody. "This is my coronation day! I have been looking forward to it for years." His face suddenly lit up. "Dwight! Irene! I see the children's faces!" His funeral was conducted at 10 A.M. on December 26, 1899, by C. I. Scofield, and he was laid to rest atop Northfield's Mount Hermon. ✹ Jozsef Mindszenty, a Hungarian Roman Catholic bishop, suffered imprisonment for his faith during the Nazi era and was later persecuted by the Communists. When he realized he was in again in danger of imprisonment, he wrote his mother, saying, "If . . . you should read that I have confessed or resigned . . . in advance, I declare all such actions null and void." On December 26, 1948, he was arrested in Budapest by Communist officials. He was later convicted of treason and imprisoned for 23 years.

STATS, STORIES AND MORE

There was a Marine in World War II named James (Ted) Colson. He had a Baptist background, but he wasn't a genuine Christian. He spent all his time drinking and partying and running from God. But he had a New Testament that had been given to him by the Gideons before he sailed out of San Diego on the *U.S.S. President Adams*, and he knew his Bible enough to know one verse, a verse from Romans chapter 10: "If you confess with your mouth Jesus as Lord and believe in your heart that God has raised Him from the day, you will be saved."

At Guadalcanal, Ted Colson found himself under intense bombardment. Japanese were shelling around the clock. Colson had dug a foxhole under a tall tree, and one day during a particularly intense period of naval shelling, he and his buddy, Kenneth Pauls, jumped into the foxhole. Just then, a large naval shell whistled out of the air and landed just a few feet in front of the foxhole. Colson had seen the craters made by those shells, and he knew that if it went off, he'd be blown to bits and that he would go to hell.

Instantly, he yelled over to his buddy, Kenneth Pauls. He shouted, "Kenny, I want you to know I'm confessing Jesus as my Savior!"

"So am I, Ted," was the reply.

Ted Colson survived World War II, but he never got over that moment when he confessed Jesus Christ as his Lord. He returned home and spent the rest of his life loving and serving Jesus Christ.

WORSHIP HELPS

Call to Worship:
Unto You I lift up my eyes, O You who dwell in the heavens. Behold, as the eyes of servants look to the hand of their masters, as the eyes of a maid to the hand of her mistress, so our eyes look to the Lord our God until He has mercy on us (Ps. 123:1–2).

Welcome:
I've noticed something becoming more frequent on our highways: truckers who advertise for churches. I've often been delighted to drive by a truck on the interstate with a large decal that says "Attend the church of your choice!" Though they're confined to one small space—the cabs of their trucks—for long periods of time, they've found ways of inviting others to church all over the country! If you're a guest today, thank you for making this the church of your choice.

Scripture Reading:
But concerning the times and the seasons, brethren . . . the day of the Lord so comes as a thief in the night. For when they say, "Peace and safety!" then sudden destruction comes upon them, as labor pains upon a pregnant woman. And they shall not escape. But you, brethren, are not in darkness, so that this Day should overtake you as a thief . . . But let us . . . be sober, putting on the breastplate of faith and love, and as a helmet the hope of salvation. For God did not appoint us to wrath, but to obtain salvation through our Lord Jesus Christ, who died for us, that whether we wake or sleep, we should live together with Him. Therefore comfort each other and edify one another, just as you also are doing (1 Thess. 5:1–11).

Additional Sermons and Lesson Ideas

What the Death of Christ Has Secured Us
By Evan H. Hopkins

Date preached:

SCRIPTURE: Various

INTRODUCTION: For years, people have trusted "safety deposit boxes" at their local banks to store their most treasured items; there they are most secure. Our spiritual treasures are secured by Jesus Christ Himself:

1. A New Position (Rom. 3:23–24).
   A. Of Acceptance before God (Rom. 8:15).
   B. Of Victory over Satan (Col. 1:13).
   C. Of Delivery from the World (Gal. 1:4).
2. A New Emancipation (Rom. 6:5–7).
3. A New Character (2 Cor. 5:17).

CONCLUSION: Have confidence in your relationship with God, which Jesus has secured for eternity!

Fear or Faith
By Joshua Rowe

Date preached:

SCRIPTURE: Daniel 2

INTRODUCTION: Imagine your boss giving you the most difficult assignment of your career with this ultimatum: "Have this finished by the end of the day or I'll kill you—literally." If you can imagine this, you've just put yourself in Daniel's shoes.

1. The Fury of the King (vv. 1–12). King Nebuchadnezzar had a vivid, recurring dream. He also had magicians, sorcerers, astrologers, and other "wise men" on his payroll, so he expected the interpretation; he sentenced death to all of them should they be unable!
2. The Fear of the "Wise" (vv. 8, 10–11). These "spiritual" men of Babylon supposedly had connections with the gods, but fearfully stalled for time and eventually admitted their inability. Their gods' "dwelling (was) not in the flesh" (v. 11; see also Ex. 33:11).
3. The Faith of Daniel (vv. 14–19). Daniel wasted no time; he organized a prayer meeting. As a result, the dream was revealed to him!
4. He Gave God the Glory (vv. 27–30). Daniel didn't dare take credit for God's revelation.
5. He Shared the Salvation (vv. 24, 48–49). Daniel asked that the "wise men of Babylon" not be killed, and that his friends (who prayed with him) be exalted with him.

CONCLUSION: Despite the fury and the fear of this world, the Lord reigns, who reveals Himself to His people of faith. Won't you give God the glory, and share His salvation?

WEDDING SERMON

A Traditional Wedding

Dearly beloved, we are gathered together here in the sight of God and in the face of this congregation to join together this man and this woman in holy matrimony; which is an honorable estate, instituted of God in the time of human innocence, signifying unto us the mystical union that is between Christ and His church; which holy estate Christ adorned and beautified with His presence and first miracle in Cana of Galilee; and is commended in the Book of Hebrews to be honorable among all: and therefore is not by any to be entered lightly or casually; but reverently, discreetly, prayerfully, and in the fear of God, duly considering the causes for which matrimony was ordained. It was ordained to provide companionship between two people who need each other, love each other, and seek to glorify God by the uniting of their lives for His glory, even as God said to Adam, "It is not good for man to be alone."
It was ordained, too, for the sake of children, to give them a loving home in which they may be raised in the nurture and admission of the Lord.

Third, marriage was ordained for a remedy against sin and as a safeguard against immorality.

Fourth, it was ordained for the benefit of human society; our communities are made up of homes, and the family unit is the basic building block of a healthy society. A strong nation needs sturdy homes and healthy marriages.

Therefore, God has ordained the ordinance of marriage, and into this holy estate these two persons present come now to be joined.

_____, will you have this woman as your wedded wife, to live together after God's ordinance in the holy estate of matrimony? Will you love her, comfort her, honor and keep her in sickness and in health; and, forsaking all others, keep only unto her so long as you both shall live?

The groom answers: I will.

_____, will you have this man as your wedded husband, to live together after God's ordinance in the holy estate of matrimony? Will you love him, comfort him, honor, and keep him in sickness and in health; and, forsaking all others, keep only unto him so long as you both shall live?

The bride answers: I will.

(To the groom): Will you then repeat after me: I _____ take you, _____, to be my wedded wife, to have and to hold from this day forward, for better for worse, for richer for poorer, in sickness and in health, to love and to cherish, as long as we both shall live.

(To the bride): Will you then repeat after me: I _____ take you, _____, to be my wedded husband, to have and to hold from this day forward, for better for worse, for richer for poorer, in sickness and in health, to love and to cherish, as long as we both shall live.

Have you rings as a sign and seal of this marriage? _____, will you place the ring on your bride's finger and repeat after me: With this ring I thee wed, in the name of the Father, and of the Son, and of the Holy Ghost. Amen.

_____, will you place the ring on your groom's finger and repeat after me: With this ring I thee wed, in the name of the Father, and of the Son, and of the Holy Ghost. Amen.

Let us pray. O Eternal God, Creator and Preserver of all mankind, Giver of all spiritual grace, the Author of everlasting life; Send thy blessing upon these Your servants, this man and this woman, whom we bless in Your Name; that this couple may surely perform and keep the vow and covenant between them made, whereof this Ring given and received is a token and pledge, and may ever remain in perfect love and peace together, and live according to Your laws and in Your love; through Jesus Christ our Lord. Amen.

_____, you may now kiss your bride.

Ladies and gentlemen, it is my pleasure to present to you Mr. and Mrs.

_____ _____

WEDDING SERMON

A Wedding from 1 John 1:7

Dear friends: We are gathered here in the presence of God and these witnesses to unite this couple in holy marriage. _____ and _____, the two of you are embarking upon an adventurous voyage across the restless sea of the rest of life. You're standing now at the helm of a home about to be launched. The water here in the bay is calm, but soon, within days and months, the winds will blow harder and the waves will curl higher. As you plow the deep, you'll pass over the watery graves of millions of sunken ships of marriages that were overcome by the billows, smashed by the rocks, and confused in the storms by defective compasses.

Today (Tonight) I'm going to give you a compass that works. It has two points, and if both of you keep both of these points aligned, you'll surely and safely arrive at the heavenly harbor together at the end of your earthly voyage. The two compass points are two simple instructions based on a verse of Scripture 1 John 1:7.

The first needle of direction is this: Walk with the Master. The second compass point is: Work on the marriage. One of these without the other is as useless to your union as one of you without the other. But both of them aligned in both your lives will provide accurate navigation even in the wildest typhoons. Walk with the Master and Work on the marriage.

The reason I can give you this golden compass with such confidence is because, based as it is upon 1 John 1:7, it comes straight from the Lord Himself who said in that verse: If we walk in the light of His presence, we will have fellowship with one another and the blood of Jesus Christ cleanses us from all sin.

Now if this ship that we are launching today (tonight) on the sea of matrimony is the fellowSHIP of 1 John 1:7, Jesus Christ will be the Captain, and the relationSHIP will be a godly partnerSHIP, not a godless battleSHIP.

It will sail on, when the soft winds of pleasant days blow across it.

It will sail on, when the whirlpools of financial hardship swirl around it.

It will sail on, when the bright clouds of parental responsibility drift above it.

It will sail on, when the billows of misunderstanding, sickness, tragedy, and death crash against it.

Because it will be steered by Jesus Christ, blown on its way by the winds of the Holy Spirit, steadied by the anchors of daily Bible study, prayer, and regular church attendance. And it will be loaded with the priceless cargo of that biblical sort of love that does so much, remains so constant, forgives so frequently, and acts so sensibly.

The Bible says, "Let your hearts be knit together in love," but there will be times when it will seem easier to quit than to knit—but it's not. Just keep on knitting your hearts together, committing yourselves to Christ, submitting yourselves to each other, omitting the black curse of bad habits from your home, and emitting the fruit of the Spirit in the context of a godly family life.

This is God's plan for you—His fellowship of love and excitement for all those who walk with the Master and work on the marriage.

If you, then _____ and _____ have freely and deliberately chosen each other as partners in this holy estate, and know of no just cause why you should not be so united, in token thereof, will you please join your right hands.

_____, will you repeat after me: *In taking the woman I hold by the right hand to be my wedded wife, before God and these witnesses I promise to love her, to honor her and cherish her in this relationship, and leaving all others, cleave only unto her, in all things a true and faithful husband, as long as we both shall live.*

_____, will you repeat after me: *In taking the man I hold by the right hand to be my wedded husband, before God and these witnesses I promise to love him, to honor him and cherish him in this relationship, and leaving all others, cleave only unto him, in all things a true and faithful wife, as long as we both shall live.*

Then you are each given to the other for richer or poorer, for better or worse, in sickness and in health, till death shall you part.

The wedding ring is a fitting symbol of these vows in two ways. The shape of the ring reminds us that marriage is a never-ending relationship which grows sweeter through the ever-encircling years. And the gold gives us a lesson about the glory and the purity of the home.

_____, will you please place the ring on _____ finger and repeat after me: *With this ring I thee wed, with love and joy, through the grace of the Father, and of the Son, and of the Holy Spirit.*

_____, will you please place the ring on _____ finger and repeat after me: *With this ring I thee wed, with love and joy, through the grace of the Father, and of the Son, and of the Holy Spirit.*

Now, upon your mutual promise, made in the presence of God and these witnesses, and according to the authority invested in me as a minister of the gospel of Jesus Christ, I pronounce you husband and wife.

WEDDING SERMON

A Wedding Ceremony about Love

Dear friends, we have assembled in this place with joyful thanksgiving as witnesses for the uniting of these two persons into one wedded union. _____ and _____ have come, pledging their love for one another because of their prayerful and steadfast conviction that the Lord of Love has led them all their lives towards this divinely appointed moment.

In my remarks today, I want to say a word about the glue of marriage—love—and then quote some wonderful Scriptures on this topic. Contrary to popular opinion, love is not having a trouble-free relationship. Love is caring deeply about the needs of the other person even if and when there is stress and strain in the relationship. Love means putting up with the faults, flaws, and failures of others. Love grows and glows and shows, ever richer, ever deeper, a friendship indivisible, a companionship eternal. This kind of love isn't of the earth, but from above. This kind of love flows into imperfect hearts and heals imperfect circumstances because it comes from an infinite and infallible God who loved us. For thus says the Scriptures:

Behold what manner of love the Father has bestowed on us, that we should be called children of God![i] The Lord . . . appeared of old . . . saying: "Yes, I have loved you with an everlasting love; Therefore with lovingkindness I have drawn you."[ii] For God so loved . . . [iii] God is love . . . [iv] Jesus loved . . . [v] See how He loved . . . [vi] He didn't choose you and pour out His love upon you because you were a larger nation than any other, for you were the smallest of all! It was just because He loves you, and because He kept His promise to your ancestors. That is why He brought you out of slavery in Egypt with such amazing power and mighty miracles.[vii]

And when the kindness and the love to men of God our Savior did appear . . . He did save us, through a bathing of regeneration, and a renewing of the Holy Spirit, which He poured upon us richly, through Jesus Christ our Savior.[viii]

Understand, therefore, that the Lord your God is the faithful God who for a thousand generations keeps His promises and constantly loves those who love Him and who obey His commands.[ix] Choose to love the Lord your God and to obey Him and to cling to Him, for He is your life and the length of your days.[x]

Dear friends, since God so loved us, we also ought to love one another.[xi] A new commandment I give to you, that you love one another; as I have loved you, that you also love one another. By this all will know that you are My disciples, if you have love for one another.[xii]

Husbands, love your wives, just as Christ also loved the church and gave Himself for her.[xiii] Husbands ought to love their own wives as their own bodies . . . [xiv] Go, show your love to your wife.[xv] Let each one of you in particular so love his own wife as himself, and let the wife see that she respects her husband.[xvi]

Bid the older women likewise to be reverent in behavior . . . ; they are to teach what is good, and so train the young women to love their husbands.[xvii]

Better a meal of vegetables where there is love than a fattened calf with hatred.[xviii] Better a little with righteousness than much gain with injustice.[xix] Better a little with the fear of the Lord than great wealth with turmoil.[xx] Better a dry crust with peace and quiet than a house full of feasting, with strife.[xxi] Hatred stirs up dissension, but love covers over all wrongs.[xxii]

Love never gives up. Love cares more for others than for self. Love doesn't want what it doesn't have. Love doesn't strut, doesn't have a swelled head, doesn't force itself on others, isn't always "me first," doesn't fly off the handle, doesn't keep score of the sins of others, doesn't revel when others grovel, takes pleasure in the flowering of truth,

puts up with anything, trusts God always, always looks for the best, never looks back, but keeps going to the end. Love never dies.[xxiii]

And hope does not disappoint us, because God's love has been poured into our hearts through the Holy Spirit that has been given to us.[xxiv]

And now abide faith, hope, love, these three; but the greatest of these is love.[xxv]

If you then _____ and _____ are willing to let the Lord Jesus Christ pour His love into your hearts by His Holy Spirit, making you one, then join your hands and hearts for the pledging of your marriage vows.
_____, do you take this woman as your wedded wife, to live together after God's ordinance in the holy estate of matrimony, to love her, comfort her, honor, and keep her in sickness and in health; and, forsaking all others, keep yourself only unto her, so long as you both shall live?
The Man shall answer, I Do.

_____, do you take this man as your wedded husband, to live together after God's ordinance in the holy estate of matrimony, to love him, comfort him, honor, and keep him in sickness and in health; and, forsaking all others, keep yourself only unto him, so long as your both shall live?
The Woman shall answer, I Do.
Then you are each given to the other, to have and to hold from this day forward, for better for worse, for richer for poorer, in sickness and in health, to love and to cherish, as long as you both shall live on earth, according to God's holy ordinance.

---

i	1 John 3:1
ii	Jeremiah 31:3
iii	John 3:16
iv	1 John 4:8
v	John 11:5
vi	John 11:36
vii	Deuteronomy 7:7–8 (The Living Bible)
viii	Titus 3:4–6 (Young's Literal Translation)
ix	Deuteronomy 7:9 (The Living Bible)
x	Deuteronomy 30:20 (The Living Bible)
xi	1 John 4:11 (New International Version)
xii	John 13:34–35
xiii	Ephesians 5:25
xiv	Ephesians 5:28
xv	Hosea 3:1 (New International Version)
xvi	Ephesians 5:33
xvii	Titus 2:3–4 (Revised Standard Version)
xviii	Proverbs 15:17 (New International Version)
xix	Proverbs 16:8 (New International Version)
xx	Proverbs 15:16 (New International Version)
xxi	Proverbs 17:1 (New International Version)
xxii	Proverbs 10:12 (New International Version)
xxiii	1 Corinthians 13:4–8 (The Message)
xxiv	Romans 5:5 (New Revised Standard Version)
xxv	1 Corinthians 13:13

FUNERAL MESSAGE

How God Comforts Us

Today we have gathered in loving memory of _____
(Personal comments)

Scripture: Isaiah 51:12: I, even I, am He who comforts you.

Introduction: Today is a day of mourning, of sorrow and separation, of tears. But it is also a day when our hearts are in need of, and open to, a special ministry the dear Lord provides—the ministry of comfort. The word *comfort* occurs 112 times in the Bible, and Scriptures containing that precious word are among our very favorites. Let me quote some of them for you:

As one whom his mother comforts, so I will comfort you; and you shall be comforted.
Blessed are those who mourn, for they shall be comforted.
For whatever things were written before were written for our learning, that we through the patience and comfort of the Scriptures might have hope.
Be of good comfort.
Yea, though I walk through the valley of the shadow of death, I will fear no evil: for thou art with me; thy rod and thy staff they comfort me . . .
Blessed be the God and Father of our Lord Jesus Christ, the Father of mercies and God of all comfort, who comforts us in all our tribulation, that we may be able to comfort those who are in any trouble, with the comfort with which we ourselves are comforted by God.
May our Lord Jesus Christ Himself, and our God and Father, who has loved us and given us everlasting consolation and good hope by grace, comfort your hearts and establish you in every good word and work.
(Is. 66:13; Matt. 5:4; Rom. 15:4; 2 Cor. 13:11; Ps. 23:4; Ps. 94:19; 2 Cor. 1:3–4; 2 Thess. 2:16–17)

How does God convey His comfort into our hearts during times like these? What are His means and methods?

1. **The Consolation of Friends.** When Lazarus died, the friends of that little Judean family gathered—Jesus among them—to comfort Mary and Martha (see John 11). When we lose someone near and dear to us, we're left with a deep sense of loneliness. There is a vacant spot in our hearts of immense size. More than ever, we need the prayers, the love, and the presence of our dearest friends to remind us that, despite our loss, we are not entirely alone. Our friends bring food, they answer the phone, they help make arrangements, they sit with us, they weep with us, they give their hugs, and the silent support of their loyal presence. But sometimes the Lord also gives them a word for us. In 1 Thessalonians 4, Paul told us to comfort one another in times of grief with the sure hope of the coming resurrection.

2. **The Confirmation of Scripture.** We also have an even richer source of comfort, the words of the Lord Himself as the Holy Spirit whispers them to our hearts. In her wonderful book, *To Live Again,* Catherine Marshall tells of her struggle with overwhelming grief following the unexpected death of her husband, Peter. One day she opened her Bible to Hebrews 12, and there were just the words she needed to begin the healing process in her life. When the great Reformer Martin Luther died, his wife, Katherine von Bora, found comfort in Psalm 31. There was a dear woman in Middle Tennessee named Agnes Frazier who began each day for fifty years by having devotions with her husband, Emmett. The morning after his passing, Agnes didn't think she could sit at the breakfast table and read the Bible. But she did, and the text she came to was this verse: *I, the Lord, will be a husband to you* (Is. 54:5). She smiled and said, "Thank you, Lord." We must learn to open our Bibles and claim the word God has for each of us in our time of need.

3. **The Contemplation of Heaven.** In his book on heaven, evangelist D. L. Moody quotes an acquaintance as saying: "When I was a boy, I thought of heaven as a great, shining city, with vast walls and domes and spires, and with nobody in it except white-robed angels, who were strangers to me. By and by my little brother died; and I thought of a great city with walls and domes and spires, and one little fellow that I was acquainted with. He was the only one I knew at that time. Then another brother died; and there were two that I knew. Then my acquaintances began to die; and the flock continually grew. But it was not till I had sent one of my little children to

his Heavenly Parent—God—that I began to think I had a little in myself. A second went, a third went; a fourth went; and by that time I had so many acquaintances in heaven, that I did not see any more walls and domes and spires. I began to think of the residents of the celestial city as my friends. And now so many of my acquaintances have gone there, that it sometimes seems to me that I know more people in heaven than I do on earth." Mrs. A. S. Bridgewater wrote:

> *We read of a place that's called Heaven,*
> *It's made for the pure and the free;*
> *These truths in God's Word He hath given,*
> *How beautiful Heaven must be.*
> *In Heaven no drooping nor pining,*
> *No wishing for elsewhere to be;*
> *God's light is forever there shining,*
> *How beautiful Heaven must be.*
> *Pure waters of life there are flowing,*
> *And all who will drink may be free;*
> *Rare jewels of splendor are glowing,*
> *How beautiful Heaven must be.*
> *The angels so sweetly are singing,*
> *Up there by the beautiful sea;*
> *Sweet chords from their gold harps are ringing,*
> *How beautiful Heaven must be.*

FUNERAL MESSAGE
What to Avoid at Funerals

Today we have gathered here in memory of _____
(Personal comments)

Scripture: 1 Thessalonians 4:13

Introduction: This verse is God's Word for us today, for we could find no better verse to tell us how to think and feel at funerals than this one. This verse gives us the divine protocol for dealing with death. What does God have to say about our duty and decorum at funerals? He gives us two prohibitions, two things to avoid today, two gentle warnings.

1. **Do Not Be Uninformed As To Your Hope.** *I do not want you to be ignorant, brethren, concerning those who have fallen asleep.* The word "brethren" indicates Paul was speaking to Christians who were alive, talking about Christians who have passed away. He told the Thessalonians not to be ignorant about what has happened to these departed loved ones. The word "ignorant" is not used here in the sense of stupid or senseless, but in the sense of being uninformed. God is reminding us that the Bible is full of information about those who have fallen asleep, and we need to keep that information in mind during times of sorrow. After all, the word "everlasting" occurs one hundred times in the Bible. The word "eternal" occurs fifty times. The word "hope," 142 times. The word "heaven," 539 times.

Once a group of people, the Sadducees (who didn't believe in the resurrection of the dead or in eternal life), challenged Jesus on those issues, He told them that they were in error because they did not know the Scriptures nor the power of God. He asserted to them, "God is not the God of the dead, but of the living" (Matt. 22:32; See also John 4:14; 5:24; 6:40). All four of the Gospels end with a thrilling description of the resurrection of Jesus Christ, and the Bible clearly teaches that in His Resurrection we have the guarantee, the pattern, and the power for our own Resurrection when He comes back. Jesus said, "Because I live you will live also" (John 14:19;

See also 1 Cor. 15:20–22; Rom. 8:11; and Ps. 23:6). So when the Lord tells us He would not have us ignorant regarding those who have fallen asleep, He is telling us to get our Bibles, search out all that the Lord has for us, and claim it by faith. When most of us go on a vacation or visit a distant city, we read all we can about the place we're going. The anticipation is part of the joy of the trip. How much more should we read about and anticipate heaven.

2. **Do Not Be Uncontrolled As To Your Sorrow.** . . . *lest you sorrow as others who have no hope.* Paul is not saying we shouldn't grieve, of course. Jesus wept by the tomb of Lazarus. He groaned in Himself, and His grief was so visible that those around exclaimed, "See how He loved him!" (John 11:36). When Stephen was slain for his faith in Acts 8, we read that "devout men carried Stephen to his burial, and made great lamentation over him" (Acts 8:2). But 1 Thessalonians 4:13 says that we should not sorrow *as others who have no hope.* Our grief is different. It is bearable. It is measured. It gives way to joy. One of the greatest preachers in Christian history, John Chrysostom, once preached a sermon entitled, "Excessive Grief at the Death of Friends." He told his listeners that when their loved one dies, they should not think of him or her as a lifeless body with closed eyes and speechless lips, but think of the person as having gone on to be with the Lord, in glory unspeakable and amazing. "Direct your thoughts," said Chrysostom, "from the present sight to the future hope."

Conclusion: Winston Churchill wanted his funeral done his way, and at the end of it he had planned a little surprise. After the stately hymns and majestic service at St. Paul's Cathedral, after the benediction, he had arranged for a bugler high in the dome of St. Paul's Cathedral on one side to play "Taps," then, after a pause, a bugler on the other side played "Reveille," the signal of a new day beginning. Churchill's message was that it may be "Good night" here, but it is "Good morning" up there! Today, there are tears in our eyes, but joy in our heart. This service is both a memorial and a celebration. We don't want to be unaware as to our hope, nor unrestrained in our grief. Jesus Christ said, "I am the resurrection and the life. He who believes in Me, though he may die, he shall live" (John 11:25).

FUNERAL MESSAGE

Death Swallowed Up in Victory

Today we have gathered here in loving memory of _____
(Personal comments)

Introduction: The Bible is rich in comfort, and its many books and chapters contain beautiful portions that soothe and strengthen our hearts. Some of them are familiar to many of us. (see John 14:1–6; Ps. 23; 1 Thess. 4 and 1 Cor. 15). But today I want to read a lesser-known passage, one placed in the Scriptures just for times like these. It's found in the Book of Isaiah, written about seven hundred years before Christ. One of Isaiah's shortest chapters is chapter 25, containing an even dozen verses; and this is the passage I want to lay upon your hearts and minds today.

Scripture: Isaiah 25:8 (with 1 Cor. 15:54–57)
He will swallow up death forever.

Verse 1: Isaiah 25 begins with praise and thanksgiving. There's never a time when we cannot praise the Lord, never a time when we cannot thank Him. It may be that all seems dark and doubtful for you today. This most precious companion is gone, and we know that our earthly lives will never be the same. But nothing has taken God by surprise. He marks our days and our years, and He knows what He is doing. It is healthy and healing for us to lift our tear-stained eyes to Him in praise and thanksgiving. Worship helps restore our perspective, for it refocuses our attention on what is invisible, eternal, durable, and unchanging.

Verse 4: In the next several verses, Isaiah lists some of the reasons we should praise and thank our God. Verse 4 says that even if troubles should strike us like a rainstorm against the walls of our houses, we still have safety and strength within. Our lives are hidden with Christ in God, and in that place I find a refuge from the storm.

Verse 6: Here we come to the most wonderful part of the chapter. Isaiah, more than any of the other prophets, spoke of Christ. He's the Old Testament Gospel writer, and the Book of Isaiah is full of the Lord Jesus. In verse 6, Isaiah talks about Mount Calvary as though he had seen that old rugged cross on a hill far away; and He *did* see Mount Calvary with the eyes of faith and through the telescope of prophecy. On this mountain, God is going to meet the needs of His people, He is going to feed them Living Bread, and He is going to spread a table before them in the presence of their enemies. On a particular mountain, Isaiah said, God is going to meet the needs of the people of this planet.

Verses 7–8: On this same mountain God is going to destroy something, "the covering cast over all people, and the veil that is spread over all nations. He will swallow up death forever . . . ." The New International Version puts it: "On this mountain He will destroy the shroud that enfolds all peoples; the sheet that covers all nations. He will swallow up death forever." Isn't that a vivid picture? Just visualize this planet, suspended in space, spinning on its axis, yet covered in a shroud and existing in darkness. The pall of death covers every human being who lives, who has ever lived, and who will ever live. But Isaiah predicted a coming day when, on a particular mountain, the Eternal, Almighty God would jerk away the shroud, remove the pall of sorrow, and swallow up death forever.

Verse 9: This is our God. On the cross, He swallowed death in victory. (see 1 Cor. 15:54–57).

Conclusion: Today we're aware of shrouds and death. But what Jesus did on Calvary when He died on the Cross and rose from the tomb changed everything for us. He prepared a feast of abundant, eternal life for us, and He destroyed the shroud that covers this planet, swallowing up death forever. Despite our tears, we wait today on the Lord, and we will be glad and rejoice in His salvation.

> *Thine is the glory, risen conqu'ring Son,*
> *Endless is the vict'ry, Thou o'er death hast won.*

Special Services Registry

The forms on the following pages are designed to be duplicated and used repeatedly as neeeded. Most copy machines will allow you to enlarge them to fill a full page if desired. Since they also are included in the CD-ROM in the back of the book, you may use that digital file to customize the forms to fit your specific needs.

Sermons Preached

Date	Text	Title/Subject

Sermons Preached

Date	Text	Title/Subject

Marriages Log

Date	Bride	Groom

Funerals Log

Date	Name of Deceased	Scripture Used

Baptisms / Confirmations

Date | Name | Notes

Baby Dedication Registration

Infant's Name: _____

Significance of Given Names: _____

Date of Birth: _____

Parents' Names: _____

_____

Siblings: _____

_____

_____

_____

Maternal Grandparents: _____

Paternal Grandparents: _____

Life Verse:_____

Date of Dedication: _____

Wedding Registration

Date of Wedding: _____

Location of Wedding: _____

Bride: _____

    Religious Affiliation: _____

    Bride's Parents: _____

Groom: _____

    Religious Affiliation: _____

    Groom's Parents: _____

Ceremony to be Planned by Minister: _____ by Couple: _____

Other Minister(s) Assisting: _____

Maid/Matron of Honor: _____

Best Man: _____

Wedding Planner: _____

Date of Rehearsal: _____

Reception Open to All Wedding Guests: _____ By Invitation Only: _____

Location of Reception: _____

Wedding Photos to be Taken: _____ During Ceremony

                      _____ After Ceremony

Other _____

Date of Counseling: _____

Date of Registration: _____

Funeral Registration

Name of Deceased: _____

Age: _____

Religious Affiliation: _____

Survivors:

    Spouse: _____

    Parents: _____

    Children: _____

    Siblings: _____

    Grandchildren: _____

Date of Death: _____

Time and Place of Visitation: _____

Date of Funeral or Memorial Service: _____

Funeral Home Responsible: _____

Location of Funeral or Memorial Service: _____

Scripture Used: _____ Hymns Used: _____

Eulogy by: _____

Other Minister(s) Assisting: _____

Pallbearers: _____

Date of Interment: _____ Place of Interment: _____

Graveside Service: _____ Yes   No _____

Subject Index

Abortion, 22–23
Aging/Old Age, 211
Angels, 145
Anskar, 339
Baptism, 246–47
Bible study/Meditation, 55, 127
Blood of Christ, 67
Bounds, E. M., 248–49
Change, 13
Children's ministry, 178–79
Christian flag, 296
Christmas, 13, 362–64, 366, 367, 368–79
Church attendance, 95
Compassion, 56–59
Crosby, Fanny, 265
Cross, XIV, 103, 104–05
Decision-making, 233
Discipleship, 345
Discouragement, 292–95
Easter, 106–09
Evangelism, 62–65
Faith, 73, 92–94, 97, 218–21, 324–26
Fathers, 186–89, 346–48
Favoritism, 304–07
Fear, 73
Finney, Charles, 224–27, 264
Forgiveness, God's, 65, 282–84, 374
Friendship, 281
Funerals, 393–99
Giving/offertory, 20, 21, 66, 84, 144, 266, 350
Gospel, 103
Grace, 24–27, 91, 154–56
Hamilton, Patrick, 64
Hell, 68–71
Holy Spirit, 55, 166–69
Humility, 21, 114–15
Hyde, John, 19

Integrity, 132–34, 137
Jesus, 41, 56–58, 67, 86–88, 111, 185, 201, 228–30, 245, 287, 297, 362–64, 367, 368–70, 371, 373
Luther, Martin, 324–28
Leadership, 7, 36–38, 80–83
Legalism, 297
Love, 176, 303, 309
Marriage, 29, 48–49
Maturity, 171, 318–20
Money, 151
Mothers, 140–43
Missions, 8–11, 47, 164–65, 339
Obedience, 177, 217, 315
Palm Sunday, 98–101
Pentecost, 166–69
Power, XIII–XVIII
Prayer, XV–XVI, 19, 159–60, 186–89, 192–95, 248–49, 256–59, 323
Preaching, 74–77
Presence of God, 201
Prodigals, 157, 192–95, 279
Purity, 172–75
Renwick, James, 153
Reading, 268–69, 316–17
Resting in Christ, 7
Revival, 16–18
Sanctity of life, 22–23
Second Coming, 250–54, 380–82
Simpson, James, 78–79
Sin, 129
Stress, 180–83, 309
Television, 175
Temptation, 85, 172–75
Thanksgiving, 185, 276–79, 352–53, 354–56
Time management, 30–35, 184
Tongue, 97, 132–35, 137, 345
Tozer, A. W., 138–39

Trials and troubles, 92–94, 116–19, 159, 191–92, 275, 287, 351, 360, 367
Trinity, 215
United States of America, 202–04, 211
Unity, 212–15
Voice, care for, 130–31
Waiting on God, 145, 191–92
Watson, Thomas, 14–15
Watts, Isaac, 288–91
Weddings, 386–92
Witnessing, 50–53, 129, 240–42, 261, 262–65
Worship, 61, 112–13, 333, 335
Zeal, 160–63

Scripture Index

Genesis 2:7, 22–23
Genesis 2:18–25, 29, 140–43
Genesis 5:18–24, 351
Genesis 5:25, 124–27
Genesis 27:18–40, 85
Genesis 28:15, 154–56
Genesis 29—31, 121–22
Genesis 32—33, 196–98
Genesis 48:1–22, 177
Exodus 13:17–22, 239
Exodus 14:1–30, 309
Numbers 6:22–27, 2–4
Joshua 7:1–26, 129
1 Samuel 1:1–24, 159–60
1 Samuel 13:1–14, 146–49
1 Samuel 15:1–23, 21
1 Samuel 17:1–54, 92–94
2 Samuel 6:12–22, 61
1 Kings 2:1–9, 346–48
1 Kings 10:13, 323
1 Kings 19:1–18, 73
2 Kings 4:1–7, 116–19
2 Kings 5:1–14, 240–42
2 Kings 7:3–16, 261
2 Kings 13:14–15, 206–08
2 Chronicles 7:12–16, 16–18
Nehemiah 1:1–11, 36–38
Job 11:17, 211
Job 23:3, 281
Psalm 1, 267
Psalm 19, 255
Psalm 24:3–4, 172–75
Psalm 27, 73, 354–58
Psalm 31:1, 97
Psalm 32, 282–85
Psalm 44:4, 97
Psalm 46, 40
Psalm 86, 79
Psalm 100:4, 185
Psalm 101, 217
Psalm 111, 255
Psalm 113, 335
Psalm 130, 191–92
Psalm 147:3, 367
Ecclesiastes 4:9–12, 281
Isaiah 1:1–31, 62–65
Isaiah 2:1–22, 315
Isaiah 6:1–10, 330–33
Isaiah 9:1–7, 335
Isaiah 30:18, 315
Jeremiah 23:1–8, 245
Ezekiel 47:1–12, 55
Daniel 2, 385
Daniel 2:18–23, 323
Daniel 9, 287
Daniel 9:25, 287
Micah 5:1–5, 374–76
Zephaniah 3:17, 201
Haggai 1, 234–37
Haggai 2, 292–95
Malachi 1:1–5, 261
Malachi 1:6–14, 303
Malachi 2:1–9, 329
Malachi 3:13–18, 345
Matthew 1:18–25, 362–64
Matthew 1:25, 367
Matthew 2:1–18, 379
Matthew 2:2, 373
Matthew 4:1–11, 85
Matthew 5:4, 340–42
Matthew 5:6, 310–12
Matthew 7:24, 267–68
Matthew 9:35–38, 8–10
Matthew 13:54–56, 42–45
Matthew 22:42, 297
Matthew 23, 297
Matthew 24:32–35, 250–53
Matthew 26:47–56, 329
Matthew 26:69–73, 345
Mark 1:9–13, 246
Mark 7:1–30, 239

Mark 8:1–13, 56–59
Mark 8:27–38, 228–30
Mark 10:46–52, 275
Mark 11:1–11, 98–101
Mark 14:32–37, 360
Luke 2:16, 373
Luke 2:19, 13
Luke 3:5, 47
Luke 5:1–11, 177
Luke 10:38–42, 180–83
Luke 12:16–21, 191
Luke 14:26–27, 345
Luke 15:11–32, 151–52
Luke 16:19–31, 68–71
Luke 21:1–4, 21
Luke 23:32–43, 104–05
John 3:1–16, 298–300
John 6:1–13, 164–65
John 9, 262
John 11:1–46, 145
John 13:35, 309
John 14:19, 111
John 15:5, 111
John 17:20–25, 212–16
John 19:30, 103
Acts 2:1–38, 166–69
Acts 8:26–40, 129
Acts 12, 145
Acts 17:6, 50–53
Acts 20:27, 245
Acts 24:1–21, 233
Acts 26:19, 217
Acts 28:17–30, 223
Romans 1:1–4, 106–09
Romans 1:16, 103
Romans 1:23, 13
1 Corinthians 2:1–5, 211
1 Corinthians 3, 171
1 Corinthians 3:2, 318–20
1 Corinthians 13, 303
2 Corinthians 4:16, 211
2 Corinthians 5:17–21, 47

2 Corinthians 9:15, 368–70
2 Corinthians 12:1–10, 351
2 Corinthians 12:7–10, 159
Ephesians 1—6, 336–38
Ephesians 1:19–23, XIII–XVII
Philippians 1:1–11, 256–59
Philippians 1:1–26, 7
Philippians 1:27—2:30, 29
Philippians 3:1—4:1, 91
Philippians 4:2–23, 137–38
Philippians 4:4–8, 276–78
Colossians 3:17, 352–53
1 Thessalonians 2:1–12, 80–84
2 Timothy 3:14–17, 55
Titus 1:5–9, 7
Titus 2:11–14, 24–27
Hebrews 2:14–18, 379
Hebrews 11:5–6, 351
Hebrews 12:1–2, 121
James 2:1–7, 304–07
James 2:14–20, 218–21
James 5:1–6, 151
James 5:12, 132–35
James 5:16–18, 186–89
1 Peter 1:9, 67
1 Peter 2:1–2, 223
1 Peter 2:4–12, 86–88
2 Peter 1, 171
2 Peter 3:1–12, 380–82
2 Peter 3:18, 91
1 John 1:3—2:11, 137
1 John 2:1–2, 41
1 John 2:13, 185
1 John 4:4, 201
Jude 1–25, 61
Jude 14–15, 351
Revelation 1, 67
Revelation 1:1–3, 270–73
Revelation 1:4–7, 275

SOFTWARE LICENSE AGREEMENT

CAREFULLY READ THE FOLLOWING TERMS AND CONDITIONS BEFORE USING THIS SOFTWARE. USING THIS SOFTWARE INDICATES YOUR ACCEPTANCE OF THESE TERMS AND CONDITIONS. IF YOU ARE NOT IN AGREEMENT, PROMPTLY RETURN THE SOFTWARE PACKAGE UNUSED WITH YOUR RECEIPT AND YOUR MONEY WILL BE REFUNDED.

LICENSE

The SOFTWARE may be used on a single machine at a time. This is a copyrighted software program and may not be copied, duplicated, or distributed except for the purpose of backup by the licensed owner.

The SOFTWARE may be copied into any machine-readable or printed form for backup, modification, or normal usage in support of the SOFTWARE on the single machine.

You may transfer the SOFTWARE and license to another party if the other party agrees to accept the terms and conditions of this Agreement. If you transfer the SOFTWARE, you must either transfer all copies, whether in printed or machine-readable form, to the same party or destroy any copies not transferred; this includes all modifications and portions of the SOFTWARE contained or merged into other software and/or software programs.

YOU MAY NOT USE, COPY, ALTER, OR OTHERWISE MODIFY OR TRANSFER THE SOFTWARE OR DATABASE(S) OR ANY ADD-ON PRODUCT'S TEXT EXCEPT AS EXPRESSLY PROVIDED FOR IN THIS LICENSE.

IF YOU TRANSFER POSSESSION OF ANY COPY OR MODIFICATIONS OF THE SOFTWARE TO ANOTHER PARTY, EXCEPT AS EXPRESSLY PROVIDED FOR IN THIS LICENSE, YOUR LICENSE THEREUPON IS AUTOMATICALLY TERMINATED.

LIMITED SOFTWARE WARRANTY

LIMITED WARRANTY. *Nelson Electronic Publishing* warrants that, for ninety (90) days from the date of receipt, the computer programs contained in the SOFTWARE will perform substantially in accordance with the *User's Guide*. Any implied warranties on the SOFTWARE are limited to ninety (90) days. Some jurisdictions do not allow limitations on the duration of an implied warranty, so the above limitation may not apply to you.

CUSTOMER REMEDIES. *Nelson Electronic Publishing's* entire liability and your exclusive remedy shall be, at our option, either (a) return of the price paid or (b) repair or replacement of SOFTWARE that does not meet *Nelson Electronic Publishing's* Limited Warranty and that is returned to us with a copy of your receipt. This Limited Warranty is void if failure of the SOFTWARE has resulted from accident, abuse, or misapplication. Any replacement SOFTWARE will be warranted for the remainder of the original warranty period or thirty (30) days, whichever is longer. Outside the United States, neither these remedies nor any product support services are available without proof of purchase from an authorized non-U.S. source.

NO OTHER WARRANTIES. To the maximum extent permitted by applicable law, *Nelson Electronic Publishing* and its suppliers disclaim all other warranties, either expressed or implied, including, but not limited to, implied warranties of merchantability and fitness for a particular purpose, with regard to the SOFTWARE and the accompanying written materials. This Limited Warranty gives you specific legal rights. You may have others, which vary from state to state.

NO LIABILITY FOR CONSEQUENTIAL DAMAGES. TO THE MAXIMUM EXTENT PERMITTED BY APPLICABLE LAW, IN NO EVENT SHALL *NELSON ELECTRONIC PUBLISHING* OR ITS SUPPLIERS BY LIABLE FOR ANY DAMAGES WHATSOEVER (INCLUDING WITHOUT LIMITATIONS, DAMAGES FOR LOSS OF BUSINESS PROFITS, BUSINESS INTERRUPTION, LOSS OF BUSINESS INFORMATION, OR ANY OTHER PECUNIARY LOSS) ARISING OUT OF THE USE OF OR INABILITY TO USE THIS PRODUCT, EVEN IF *NELSON ELECTRONIC PUBLISHING* HAS BEEN ADVISED OF THE POSSIBILITY OF SUCH DAMAGES. BECAUSE SOME STATES DO NOT ALLOW THE EXCLUSION OF LIABILITY FOR CONSEQUENTIAL OR ACCIDENTAL DAMAGES, THE ABOVE LIMITATION MAY NOT APPLY TO YOU.

Should you have any questions concerning this Agreement, please contact:
Nelson Electronic Publishing
Thomas Nelson, Inc.
501 Nelson Place
Nashville, TN 37214-1000
615/889-9000